Jihadism in Pakistan

Jihadism in Pakistan

Al-Qa'ida, Islamic State and the Local Militants

Antonio Giustozzi

I.B. TAURIS
LONDON • NEW YORK • OXFORD • NEW DELHI • SYDNEY

I.B. TAURIS
Bloomsbury Publishing Plc
50 Bedford Square, London, WC1B 3DP, UK
1385 Broadway, New York, NY 10018, USA
29 Earlsfort Terrace, Dublin 2, Ireland

BLOOMSBURY, I.B. TAURIS and the I.B. Tauris logo are
trademarks of Bloomsbury Publishing Plc

First published in Great Britain 2023

Copyright © Antonio Giustozzi, 2023

Antonio Guistozzi has asserted his right under the Copyright, Designs and
Patents Act, 1988, to be identified as Author of this work.

For legal purposes the Acknowledgements on p. vii constitute
an extension of this copyright page.

Cover design by Charlotte Daniels

All rights reserved. No part of this publication may be reproduced or transmitted
in any form or by any means, electronic or mechanical, including photocopying,
recording, or any information storage or retrieval system, without prior
permission in writing from the publishers.

Bloomsbury Publishing Plc does not have any control over, or responsibility for,
any third-party websites referred to or in this book. All internet addresses given
in this book were correct at the time of going to press. The author and publisher
regret any inconvenience caused if addresses have changed or sites have ceased
to exist, but can accept no responsibility for any such changes.

A catalogue record for this book is available from the British Library.

A catalog record for this book is available from the Library of Congress.

ISBN:	HB:	978-0-7556-4735-4
	PB:	978-0-7556-4738-5
	ePDF:	978-0-7556-4736-1
	eBook:	978-0-7556-4737-8

Typeset by Integra Software Services Pvt. Ltd.

To find out more about our authors and books visit www.bloomsbury.com
and sign up for our newsletters.

Contents

List of figures	vi
Acknowledgements	vii
List of acronyms	viii
Introduction	1
1 How Pakistan's deep state, AQ and the jihadists met 1980–2001	15
2 The strategies of the global jihadists in Pakistan after 2001	27
3 The TTP: Bastard offspring of global jihad	65
4 The Sunni supremacists: Deviant allies of AQ	123
5 Global jihad and the Kashmiri jihad: Co-opting or being co-opted?	141
Conclusion	173
Notes	188
References	226
Index	237

Figures

1. AQ numbers in Pakistan and Afghanistan, 2008–16. Sources: Meeting with AQ cadre, 2014; meeting with Q*, assistant of Taliban leader Akhtar Mohammad Mansur, 2014; meeting with Q*M, senior Taliban cadre, Pakistan, March 2014 — 30
2. Splinters and mergers of the TTP, 2007–19 — 81
3. Terrorist attack by TTP and related organizations, 2012–18. Source: PIPS — 103
4. Victims (killed) of terrorist attack by TTP and related organizations, 2012–18. Source: PIPS — 103
5. Estimates and claims of TTP fighting strength, 2007–20 (excluding splinter groups) — 112
6. The changing structure of the TTP (fighters by faction) — 112
7. Sectarian violence in Pakistan. Sources: https://www.satp.org/type-of-attack/Sectarian-Violence/pakistan-2018; https://www.satp.org/type-of-attack/Sectarian-Violence/pakistan-2019 and https://www.satp.org/type-of-attack/Sectarian-Violence/pakistan-2020 — 128
8. The factionalization of LeJ. Sources: see text above — 135

Acknowledgements

This book is the result of a research project run by the author with his own limited financial resources and drawing from a range of small consultancy projects and articles produced for specialized media outlets. The project was particularly difficult to research due to the controversial character of the topic. For the author in particular, arranging any meetings with informed individuals was very challenging and research had to depend largely on local researchers.

The author thanks all those involved in preparing the volume at Bloomsbury's and the anonymous reviewers for their constructive criticism of the original manuscript.

Special thanks to friends and colleagues who read the book and provided comments and advice. The author also wishes to thank all those who contributed to the development of his ideas and views on the subject in meetings, workshops and conferences. They are far too many to be mentioned individually here.

Special thanks go to the researchers, who carried out the bulk of the interviews in Afghanistan and Pakistan. They have to remain anonymous for security reasons, but their efforts were essential to the research project. The author assumes all responsibility for the analysis contained in this text, of course.

Acronyms

AQ	al Qa'ida
AQIS	al Qa'ida in the Indian Subcontinent
ASS	Anjaman Sipah i Sahaba (Society of the Companions of the Prophet of Islam)
FATA	Federally Administered Tribal Areas
HM	Hizb ul Mujahideen
HuA	Hizb ul Ahrar
HuJI	Harakat ul Jihad al Islami
HuM	Harakat ul Mujahidin
IMU	Islamic Movement of Uzbekistan
IS	Islamic State
ISI	Inter-Services Directorate (Pakistan)
IS-Central	Acronym used in this book to identify the central leadership and command structure of IS, based in Iraq and Syria
IS-H	Islamic State Hind (*ad-Dawlah al-Islāmiyah fi Hind*)
IS-K	Islamic State in Khorasan (*ad-Dawlah al-Islāmiyah fi Khorasan*)
IS-P	Islamic State Pakistan (*ad-Dawlah al-Islāmiyah fi Pakistan*)
JeI	Jama'at e Islami
JeM	Jaish e Mohammad
JKLF	Jammu and Kashmir Liberation Front
JuD/LeT	Jama'at-ud-Dawa/Lashkar e Taiba
JuA	Jama'at ul Ahrar
JuI	Jama'at Ulema e Islam
LeJ	Lashkar e Jhangvi
LeJ (aA)	Lashkar e Jhangvi (al-Alami faction)
LeJ (Lahori)	Lashkar e Jhangvi (Lahore faction)

LeT	See JuD above
LeI	Lashkar e Islam
MDI	Markaz Dawat wal'Irshad
MI	Military Intelligence (Pakistan)
MQM	Mujahir Qawmi Movement
NDS	National Directorate of Security (Afghanistan)
PATA	Provincial Administered Tribal Areas
SSP	Sipah e Sahaba Pakistan
TKP	Tehrik e Khilafat Pakistan
TNSM	Tehreek e Nafaz e Shariat e Mohammadi
TTI	Tehreek e Taliban Islami
TTP	Tehrik e Taliban Pakistan
Wilayat	Province (Arabic)

Introduction

Pakistan is host to the largest concentration of jihadist groups of the world. The relationship of the Pakistani authorities with them has been the object of many diatribes, starting from the Soviet and their allies in the Afghan government in the 1980s and continuing to date with the Indian and Afghan authorities, all of whom accused Pakistan of sponsoring local jihadist groups and of sending Pakistani volunteers to support them. In the West, hardly any analyst believes anymore that the Pakistani authorities are not involved in supporting jihadist groups. However, there is still no consensus concerning the relationship between the Pakistani establishment and global jihadist groups, such as al Qa'ida (AQ). This, of course, would be much more controversial in the eyes of Western powers, especially the Americans. After the 2011 raid that killed Osama bin Laden in Abbottabad, accusations of Pakistani complicity with AQ peaked. Still, the US authorities were cautious in pointing the finger towards Islamabad. They would certainly have taken steeper actions if a country like Iran had been involved, for example.

As a result, despite the rather astonishing 2011 raid in Abbottabad, the relationship between Pakistan and the jihadists is still a matter of debate. Pakistan's security establishment has always denied having any connection or collusion with the jihadists. It is not just a matter of whether there is a relationship with the global jihadists or not, but also:

- of the nature of that relationship,
- of Pakistan's and of the global jihadists' aims,
- of the impact of that relationship on local jihadists,
- of the impact of the relationship on Pakistani policymaking
- and of the impact on global jihadists.

Tools of Pakistan foreign policy

The origins of the massive expansion of Pakistan's jihadist movement from the 1980s onwards lie in the 1980s war in Afghanistan and in Pakistan's own sponsorship of Afghan jihadist groups. Pakistan channelled its and others' support towards Islamist groups in Afghanistan and started seeing its covert operations there as highly successful. The Pakistani military establishment started conceiving of militant groups as a potentially very useful tool of foreign policy after its success in Afghanistan. As Kapur commented,

> *Pakistan's militant strategy has enabled it to shape the strategic environment in Afghanistan, helping to install a friendly government on its critical western border.*[1]

Then the Pakistanis applied the same strategy to Kashmir. Pakistan's proxies in Kashmir forced India to commit considerable financial and military resources, 'redressing Pakistani material weakness vis-à-vis India'.[2] Moreover,

> *the strategy has enabled Pakistan to continue to undermine Indian control of Kashmir and ensure that the disputed territory remains a subject of international attention.*[3]

Although relying on jihadist groups seemed an uncontroversial success initially, problems soon started brewing. The US intervention in Afghanistan acted as a coagulant for these problems. Topich described Pakistani dictator Musharraf's policy after 2001 as 'full of contradictions', pursuing AQ members while at the same time refusing to dismantle his domestic 'terrorist network'.[4] Along similar lines Rashid had already pointed out in 2008 the 'contradictions in Pakistan's counterterrorism strategy':

> *Even as the ISI helped the CIA run down al Qaeda leaders in Pakistan's cities, Pakistani Islamist militants, with quiet ISI approval, were attacking Indian troops in Kashmir or helping the Taliban regroup in Pakistan. Yet al Qaeda itself was involved in training and funding the Islamist militants ordered to kill Musharraf.*[5]

But, of course, what appears a contradiction from a Western perspective might have looked like a reasonable compromise from Islamabad's. The rationale was, according to a general quoted by Rashid, that 'It is not possible to completely crack down on the fundamentalists, as they may be needed in any future conflict with India'.[6] Moreover, a 'Talibanized belt' in FATA

> *would keep the pressure on Karzai to bend to Pakistani wishes, keep U.S. forces under threat while maintaining their dependence on Pakistani goodwill, and create a buffer zone between Afghan and Pakistani Pashtuns.*[7]

Undoubtedly this approach was fraught with risks, as reportedly several of Musharraf's aides told him, highlighting how 'keeping one set of insurgents alive while trying to apprehend others would be virtually impossible'.[8] Indeed after 2001 Pakistan's strategy started to backfire, as it became evident in 2003 with the two assassination attempts on Musharraf, planned by jihadists based in South Waziristan.[9]

> *Recently, however, these successes of Pakistan's militant strategy have given way to serious problems. The militant organizations that Pakistan nurtured over the decades are increasingly exceeding its control.*[10]

Why and how Pakistan's jihadists started getting out of the control of the state authorities that had sponsored them is a complex matter, but one of the explanations that are usually offered is that global jihadist groups managed to drive a wedge between the state and its proxies.¹¹ The purpose of this book is to examine the relationship between the Pakistani state and jihadist groups, which, as it will emerge below, has been indeed a complicated one. It should be noted that the purpose of the volume is not to provide an exhaustive explanation of the emergence of jihadism in Pakistan, even if it does provide some background information about their history.

The nature of AQ

There is still an ongoing debate on whether an AQ core exists or not, that is whether AQ is a mere network of like-minded groups and individuals, or a disciplined and well-organized structure. In the former case, it would be hard to see how AQ could formulate a coherent strategy over a long period of time. Much of the debate is based on a focus on AQ's terrorist activities, either in the assumption that AQ is just that, an entity dedicated to carrying out terrorist attacks, or in the assumption that anything else AQ might be doing does not really matter.¹² However, the debate about the 'core' is even more relevant for AQ's 'pro-insurgency' operations, which are arguably more complex than organizing terrorist attacks.

Gartenstein-Ross and Barr have strongly argued that AQ was and remains a coherent centralized organization, not a mere collection of networks. Their findings are based on documents captured in Abbottabad and elsewhere.¹³ As a result

> *al-Qaeda's leadership continues to be essential in determining both the trajectory of the organization as well as its strategic direction. While al-Qaeda sometimes fails to resolve its internal disputes before they boil over into the public eye – a phenomenon seen in earlier years as well (there were highly public disputes in the 1990s in both Sudan and Afghanistan over the state and trajectory of the global jihadist movement) – its affiliates generally continue to adhere to the goals, objectives and strategies outlined by the organization's senior leadership. At the same time, al-Qaeda's flexible organizational model allows affiliates to adapt their tactical approach to local dynamics.*¹⁴

The AQ concept was from the start and remained an 'international vanguard charged with taking the first steps necessary to sweep an un-Islamic world order from power'. AQ central in this model retained control over the propaganda apparatus and developed a command and control mechanism to direct the activities of members, branches and affiliates. The stress has been on a hierarchical and rules-based organization, keen on professionalizing its operations. The role of bin Laden and of the leadership has been 'to craft a strategic vision through the development of annual plans, budgets and structures'.¹⁵ Gartenstein-Ross and Barr do not discuss AQ's policies towards allies.

Even for some of those who accepted the idea of a 'core' AQ, the emergence of IS in 2014 reinforced the impression of a declining AQ, as the impressive successes of IS in 2014–15 overshadowed any achievement by AQ. Well-advertised differences and even friction between AQ Central and Jabha al Nusra in Syria, as well as the defection of some AQ fronts or affiliates to IS, contributed to conjure an image of a fractured, or fracturing, AQ. The uncharismatic leadership of al Zawahiri after 2011 allegedly compounded the picture, as he was believed to be 'unable to authoritatively and effectively wrestle al-Qaeda's regional affiliates and global adherents back into line when they stray'.[16]

Despite much effort going into targeting and killing AQ leaders and cadres, the inner workings of the organization are still poorly understood. Moghadam stresses that AQ itself described its organizational approach as 'centralisation of decision and decentralisation of execution'.[17]

> *According to this principle, bin Laden 'decided on the targets, selected the leaders, and provided at least some of the funding. After that, the planning of the operation and the method of attack were left to the men who would have the responsibility of carrying it out.'*[18]

The idea of a centralized leadership, at least in terms of decision-making, has been called into question by Nelly Lahoud's book on the *bin Laden Papers*, the first one to rely extensively on the papers captured in Abbottabad. Referring of course to the period up to bin Laden's death in 2011, Lahoud comments wonders:

> *Was Usama counting on his 'Brothers' – i.e., regional jihadi groups acting in al-Qaeda's name in Iraq, Yemen, North Africa, and Somalia – perhaps? Quite the contrary. His letters reveal that he did not believe them to be reliable partners. We find him lamenting that they had become a 'liability' to global jihad. Usama had good reason to complain. Their own letters expose the fact that, beneath their vows of allegiance, the 'Brothers' had no desire to act in unison toward a common goal.*[19]

Reviewing Lahoud's book, Cole Bunzel assessed that

> *Bin Laden perceived a fundamental strategic disconnect between the regional branches with their locally oriented strategies and his own vision of global jihad. [… Bin Laden's al Qaeda was not a 'Leviathan in the jihadi landscape' as many saw it to be, Lahoud writes, but rather a weakened organization marked by operational impotence and an inability to control the groups acting in its name.*[20]

Beside the 'far enemy': AQ's local partners

Whatever the original or primary aims, it is clear from the 2020 vantage point that AQ ended up doing much more than plotting to strike at the West (the 'far enemy'). AQ's involvement in 'local conflicts and insurgencies' needs unpacking. As noted above about Lahoud's conclusions, based on the Abbottabad papers, AQ central might have been unable to assert leadership in the early post-2001 years, but its branches were active and often effective. AQ's branches started making deals with states and groups, which were not ideologically strictly aligned with AQ, even if they might have had varying degree of sympathy for its aims. AQ and/or its branch in the Indian Subcontinent (AQIS) did for sure invest considerable resources in trying to influence and strengthen various Pakistani jihadist groups. But what was the purpose in doing so? This book looks at a number of these partners of AQ, in and around Pakistan, and seeks to answer questions about why AQ and its AQIS branch went for this engagement and what came out of it. Was AQ's involvement essentially expediency, driven by pragmatism and tacticism? Or was it part of a coherent long-term strategic plan to expand its influence and presence in all directions?

Mendelsohn acknowledges, based on his discussion of the Somalian and Syrian cases, that AQ's agenda has been drifting away from a narrow focus on the 'far enemy', especially after bin Laden's replacement by al Zawahiri. Similar instances can be found in Pakistan too. For example, AQ/AQIS (it is often hard to distinguish between the two in South Asia) remained a source of support even after the TTP stopped playing any significant role in support of the Afghan Taliban's insurgency and it turned into an essentially Pakistani insurgency – against Islamabad. Was the TTP another case of 'drift'?

Jihadist groups mostly allied with the Pakistani state and focused on Kashmir, such as LeT, Jaish e Mohammad (JeM) and HuM, had early connections to AQ and developed them after 2001. Some factions within these groups turned against the Pakistani state after 2001, often with AQ's encouragement. LeT was after 2001 one of the privileged interlocutors of AQ/AQIS in Pakistan, regardless of the dramatic ups and downs in the relationship between the Pakistani security apparatus and AQ/AQIS. Was this another case of 'drift'?

Despite being mostly known for avoiding sectarian conflict with Shi'as, AQ also entertained close relations with various sectarian extremist groups, such as Sipah e Sahaba Pakistan (SSP), Lashkar e Jhangvi (LeJ) and Jundullah. When AQ severed its links to LeJ, it did so not because of its sectarian violence, but because the latter had established a strong connection to the Islamic State in Khorasan (Chapter 4). The relationship of AQ with the Sunni supremacists is a perfect example of AQ cultivating groups that did not share with it their aims and objectives.

If AQ was drifting all the time, a more ad hoc analysis is required. Byman argued that AQ

> *seeks affiliates to expand the scope and scale of its operations, gain the benefits of greater local expertise, better spread innovations, and – most important – endow itself and its mission with greater legitimacy. [...] Affiliates have hundreds or even thousands of fighters under arms, provide ties to local communities, offer knowledge of terrain (both physical and human), and are otherwise better able to fight and operate. As a result, al Qaeda is able to raise its banner in several important theaters where it would otherwise find it difficult to operate.*[21]

Byman argues that AQ's expanding list of 'affiliates' has been exactly what allows it to claim to lead global jihad, as 'having a diverse array of affiliates that bear a more localized al Qaeda name fulfills the organization's self-image as the leader of the jihadist movement throughout the Muslim world'.[22] As pressure on AQ rose, the growing number of affiliates allowed it to keep claiming that it is 'a dynamic – and ascendant – organization'.[23]

Byman provides a first possible explanation for AQ's extensive 'drift'. Another explanation could be that perhaps AQ was never as focused on striking Western targets as assumed in the early post-9/11 days. The predominant concern with terrorist attacks in the West has led many analysts to declare the decline of AQ, given the post-9/11 anti-climax on this front. Some analysts have however pointed out how AQ's main concern was never striking Western targets per se, but, in reality, to overthrow Middle Eastern regimes.[24] As noted by a team of Danish analysts,

Though the West is still its primary enemy, attacks in the West have largely been replaced by attacks on Westerners in the regions where AQ is active, and its declared range of enemies has simultaneously become broader due to its involvement in these local conflicts and insurgencies.[25]

AQ did not find managing jihadist allies necessarily easier than Pakistan found managing proxies. Gartenstein-Ross and Barr acknowledge that 'al Qa'ida's organizational model makes it susceptible to preference divergence', not least because 'geographic expansion increased the possibility that affiliates would have interests that differed significantly from those of al-Qaeda Central'.[26] Still they conclude that

The leadership's role in determining the military, political and propaganda strategy of the organization allows it to shape the behavior of affiliates, to mitigate preference divergence, and to avoid the kind of strategic incoherence that could taint al-Qaeda's global image. Al Qa'ida Central's involvement in selecting or at least approving the appointment of its affiliates' emirs similarly reduces the likelihood that commanders will deliberately deviate from al-Qaeda's strategic guidance.[27]

A similar view was expressed by Andersen.[28] This volume argues that apart from 'affiliates' who 'adhere to the goals, objectives and strategies' of AQ, AQ also established a vast network of alliances with 'compagnons de route', which had their own goals, objectives and strategies, only partially overlapping with AQ's. One would expect that managing them would have turned even tougher than managing affiliates.

The 'modus' of AQ's engagement with states and especially jihadist groups indeed matters. The dominant view of the way AQ has been expanding is that it relied on franchising. The most ambitious effort to discuss AQ's strategies for expansion so far is Mendelsohn's *The al-Qaeda franchise*. Mendelsohn distinguishes between absorption, branching out (franchising), unification, umbrella group, cooperation and advisory missions. He seems to completely discount the latter model as

groups are likely to retrench only if the move guarantees the group's survival, since it represents a scaling down of the group's profile and acknowledges its vulnerability and declining power. A retreat from active operations reduces the ability to provide economic and reputational goods for the organization's rank and file; any measure that could be interpreted as acknowledging a decline risks accelerating that process.[29]

However, as it will be shown in this book, AQ/AQIS relied massively on the 'cooperation and advisory' model in South Asia. Its reliance on this model was less visible than its involvement at the forefront of major jihads as in Syria or Africa, or of its attempts to strike Western targets around the world. It was nonetheless very extensive. One of AQ's largest 'missions' in this field was of course supporting the Afghan Taliban.[30] It was far from being the only one, as this book also shows.

Several Pakistani jihadist groups that became close to AQ, such as the Tehrik e Taliban Pakistan (TTP), Lashkar e Taiba (LeT), JeM, Hakarat ul Mujahidin (HuM), SSP, LeJ and others definitely do not fit well with Mendelsohn's argument, and Mendelsohn in fact does not even mention them. Mostly these groups did not fit well with Gartenstein-Ross/Barr's 'affiliates' either. They will be described throughout this book as 'clients', that is, groups that essentially collaborated with AQ because it extended patronage to them, or 'allies', that is, groups that were mainly motivated to collaborate because of somewhat overlapping interests and aims.

As this book will show, AQ invested major resources in supporting 'clients' and 'allies' – it could arguably have invested instead in establishing a powerful South Asian 'franchise'. Even when a 'franchise' eventually emerged (AQIS), its purpose was more to support more efficiently allies and clients, rather than carry out its own military or terror operations. The AQ mission in South Asia remained one that only fits in Mendelsohn's 'advisory mission' category, which in his view should not have been in AQ's interest. This begs the question of why AQ went for it, assuming it had control over what its local branch was doing.

In terms of impact, in South Asia AQ's advisory missions among 'clients' and 'allies' might well have been more important than the 'franchises': AQ's branch in Pakistan hardly had any major direct impact on local security, but the TTP and others definitely had. Not only the type of relationships that AQ entertained with insurgent groups cannot be reduced to a single 'franchise' model and its variations, but the near monopolistic attention for the franchises does not appear justified.

The TTP and its predecessor groups were one of AQ's first main partners, long before Al Nusra or Ash Shabaab emerged and before AQ in Iraq was established. The TTP became the most violent insurgent organization to have operated in Pakistan, despite having never risen to the status of 'affiliate' and having just been the beneficiary of help and advice. TTP had a major impact in Pakistan, which justifies moving away from Western-centred counter-terrorism concerns. In 2002–3 much of AQ's assistance and cooperation with insurgent groups was focused on the Afghanistan/Pakistan border, and the Pakistani Taliban were possibly the main beneficiaries, given the disorganized and demoralized state of the Afghan Taliban at that stage. The Afghan Taliban started receiving support from AQ at about the same time as the Pakistani Taliban, but soon the Afghans were able to diversify their sources of support to a much greater extent than the Pakistani Taliban. AQ's was soon an almost negligible contribution to the coffers of the Afghan Taliban, whereas it remained one of the main sources of financial support (if not *the* main one) to the Pakistani Taliban to this day. Still the TTP never pledged allegiance to AQ, even if as discussed in Chapter 3 it cooperated closely with it. It did not turn out to be a very dependable partner either.

Byman argued that affiliates are asked to take on 'the core's anti-American and anti-Western agenda',[31] but once they have done that

> *Affiliation offers both the core organization and local groups better propaganda opportunities to reach more potential recruits with existing resources.[...] From Somalia to Iraq, al Qaeda has used its worldwide recognition to draw attention to local struggles and, in so doing, attract recruits and funds for local fighters. Affiliates may maintain an impressive network outside their country of origin, usually for logistics and fundraising. [...] Beyond branding, affiliate relationships allow learning that improves both al Qaeda's and the affiliates' overall performance. Some of this is tactical. [...] Perhaps the more important learning occurs at the strategic level. Jihadist leaders scrutinize both supposed successes and perceived failures and from them impart lessons to affiliates.*[32]

Much of what Byman says applies to AQ's allies and clients, branding aside. Byman adds that AQ's modus operandi ran into deep trouble after 9/11:

> *al Qaeda faces a host of problems related to delegation and integration, and often affiliation is a net loss. Divergent preferences and priorities, branding problems, shirking at the local level, adverse selection, and costly control mechanisms all make affiliates of questionable value to the core organization.[...] Local groups often retain many of their original goals and missions, increasing the likelihood of preference diversion.*[33]

As a result, even if AQ *often used money to influence and shape the cause of potential allies,*[34] it

> *often finds controlling its affiliates to be difficult. Part of this problem stems simply from the nature of running a global clandestine organization whose component parts are often thousands of miles away. Al Qaeda must communicate with affiliates and uses messengers and facilitators to do so, but these communications might be intercepted by US or allied intelligence, exposing the operation and putting the operatives on both sides at risk. But if al Qaeda leaders hunker down, they are ineffective commanders. Clandestine methods of communication reduce this risk but also are far less effective.*[35]

Arguably 'preference divergence' should be even more of a problem in the case of simple allies clients, as opposed to affiliates. Byman is not alone in pointing out the difficulties faced by AQ. A 2006 CTC paper already argued that

> *Terrorist organizations [...] must execute a controlled use of violence as a means to achieving their specified political ends. Doing too much can be just as damaging to the cause as doing too little [...] However, preferences aren't always aligned. When*

they are not, the covert nature of terrorist groups necessarily implies that agents can take advantage of delegation to act as they prefer, not as their principals would like. Thus, terrorist leaders have a problem. Security concerns mean they cannot perfectly monitor what agents are doing. Moreover, the nature of the operational environment means that it is hard to punish agents, even when leaders do catch them taking unauthorized actions.[36]

So Byman stated his optimism that AQ's 'decline is for real and might even be permanent'.[37] Perhaps more than decline of AQ tout court it would be more accurate here to speak of declining efficiency of AQ's strategy. As it will emerge throughout the book, at least as far as allies and clients are concerned, the marginal efficiency of AQ's investment in allies declined as it reached out to a growing number of organizations, whose aims overlapped with AQ's less and less.

The IS model and its adaptation to South Asia

In part, the decline of the 'marginal efficiency' of AQ's investment in its allies in South Asia was the result of the appearance of IS on the scene, which introduced a strong competitor for the loyalty of jihadist groups. The literature and IS propaganda itself tend to describe IS as all bent on establishing the Caliphate as a territorial entity, as opposed to AQ which postpones the establishment of the Caliphate to a rather distant future and operates instead as a 'trans-territorial network'.[38] Turner summarizes the different strategic approaches of AQ and IS this way.[39]

- *AQ's strategic focus is not so much on controlling territory, but rather on projecting its sway over those who have significant influence in areas not under state control.*
- *AQ was working with a strategy that imagined at least a twenty year long initiative building on the events of 2001 in pursuit of a caliphate. For AQ, the caliphate is a distant objective only to be realized when the appropriate conditions have been achieved.*
- *Violence is conceived of as a political rather than a military tool, requiring restraint and selective implementation.*[40]
- *AQC seeks to win good will from the local community, […] serving as protectors against government and foreign forces.*
- *They are attempting to balance localism with internationalism.*
- *Third, they are presenting themselves as the rational moderate alternative to IS, putting themselves in opposition to the methods highlighted as part of the Islamic State's ideological correction.*
- *AQ, then, is seeking to legitimize its struggle as not simply an ideological Islamic cause, but as one that can help to fight and win against common injustices which plague Muslim communities.*
- *Its end game goals can sit in reserve until AQ becomes imbedded in the population having purchased good will.*[41]

IS, by contrast,

- *does not view itself as compromising the Salafi Jihadist ideology, rather it is AQC which has lost its legitimacy through political scheming and lethargic methods, forcing IS to pursue ideological correction.*
- *This strategic approach is aimed at the provocation of instability that the jihadists can seek to manage as state control over the territory in concerned areas diminishes.*[42]

In principle, the contrast between the two global jihadist organizations could not be starker. Was the IS' radically different approach that allowed it to make substantial inroads at AQ's expense?

Much of what was discussed about AQ and IS in the early years after IS made its appearance was based on what could be seen of IS in Iraq and Syria. It is however easy to overstate the differences between AQ and IS, especially as the latter expanded its influence beyond its original Iraqi-Syrian turf. In practice, IS

pursues a 'pragmatic' approach in its territorial practices. [...] [It] adapts to each areas' specific social and political dynamics, and behaves accordingly, only to frame its actions – in an ad-hoc manner – in religious terms by selectively invoking Islamic texts or past practices.[43]

Where IS found a 'strong enemy' and/or a 'fragmented jihadi scenery lacking the deeply entranced networks of official AQ branches', it 'nurtured alliances with AQ-linked groups', as in Libya.[44] Another example is that of the Philippines, where 'parts of Abu Sayyaf's leadership have identified with the Islamic State, but the organization as a whole has not publicly pledged bay`a to al Baghdadi'.[45] Critchley et al. describe this type of IS clients as 'bandwagoners', such as the Yarmouk Martyrs Brigade in southern Syria.[46] They conclude that

The nature of the relationship between Daesh and their affiliate groups is contingent upon the geopolitical, ideological and financial context in which them find themselves. Partner groups are those which contribute to the Daesh project more directly and are therefore shown more support by the hierarchical [sic] head. Bandwagoners are given less support due to their pragmatic or idealised motivations to affiliation but still fostered by Daesh.[47]

Hansen found during his research in Africa that

Both the Islamic State in the Greater Sahara and the Islamic State in Somalia are just as embedded in a local tribal/ clan reality as are al-Qaeda's affiliates in their areas, if not more so; and both factions of Boko Haram maintain a local focus. Al Qa'ida's affiliates in Africa are not more 'tribalised' than the Islamic State's: they are very similar in this matter. Such observations do suggest that this pattern can be repeated outside Africa: that the Islamic State will follow the path of al-Qaeda, with a weakened centre, perhaps operating in a semi-territorial configuration, and as increasingly locally focused affiliates, influenced by ethnic, tribal and clan dynamics as well as local conflicts. [...] None of the organisations studied in this book are 'puppets' of mother organisations such as al-Qaeda and the Islamic State: they have their own agenda, and it is unlikely that they will, for example, target the West outside of Africa.[48]

Azoulay goes even father and argues that

While claiming to aspire to global jihad, [IS] has been very localised in its actions, focusing on territorial gains and limited governance, according to its strategy to maintain and expand. Consequently, it has been more pragmatic and flexible. It is able to adapt to different contexts, facilitated by its thin ideology and not constrained by a very clearly defined goal of attacking a far enemy, as was the case for AQ. [...] In sum, one could argue that the IS model is less in contradiction with the local agendas of jihadi groups, thus limiting the risks of divergence of interests between local and core organisations.[49]

The approach of IS in South Asia, therefore, might not have differed from AQ's that much. If that was the case, what explains its success?

Key questions

The questions raised above can be summarized as follows:

- Did the global jihadists effectively drive a wedge between the Pakistani state and the local jihadists? What were the long-term consequences of that?
- What purpose did the Pakistani jihadists serve in AQ's strategy, justifying a large commitment of resources over a period of almost twenty years (and still counting in 2020)?
- How effective was it, from AQ's own perspective, relying on allies whose agendas and methods only partially overlapped with AQ's?
- Why, despite so many incidents of jihadist rebellion against the Pakistani state, the latter seemingly insisted on relying on jihadist groups as proxies to project power in the near abroad?
- Why did so many Pakistani jihadists continue to cooperate with the Pakistani state and with AQ at the same time?
- Was AQ pursuing a coherent strategy in South Asia, or was its decision-making driven by expediency?
- If there was a coherent strategy, what was it?
- Do AQ's activities in South Asia suggest the existence of a core structure?
- What explains the relatively successful competition of IS for the loyalty of Pakistani jihadist groups?

The five chapters in which this book is divided try to address these questions based on the information available in the literature, in the media and importantly a series of meetings with members of jihadist groups.

Methodology

This article is primarily based on a series of 114 interviews, telephone contacts or meetings with thirty-six members or former members of TTP and related groups (such as Lashkar e Islam, Jama'at ul Ahrar and Devotees of Fazlullah), twenty-three members or former members of LeT, JeM and HuM, two Afghan National Directorate of Security (NDS) officers, one Inter-Services Intelligence (ISI) officer, one Revolutionary Guards (Iran) officer, one donor to jihadist groups, six members of the Afghan Taliban, two with local elders in areas of TTP presence, twelve with members of sectarian groups (SSP, LeJ, Jundullah), one with a Baluchi jihadist group, four with members of the Islamic State in Pakistan (IS-P), fifteen with members of the Islamic State in Khorasan (IS-K) and thirteen members of the AQ branch for Afghanistan, Pakistan and South Asia. The meetings took place in 2013–20. The meetings were carried out by four different local researchers in Afghanistan and Pakistan, who all had previous experience of working with insurgent groups and were chosen for their high level of access to Pakistani jihadist organizations.

Most of the interviewers have a background in journalism and have been involved in previous research projects led by the author. They were therefore already a battle-tested team before the project began, well versed in ensuring that meetings took place safely for all those involved. Access to jihadist groups, usually not the most accessible organizations, was obtained by leveraging existing contacts with members of linked groups such as the Afghan Taliban and solicitating introductions from older contacts within the ranks of the same groups. Once contact was re-established, it became easy to access other members of jihadist groups through introductions provided by the original contacts. The research team has established a reputation for the safe handling of meetings over several years of research activity. This reputation has contributed massively in making access possible.

Secondary sources are relatively abundant on some aspects of Pakistan jihadism, even if of uneven quality. Although these sources were abundantly used, it is heavily reliant on information provided by members of jihadist organizations. In those cases where external sources (media, elders, intelligence officials) were not available to confirm the plausibility of the information provided by such members, the author relied on cross-referencing between different jihadist sources, interviewed at different time and in different places. We also considered the sensitivity of the information provided; the author focused on cross-checking the most sensitive information, while he adopted lower standards of cross-checking for information which was not very sensitive or not sensitive at all.

In this type of research work there is an obvious risk (or perhaps even a certainty) that much of the information provided will be essentially propagandistic in nature, or even deliberately misleading. While this is inevitable, the research project handled the risk by relying on

a. interviews with external observers, allowing the author to check a number of statements made by IS-K interviewees;
b. multiple meetings in different places and at different times, with different interviewers and interviewees contacted through different channels; this was meant to minimize the risk of collusion among interviewees in providing misleading information and to allow cross checking among different IS-K interviewees;
c. the inclusion in the questionnaires of questions whose answer was already known to the authors, in order to check to what degree interviewees were being honest in their answers;
d. structuring the interviewing process in successive waves, with a first 'exploratory' wave used to strengthen the questionnaires and to insert more test questions, based on the newly obtained information;
e. cross-referencing factual information provided to verify its internal consistency. Thanks to the previous research projects carried out on Taliban, IS-K and Central Asian jihadists, it was also possible to compare the data obtained with similar data about other organizations.

In addition, it is important to note that some of the sources, and particularly the AQ ones, were not approached in formal interviews, but instead contacted through researchers who had links to AQ, IS and allied organizations (either because of family or business, or because of membership of AQ partners, such as the Afghan Taliban). It was informal discussions and not formal interviews; the researchers were then debriefed. This approach was deliberately adopted to increase the willingness of the sources to speak openly.

The initial group of interviewees was selected on the basis of existing contacts; snowball sampling was used to reach out to a large number of interviewees.

The material from the meetings included in the book has been filtered by the author, who assessed the material and excluded everything that he judged to be propagandistic. Some of the material that the author decided to use in this book will nonetheless be judged to be controversial by some readers. In particular, AQ's allegations of deals being make with Pakistani intelligence units and of the level of funding received and redistributed by AQ to other jihadist groups are the most likely to raise a few eyebrows. This is why in the text these issues are discussed at length, with reference to whatever alternative sources are available.

Given the type of project, research ethics were a major concern. One of the criteria for selecting the members of the research team was their proven ability (from pervious projects) to preserve confidentiality. The meetings were anonymized at an early stage and nobody but the people directly involved in the research effort know the actual identities. In the large majority of cases, meeting transcripts were handed by hand (typically in small USB drives). Electronic transfers were done through encrypted emailing.

1

How Pakistan's deep state, AQ and the jihadists met 1980–2001

The first Afghan jihad

The Afghan jihad movement of 1978 onwards (first against the leftist Khalq government and then against the occupying Soviet army) kick-started a series of developments, which would turn the Pakistani state into a major sponsor of jihadist groups and give birth to the global jihad movement. With financial and logistical support from a number of countries (primarily the United States, Saudi Arabia and China), the Pakistani security service ISI funded, equipped and trained insurgents from a variety of Afghan groups opposed to the leftist government that had come to power in April 1978 and to the Soviet army contingent that occupied the country between December 1979 and February 1989.[1]

Almost all the groups supported by the ISI belonged to some strain of political Islam, typically Muslim Brotherhood, Deobandi or Salafi inclinations. Among the former, the most prominent was Hizb e Islami, which was also closely connected to the Pakistani Jama'at e Islami.[2] Although few Afghan mullahs would describe themselves as Deobandi, one of the resistance parties, Harakat e Enqelab e Islami, had links to Deobandi networks in Pakistan, which grew deeper and deeper during the war.[3] Finally, a few Salafi resistance groups existed in eastern Afghanistan, mostly within Hizb e Islami, but in some cases operating independently.[4]

Aside from supporting a range of Afghan jihadist groups, the Pakistani ISI encouraged Pakistani clerical networks, linked to some of the Afghan jihadist organizations, to raise groups of Pakistani volunteers to fight in Afghanistan in 1980, especially in Punjab.[5] Possibly the largest number of volunteers, at least initially, were gathered in Jami'at ul Ansar ul Afghaneen, a Deobandi organization. The participation of the group to the fighting was limited, as witnessed by the modest level of casualties taken, but from it later derived important Pakistani jihadist groups such as Harakat ul Jihad al Islami (HuJI) and Harakat ul Mujahidin (HuM). It also established links to other groups that were forming in those years, especially the SSP, which was also sending volunteers from its madrasa network to the Taliban.[6]

Jamal estimates that by 1988 its direct derivative HuJI had 4,000 members, between Pakistanis and others.[7]

On top of Jami'at ul Ansar ul Afghaneen, there were also some small Salafi groups, which became active in Afghanistan in 1986, initially among the ranks of local Salafi groups in Nuristan. Among them there was a small group led by Maulana Zakiur Rehman Lakhvi, which had been linked to the Jami'at Ansar ul Afghaneen. Gradually a variety of Salafi (Ahl e Hadith) grouplets coalesced together under Hafiz Saeed to form the Markaz Dawat wal'Irshad (MDI), the predecessor of Lashkar e Taiba (LeT). From 1987 onwards MDI started sending recruits for training to Ittehad e Islami of Prof Sayyaf in Paktia province, which was the closest to Salafism of all the main Afghan resistance parties. It also started working with Jamat ud Dawa ilal Quran wal Sunnah, another Afghan Salafi group which controlled parts of Kunar and eventually (1990) moved its training camp there, from Paktia.[8]

Alongside the Pakistani involvement in the Afghan jihad, by 1984 some of the Arab volunteers who had joined the Afghan jihad were developing the embryo of the global jihad movement, with the formation of Maktab Khidamat al Mujahidin.[9] From there, AQ eventually emerged. Stenersen argues that in the 1980s–90s AQ's main reason for being in Afghanistan was preparing for taking jihad to the Middle East and beyond. AQ was originally intended to be

> *an elite Muslim combat unit which would spread 'the sentiment of jihad' by participating directly at the frontlines, and by promoting a culture of martyrdom and self- sacrifice.*[10]

From the beginning AQ insisted on professionalism and very selective in recruitment.[11] In Afghanistan AQ shared the same environment with Pakistani groups. Rana says that HuM was collaborating with bin Laden already in the 1980s.[12] Up to 1992, however, the role of AQ in Afghanistan was very modest.

The impact of the Iranian revolution

At about the same time as the Afghan conflict was taking off, Shi'a mobilization in Pakistan in the wake of the Iranian revolution quickly generated a counter-mobilization of radical Deobandi groups, of which the SSP became by far the largest and best organized.[13] As many Pakistanis were finding employment in the Gulf monarchies, they were also being influenced by the local anti-Shi'a views. It is widely alleged that support from sectarian groups in Pakistan came from Gulf countries, reacting to growing Iranian influence among Pakistan's Shi'as. Reportedly rich donors from the Gulf states soon started funding anti-Shi'a outfit in Pakistan.[14]

> *Besides lavishing funding on extremist violent sectarian madrassas and jihadi groups, Saudi Arabia has for a number of years interfered in the internal affairs of Pakistan by promoting its narrow Wahhabi version of Islam. The Saudi elite have never hidden their determination to continue to use their considerable financial power and influence in Pakistan to support the more extremist forms of sectarian Deobandism opposed to the Shia and followers of Barelvi Islam. In January 2009*

Wiki Leaks revealed that the Saudi King Abdullah told James Jones, the then United States security advisor, that the Shia president, Asif Ali Zardari, was weak on terrorism and a 'rotten head that was infecting the whole body'.[15]

The Saudis rationalized their attitude alleging concerns of an emerging alliance between Iran, the Shi'a-dominated government in Iraq and Pakistan under Zardari, which would represent a direct threat for Saudi Arabia and other Gulf monarchies.[16]

The main sectarian organization in Pakistan, SSP (Sipah e Sahaba or Army of the Prophet's Companions), was originally established by controversial Sunni cleric Haq Nawaz Jhangvi (member of the Jama'at Ulema e islam) in September 1985. Originally active under the name of Anjaman Sipah i Sahaba (Society of the Companions of the Prophet of Islam, ASS), it was renamed shortly thereafter.[17] Gradually the SSP expanded its presence throughout Pakistan, opening offices in mosques everywhere and branches even in Europe. In its campaign of violence, it targeted 'prominent Shia religious leaders, politicians and community leaders, especially high profile, respected professionals such as doctors'. It also carried out 'indiscriminate attacks on Shi'a mosques and other Shi'a gatherings' and was involved in a number of attacks on Iranian diplomats and buildings in Pakistan.[18]

There is nowadays a near consensus among analysts that SSP has received considerable financial and logistical support from Saudi Arabia and the other Gulf states.[19] Reportedly even Pakistani intelligence believed the Saudi embassy was the conduit for funding to SSP.[20] Maulana Jhangvi knew the Saudis were already the main source of funding to Deobandi groups in Pakistan and 'began visiting Arab embassies in Islamabad to solicit financial support and soon succeeded in solidifying Saudi patronage for ASS/SSP'.[21] According to Jamal,

The Saudis were looking for groups to wage a proxy war on the model of the Afghan jihad inside Iran at that time. [...] They were particularly interested in setting up jihadi training camps along the Pakistan-Iran border. The aim was to execute incursions inside Iran and incite Sunni minority populations against the Shia rulers of the country. None of the existing groups they had funded were ready or able to do this. The Saudis had invited some Kashmiri commanders from Indian – controlled Kashmir to Saudi Arabia in the early 1980s and offered large sums of money to wage an Iranian jihad instead of the jihad in Kashmir, but ultimately failed to convince them.[22]

At that time Maulana Jhangvi was a regular visitor to Arab embassies such as those of Iraq and Saudi Arabia. He and his group emerged as the only willing candidate for the Saudi request of establishing

Sunni terrorist infrastructure – such as military training camps – along the Pakistan-Iran border so that terrorists could carry out attacks inside Iran to incite the Sunni population against the Shi`a regime; after conducting attacks, they could flee back across the border to their sanctuaries in Pakistan.[23]

The SSP ended up as a result setting up a sizeable infrastructure in Baluchistan, kick-starting the massive organizational development of SSP, even if these capabilities were never used against Iran directly.[24]

According to Kamran, 'Zia lent unequivocal support to the SSP after he had a "bad meeting" with Khomeini. He used the SSP to resist Shia mobilization and contain Iranian influence'.[25] Jamal agrees:

> *Maulana Jhangvi understood that General Zia-ul-Haq continuously needed mujahideen to wage the U.S.- funded jihad in Afghanistan, which his group could provide. In return for this quid pro quo, his group could receive militancy training in the camps set up for the mujahideen fighting in Afghanistan.*[26]

After Haq Nawaz Jhangvi was killed, several other leaders succeeded each other, such as Mawlana Tariq Azam, Isra ul Haq Qaseemi, Ali Shir Haydari, Zia ul Rahman Faroqi – all were assassinated.[27] After the death of founder Haq Nawaz Jhangvi the SSP splintered in many different factions, mostly led by the provincial leaders of the group: Lashkar e Jhangvi (LeJ), the Al Badr Foundation, Al Farooq, Allah Akbar, Tanzeem ul Haq, Jhangvi Tigers and Al Haq Tigers. Later the Jhangvi Tigers, Al Haq Tigers and Allah Akbar factions merged with LeJ.[28]

LeJ was born as a split of SSP in 1996. It was the largest of the splinters and had much greater resonance than the other splinters mentioned above, and others such as Tanzeem ul Haq, Al Farooq and Al Badr Foundation.[29] It emerged mainly because as the mother organization was getting involved in mainstream politics, a group of militants decided to continue with their terrorist activities. Reportedly LeJ continued being supported by Saudi money, 'funnelled through Ahl e Hadith madrassas'.[30] LeJ had the dubious distinction of introducing suicide bombing to sectarian warfare in 2003.[31]

LeJ was characterized by a tight discipline including the requirement of a vow until death, and never tried to develop a mass base. External estimates of its strength did not exceed 1,000. In its first five years of existence, LeJ carried out an average of seventy attacks a month.[32]

It has been repeatedly alleged that SSP created LeJ under its control in order to be able to combine political activities with terrorist operations.[33] It was also alleged among other things that LeJ's real leader was Maulana Alam Tariq, the brother of SSP's future leader Maulana Azam Tariq.[34] It is possible, in any case, that SSP might have lost control of LeJ or part thereof at one point, and that LeJ might have lost control of part of its members.[35]

Jihad in Kashmir

The beginnings, Afghan style

It has been argued that for Pakistan the Afghan war of the 1980s was a multiple opportunity not only to expand its influence in Afghanistan to unprecedented levels, but also to develop a new strategy for undermining Indian control over Kashmir, fostering an insurgency that was intended to make the cost of occupation unbearable to India.³⁶ Already in 1984 plans started reportedly being drafted in Pakistan, following a direct order of President/dictator Zia ul Haq, for sponsoring an insurgency in Kashmir.³⁷ Soon Kashmiri separatists were being trained in the camps of Jama'at e Islami, the main Pakistani Islamist party and a close ally of Zia.³⁸ The Pakistani leadership reportedly reasoned that after the Afghan jihad, which was supported by Western powers, it would be hard for the Americans not to support the Kashmiri jihad.³⁹ Moreover, according to Kapur,

> *General Zia believed that if Pakistan could serve as the primary conduit for international aid to the Afghan resistance, it could inflate the cost of its support for the war effort and then divert the profits from US reimbursements to Kashmiri rebels. He maintained that the United States, preoccupied with its goal of damaging the Soviet Union, would ignore the Pakistani scheme. The Afghan conflict would thus serve as a 'smokescreen' behind which Pakistan could wage a renewed militant campaign in Kashmir. Indeed, Zia reportedly referred in private to the war in Afghanistan as 'the Kashmir jihad.'*⁴⁰

By the mid-1980s, the Pakistanis were already providing support to the Jammu and Kashmir Liberation Front (JKLF).⁴¹ The Kashmir operation rapidly escalated to the point when in 1990 'several hundred Kashmiris per month were crossing into Pakistani territory for military training and then returning to Kashmir to fight the Indian occupation'.⁴²

Although the covert operation in Kashmir inflicted major damage on India, managing it turned out to be a complex matter for Pakistan. As Kapur put it,

> *The biggest challenge that Pakistan faced was ensuring proper alignment between Pakistani national interests and the interests and capabilities of its militant proxies.*⁴³

The nationalist tendencies of the JKLF were not to Pakistan's liking.⁴⁴ For this reason the Pakistani ISI abandoned the JKLF and started supporting other groups, primarily Hizb ul Mujahideen (HM), an Islamist group linked to Jama'at e Islami (JeI), which, contrary to the JKLF advocated the accession of Kashmir to Pakistan.⁴⁵ But even the HM, was not entirely suitable for Pakistan's aims, as it was largely a Kashmiri organization, which was reluctant to use extreme violence and not sufficiently controllable by the ISI.⁴⁶

> *HM members thus worried about the consequences of their militant activities and were less inclined to engage in extremely violent actions against the Indian authorities than the Pakistanis wished. In addition, in important instances, HM leaders were willing to strike compromises directly with the Indian government.*⁴⁷

The faith of the Pakistani establishment in HM was undermined.⁴⁸ According to Shahzad, another reason why the ISI eventually opted to favour HuJI as opposed to JeI was the former's 'simple rural background' was deemed to be more suitable as opposed to the 'middle-class' background of the typical JeI member.⁴⁹

According to Kapur, the Pakistanis decided that they needed forces 'willing to employ extreme violence', 'able to pose a significant tactical challenge to Indian security forces' and 'utterly unwilling to compromise'.[50] Hence the decision to shift support to non-Kashmiri groups, who relied on foreign volunteers (mostly Pakistanis). Among them HuM, LeT and Jaish e Mohammed (JeM) emerged as the most prominent (see below).

The 'professionalization' of the jihad for Kashmir in the 1990s

As discussed above, by the early 1990s the Pakistani ISI had lost faith with both the JKLF and HM. It started looking for new blood. HuM and HuJI started operating in Kashmir in 1991.[51] By 1994, the local Kashmiri insurgent groups supported by Pakistan were running out of steam also because the Indian security force were gaining the upper hand. This accelerated the transition to Pakistani jihadist groups, according to Swami:

Pakistani strategists sought to respond to this situation by pumping in growing numbers of battle-hardened personnel, often its own nationals and those from West Asia. A welter of Pakistan-based organizations, such as the LeT, HuJI, Harkat-ul-Ansar and HuM, began to play an ever-greater role.[52]

The HuJI grew quickly in the early days of the Kashmir jihad, but it suffered from the defection of a large faction, led by Maulana Fazlur Rehman Khalil and Maulana Masood Kashmiri, who founded HuM in 1991. The HuJI's donors in Saudi Arabia put pressure on the two factions to reunify, with they did in October 1993, under the name Harakat ul Ansar.[53] The merger did not last and soon HuM was re-established as a separate organization.

By 2000 HM had been eclipsed by HuM, LeT and JeM. From 2000 these Pakistani groups were also instrumental in the new strategy to expand the jihad in Kashmir to the rest of India.

HuM first emerged as the most prominent of the Pakistani groups, thanks to its ability to deploy large numbers of foreign fighters, which the ISI reportedly considered more dependable.[54] Although free of Kashmiri nationalist tendencies, HuM was not particularly effective in fighting. Indeed, as mentioned above HuM was already in crisis in the early 1990s, when it was the largest of the Pakistani groups active in Kashmir. The establishment of JeM took away much of its membership. HuM was the first victim of the decision of the ISI to concentrate its funding on more radical and better organized groups such as JeM and LeT. At the peak of its power HuM had thousands of fighters, but as a result of decreased funding some 70 per cent of them joined JeM after it was founded.[55] Many HuM fighters also joined LeT.[56] Soon HuM was overshadowed by LeT and JeM.[57]

Meyerle noted that the Pakistani jihadists

possessed much greater striking power, not to mention a reputation for extreme brutality. It was these hardcore fundamentalist outfits that had come to dominate the headlines through daring, gruesome, and relentlessly vicious attacks. These Pakistan based guerrillas escalated their attacks through 2000 and 2001 with bigger, bolder operations – thereby demonstrating that they, and not the HM, were the primary force behind the insurgency.[58]

The Pakistani jihadists (read JeM and LeT) indeed 'professionalized' the insurgency in Kashmir from the 1990s onwards, deploying with much better training and better equipment, including advanced communications equipment and large quantities of military grade explosive. They also proved able to deploy committed recruits, even willing to engage the Indian army in open battle. The jihadists organized in small units, operating autonomously, enabling an insurgency centred on commando-style strikes. The Pakistani groups were also much harder to infiltrate for the Indians.[59]

By 2000, [...] while the HM's fighting power withered under continual crackdowns, more decentralized outfits continued to innovate and carry out increasingly bold and damaging attacks.[60]

In addition, the new insurgent groups also started taking the jihad to India itself. The first strike was in December 2002, against the Red Fort in Delhi, and it left a very strong impression in India.[61]

The main protagonist of this transformation was LeT. What was at that time still MDI started getting involved with Kashmir by training Kashmiri recruits in 1988, on request of the ISI. By 1989 MDI was already sending some of its own to Kashmir, to fight alongside groups such as al Baqr and Tehreek ul Mujahideen (another Salafi group). From 1989 onwards, however MDI was setting up its infrastructure in and around Kashmir and in August 1992 for the first time it began operating independently. By the summer on 1993 LeT was established as a separate department.[62] Initially LeT was the only Pakistani jihadist group to show any interest in Kashmir, the others being more interested in India proper.[63] Not that LeT was not interested in India: in 1994 LeT however announced for the first time that its forces had entered India, from Kashmir.[64]

Kapur believes that exactly because LeT was initially just a small group with a limited Ahl e Hadith base (contrary to Deobandi groups such as JeM, HuM and HuJI), the ISI assumed it could control it easily and therefore decided to invest large resources on it. LeT's ideology also offered guarantees that it would never seek compromise with India, or turn against the Pakistani authorities. Despite the low starting base, the ISI eventually turned LeT into a very capable force. 'Numerous army and ISI personnel also contributed their expertise by joining LeT following their retirement.'[65] Members of the Indian security forces agreed that LeT emerged as the 'most capable' of the groups involved in Kashmir.[66] LeT's philosophy involved giving the recruits a strong religious indoctrination first, and only later train them militarily.[67] LeT successfully reinvigorated the insurgency deploying its fedayin (self-sacrificing) tactics from 1999 onwards.[68]

According to Meyerle, LeT's superiority on local Kashmiri insurgents derived from 'its unique combination of decentralized cells and centralized military command'.[69]

The bottom rungs of the LeT, which are organized in small cells rather than large units, are more autonomous and self-directing than those of the HM. If their leaders in the district command are captured or killed, they can act on their own or even reconstitute the district-level leadership. [...] the group's organization on the Indian side of the LOC includes autonomous cells managed directly from Pakistan, as well as district commanders with their own units. These special cells are charged with carrying out important, super-secret missions, such as the attacks on the Red Fort and market areas in New Delhi.[70]

Schmidt notes LeT's specialization in fedayin attacks, consisting of small teams, highly trained, attacking large Indian targets with the purpose of inflicting as many casualties as possible before being overcome. The new tactic was meant to overcome the problem posed by the saturation of Jammu and Kashmir with Indian security forces.[71]

As Fair put it, LeT became the ISI's favourite in the early 1990s because of 'its demonstrable superior capabilities', which would allow to 'intensify the conflict in Kashmir' and expand the insurgency.[72] Lieven commented that

the militants in Kashmir began to alienate much of the native Kashmiri population with their ruthlessness and ideological fanaticism; to splinter and splinter again into ever-smaller groups and fight with each other despite ISI efforts to promote co-operation, and to prey on Kashmiri civilians. LeT's greater discipline in this regard was reportedly one factor in the increasing favour shown to it by the ISI.[73]

The fact that Hafiz Saeed had previously worked in the ISI must have helped reinforce the trust in his organization. His links to Saudi Arabia and Qatar helped raise funds for LeT.[74] Most sources inside LeT have been portraying it as internally homogeneous and fully united.[75]

JeM was the other protagonist of the new wave of Kashmiri groups. JeM was a more recent innovation, having been formed in February 2000 as a splinter of HuM. A source in HuM confirmed that JeM was formed out of HuM and SSP, perhaps as a Deobandi pendant of LeT.[76] Incidentally, a JeM source claimed that was founded with the support of Osama bin Laden.[77] It positioned itself as the most radical of the groups active in Kashmir and attracted widespread support by radical clerics. It pioneered suicide attacks in Kashmir.[78]

JeM might also have benefited from a deliberate ISI divide and rule effort, to keep jihadists divided in order to better control them.[79] It is often argued that the ISI sponsored JeM's creation in order to check LeT's growing power and to be able to deploy proxies to Kashmir.[80] Zahab and Roy indeed believed that the appearance of JeM weakened LeT.[81]

A partially alternative interpretation is provided by Mir, who believes JeM grew rapidly because of the links to SSP and LeJ and because of the support of leading radical clerics.[82] In other words, JeM mobilized the more radical Deobandi groups for the jihad in Kashmir.

In contrast to LeT, JeM was even more decentralized and lacked a central command altogether:

adopted an extremely fluid and decentralized command structure. It is a small group of no more than 300 cadres that operates a number of cells loosely coordinated by a handful of leaders in Pakistan. [...] It operates underground in both India and Pakistan, and so has no centralized command or infrastructure.[83]

Technically banned already in 2002, JeM split into two factions in 2003 (Khuddam ul Islam and Jama'at ul Furqan), but the split seems to have had little impact and to have been soon re-absorbed.[84] In 2001 JeM claimed around 10,000 active members.[85]

The involvement in the 1990s civil war in Afghanistan

After the emergence of the movement of the Taliban in 1994, various groups of volunteers, encouraged if not sponsored by the Pakistani authorities, joined the Afghan Taliban's fight in the second half of the 1990s.[86] These were largely Deobandi groups. Jama'at Ulema e Islam (JuI), the leading Deobandi group, lobbied the Pakistani government in favour of the Taliban in 1994 and soon started sending thousands of volunteers (including many Pakistanis) from the madrasas it controlled and more in general from the FATA.[87] Several other leading supporters of the Afghan Taliban were splinters of the JuI. Among them, HuJI was one of the most consistent supporters of the Afghan Taliban with its volunteers in the 1990s; it was so close to the Taliban that it had three ministers and twenty judges appointed by them and leader Qari Saifullah served as adviser to Mullah Omar. HuJI lost some 300 men fighting alongside the Taliban before 2001.[88] The SSP also lost many, especially in the battle of Kunduz in 2001.[89] HuJI's splinter too, HuM, fought alongside the Taliban in the 1990s and took significant casualties.[90] Separately, Darul Uloom Haqqania, a splinter of JuI led by Mawlavi Sami ul Haq, also sent hundreds of volunteers to the Taliban in the 1990s.[91] Yet another splinter of JuI, the Jamiat ul Uloomi Islamiyyah of Maulavi Mohammed Yousuf Binori, reportedly sent 600 volunteers to the Taliban in 1997.[92]

Other groups linked to the JuI also contributed. The paths of the Afghan jihadist movement and of the Sunni supremacist movement, mobilized in response at the waves caused by the Iranian revolution, eventually met in the 1990s. The SSP had an armed militia, which it deployed in Afghanistan.[93] 'Thousands' of volunteers went to fight on the Afghan Taliban's side in the 1990s.[94] It is in the training camps of Afghanistan that AQ forged links with the sectarian groups (see also *The first Afghan jihad* above).[95] Possibly to please the authorities and certainly to obtain military training, LeJ too participated in the fighting in Kashmir alongside HuJI and JeM in the 1990s.[96] The relationship with the 'Kashmiri' jihad was already established years earlier, when LeJ trained its members in HuM's training camp 'Khalid Bin Walid' in Afghanistan.[97]

JuI was part of the ruling coalition in Pakistan when it got engaged on the Taliban's side, so its direct support for them must have been welcomed by the Pakistani authorities.

By contrast, non-Deobandi groups were only marginally involved with the Taliban. The main exception was the Tehreek e Nafaz e Shariat e Mohammadi (TNSM), a Panjpiri-dominated outfit, which established close relations with the Afghan Taliban after 1994. However, it is not clear whether it put in practice any organized effort to send volunteers to them, before the US intervention in autumn 2001. At that point the TNSM led the solidarity movement with the Taliban, sending in the largest contingent of volunteers (some 6,000 out of a total of 10,000).[98]

JeI, which was supporting Hizb e Islami in Afghanistan in the 1990s, did not support the Taliban until after 2001.[99] LeT played a very marginal role in Afghanistan before 2002, with only five of its members dying in combat there. Its Ahl e Hadith links made it not too sympathetic to the Deobandi-linked Taliban.[100]

Although the literature usually refers to Pakistani volunteers being sent to the Taliban from the madrasas, clearly volunteers were accruing from a somewhat wider pool of sympathizers. The case of the first leader to emerge among the Pakistani Taliban, Nek Mohammed (see Chapter 2), is emblematic: he dropped out of the madrasa where he was studying years before volunteering for Afghanistan and was instead running a shop in Wana when he enlisted.[101] Beitullah Mehsud too was reportedly working as a gym instructor before volunteering for Afghanistan in the 1990s.[102] Hakimullah Mehsud also appears to have dropped out of his madrasa before he volunteered to fight with the Taliban in the 1990s.[103]

The Afghan civil war of the 1990s is particularly important from this book's perspective because it saw the role of AQ in Afghanistan expand considerably, even if at the same time AQ was starting to get involved in other jihads, as in Tajikistan and Somalia.[104] In Afghanistan it started building relations with other groups, which would become long-term partners, such as the IMU (Islamic Movement of Uzbekistan).[105] With other groups, such as the SSP, the relationship was more superficial, as they were more closely connected with the Taliban.[106] AQ allied with the Afghan Taliban from 1997 onwards, although initially there was friction between AQ and Taliban over the need to resolve the Afghan issue, before getting involved in other conflicts, and over the concept of global jihad.[107] Only in spring 2001 bin Laden pledged allegiance to Mullah Omar.[108] AQ's focus was not on Afghanistan. Even after AQ expanded operations, towards the end of the Emirate,

> The main goal was to educate military leaders for al Qa'ida's organization that could take on a range of tasks – from leading units on a battlefield to building clandestine underground networks in the 'interior' (i.e., the Middle East), to providing military assistance to local insurgencies.[109]

Pakistani volunteers for the Afghan jihad often trained at AQ-run camps. AQ and its predecessor Maktba al Khidamat had links to Pakistani Deobandi clerics and interacted with Pakistani jihadist groups present in Afghanistan, such as Harakat ul Ansar, HuJI and MDI (the predecessor of LeT), although there was also friction.[110] When in 1998 bin Laden launched the World Islamic Front for Jihad, two South Asians signed the edict, Mir Hamza (head of Jamiat Ulema e Pakistan) and Fazlul Rahman Khalil (member of HuJI and the future leader of HuM).[111] The link with Pakistani jihadism was therefore there already.

The collaboration of AQ with Pakistani jihadist groups was the object of gossip and speculation in the 1990s. For example, it was also claimed that bin Laden was involved in setting up LeT.[112] Some sources even see a link between AQ and the Pakistani ISI. Benazir Bhutto alleged in her memoirs that bin Laden had cooperated with the ISI against her.[113] American investigators also alleged a relationship between bin Laden and the ISI in the 1980s and 1990s.[114] Such allegations would imply that AQ had already before 2001 a significant presence inside Pakistan and operational links to Pakistani groups, but there is little or no hard evidence of this.

2

The strategies of the global jihadists in Pakistan after 2001

The second Afghan jihad (2002–) and AQ's expanding role with Pakistan's jihadists

In 2001 the Kashmir campaign was in full swing, while the Afghan civil war seemed to be drawing to a close with an impending Taliban victory. Almost everybody was surprised when a new front was opened in Afghanistan, following the 9/11 attacks in the United States. AQ of course caused the start of the second Afghani jihad with its 9/11 attacks in New York. Opinion among analysts is still divided on whether AQ did intend to draw the Americans into Afghanistan, or miscalculated assuming that the Americans would not react strongly.[1] In any case, the American invasion of Afghanistan in October 2001 pushed AQ members into Pakistan and that is when it started getting more deeply involved with Pakistani jihadists, who soon were expanding further due to their role in the jihad in Kashmir and in supporting Taliban remnants in Afghanistan. The American occupation of Afghanistan after 2001 acted as a magnet for jihadist groups of all description and especially global jihadists, volunteering to fight alongside the Afghan Taliban, who had been ejected from power by the US intervention.[2] AQ cadres and members in the region were fully on board. As one AQIS source would put it years later:

> One of the major objectives of [AQIS] is strengthening the Islamic Emirate of Afghanistan, defending it, and bringing stability to it. In pursuit of this objective, [AQIS] engages the enemies of the Islamic Emirate outside Afghanistan, and also takes part in the battles inside it – fighting shoulder-to-shoulder with the mujahideen of the emirate. Moreover, it invites the Muslims of the Subcontinent to pledge their allegiance to the Islamic Emirate and to support it.[3]

The rationale for pledging to the Emirate was that 'a useful and constructive alliance in the region is only possible with the allegiance to the Islamic Emirate of Afghanistan'.[4] The support extended to the Afghan Taliban was therefore instrumental to building a viable jihadist alliance. We also know that AQ's leadership had just moved into Pakistan's tribal areas in 2002 and needed to be protected. The American intervention in Afghanistan in other words represented both a major threat and an immense opportunity for AQ, which had to juggle its strategic choices to manage a complex situation. The sense of threat permeates the account provided by Lahoud, based on bin Laden's correspondence. The sense of opportunity much less so.⁵ This is quite obvious, given that the leadership was more affected by the threats and had less to gain from the opportunities that were arising, which benefited primarily AQ's local branch and operatives. This was particularly the case because, as Lahoud notes, bin Laden was still focused on the 'far enemy' and on the Middle East, maintaining an instrumental attitude towards Afghanistan and Pakistan.

The primacy of Pakistan 2002–14

According to Shahzad, after the Americans entered Afghanistan, Musharraf asked the Pakistani jihadi leaders to wait until the Americans would pull out of Afghanistan, which he thought would happen within five years. Then they would be allowed to resume their activities. But Musharraf was not believed by many jihadists, and quite a few of them headed for the tribal areas to escape the expected forthcoming crackdown.⁶ That created opportunities for AQ to expand its influence.

After initially lingering on in the tribal areas, AQ elements started supporting jihadist groups deeper inside Pakistan in 2004–5, including LeT, JeM, HM, HuM, LeJ and Al Badr Mujahidin. A source in LeJ said that AQ members in 2001–2 approached LeJ asking for safe haven, protection and support in fighting the Americans in Afghanistan.⁷

According to an AQ source, the funds were obtained from the Gulf States and to a lesser extent from Pakistani donors in Karachi and some other wealthy cities of Pakistan. AQ members encouraged all these Pakistani groups to take part in the Afghan jihad.⁸ Given the poor state of AQ Central's finances in those years, it would appear that these funds did not go through the central leadership and that the latter had little or no say about them.⁹ Support from AQ members included funds, but also advice and training. According to a source inside AQ, as late as mid-2020, the local branch of AQ (AQIS) still had 375 agents busy training and advising jihadist groups based in Pakistan, providing 'weapons trainings, planning, resources management, capacity building, improving organizational structures and recruitment and help in other different fields and areas'.¹⁰

The South Asian AQ branch developed greater ambitions than simply 'supporting' Pakistani jihadist groups and the Afghan jihad. AQ was clearly trying to expand its influence. An AQ cadre depicted AQ's role in the post-2001 years this way:

> We are here to help the other groups. We want to show them that we are always with them. We are giving good advice to them on how to fight against Americans and westerners.¹¹

In the words of another AQ source, 'we want to become very powerful and all the jihadi groups to be under our control.'¹² The desire to consolidate legitimacy as the leader of global jihad, discussed in the *Introduction*, clearly resonates here. This had not been the case before the American invasion on 2001. In fact, the ambitions of the AQ branch in Afghanistan and Pakistan expanded greatly year after year after 2001. For quite a few years into the second Afghan jihad, this branch and the groups it supported (mostly various Pakistani and Central Asian outfits and of course the Afghan Taliban) mainly operated from across the Afghan-Pakistan border. Their permanent presence inside Afghanistan was minimal. A senior Taliban source estimated that as late as 2008 AQ only had 50 full members in Afghanistan, while 200 other members were in Pakistan. In subsequent years, at least according to AQ sources, there was a steady increase in the number of AQ members arriving to Pakistan (from where some would then be deployed to Afghanistan), with numbers growing steadily every year. By 2014, according to an internal source, AQ had 430 members in Pakistan and half that number in Afghanistan. In Pakistan the main centre of AQ presence was Waziristan (58 per cent), followed by Bajaur (24 per cent), Lahore (5 per cent), Quetta (8 per cent) and Kashmir (5 per cent) (see Figure 1).[13]

Renewed primacy of Afghanistan 2014–16

Despite the deep involvement with Pakistani jihadist groups, protecting AQ leaders remained a priority for AQ members in Pakistan throughout. As late as September 2020, an AQIS source still described one of the primary tasks of AQIS as protecting AQ leaders in Pakistan.[14] Once chased from the FATA, AQ members relocated to the cities of Lahore, Faisalabad and Karachi.[15] Many of its cadres and leaders remained in Karachi and Lahore at least until mid-2020.[16]

Throughout the post-2001 period and at least until 2019, AQ continued to see Afghanistan as the ideal base for its leaders, or at least as the least bad option. An AQ source for example claimed that al Zawahiri as of 2016 was still hoping to be able to return to Afghanistan:

> Our main objective in Afghanistan is to make our bases here like in 1996. We want AQ's centre to be in Afghanistan. This is our mission and we will achieve our mission because Ayman Al Zawahiri also wants to come to Afghanistan.[17]

The acceleration in the build up from 2013 onwards was due to the hope that year 2014 was hoped to represent a turning point, thanks to the US withdrawal decided by President Obama, which was supposed to leave only a token US combat capability in the country. In the wake of the US withdrawal, AQ decided to massively increase its presence in Pakistan and Afghanistan and was planning to send 500 more members, according to Afghan Taliban sources, which had close contacts with AQ.[18] One should note that the establishment of AQIS was announced in September 2014.

Soon afterwards, in late 2014 or in 2015, the new AQIS leadership decided to move the bulk of its men from Pakistan to Afghanistan. Pakistani government operations against TTP in North and South Waziristan created an unsafe environment for AQ, at a time when the risk to AQ's camps in Afghanistan had reduced thanks to the US withdrawal. AQIS' headquarter for Pakistan had been moved to Bajaur, from Waziristan, and AQ also moved other members from Waziristan to Karachi,

Faisalabad, Bajaur, Chitral and Kashmir.[19] At the beginning of 2016, an AQ source put the number of members in Pakistan at 304, while Afghanistan had risen to 518, having overtaken Pakistan during 2015.[20] In just three more months AQIS reached 540 members in Afghanistan, according to another internal source.[21] The increase in the numerical strength of AQ was therefore well underway and the Afghan branch was the main beneficiary (see Figure 1).

As its numbers grew, the local branch of AQ was also mobilizing growing resources to its operations in Afghanistan and Pakistan. An AQ source indicated that by 2009 its budget was already $35 million for the two countries and if it rose only marginally to $37 million in 2010, it accelerated in subsequent years. Reportedly it reached $45 million in 2011, $55 million in 2012, $68 million in 2013 and $85 million in 2014, the year of the American withdrawal.[22] According to a Taliban source close to AQ, in 2014 the AQ branch sourced the funds for Afghanistan and Pakistan from private donors in Saudi Arabia (41 per cent), Egypt (18 per cent), UAE (6 per cent), Qatar (9 per cent), Oman (6 per cent) and Europe (5 per cent), as well as from the Iranian authorities (14 per cent).[23] While it is impossible to probe these figures, the trends highlighted by different sources seem consistent, highlighting an upsurge in funding and in strength in the years leading up to the 2014 US withdrawal.

The shifting focus led to the subordination of the Pakistan branch to the Afghan one. An AQ source for example said in 2016 that the AQ finance commission for Pakistan was subordinated to the Afghan one, under the leadership of Mustafa Hamid Al Falestini.[24] According to another AQ source, in 2017 the Afghan and Pakistani branches of AQ were still united under one leadership (Abdul Rehman Al Aziz Al Awda, a Palestinian appointed on 4 May to replace Qari Yaseen, killed in an airstrike).[25] The primacy of Afghanistan was asserted despite the fact that AQ's top leaders (at least bin Laden until 2011) were based in Pakistan. In 2017, one AQ cadre claimed that al Zawahiri, together with other senior AQ figures such as Abd Al Aziz, Abd Al Hamid and Abu Bakr, was based in Karachi.[26] This might contradict another claim, discussed below, that al Zawahiri travelled to Pakistan from Yemen in 2020, although it cannot

Figure 1 AQ numbers in Pakistan and Afghanistan, 2008–16.

Sources: Meeting with AQ cadre, 2014; meeting with Q*, assistant of Taliban leader Akhtar Mohammad Mansur, 2014; meeting with Q*M, senior Taliban cadre, Pakistan, March 2014.

be ruled out that al Zawahiri moved back and forth. Whether or not al Zawahiri was in Karachi, the city was becoming a centre of AQ activity, as 'most of the group's banking transactions were funnelled through the city'.[27]

Pakistan primacy again 2016–

The renewed 'primacy of Afghanistan' did not last long. The dream of re-establishing a dependable safe haven in Afghanistan petered out quickly as it became clear that the Americans were not the only obstacle to that happening. Already during 2016 a new turn took place as AQ started taking members out of Afghanistan as well. According to an internal source, from a peak of over 800 in spring 2016, by mid-2017 the number had already fallen to 480, of which 200 were in Pakistan (see Figure 1). The decision seems to have been linked to friction with the IS in eastern Afghanistan, where most AQ bases were, and to the Taliban establishing relations with Russia, a development that raised new doubts among AQ's ranks about the trustworthiness of the Taliban.[28]

In parallel to numerical strength, the budget of the local branches too continued to rise vertically in 2015 and 2016, by which time it had reportedly reached $200 million, of which $90 million were for Pakistan and the rest for Afghanistan. For 2017 it was projected to reach $180 million for Afghanistan and $120 million for Pakistan, but it is unlikely to have been met due to the change in plans discussed above.[29]

These numbers cannot be verified, but would suggest that the local branches of AQ were spending not just on keeping a few hundred members in the two countries, but was distributing widely to allies and clients. Indeed, even as late as 2019, AQIS was not able to carry out operations independently of its local allies in South Asia.[30] Most of the money went into supporting Afghan and Pakistani groups.[31] As it will be discussed below and in the following chapters, sources in several Pakistani jihadist groups confirm that they had been receiving substantial amounts of funds from AQ sources over the years. This confirms that AQ as a whole was able to mobilize funds comparable to what the sources above alleged, and that it was being redistributed.

In Pakistan, the primary recipient of AQ support has always been the Pakistani Taliban, both before and after the establishment of the TTP. The Pakistani Taliban emerged after 2001 as a result of the convergence of different trends. The movement of solidarity with the Afghan Taliban was a short-term factor. It was then boosted by an underpinning trend such as the growing power of clerics in the tribal environment of the FATA and PATA, itself a consequence of the effort to support the Afghan mujahidin in the 1980s. The disparate groups that organized in the FATA in 2001–4 had in common the readiness to fight a jihad in support of the Afghan Taliban. This desire brought them in close contact with other groups that had at that time the same aims, such as AQ and allied groups, mostly Central Asians and some Chechens. Clerical influence, according to some authors, favoured the drift of the movement towards sympathizing with global jihadists as well (see Chapter 2).[32]

In addition, as hinted already, AQ sources provided some degree of support to almost all other main jihadist groups in Pakistan, including the groups active in Kashmir. LeT was a major beneficiary, followed by JeM and HuM (see Chapter 5). An AQ source claimed that AQ was also supporting HuJI with $13 million in 2014.[33]

Other groups that received support were the sectarian ones (LeJ, SSP and Jundullah, see Chapter 4). All these groups were to various degrees engaged in supporting the Afghan Taliban's jihad, sending volunteers. But AQ's support was not just motivated by the aim of helping the Taliban in their jihad. For example, a senior Taliban source indicated that in 2014 AQ elements were advising and training the Indian Mujahidin as well.[34] AQ's practice of distributing funds to earn the support of as many jihadist groups as possible, a technique of 'influencing and shaping' the aims of its allies, was highlighted by Byman (see *Introduction*). The fact that this might not have been coordinated by AQ Central might be relevant to counter-terrorism operations, but did not change the impact on Pakistani jihadism. As Markey noted in 2013,

> *Even if al-Qaeda is never able to reconstitute, other like-minded Pakistani terrorist groups have been influenced and strengthened by their contact with al-Qaeda operatives. They have learned new, more sophisticated tactics and adopted aspects of al-Qaeda's worldview, at times trading local and parochial grievances for the rhetoric of global jihad.*[35]

Beyond the Afghan jihad: The 'regionalization' of AQ

The anonymous author of an AQ booklet, dated c. 2005–6, already rationalized the need for AQ to recruit local members in order to spread the jihad movement among the local population. First the author argued the need to reach out to social constituencies:

> *Just as it is unavoidable to anchor strong brotherly relation with local Taliban to establish an effective Mujahid movement in tribal society, likewise, it is unavoidable to anchor relationship with local scholars, tribal leaders, and neo-cultured through continuous communication with them, and proposing the (Islamic) call to them in unique fashion; this is because these are the effective cross-section of tribal society. So, if we could explain to this cross-section, the war theory according to their intellectual level, and they comprehend it, with the help of God, the Jihad would take root.*[36]

Second, he focused on the need for 'Pakistani Mujahidin' to achieve such an impact:

> *In my opinion, in order to achieve this important objective, it is a must to form a designated apparatus that will include Pakistani Mujahidin who will be able to influence this societal cross-section, as they are knowledgeable about tribal traditions and its languages. [...] If communicating with the society's effective cross-section is of great importance on one hand, likewise, the selection of pious and intelligent youths from every tribe is of no lesser importance, having them undergo a comprehensive military and religious training. Those youth will be natural Mujahidin leaders for their tribes. So we have to elevate the scientific (religious sense) level of those youths, build their dexterity in military science, teach them enemy war tactics in addition to the special emphasis of enlightening their hearts with the benefits of Shari'ah religious sciences.*[37]

It is not clear from the booklet quoted above whether AQ saw allies and clients in Pakistan as potentially turning into useful vehicles for such an elite of ad hoc trained Pakistani Mujahidin. AQ had been for long years very selective in its recruitment of Afghans and Pakistanis. According to an internal source, as late as spring 2016 (two years after the launch of AQIS), of 540 members it had in Afghanistan, some 30 were from Afghanistan and some 40 from Pakistan, as well as 27 from India.[38] There were likely more Pakistanis and Indians in Pakistan (where some 300 members were based at that time), but the figures are not known. Still the poor South Asian representation in the Afghan branch is striking, given also the low overall numbers. This might be due to the low 'quality' of prospective recruits, especially from Afghanistan, but it might also be taken as a sign that AQ's interest in Afghanistan, Pakistan and India had for a long time been secondary and/or transitory, in line with Stenersen's argument that AQ's real aim was taking jihad to the Middle East. It is also quite possible that the Afghan branch of AQ did not want to irritate the Taliban by recruiting Afghans.

Shahzad detected signs of AQ getting closer to the Pakistani jihadists and gradual 'indigenization' as early as late 2009, when Muhammad Ilyas Kashmiri was appointed to lead Lashkar e Zil. For Shahzad, Kashmiri was one of the most prominent South Asian members of AQ. He was radicalized by the US invasion of Afghanistan and by the two detentions that ISI inflicted on him after 2001. He then attracted hundreds of Kashmiri militants to the Afghan front. According to Shahzad, Kashmiri was particularly valuable because AQ was struggling to find Pakistani jihadist commanders that met its needs:

These AQ leaders had earlier interacted with many Jihadi commanders including Fazlur Rabman Khalil (of HuM), Masood Azhar (of JeM), and Abdullah Shah Mazhar, and feared that the Pakistani Jihadi commanders could not emerge from the steel frame constructed for them by the ISI. Their assessment was that the Pakistani Jihadi commanders could never think beyond the strategic boundaries drawn in their minds by the ISI. They knew too that the local tribal commanders were prey to a thought process constrained by tribal and Pashtun traditions. They were incapable of thinking beyond Afghan or Pashtun boundaries. Kashmiri, however, was different.[39]

As an 'original thinker' Kashmiri was rapidly brought into AQ and promoted fast up the ranks; by 2007 he reportedly was already member of the AQ Council. Shahzad wrote that Kashmiri came up with the plan of causing friction or even war between India and Pakistan, eventually forcing Pakistan to quit its alliance with the Americans. The first practical result of the new strategy was the Mumbai attack of 2008, which according to Shahzad was drafted by Kashmiri.[40]

Dasgupta too argued that the appointment of Ilyas Kashmiri as the head of Lashkar al Zil (reported in the media in early 2010) could be read as the first attempt by AQ Central to establish a South Asian branch or affiliate. Lashkar e Zil had existed for years, but had been earlier led by Arabs.[41] AQ had only limited influence and control over the TTP, and the TTP often indulged in activities to which AQ objected. The same applied to the Afghan Taliban. Lashkar e Zil was believed by Shahzad to have originally been a tool to strengthen AQ's influence, 'provid[ing] support through expertise to various Taliban factions in Pakistan and Afghanistan against NATO and Pakistan's armed forces'.[42] The new Lashkar e Zil was reportedly intended to

> *gather under one umbrella all of the Muslim guerrilla outfits and strategic experts previously working separately for the Islamist cause, and transform them into 'blood brothers.' Al Qa'ida's ultimate aim is to control the dynamics of all the local Muslim armed resistance movements [...] and create an environment in which local agendas are surrendered to synchronize with al Qa'ida policies.*[43]

Other analysts too have later accepted the idea that by appointing a South Asian to lead Lashkar e Zil, AQ Central seemed to be aiming to start putting local roots finally.[44]

An AQ source, contacted long after Kashmiri's appointment, explained that Lashkar e Zil (aka Jaish ul Usra) was a 'military brigade' of AQ, based in Lahore and North Waziristan, and also provided information about what its original intent was:[45]

> *This brigade was formed by our leader in response to American drone airstrike on our positions in Pakistan. The group was formed jointly from foreign and Afghan loyalists such as Hezb e Islami, Afghan Taliban, Pakistani Taliban and LeT. The group was tasked to train Afghan Taliban suicide bombers and also plan military operation against American military and intelligence bases in south and south eastern Afghanistan.*[46]

It would seem therefore that Lashkar e Zil was aimed at intensifying the effort in Afghanistan. The source did not however mention any upgrade of Lashkar e Zil to an umbrella structure, gathering all jihadist groups in the region. He added that Lashkar e Zil was disbanded in 2014, that is, when AQIS was launched.[47] The timing of Lashkar e Zil's disbandment is compatible with the claim that Lashkar e Zil had a role somewhat similar to the one AQIS came to play. It is nonetheless not clear whether Lashkar e Zil was indeed meant to 'regionalize' AQ, nor why (if that was indeed the case) it did not succeed.

The establishment of Al Qaida in the Indian Subcontinent (AQIS) in 2014 appears to have been a clearer turning point towards regionalization. If in 2016 (at least in Afghanistan) there were still few South Asians in its ranks (see above), according to an internal source by 2019 of the total core membership of AQIS (742), 256 were Pakistanis, 198 Indians, 238 Kashmiris and 50 of other nationalities (mostly Arabs).[48] Full members of AQIS were typically recruited from the ranks of other jihadist groups, such as LeT, Jama'at ul Ansar ul Shari'a, a small group established in 2017, and others.[49] It is worth noting how Afghans appear to have remained nearly insignificant, perhaps due to some AQ-Taliban agreement that AQ would not target Afghans for recruitment as full members, as mentioned above.

When AQIS was established, commentators again assumed that all or at least many of the groups that had been linked to AQ beforehand would merge into it: Afghan and Pakistani Taliban, HuM, HuJI, JeM, LeJ, the Indian Mujahidin (a front for Lashkar e Taiba), the IMU, the Turkistan Islamic Party, Junood al Fida, etc.[50]

In this interpretation, AQIS was assumed to be a follow up on the 'new incarnation' of Lashkar e Zil, assuming the latter was ever intended by AQ to be that. The explicit use of AQ in the name of the 'affiliate' surprised, as it attracted immediate American attention, making the growth and development of AQIS much harder. Hence it has been speculated that the choice of the name might have been an attempt to advertise the innovation, probably to signal dynamism in the face of the competition posed by the recently established IS.[51] This is the argument advanced by the Soufan Group:

> *The disagreements between al-Qaeda's senior leadership and al-Qaeda in Iraq (AQI), the precursor to IS, in the mid-2000s fundamentally shaped al-Qaeda's strategic shift. The failure of AQC [Al Qai'da central] to reign in the brutality of AQI provided an important lesson to the parent organization, namely, that it needed to exercise more moral, and at times operational, control over its affiliates. Further, the success of IS in Iraq, which was predicated upon support it received from local Sunni groups, solidified AQC's realization of the need to focus more aggressively on developing local roots, cultivating these ties and ultimately strengthening its base in South Asia – the region that hosted its fighters for more than a decade and a half.*[52]

Indeed, years later an AQIS source admitted that

> *One of the main reasons for establishing and announcing AQIS was to compete with Daesh. As you know better, in the past years and before their defeat, Daesh was trying their best to promote and expand their influence among Pakistani based jihadist groups. They were using funding and other techniques to urge groups to join their Islamic state and accept their aims.*[53]

An AQIS source saw the establishment of Wilayat Pakistan (IS-P) by IS as 'not good nor healthy'. 'Indeed, they only tried to disrupt our plans and start competing with us.'[54]

> *We [AQIS] are worried by Daesh competition in Pakistan. We're worried about our current place among different groups here in Pakistan. We are also worried about the groups with which we have alliances, if we might lose our alliances with these groups, that can definitely worsen our position and further damage our credibility and image.*[55]

A 2017 AQIS document suggests the same when it stresses that the jihadist

> *bases its actions on Shari'ah's clear and established evidences, and not on irrational interpretations and ambiguous texts.*[56]

and that AQIS

> *forbids hitting or killing targets permissible in Shari'ah when hitting or killing such targets does more harm than good to the jihadi movement. Moreover, the Jama'ah*

*forbids carrying out operations that are beyond the understanding of Muslim masses, and repulses them from jihad.*⁵⁷

This does not mean that the purpose of AQIS might not have gone beyond a propaganda response to IS. AQ media for their part attributed the establishment of AQIS to the US withdrawal from Afghanistan and by the need to re-orient the focus towards the local impious governments of South Asia, that is, the 'near enemy, and especially India'. It was also alleged that the desire of AQ Central to move its centre away from South Asia might also have had to do with the establishment of a local branch, although as it was discussed above in 2014–16 AQ sources were claiming the contrary, that is, that AQ Central wanted to re-establish itself in Afghanistan.⁵⁸

In terms of actual changes, however, analysts have been at pain to identify what the establishment of AQIS meant operationally, and they have not been very successful, aside from the 'formalisation of the already close working relationships of the different Jihadi groups in South Asia'.⁵⁹

al Zawahiri's claim of a 'merger' with other jihadist groups appears to have been largely propagandistic as well. AQIS in fact continued to preside over a rather loose network of allied jihadist groups, around a core barely larger than the old AQ.⁶⁰ An AQIS document, published in 2017, insisted on presenting AQIS as an umbrella group of jihadist organizations:

*In the early days following its inception, mostly those groups were incorporated into AQS that had been engaged in jihad in this region under the umbrella of al Qa'ida for a long period.*⁶¹

While it is clear that AQIS did not absorb any jihadist group of any importance, it is more plausible that it would have played some kind of coordination role between them. Indeed, the description of the role attributed to AQIS in the same document provides points in such a direction:

*[AQIS] would try to bring about an environment of mutual constructive criticism and reform with jihadi groups [...]. Jihad can progress in a positive direction only when the jihadi groups fighting in Pakistan, agree on some clear principles with regard to selecting targets for military operations. To bring about that required agreement, [AQ] would try, as an act of advising, to bring together the jihadi organizations on one and the same strategy, despite their being distinct from one another.*⁶²

Moreover, AQIS appears to have started recruiting non-core (second-tier) members from within the ranks of its most closely allied organizations, aside its core members, few in numbers. As late as September 2019, while an AQIS source claimed 742 members in all of South Asia, he also claimed 4,000 non-core members, of which about 60 per cent were Pakistanis and 20 per cent Afghans. They came from organizations such as LeT, Haqqani network, IS-K, LeJ, HuM, HuJI, TTP and IMU.⁶³

It is not clear whether recruiting second-tier members was specifically an AQIS innovation, even if it seems likely. Certainly, recruiting second-tier members must have helped AQIS play a coordinating role. The members of the second tier were selected from within the ranks of allied organizations, and stayed with those organizations, so it might have been a way of inserting AQ's DNA (the specially trained Pakistani Mujahidin) into the wider jihadist movement. It was a way of going local, without the core membership being unduly influenced by local causes. This however suggests that AQ was either not yet so interested in putting deep roots in South Asia or considered that it would have been tactically more effective or appropriate to maintain some insulation from the bulk of Pakistani jihadists. The close relations between many jihadist groups and the Pakistani deep state must have worried AQ because of the risk of infiltration of its core. Hence the rationale for the second tier.

For some time AQ maintained a structure in Pakistan, parallel to AQIS, but the two were integrated 'recently', said a source in September 2020.[64] The merger adds to doubts concerning the actual impact of the establishment of AQIS. Indeed, the Soufan group concluded that 'The decision behind the creation of a South Asian affiliate, therefore, was perhaps "less operational than political".[65] In the end, the establishment of AQIS boiled down to rather little:

> *Because of the relative geographical proximity of AQIS and the AQ core, differentiating between the two is difficult, but some key distinctions exist. Overall, AQIS represents an attempt by AQ to establish a more durable presence in the region by enhancing links with local actors.*[66]

But, as discussed throughout this chapter, there seems to be little question that a core did exist. All the accounts provided by the sources imply that and without that, managing the 'loose' groups and networks would have been unmanageable. How the core dealt with the loose jihadist allies is discussed in the following chapters. The aims of the Qaidists in dealing with its host of allies in South Asia vary from case to case. Its alliance with the TTP and with the Sunni supremacist groups might well have been a largely pragmatic step, dictated by the need to enjoy some protection in Pakistan, as well as to support jihad in Afghanistan. Support to Kashmir-focused groups such as LeT, HuM and JeM might have started in a largely similar way, but then evolved into something different. Despite a slow start, driven by the need to respond to IS, a new focus on India and Kashmir appears to have emerged over the years, when AQIS' media started focusing away from Afghanistan towards India and Kashmir.[67]

AQ and the Pakistani authorities

Considering that the Pakistani security establishment long maintained close to very close relations with a variety of groups close to AQ, including the Afghan Taliban and several Pakistani jihadist groups active in Kashmir, the idea of it having relations with AQ should not be particularly outlandish. AQ's relations with the Pakistani army and the ISI date back to the 1980s jihad and the 1990s civil war in Afghanistan and the relationship did not evaporate in later years, as a member of AQIS claimed in 2020, perhaps with some overstatement:

Many Pakistani senior Army and ISI generals have remained very close with us from that time. Still, we have big influence in Pakistani Army and ISI. Many retired generals and people in ISI and Army are still actively supporting our leadership, ideology and ambitions against the crusaders in the region. [...] There're many people in the Pakistani army and the ISI who are compassionate and sympathetic toward us.[68]

The post-2001 relationship between the Pakistani authorities and AQ was however greatly complicated by the changing environment. On the one hand, US intervention and Musharraf's desire to maintain good relations with the Americans pushed AQ and Pakistan apart. The extent of sympathies for AQ among Pakistan's jihadist sub-culture on the other hand advised elements of the Pakistani security establishment to keep good relations with AQ. By 2004–5 the Pakistani Ministry of Interior estimated that there were 50,000 trained militants belonging to the main jihadist groups.[69] Islamabad certainly did not want to see them turn against the Pakistani state en masse.

The top leaders of AQ, such as bin Laden himself, did not have operational control over their men in Pakistan and Afghanistan until 2004.[70] The Qaidists were managing nonetheless, if, as Rashid assessed, they were becoming increasingly confident about its hideout in the tribal areas, allegedly also because of the tolerance, if not cooperation, showed by ISI officers.[71] British journalist Carlotta Gall was told by a former senior intelligence official that while some departments of the ISI were hunting down militants, other departments were working with them. The police used to refuse carrying out arrests of militants, in the assumption that the ISI was still protecting them.[72] Gall, who investigated the issue, found that al Zawahiri and bin Laden spent years moving from place to place in the FATA, trying to avoid capture or killing. Only in 2004, when the Pakistanis started intensifying their large-scale military raids, and the Americans started their drone strikes, the FATA started feeling insecure for the AQ leaders and moved to Pakistani cities.[73] In 2004 al Zawahiri issued his first message, calling for Pakistan's military to turn against Musharraf.[74]

An AQIS source confirms that this was not a smoke screen and that in the early Musharraf years the Qaidists reached the point where it genuinely would have liked to overthrow the Pakistani state. In the words of the source, 'Our leaders were saying that we will free Pakistan from apostates, kafirs; who are working at the behest of Americans and British.'

Our leaders had serious problems with Gen. Musharraf since he was a puppet of the British and American crusaders. From the time when he was in power, we lost so many leaders and mujahidin in crusader attacks inside Pakistan. General Musharraf provided safe heaven to crusaders inside Pakistan to target and kill our leaders. Gen. Musharraf was the person, who signed agreements with American crusaders, through which they have targeted many of our senior leaders and allies in drone strikes inside Pakistan.[75]

In response to the Pakistani crackdown on its operatives, bin Laden and his deputy Zawahiri repeatedly called for Musharraf's overthrow and reportedly plotted to kill him. Up to nine assassination plots against Musharraf have been reported.[76] Assassination attempts aside, as angry and hateful the Qaidists might have been in 2004, another AQ source admitted much later that overthrowing Musharraf and his regime was never a real possibility.[77]

> *Musharraf was a powerful general and leader during his time in power. We never thought that overthrowing him was a possibility because he had strong control over the government, army and intelligence. He had friends in almost every administration of his government and army. He had broad relations with Islamist groups and political parties, which strengthened his grip on power.*[78]

Even failed assassination attempts, while generating a repression in the short term, contributed to the overall strategy of putting pressure on Islamabad, to force it to back off and pull out of the tribal areas. The Qaidists even developed its ideological indictment of the Pakistani state. In Semple's words:

> *The AQ narrative for Pakistan asserts that the Pakistani state is a hangover from colonialism and is therefore inherently un-Islamic. According to this narrative, by clinging to a colonial era legal system and western-style constitution, the Pakistani state is a bulwark for western influence in the Muslim world. The Pakistan army epitomises the colonial character of the Pakistani state.*[79]

For all the rhetoric deployed by the Qaidists, direct confrontation with the Pakistani authorities was a risky path for an organization that had its leaders on Pakistani territory.

AQ tries to exploit cracks in the US-Pakistan alliance 2005-8

After 2004, gradually US and Pakistani interests started diverging, as the Pakistanis started making deals with some groups of Pakistani Taliban. One example was Mullah Nazir, whom the Pakistanis protected and the Americans wanted dead, because he supported the Afghan Taliban.[80] The Pakistani authorities started supporting the Afghan Taliban in 2003 (at modest levels), again entering a path convergent with AQ's interests.[81] AQ of course had been supporting the resurgence of the Afghan Taliban from 2002 onwards and cooperated closely with them, despite their refusal to commit to the global jihad. By 2004 or 2005, AQ elements was involved in other efforts potentially converging with Pakistan's interests, for example, intensifying its cooperation with LeT, of course knowing full well about the latter's close relationship with Pakistani intelligence (see Chapter 5). The apparent contradictions in the attitudes of both the Qaidists, between their denunciation of the Pakistani authorities and its willingness to support ISI proxies, and of the Pakistani authorities, collaborating with the Americans and supporting their enemies in Afghanistan, suggest that deal-making between Qaidists and the Pakistani authorities was not beyond the realm of possibilities.

Indeed, some actors on both sides started seeing reaching an understanding as feasible. An AQ source indicated that a first 'agreement' with the 'Pakistani authorities' was actually reached as early as 6 September 2005 and remained in place until bin Laden's killing in 2011. It is not clear at what level of seniority this deal was signed on the Pakistani side and, as it will be discussed at length below, nor it is clear whether this agreement was a formal one or just an understanding between AQ elements and ISI operatives. This first 'agreement' or understanding reportedly included a provision, according to which bin Laden would be taken under the protection of the Pakistani authorities and other senior figures would be offered 'safe sanctuaries'. The Pakistanis also promised not to take any action against AQ, while AQ promised to share information about other jihadist groups, to stop all its violent attacks inside Pakistan and to support the jihad in Kashmir.[82] The Abbottabad papers show that bin Laden was not privy to any such agreement, but the papers also show that bin Laden knew little of what was going on even in Pakistan and had no control over the local branch of AQ.[83] It is quite possible that the Qaidists negotiating with ISI counterparts might not have informed bin Laden, possibly to avoid facing rigidities at a time when they were trying to save their own and his skin.

There is some partial non-AQ backup for this claim. Several sources mention that Gen. Hamid Gul of the ISI had been talking to AQ about providing security for bin Laden in 2005; Gul was already retired at that time, but he is known to have worked as a 'consultant' for the ISI, covering the Afghan theatre of operations.[84] The bi-partisan Pakistan Working Group in its 2008 report described Pakistan as having 'at times' pursued AQ aggressively, concluding that 'it is unclear whether Pakistani agencies are working at cross-purposes or the Pakistani leadership is intentionally playing a double game'.[85] Then in 2009 Clinton, at that time Secretary of State, suggested that 'some Pakistani officials bore responsibility for allowing terrorists from Al Qaeda to operate from safe havens along this country's frontier', disbelieving that nobody in the Pakistani government knew where the terrorists were.[86] More in general, American officials were reported to have been suspicious of the activities of the 'deep state', thinking that at least some Pakistanis might have been working with the other side.[87] Nonetheless, even the Abbottabad report, produced by an ad hoc commission of Pakistani officials, does not exclude the possibility of complicity by elements of the ISI, but says no evidence was found of that.[88] Kiessling, among others, believes that the ISI could not have ignored the presence of bin Laden in Abbottabad; intelligence data retrieved in bin Laden's house suggested that a dozen ISI agents were informed about bin Laden's whereabouts.[89] Gall also believes that the weight of evidence is that the authorities knew about bin Laden's whereabouts.[90] In the wake of the 2011 Abbottabad raid, some Pakistani officials indicated that even senior elements of the 'deep state' might have established relations with AQ, according to sources gathered by Gall.[91] CIA deputy director Morrell wrote in 2015 that he knew that

> *it was impossible at some level to dismiss the notion that some Pakistani security officials at some level might have been aware of [bin Laden's] presence.*[92]

As McNally and Weinbaum noted in 2016, 'only nominal attempts have been made by Pakistan to dislodge al-Qaeda from its strongholds' in the tribal belt.[93] Senator Cardin noted at a hearing in 2016 that Pakistanis had been 'selective' in helping the

United States in their campaign against AQ in Pakistan. At the same hearing, Dr Markey described the Pakistani alliance with the United States against AQ as 'fleeting and inadequate'.[94] President Obama wrote in 2020 that:

> *Although Pakistan's government cooperated with us on a host of counterterrorism operations and provided a vital supply path for our forces in Afghanistan, it was an open secret that certain elements inside the country's military, and especially its intelligence services, maintained links to the Taliban and perhaps even al-Qaeda, sometimes using them as strategic assets to ensure that the Afghan government remained weak and unable to align itself with Pakistan's number one rival, India.*[95]

Moreover, year 2005 does appear to have been a turning point in the AQ-deep state relationship. Coll noted that in 2006 there was a massive upsurge in the propaganda output of AQ from Waziristan, which perhaps suggests greater freedom of operating for AQ.[96]

The known timelines of bin Laden's movements match. Analysts believe that based on the available evidence, bin Laden moved into his Abbottabad compound sometime between 2005 and 2008, which is compatible with the claim of a 2005 deal, discussed above.[97] Could the preparation of the Abbottabad compound and bin Laden's transfer there have been agreed with ISI elements, without bin Laden knowing? Again, pragmatic elements in AQ could have kept the leader in the dark, for his own good. The Abbottabad Commission Report, written as a result of the enquiry started by the Pakistani authorities, found that the Pakistani security services stopped pursuing bin Laden in 2005 and that he and his family members moved into Abbottabad in the same year. Again, this timeline is even more in line with what is claimed by the AQ sources.[98]

All this seems supportive of the hypothesis of some kind of 'agreement' or understanding having been in place.

For some time, the agreement, if it was really in place, seemed to have an impact. In 2006 Qaidist advisers were reportedly telling the Pakistani Taliban against starting a jihad with Islamabad (see *AQ and the birth of the TTP* below). The Pakistani authorities continued to occasionally detain AQ members after 2005, but usually following tips from US agencies, contributing little or nothing to the American effort to crush AQ. In other words, after 2005 the Pakistani authorities were already cautiously distancing from the Americans, and their campaign against AQ was not an all-out one. They were acting only when they could not avoid doing so due to US pressure. By 2007, the ability of the CIA to kill or capture AQ members in the cities and in the tribal areas had seriously declined due to decreasing Pakistani cooperation.[99]

However, before the end of 2007 relations between the 'pragmatic' Qaidists and the Pakistani 'deep state' hit a bump. In the wake of the Lal Masjid incident, bin Laden himself called for the overthrowing of Musharraf.[100] There was more in general a shift in AQ's approach. Rassler details it, quoting statements by bin Laden, al Libi and al Zawahiri, all justifying the diversion from the focus on the 'far enemy'.[101] How to explain bin Laden's and AQ's rhetorical attack and incitement to fight the Pakistani state in 2007 if he was already under the protection of the Pakistani authorities? The pragmatists, as already discussed, clearly had not informed bin Laden if the 2005 agreement really took place, and were not in a position to restrain their top leaders. Significantly, Atiya, at that time AQ's point of contact with Pakistani and Afghan jihadist groups, tried to discourage bin Laden from his heavily charged rhetoric after the Lal Masjid affair, which resulted in groups loosely connected to AQ starting indiscriminate attacks around Pakistan. He asked in a letter to bin Laden whether he 'could clarify the issue of jihad in Pakistan and how it fits into our policy and strategy' and added that 'the Pakistani brothers who are with us are asking a lot about this, and also relayed to us the concerns of other Pakistani elites, Islamists, and others'. He also asked bin Laden to stress that AQ was only fighting Pakistan because it was a 'tailpiece and a helper to the Americans'.[102] Could it be that Atiya had been involved in the contacts leading to the 2005 agreement and was trying to salvage what he could of the relationship with ISI elements? Atiya and others on the ground had strong incentives not to inform bin Laden of anything that might have been happening at the ground level, away from the eyes of the opposite leaderships, even beyond the need to keep any relationship with the ISI as discrete as possible and avoid referring to it in written messages.

If Gul was indeed the signatory to the 2005 'agreement', he might well have oversold to the AQ pragmatists his ability to have it implemented. It must have rapidly become clear to the Qaidists involved that Gul did not have the power any longer to guarantee any deal with them. Incidentally, in the wake of the Lal Masjid incident (when relations between AQ and the Pakistani authorities reached a new low), Hamid Gul himself turned against Musharraf, possibly exasperated that the president was not supporting his work with jihadists. Musharraf jailed Gul, who never forgave him.[103] Interestingly, Gul was rehabilitated after Musharraf lost power (see below). This falling out coincided with the new crisis in AQ-ISI relations.

The same AQ source which mentioned the agreement said that for some time even after the 2005 deal the Pakistanis 'kept cheating our leaders and members', 'helping with the Americans against us particularly in targeting and killing of our members in North Waziristan and Baluchistan', allegedly because 'Pakistan was receiving a lot of funding and support'.[104]

Sometimes, the relations were good, but there were times that we had experienced very bad relations with Pakistani authorities during Musharraf's presidency and power.[105]

For sure, in 2005–11 the implementation of the 'agreement' was far from being a smooth path and there was constant friction over occasional US-ISI cooperation and over some of the bluntest actions of the Pakistani authorities, such as the Lal Masjid affair. Overall, the type of agreement with the Pakistani 'deep state' that the AQ source allege looks plausible on the basis of that similar deep state's relationship with other jihadist groups, such as LeT and JeM. It is striking, for example, that JeM's leader Azhar was eventually allowed to escape unscathed the attempted murder of Musharraf by one of the members of his organization, despite Azhar himself having called in public for Musharraf's assassination (see Chapter 5). This seemingly incoherent behaviour appears to betray the complexities of efforts to re-absorb the bulk of the disaffected militants, while slowly transitioning away from extensive cooperation with the Americans. The leaders on either side did not need to know.

Another AQ source stressed that the problem was Musharraf and what the source described as his 'corruptibility' by the Americans:

We tried several times to forge relations with him, but each time, our efforts were in vain since he was receiving a good amount of money from the crusaders.[106]

So, despite the 2005 'agreement', there were crises in the relationship, leading to renewed friction, even if the 'agreement' was not abolished. This would be easier to explain if the 2005 deal had been signed or agreed at a relatively junior level not only within the ranks of AQ, but also within the ISI, possibly by a single department or unit within it. In particular, it seems unlikely that Musharraf would have been fully and perhaps even partially supportive of the deal. After the 2007 crisis, in any case, bin Laden kept quiet about the Pakistani authorities in his public statements, suggesting that he was himself moving towards seeking an arrangement with the Pakistani security establishment. This is also confirmed by the papers captured in bin Laden's house in Abbottabad, showing that he had been trying to reach a deal with the Pakistani security services for some time (see *Towards a breakthrough* below).

Rassler sees AQ's strategy as being to force the Pakistani authorities to abandon their support for US efforts in Afghanistan.[107] From that perspective, it would have made sense for AQ to vary the pressure it exercised on Islamabad and combine stick and carrot tactics, according to the line adopted by the Pakistani government in dealing with US requests. At least one AQIS source confirmed that indeed AQ's Pakistani branch had a strategy of putting pressure on Pakistan to force it to stop its collaboration with the Americans:

In the past, we have continuously threatened the Pakistani state and system to force it to cut off relations with the crusaders. In fact, we are happy in some cases with their achievements. They did what we wanted. They played a good game with the crusaders. They looted and burned the crusaders' supply lines inside and outside Pakistan. Plus, they supported us and our allies to continue jihad against them in Afghanistan.[108]

Of course, there might well be multiple and probably more compelling reasons for the Pakistani authorities to turn against US intervention in Afghanistan, but from the perspective of the pragmatists in AQ it made sense to apply a mix of pressure and incentives as it did. Although a single source is insufficient to make a final statement, it is at least highly plausible that AQ would engage in such tactics, at least for the period up to 2008.

Towards a breakthrough 2008–14

Relations between AQ and the Pakistani deep state started improving after Musharraf quit power in 2008, as a source implied by saying that AQ's position improved: 'Praise be to God, from the time that he lost power, we steadily became stronger.'[109]

Musharraf's departure might have reduced the interference of the political authorities and of the army in the 'agreement' between the elements of AQ and of the ISI involved. From 2008 onwards the campaign against AQ was mostly waged through US drone strikes, reportedly secretly authorized by the Pakistani authorities, despite official denials.[110] That removed the need for the Pakistanis to take part in operations against AQ members. Kiessling noted that from 2010 onwards the ISI became reluctant to share any intelligence with the CIA, and the quality of the intelligence shared also started declining.[111] That is probably an indicator of relations with AQ improving markedly and of contacts intensifying at a higher level than had been the case in 2005.

An AQIS source, different from the one quoted about the 2005 'agreement', confirmed that when bin Laden was killed in the Abbottabad raid, he was under the direct protection of the Pakistani ISI and military.[112] As discussed above, this does not mean that he even had to be aware of it. The obvious difference between Kiessling and AQ sources is that Kiessling believes that the Pakistanis did not want to hand over or kill bin Laden, not because of an agreement with AQ, but because Pakistan did not want to be seen as responsible for the downfall of the 'al-Qaeda icon'.[113]

Among the correspondence found in bin Laden's Abbottabad's home was reportedly some that showed how he and his closest collaborators were discussing as late as 2010/11 the possibility of making a deal with Pakistan, trading a safe haven for giving up on violent attacks within Pakistan. Pakistani journalists told Gall that they viewed bin Laden as in favour of a deal with Pakistan, whereas al Zawahiri opposed it.[114] The Abbottabad papers show that Atiya, the AQ cadre in charge of the region, tried to reach out the Pakistani authorities in June 2010 for a truce, claiming that they were withholding TTP and others from escalating violence inside Pakistan, but would give the green light if the Pakistanis failed to respond. It was a bluff, but prompted a response from the Pakistani ISI through HuM that then ISI head, Shuja Shah, was ready to speak to them directly. Interestingly, Hamid Gul was involved in handing the messaging through HuM. Gul reportedly claimed to HuM that the ISI had been trying to convince the Americans to negotiate with the Taliban and AQ. Atiya said in the message to bin Laden that he was not convinced at that stage.[115] Other sources too mention meetings held by intermediaries such as Fazal ur Rahman of the JuI and Hamid Gul (an ISI 'consultant' at that point) between AQ and ISI chief Pasha in 2010, promising to work towards some formal deal, while asking for 'wait a little bit'. Bin Laden agreed to pursue further talks.[116]

Before the Abbottabad raid, bin Laden appeared interested in maintaining relations as good as possible with the ISI and the army, regardless of the limited impact of the 'agreement' on 2005 and with the exception of the Lal Masjid crisis. According to an intelligence report, bin Laden refused to help Akhtar, the leader of HuJI, carrying out an attack against the army headquarters in Rawalpindi. Reportedly bin Laden also advised Akhtar and other militants not to carry out attacks in Pakistan, in order not to endanger AQ's members there.[117] This despite internal divisions within AQ about it, as mentioned above. After Musharraf left power, according to an AQIS source AQ members played an important role also in mediating between JeM and the Pakistani authorities. The mediation was successful and led to the full rehabilitation of JeM.[118] If all or at least a substantial part of it this is true, it would again confirm that the 2005 deal claimed by the AQ source was involving only some ISI elements. Coll too refers to the possibility of a compartmented ISI approach to bin Laden (and by extension implicitly AQ), with a department dealing with him and other not being involved or even not informed at all, similarly to police and army.[119] The constant breaches mentioned by the AQ source quoted above made the 2005 'agreement' only a partial improvement on the pre-2005 situation and the repeated incidents and friction that occurred have already been noted above. Presumably, then, bin Laden would have wanted a more comprehensive deal.

Despite the improving relations, AQ's propaganda remained highly critical of the Pakistani state. An example of AQ's rhetoric against the Pakistani state was an interview of AQ's Ustadh Ahmad Farooq's with al-Qaeda's media wing:

We are trying to create and to liberate a Pakistan that will be a pure Shari'a governed state and that will be a safe center for all Muslims from any place in the world, irrespective of their color, race or geographical origin. We are doing jihad for a Pakistan that will be a center of the mujahideen and of Muslims who would be able to come to Pakistan without any restrictions. (As Sahab Media Productions, 12 July)[120]

This propaganda aimed at the Pakistani state was logical, within the context of the carrot-and-stick strategy discussed above, of AQ trying to drive a wedge between the Pakistani authorities and the Americans. Unsurprisingly, the killing of bin Laden once again reignited tensions between AQ and the ISI. AQ suspected the Pakistani military establishment of complicity:

In fact, the compound was closely watched by Army and ISI, but a Pakistani doctor and several other army generals disclosed the location and betrayed us and our leadership. Perhaps they have received big bribes from the crusaders.[121]

Indeed, even Pakistani army sources have signalled that they had some awareness of the raid on Abbottabad, implying (if true) divergence between the ISI or part thereof and the Pakistani army (or part thereof).[122] Authoritative sources, however, insist that the Pakistani military was not aware.[123] In any case, with the Abbottabad raid, the 'agreement' signed in 2005, which had never been fully implemented anyway, finally collapsed completely, as even the AQ pragmatists had no option but to walk out.[124] Soon all that was left to AQ was bribing Pakistani officers for sensitive information.

Nonetheless, the 2005 'agreement' does not however appear to have been pointless from AQ's point of view. It was one step in a long-term strategy.

Breakthrough 2014–21

It took a while for AQ to accept as likely that the Pakistani generals had not been responsible for the Abbottabad raid. That realization, together with the fact that Pakistan-US relations worsened and cooperation decreased further after the raid on bin Laden, laid the bases for a new thaw between AQ and the Pakistani army.[125] Relations started warming up again and a second agreement was reached in May

2014, this time at a high level.[126] The fact that deal-making with the deep state was not the remit of local operatives anymore was the result of AQ having consolidated and having re-established a more functional chain of command. For a few months in 2014, as one AQ source confirmed, AQ eventually managed to reach a good understanding with the ISI:

> *our relationship was at a senior level and they were transferring our leaders from place to place. They were helping us a lot.*[127]

During the period inaugurated by the May 2014 deal, an example of AQ's 'constructive' relationship with the ISI was that of the so-called Punjabi Taliban (aka Tehrik e Taliban Punjab). The Punjabi Taliban emerged gradually from 2002 onwards. Even before the Lal Masjid incident, an estimated 2,000 Punjabi militants had moved to South Waziristan, probably originally to raise funds, where they linked up with the TTP. The Pakistani security forces were always particularly worried about them, due to their greater ability to penetrate Punjabi cities, than the Pashtun TTP. The security forces viewed them as influenced by Arab jihadist. These militants were from LeJ, SSP and JeM mainly. Mosques linked to LeJ and SSP were suspected of helping the Punjabi Taliban.[128]

After the Lal Masjid incident, another estimated 5,000 Punjabi Taliban flocked to North and South Waziristan. Abbas believes that in the wake of Lal Masjid, efforts escalated 'to engage Punjabi militants and draw them into their fight against Pakistani security forces'.[129] Their relationship with AQ long remained obscure. Abbas wrote that the 'authorities believe that the relationship largely remained tactical':

> *The Pashtun Taliban and the Arab-led al Qa`ida organization provide money, sanctuary, training facilities and suicide bombers, while Punjabi Taliban factions provide logistical support in Punjabi cities, including target identification and managing and assisting suicide bombers from the northwest. The nexus reportedly share each others' seminaries, sanctuaries, training facilities and jihadist cadres to conduct terrorist activities across Pakistan.*[130]

An AQIS source however acknowledged later that AQ was involved in setting up the Punjabi Taliban, with funding and other support. AQ also encouraged other groups, including the Afghan Taliban, to help as well.[131] That happened in the wake of the Lal Masjid incident, when relations between AQ and the Pakistani authorities were at a low, even if the AQ 'pragmatists' involved in the 2005 agreement had not cut off relations altogether. However, as relations improved again later, another source in AQIS stated that then AQ agreed to cut off relations with the Punjabi Taliban under ISI pressure.[132] Eventually the bulk of the Punjabi Taliban disbanded in 2014, with a small group remaining active underground (see also *AQ's role in the resurgence and adaptation of the TTP* below).[133]

Despite the successful handling of the Punjabi Taliban crisis, a new crisis followed very soon. According to an AQIS source, an unspecified attack launched by some AQ members soon led to a new deterioration in relations at an unspecified date.[134]

It is quite possible that the incident referred to was the 6 September 2014 attempt to start a war with India by seizing control of a Pakistani navy warship in 2014, which AQ claimed responsibility for.[135] Given the gravity of the episode, it seems highly plausible that it would have repercussions on the 2014 agreement. Distrust erupted again:

> *Now our relations are not at such levels. Now our relationship is not good at the senior level, because they did operations against us. They shared information about us with the Americans.*[136]

The 2014 deal was frozen. The AQ-deep state relationship defaulted to low-level cooperation with mostly commercially oriented officers, who took bribes for information:

> *AQ has relations with some members of ISI, but not with all the members of ISI. Some members are giving information to us, such as 'Americans want to perform attack here with a drone so you should leave this area'. This is secret information. They are giving this information to us in exchange for money.*[137]

This commercial relationship, which continued in later years, is confirmed by another AQ source:

> *There are some corrupt officials in both Army and ISI, who receive funding and money from us in exchange for maintaining close relations with us.*[138]

In this period, AQIS adopted again an aggressive rhetoric against the Pakistani state, as a 2017 document shows:

> *The oppressive British system imposed over Pakistan is an important priority, [...]. In the face of the secret machinations and plotting of Pakistani intelligence agencies and the open war being waged by the military, the people of faith have no course left other than fighting. In fact, jihad against these enemies of Shari'ah is really the beginning of the Battle of Hind. These armed forces imposed over Pakistan by the British imperialists are the foremost enemies of Shari'ah, and the best defenders of the global system of infidelity. That is why this military has always stabbed Islamic movements in the back to protect the interests of global infidelity. In the war against Islam and its people, it is this very military that is playing the role of a frontline ally. It is this very military whose support made the fall of the Islamic Emirate of Afghanistan possible at the hands of America.*[139]

The document then openly calls for targeting army, police and intelligence officers, as well as politicians and senior bureaucrats.[140] Another AQ document, authored by Muhammad Miqdaad and similar in tone, appeared in November 2017. This document especially targeted the Pakistani army, characterizing it as 'apostate army' and a British creation.[141]

With the electoral victory of Imran Khan in 2018, the third thaw between AQ and the Pakistani military took place.[142] A new high-level agreement, this time seemingly with the ISI as such, was reportedly reached in July 2019, after Asim Umar (AQIS's leader) was detained on 19 July and then released shortly. The new deal allowed AQIS to use Pakistan as a base for operations in India, Afghanistan and Bangladesh and as a recruitment area as long as AQIS restrained from carrying out attacks in Pakistan. According to an AQ source, the deal also included the ISI supplying AQIS with 'advanced weapons' and 'logistical support' and AQIS promising cooperation in 'targeting and eliminating all other groups which are operating against the Pakistani State'.[143] In particular, AQ was supposed to cut off relations with TTP and LeJ, as it had been the case during the previous negotiations.[144] AQIS was allowed to maintain relations with Pakistani jihadists groups, not opposed to the Pakistani authorities. The deals were guaranteeing security and safe havens for AQIS members, but also training and assistance, in addition to suspending all Pakistani operations against AQIS. In exchange AQIS accepted the Pakistani government as a legitimate Islamic government and stopped all attacks against it. Contrary to the first AQ/Pakistani military agreement of 2008–11, the Pakistani authorities were from 2019 onwards no longer directly providing security, but simply abstained from keeping track of AQ's leaders.[145]

Whether as a result of the strategic orientation sanctioned by the 2019 agreement, or of previous shifts in strategy, AQIS in 2019 was spending 70 per cent of its Pakistan-India budget on India, and only 30 per cent in Pakistan, to support India operations.[146]

The 2019 agreement did not mean that AQIS was then fully trustworthy of the Pakistani authorities and saw its interests as fully aligned with theirs. AQIS remained critical of the Pakistani establishment, which one source described as a 'traitor state':

They seem good, but suddenly they turn their back on you. They can never be trusted. The Pakistani state and system are working at the behest of Americans crusaders and the Brits. This system continues to betray their nation and the Holy Quran and Shari'a. We know about their close relations with Americans crusaders and Brits.[147]

In this context, for AQ to keep maintaining relations with the TTP made sense as a hedging strategy (see Chapter 3), despite the provisions of the agreement. An internal source also claimed that AQIS even established an alliance with the Mujahir Qawmi Movement (MQM), another group opposed to the Pakistani authorities.[148]

Still, the source argues, AQIS

cannot give up [its] relations with this corrupt system and state. [...] We have very good relations with Pakistan-based allies and partners. In order to keep these allies safe and alive, we should continue with the current approach. [...] Also, we cannot forget their support they have provided to the Mujahidin in the Afghan Jihad.[149]

Pakistan was in fact becoming more and more important for AQIS in 2020, as the Taliban-US peace deal encouraged AQIS to plan moving its leaders and then the bulk of its structure from Afghanistan to Pakistan. One additional, very important reason for the shift, according to an AQ source, was that al Zawahiri moved from Yemen to

Pakistan in 2020. al Zawahiri's presence in Pakistan would clearly represent a strong incentive for AQ to minimize the risk to him.[150]

Relocation had to happen gradually for security reasons, but as of June 2020 most of the senior AQIS members had already been relocated from Afghanistan to Karachi and Faisalabad (see also below). Despite Afghan Taliban reassurances, AQIS decided not to trust them anymore.[151]

Despite the rhetoric of the Lal Masjid years and of 2011, eventually the AQ leaders found that 'better have deals' with Pakistani intelligence. In 2005–8 AQ had been uneasily tolerating US drone strikes as the lowest price AQ could pay for maintaining a presence in Pakistan and securing at least its top leaders. In 2008–11, it tried to go beyond that. There seemed to some interest high up in the ISI, as negotiations involving bin Laden had lasted a while, but the Abbottabad raid unravelled all. In 2014, finally AQ seemed to have established a relationship with the top level of ISI, but it soon collapsed again, due to an AQ breach. In July 2019, AQ was able to reach again an agreement with the ISI.

Throughout these phases, AQ did not surrender its relationship with the Pakistani jihadists; at most it tried to get them to reach their own understanding with the Pakistani authorities, and even that not always. AQ struggled to reconcile relations with anti-Islamabad groups such as the TTP and that with the ISI. An AQ source acknowledged that

> *Our relationship with TTP is a very big problem for the Pakistani authorities. They're consistently pressuring our leaders on our relations with TTP. They're not happy about these links and relations. They want us to completely cut off relations with TTP. But considering our agreement with Pakistani authorities, we are forced to maintain limited contacts and relations with TTP. I mean, we are maintaining relations with TTP leaders that are not in favour of attacks inside Pakistan or against Pakistani Army.*[152]

AQ defended its cooperation with anti-Islamabad Pakistani jihadist groups as being 'based on specific needs and partnership'.[153] As of September 2020, an AQIS source was confident enough in the organizations' deal with the Pakistani authorities not to be worried that Islamabad's efforts to improve relations with America would have a negative impact.[154]

> *In case, they break the agreement and take measure against our organization, in that time, we will also take similar measures against them. Pakistani government and military have assured our leaders that they will not give up on our leaders and organization since they'll remain committed to the agreement.*[155]

The source seems more worried about Pakistan's ever tightening relations with China:[156]

> *We are worried about Pakistan getting too close to the Chinese government. Indeed, Pakistan closer relations with Chinese government is a threat to our people in Pakistan. We know that Chinese government is pressing Pakistani government about our Uyghurs members in Pakistan.*[157]

Confidence in the deal aside, the worsening relations with the Quetta Shura were forcing AQ to relocate members to Pakistan from Afghanistan, making it more dependent on the Pakistanis as long as a new safe haven could not be established in the east of Afghanistan.[158]

The 2019 AD-deep state deal is the most difficult one to confirm, of the three discussed above. It goes by itself that Pakistani officials would not confirm any deals with AQ and circumstantial evidence is also hard to find, given the limited time which has elapsed. However, it is worth noting that after the deal was reportedly signed, killings of AQ leaders and cadres all happened inside Afghanistan, with none in Pakistan, and no detentions of AQ members were reported in Pakistan.

Distancing again 2021–

The argument that the relationship between AQ and the 'deep state' has always been opportunistic and pragmatic is reinforced by the next turn that it took in autumn 2021, when the deal reached in July 2019 collapsed, according to an AQ source.[159] The exact causes of that collapse are not clear, but at least three developments appear likely to have influenced that.

The first development was the US withdrawal from Afghanistan and the conditions under which it happened, which seemed to undermine for good Taliban-US relations. At that point, remote parts of Afghanistan started appearing safer for AQ leaders and apparatus than Pakistan's.

The second reason, which is actually stated by the AQ source mentioned above, is that tension between AQ and the 'deep state' was rising as the former was upping pressure on the latter to address the TTP issue, and the latter was failing to take action.[160]

The third development was the likely existence of a growing perception, within AQ's ranks, that the Pakistani military establishment remained keen on improving relations with the US government, despite the failure of their approach to facilitating a US exit from Afghanistan. AQ's fears were that the Pakistanis could try to gain some American good will back by offering help in targeting AQ leaders. At the same time, as discussed in detail in *Thaw between AQ and IS* below, relations between AQ and IS had been improving for some time, which by late 2021 gave AQ some confidence that IS would not represent a danger for AQ leaders and cadres in eastern Afghanistan.

These views were later confirmed by the role of the Pakistani army in April 2022, in forcing PM Imran Khan out and fostering his replacement by one more acceptable by the United States. These fears too were later confirmed when a US drone strike took place against an AQ camp in Shorabak (southern Afghanistan) in April 2022. The drone had clearly entered Afghanistan via Pakistan and some US-Pakistan agreement must have been in place for that to happen.[161]

AQ seems to have remained uncertain about the safety of Afghanistan for its leaders. Despite having been sick for at least a couple of years, al Zawahiri continued to linger across the Pakistan-Afghanistan border, constantly changing location between Kunar and Nuristan and even crossing into Chitral from time to time.[162]

Although AQ sources described these developments as positive steps on the jihadist path, the overall picture is one of AQ still struggling dramatically to secure its top leaders after the change of regime in Kabul. As mentioned several times before in this study, the need to protect the leadership and the core apparatus that supported it was a major concern and constraint for AQ. The drone strike in Shorabak, mentioned above, likely reawakened AQ's feelings that within the Taliban were senior figures ready to cooperate even with the Americans to put the foreign jihadists in their place. The strike hit a small AQ camp within a larger Taliban base with great precision and could conceivably only have taken place with a tip off from Taliban present in Shorabak, probably routed through more senior Taliban to the Americans.[163]

Considering the lack of unified policymaking in the early post-2001 years, it is not clear whether we can speak of an AQ strategy. The policies that the leadership ended up adapting after bin Laden's death were likely the result of the expediency characterizing the decision taken by AQ members running affairs without direction from the leaders in the preceding ten years. Overall, despite multiple difficulties and considering the odds, whether a strategy or mere expediency, AQ's approach to handling Pakistan was quite successful. If as suggested AQ meant to push Pakistan away from the United States, those goals were achieved to a considerable extent after 2007. During this period the Pakistani authorities invested massively in support of the Afghan Taliban and even worked out a close cooperation with Iran's Revolutionary Guards.[164] These were not small steps to take, considering the extent to which they went against US interests. Of course, it is hard to say to what extent they were due to AQ's efforts or to other factors, but from AQ's perspective its efforts seemed to be bearing fruit.

Are Qaidist accounts credible?

The main argument contra the existence of a deep state-AQ relationship is the fighting that took place between them, with AQ sponsoring or participating in attacks against Pakistani assets and the Pakistani security services assisting US security agencies in tracking down AQ members. However, the fact is that clearly such collaboration weakened over time and seemingly even ended altogether.

Another key argument contra the thesis developed in this chapter is that hosting, protecting or holding bin Laden would have been too risky for the Pakistani authorities, a view held by many ex post, once the Abbottabad raid had happened. This argument does not really hold because it is now known beyond doubt that throughout 2002–21 the Pakistani state (and not just the 'deep' one) supported financially and logistically the Afghan Taliban, helping them kill thousands of US, British and other servicemen. Surely, if the Pakistani state felt this was a risk worth taking, making deals with bin Laden and AQ could plausibly also be considered worth the risk, not least given that AQ and its jihadist allies in Pakistan also contributed to the Taliban's military effort. In the end, as in the case of their support for the Taliban, even if the Americans were to find out about bin Laden (as they did), the disruption in bilateral relations would have been temporary and they would have had little choice but to leave Pakistan off the hook (as they did). US intelligence officers ended up telling the world that there was no evidence that Pakistani officials knew about bin Laden's presence in Abbottabad.[165]

Such caution is likely to be dictated by the desire to prevent an unmanageable crisis in the relations with Pakistan (a nuclear power with a track record of proliferation), rather than deriving from genuine conviction. However, the claims are definitely plausible and in part at least credible, given the existence of at least some supporting evidence and the fact that they help coming up with an interpretation of events that reconciles apparently contradictory behaviour on both the AQ's and the deep state's side.

Other dramatic realignments in the region were doubted by analysts for years and labelled as implausible or impossible, until they were confirmed and had to be universally accepted. A typical example is that of the Iranian regime starting to support the Taliban in 2005 and then increasingly so, despite their previous history of deep hostility.[166]

Competition for AQ: The arrival of IS

The Islamic State arrives in Pakistan

The Islamic State first gained support among some groups of disgruntled TTP commanders, who were in bad terms with Fazlullah, who was reportedly starving them of supplies (although he might in reality simply have lacked the resources to support them).[167] Some of them had been involved in sending volunteers to Iraq for some time. During 2014 seven TTP commanders started coming together with the aim of founding a group aligned with IS in Pakistan. The group took the name of Tehrik e Khilafat Pakistan (TKP) in July 2014.

Among these commanders, some of whom at least were of Panjpiri background, the most prominent was Hafiz Saeed Khan. One of his merits had been to be among the first to despatch a contingent to Syria and Iraq and another one, of having already joined the IS on 11 May 2013.[168] Hafiz Saeed himself had a strong Panjpiri reputation and had reportedly been involved in attacks on Hanafi madrasas in Orakzai.[169] Hafiz Saeed was then chosen as governor of Wilayat Khorasan in early 2015, when it was launched. The other main commanders took the other honorific positions available: Abdul Bahar Mehsud was initially appointed representative of Al Baghdadi in Pakistan as well as leader of TKP, and Hafiz Dawlat Khan was appointed his first deputy. The original bulk of TTP fighters was soon joined by some LeJ and LeT fighters, mostly veterans of Syria and Iraq, after coming back from Syria, and by a number of Afridi tribesmen from the ranks of Mangal Bagh's LI.[170] Similarly some other small groups declaring their allegiance to IS were brought into the TKP, like Ansar ul Khilafat Wal-Jihad (Partisans of the Caliphate and of Jihad).[171]

It is not clear, on the basis of the available evidence whether on balance IS-K attracted more Panjpiri Taliban than Deobandi. Fazlullah himself being of Panjpiri inclinations, Debandism was not a grudge that TTP Panjpiris defecting to IS-K could hold against him.[172]

Soon smaller Pakistani groups also aligned with IS-K, without merging with TKP. The group of Mullah Bakhtwar, a small TTP splinter known as Khilafat Speen Ghar Bakhtwar Group, joined in 2016. This group had operated in Bara and was of mixed composition (see also *The fragmentation of the TTP* below).[173] The group was seen as close to the Pakistani services.[174] In autumn 2016 Bakhtwar was killed in a drone strike in Nangarhar and his group merged into the TKP, ceasing to exist as a separate force.[175]

Yet another group that joined IS-K without going through TKP was Jaysh ul Islam (Army of Islam). Active for years in Pakistani Baluchistan, it merged into IS-K on 4 November 2015. At the time of joining IS-K, it claimed almost 700 members. The group was targeting Shi'as even before, so the ideological attraction of IS-K is easily explained. The leader of Jaysh ul Islam was initially Mehmud Rahman, replaced after his death by Maulana Mohammad Tahir Baluch.[176]

IS-K also started recruiting fresh members, initially among madrasa students from 'North and South Waziristan, Bajaur, Peshawar, Quetta, Karachi, Islamabad, Lahore and Kashmir'.[177] TKP itself in 2015 had been incorporated into IS-K, surviving only as an informal component.

By early 2017 an internal source claimed that IS-K was making progress in building a presence in Pakistan's main cities, with about 1,200 members in Peshawar, 700 in Lahore, 240 in Islamabad and 750 in Quetta; at least 40 per cent of its members on Pakistani territory were in cities at that point.[178] More than an indicator of preparations for a sustained terrorist campaign, however, this growing concentration in cities seems to be the result of the role of TKP in supporting logistically the campaign in Afghanistan, as well as of recruitment among young end educated urbanites.

The original strategy of IS-K had a clear focus on Afghanistan, with Pakistan and other countries (Iran, India, China, Central Asian countries) playing second fiddle. Its presence in Pakistan was limited; the majority of the Pashtuns recruited in Pakistan were either operating in a support role, or were deployed most of the time to Afghanistan, and spent time in Pakistan only resting and recuperating. To the extent that IS-K had any activity within Pakistan, it seemed oriented towards Baluchistan, where sectarian conflicts ran high (see *Enter IS-P* below). Pakistan also played the role of recruitment ground, especially from within the ranks of other jihadist groups (especially TTP, LeJ, SSP), and of logistical rear for the Afghan front. As it will be discussed in detail in Chapter 4, IS-K clearly had the ambition of absorbing the Pakistani Sunni supremacist groups, presumably with the intent of reinvigorating their campaign. But what about its attitude to the Pakistani state?

IS-K and the Pakistani state

In its early years, IS-K sources presented the Pakistani government as an enemy, in line with the extremist ideology of the Caliphate. In reality, however, IS-K for the first year and a half of existence of IS on Pakistani ground, no significant attacks were carried out against the Pakistani authorities, despite many terrorist attacks against civilians, especially Shi'as, taking place.[179] IS sources indicated in September 2014, when Wilayat Khorasan had yet to be announced, that fighting the Pakistani authorities was a premature aim for them and the Pakistani authorities reciprocated by limiting themselves to 'monitoring' IS activities.[180] One IS-K source claimed then to have carried out several attacks against the Pakistani army in July–September 2015, and to have been targeted in army operations in Tera, Bajaur and Orakzai. However, these clashes were not reported in the media and it is therefore unclear whether they ever happened.[181] Moreover, another ISI source admitted that as of January 2016 IS-K had only been carrying out attacks against Shi'as in Kurram, Baluchistan and Quetta city, and never against the Pakistani government. Although they were known to recruit and raise funds on Pakistani territory, their targets were Western interests, Shi'as, the Iranian and the Central Asian states.[182]

One of the few seemingly confirmed attacks involving Pakistani military personnel was the decapitation of a Pakistani army prisoner, shown on a video released on 11 January 2015, which also featured Shahidullah Shahid (ex TTP) pledging allegiance to IS.[183] The attack against the Pakistani consulate in Jalalabad in January 2016 also was attributed to IS-K, but was a rather isolated act and did not have lethal consequences.[184] It looks as if IS-K was trying to portray itself as more hostile to the Pakistani state than it actually was. One source in Jaysh ul Islam mentioned that after the group joined IS-K, it was ordered not to carry out attacks on Pakistani territory, but help instead start operations in Iran (as Jaysh operated in Baluchistan).[185]

A source in the Pakistani intelligence indicated that they were not taking the IS-K threat too seriously, at least as of January 2016, seeing its members in Pakistan as opportunists raising the flag in the hope for financial support and of benefiting from IS' aura of invincibility.[186]

Indeed, IS-K sources indicated that for a period in 2015 Pakistani repression was limited to making obstacles to IS-K logistics.[187] An Afghan member of IS-K also believed ISI was essentially adopting a neutral attitude towards them.[188] According to a source in IS-K's Finance Commission, the Pakistani authorities were aware that IS-K was transferring money to Pakistan via the hawala system, but had not tried to prevent that from happening.[189]

Relations with the Pakistani deep state somewhat worsened between end 2015 and early 2016. The Pakistani authorities claimed having arrested a number of Pakistani citizens for supporting IS-K financially and then to have arrested numerous members of IS-K in Karachi and Lahore, including at least one Arab. They claimed to see some threat of IS-K aggravating sectarian conflict in Pakistan, not least because the Iranian Pasdaran are expected to retaliate by arming Shi'a militias.[190] In January 2016 the ISI claimed that they had dismantled IS-K networks in Karachi and confined it to the Pashtun north-west: Bajaur, Khyber, Lal Masjid, Lakki Marwat, Kurram, Hangu, Peshawar and Orakzay.[191] Indeed there is evidence that the Pakistani authorities eventually did clamp down on IS-K's attempts to develop a network in urban Pakistan, attracting elements of other jihadist groups, particularly from Jama'at ud Dawa/Lashkar e Taiba (JuD/LeT).[192] An IRGC officer pointed out that the IRGC passed on information about IS-K locations and individuals to the Pakistanis, who were however failing to follow up throughout most of 2015, he believed because of Saudi pressure. However, this same officer believed that by late 2015 the Pakistani authorities were turning against IS-K and he correctly foresaw that IS-K would start operations in Pakistan soon as a result.[193] The early 2016 crisis between IS-K and Pakistani authorities lasted a few months. By mid-2016 that has ceased as well. IS-K logistics was allowed to flow.[194]

A source inside IS-K explained that the Pakistani authorities then started establishing relations with IS-K after their relations with the Afghan government worsened further following the June 2016 border clashes. Offers of logistical support were made, and repression inside Pakistan abated.[195]

While the Pakistani authorities were trying to assess IS-K and see whether there was room for co-optation, they were also beginning to infiltrate it, for information gathering purposes initially, and perhaps more. A source in Mullah Bakhtwar's group claimed to have been receiving support from the Pakistani authorities and that the latter were trying to improve relations with IS-K in general. The source admitted that Mullah Bakhtwar's group is the only one in IS-K that had Pakistani advisers and not to oppose (even rhetorically) the Pakistani state.[196] Some in IS-K believed that even the 'defectors' coming from LeT might have been infiltrators of the Pakistani services.[197]

Telling apart propaganda claims from the two sides is hard, IS-K being interested in appearing more aggressive towards the Pakistani authorities than it actually was and the Pakistani authorities being interested in appearing more committed to the struggle against IS-K than they were. Official Pakistani sources will not admit to any relationship with IS-K, but as shown above the fluctuation of operations against IS-K roughly matches IS-K accounts of how the relationship was developing. The weight of this evidence is that the Pakistani authorities oscillated between a wary tolerance of IS-K activities, with occasional effort to contain them, and ad hoc support when it suited their interest. While commentators and observers alleging deep state support for IS-K have appeared in the India media, occasionally taking these allegations to western media too.[198] One of the IS-K's Afghan founders, Muslimdost, criticized his Pakistani colleagues for having allowed the ISI hijack the movement already in 2015 and then again in 2019.[199] After he reconciled with the Taliban in 2022, Muslimdost alleged in a public speech that the ISI used to pay IS-K.[200] Contrary to what was the case for AQ, IS-K/deep state relations were not the object of scrutiny by eager American congressmen, possibly because IS-K did not have significant activities against US forces, a fact also reflected in the scant literature that appeared on IS-K.

The mid-2016 thaw between IS-K and the Pakistani deep state was very short lived, in any case. By mid-summer 2016 the picture was shifting again, with a series of bloody attacks claimed by IS-K against both civilian and Pakistan government targets. The August 2016 attack on the Quetta hospital, the October 2016 attack against the Quetta Police Academy and the attack on a Sufi Shrine in Baluchistan in November 2016 were all claimed by IS-K, and their factual participation was in part confirmed.[201] The suicide bombing attack against a crowd at Quetta's hospital in August 2016 was explicitly justified with the presence of personnel of the Ministry of Justice and of Pakistani Police. Seventy people were killed.[202]

An IS-K source indicated that the organization's main donors were opposed to jihad against the Pakistani state.[203] This is plausible, given the profile of those donors, mostly concentrated in the Gulf monarchies. Undeterred, IS-K sources were still discussing plans to escalate attacks in December 2016. During this second crisis, IS-K sources talked of planned future attacks against Chinese interests in Pakistan, of which there are plenty, many of which are soft ones, such as schools, company sites, etc. Reportedly IS-K was pushed towards these targets by Uyghurs and Huis within its ranks, and some of its donors, who were interested in a Chinese jihad, were threatening to reduce funding if IS-K would not fulfil its promises to carry out attacks against them.[204]

As in the case of AQ in 2002–7, this new violent campaign might have been a negotiations technique in order to extract concessions from the Pakistani authorities. IS-K had an interest in putting pressure on Pakistan with attacks that would not be enough to destabilize Pakistan, but enough to remind its authorities and pro-Pakistan donors of IS-K's disruptive power and of the opportunity of distracting IS-K with incentives to focus its attention elsewhere.

The uneasy relationship between IS-K and the deep state evolved towards greater stability only from mid-2017 onwards. A key development was the willingness of the majority of the IS-K senior military commanders to choose a governor of Khorasan, who would be acceptable to the Pakistani authorities. In May 2017 the majority of the Military Council of IS-K chose Aslam Farooqi, a former LeT commander, as the new governor, against the advice of a strong and determined minority, who saw him as an infiltrator of Pakistan's intelligence. Farooqi was not recognized as governor by IS-Central then, because the Caliphate insisted on demanding a unanimous decision, and for many months IS-K would de facto be split into two rival factions. The relationship of at least portions of the IS-K with the ISI, which emerged at that point, is thus described by one internal source:

inside the Daesh leadership there are different connections and links. Some members who are from Pakistan have very good connection with ISI, they fulfil the program of ISI.[205]

But Farooqi's faction was largely predominant in Pakistan and along the Afghanistan-Pakistan border. It immediately proceeded to establish good relations with the Pakistani services, in exchange for unimpeded access to its bases and camps in Pakistan (Dera, Hangu, Bajaur, Momand Dara, Naryab and North Waziristan).[206]

The relationship of IS-K with the Pakistani deep state intensified after 2017, as IS-K started losing strength due to the declining ability of the Caliphate to fund it, some loss of enthusiasm among donors in the Gulf and the first significant defeats in Afghanistan. From that point onwards IS-K needed the Pakistani services more than they needed it and seemingly avoided provoking them. From that point onwards, IS-K was on the defensive even with them and could only try to resist their pressure to align with Pakistan's geopolitical priorities (see *Global jihad arrives in Kashmir* below). The dependence of IS-K on the Pakistani ISI continued growing as IS-K was weakened by the eradication of the last vestiges of Caliphate power in Syria. The killing of Al Baghdadi in October 2019 was a further shock that impacted very negatively on morale.[207]

As for previous allegations of IS-K/deep state relations, the link of Aslam Farooqi to the ISI is a matter of contention, with the Afghan authorities and India media being very supportive of it, in the face of flat Pakistani denials. Among analysts, few have commented. Gohel and Winston support the idea of a link, drawing on the Afghan government claims that Farooqi confessed to his cooperation with LeT, JeM and other deep state clients when he was interrogated by Afghan security officers in March 2020.[208]

IS-K sources suggest in any case a more problematic relationship, even aside from the ups and downs described so far. The relationship of IS-K with the Pakistani authorities remained problematic due to support being limited to the ISI; most of the army remained hostile, not least because of the presence of many former members of TTP and LeJ in IS-K's ranks, as well as former IMU members. This dualistic approach of the Pakistani military establishment towards IS-K continued throughout 2020.[209]

From the summer of 2018 IS-K started suffering defeats after defeats inside Afghanistan, mostly at the hand of the Taliban.[210] This further weakened IS-K vis-à-vis the Pakistani military establishment. Short of funding and with morale low, by September 2018 even IS-K sources were putting membership down to as little as 7,000 men all told, compared to a peak of 12,000.[211] This does not mean that IS-K did not try to fight back. Between late 2018 and early 2019, IS-K managed to obtain new funding and to go on the offensive once again in Afghanistan and started negotiating with groups previously close to AQ, such as TTP, as well as eventually AQIS itself. The ongoing negotiations between the Taliban and the Americans produced a new wave of defections to IS-K from the TTP.[212]

A series of very hard defeats suffered from the Taliban in late 2019 and early 2020 threw IS-K off the tracks again.[213] Defeat and losses aside, what was perhaps as worrying for IS-K was a clear sense that the Taliban onslaught against IS-K of late 2019 would not have been possible without the tolerance at least of the Pakistani military establishment.[214] Perhaps the interest of the Pakistanis was to see IS-K weakened to the point where it would not be able to resist the demands of the Pakistanis anymore and align completely behind them.

By April 2020, IS-K numbers were even lower, at even less than 6,000, of which 1,500–2,000 in Pakistan. In the following months, IS-K recovered some strength thanks to an influx of new members, including some LeT ones and a larger number of Haqqani network members. IS-K sources, however, noted that the two groups were closely linked to Pakistan's ISI and interpreted the influx as a gradual takeover of IS-K by the ISI. The process of infiltration had started much earlier, perhaps even at the origins of IS-K, as already discussed above. However, tired of the never-ending ups and downs in the relationship with IS-K, the ISI might well have decided to strengthen its direct influence over IS-K, reinforcing the lobbies (primarily ex Haqqani and ex LeT) that it already maintained before. In the meanwhile, IS-K had lost the financial backup for its grand plans. By 2020, say internal sources, the budget allocated by the Caliphate to IS-K was down to $50 million (plus locally raised revenue), which would be insufficient to fund a counter-offensive against the Taliban and regain lost ground.[215]

If that was the dep state's plan, it appears to have worked. IS-K sources admit that from late summer/autumn 2020, IS-K had to accept to cooperate quite closely with the Pakistani deep state to join the campaign to put unbearable pressure on the government of Ashraf Ghani in Afghanistan, starting a campaign of targeted assassination of government officials and security officers in Kabul and Jalalabad.[216] The flow of LeT recruits into IS-K was continuing, even if at a slower pace. As of March 2021, there were still LeT members defecting to IS-P, such as a group of fifteen that switched sides in Baluchistan. Not only that, LeT was still cooperating with IS-P as well as with IS-K.[217]

Perhaps the leadership of IS-K assumed that it could benefit from being conscripted into the ISI campaign against Kabul: the ISI aim seemed to be forcing Ghani to resign and pave the way for a negotiated settlement between the political elite in Kabul and the Taliban. Then IS-K would emerge as the only remaining organization for hardline jihadists to align with. In any case, the result was the contrary of what IS-K had been hoping for, with its main enemy, the Taliban, seizing power in Kabul on 15 August 2021.

Despite having edged closer to the deep state than ever, the relationship remained opportunistic and temporary. Even in the weeks preceding the fall of Kabul to the Taliban, as the Ghani government appeared doomed, the Pakistani deep state already turned against IS-K, perhaps assuming that it had outlived its usefulness, cut off supply lines into Pakistan and unleashed LeT against IS-K bases in the east. Clashes between IS-K and ISI-linked LeT started in early August.[218] The deep state was also aware, of course, that IS had set up a Pakistani branch (see next paragraph), an ominous sign of what IS' plans for the future might have been.

Later in 2021 and early 2022 rumours started circulating among Taliban commanders that the 'deep state' had re-established connections with IS-K in order to put pressure on the Taliban's Emirate in Kabul, which was engaged in border clashes with Pakistan and was allowing the TTP to operate from its territory. There is little evidence that this was true and in fact there is some evidence of the contrary. IS-K intensified its attacks in Pakistan in 2022 and an IS-P source claimed in December 2021 that IS-K was putting pressure on IS-P to carry out more attacks inside Pakistan.[219] The Taliban are likely to have scapegoated the deep state for their own difficulties in handling the security of the Emirate.

Wilayat Pakistan

Reportedly it was Omar Khorasani, then serving as head of the military activities of IS-K for Afghanistan, Pakistan, Bangladesh and Tajikistan, who came up with the idea of establishing four new wilayats of IS, two of which were established immediately in 2019 (Hind and Pakistan) and two which were planned for later (Tajikistan and Turkey) and had not been established yet at the time of writing this book. Khorasani argued that it was highly impractical to manage so many different regions from a single centre.[220] At least two more sources agreed that there was reportedly 'miscommunication, weak leadership' and objective difficulties in managing an area as big as the historical Khorasan from Nangarhar province, where the headquarter had been.[221]

Whether Omar's idea and its justification were enough for it being approved is not clear. Whatever the case, in May 2019 Wilayat Pakistan and Wilayat Hind were announced to the public, although organizational work was slow to take off. The formation of two new provinces out of the turf that had been Khorasan, Wilayat Pakistan and Wilayat Hind, both highlighted the ongoing decline of IS-K and accelerated it. The formation of Wilayat Pakistan was in fact seen as detrimental to IS-K by some within its rank. Initially its members dismissed it as a side show and claimed that there would be no substantial transfer of members from the latter to the former. Those Pakistanis being sent to Wilayat Pakistan were merely 'on loan', it was claimed. But things turned out differently. In practice and perhaps naturally, the new Wilayat started competing with Khorasan for recruits and funds. According to the cadre contacted in November 2019, some 900 Pakistani members of Wilayat Khorasan had moved to Wilayat Pakistan in six months. That corresponds to about 8–10 per cent of the total strength claimed by Wilayat Khorasan in mid-2019. The source describes the two Wilayat suffering serious friction due to the competition for recruits. In addition, the budget allocated to Wilayat Pakistan came at least in part at the expense of Wilayat Khorasan, weakening it financially. The source might be trying to find a scapegoat for the defeat in Nangarhar, but it used unusually strong words and for the first time in tens and tens of meetings that the author organized with Wilayat Khorasan members over the years, he implicitly criticized the leadership of the Islamic State: 'the creation of Wilayah Pakistan and the immediate move of the Pakistani experienced members and fighters were a total disaster for Khorasan'.[222]

Later an IS-P source admitted that there had been initially 'a lot of problems' between IS-P and IS-K, including because of the close relationship of IS-K to the Pakistani deep state in 2019–21. Reportedly, IS-K even exercised pressure on IS-P, so that it would not carry out attacks inside Pakistan.[223] IS-P had to comply to a large degree because it was dependent on IS-K: in 2019 they had no direct communication with IS-Central and communications were routed via IS-K.[224] Relations between IS-K and IS-P remained poor until the summer of 2021 because IS-P alleged that IS-K was cooperating with the Pakistani security services.[225]

There was little sign that the two new branches of IS, IS-P and IS-Hind (IS-H) existed as actual organizations at all until spring 2020.[226] Little was known even as of end 2021 about IS-P's organization. IS-P was reportedly led by Daud Mehsud, a former TTP member who joined IS-K in 2015. Abu Mahmood is also known as the governor in official statements. Under him is a Council of fourteen members, who chose him.[227] As of mid-2020, his appointment had not been ratified by IS-Central.[228]

In 2019/20 IS-Central reportedly started allocating considerable funding to IS-P and IS-H.[229] This suggests that the intent was to set up actual organizations on the ground, and not just 'boxes' to be filled by opportunistic freelancers. Nonetheless, the perception within IS ranks was that (as of mid-2020) the priority was still reorganizing IS-K, rather than developing IS-P or IS-H, as IS still saw forthcoming opportunities in Afghanistan due to the US/Taliban peace deal.[230] IS-P in turn took priority over IS-H, which in 2020 was considerably behind in being set up.

A source in IS-P identified support for the jihad in Kashmir and bringing together the Sunni supremacist tendencies in Pakistan as the primary objectives of IS-P as of mid-2020, with a focus on 'crushing the Shi'a groups in Baluchistan'.[231] The fact that Aslam Farooqi, the pro-ISI governor of IS-K, had reportedly been pushed by the ISI for the job of IS-P governor, suggests an attempt to assert control/influence over IS-P. The ISI was also accused by IS-P and IS-K members of wanting to bring as many former IS-K as possible into IS-P as possible, perhaps because it already had established a degree of influence over them. According to an internal source, about one third of the members of IS-P were former WK members in mid-2020.[232] An IS-P source confirmed the link:

> Most of the former IS-K members who are now with IS-P came thanks to the support of the ISI. [...]Most of the members of Daesh Khurasan who moved back to Pakistan after IS-K was defeated in Nangarhar and Kunar Provinces joined back IS-P and

most of them have joined with the support of Pakistan's intelligent service. I myself was member of IS-K and was based in Achin district, after I came back to Pakistan I was visited and called several times by a member of Pakistani intelligent service, whom I had contact with when I was in Afghanistan with IS-K.[233]

The same source denied any IS-P link to the Pakistani government as such, but acknowledged connections with the ISI.[234]

Like IS-K, IS-P claimed to intend targeting Pakistani government officials (except Shi'as) and any individual opposed to its aims,[235] but in practice attacks claimed by IS-P in Pakistan in 2019–21 were few and far in between. The main attacks were focused on the Shi'a minority; it is hard to assess the sectarian background of the few government officials assassinated.[236]

This is not to say that IS-P was a mere ISI stooge. It had to bow to IS-K pressure and keep a low profile inside Pakistan, not least because of the large number of ex IS-K members within its ranks, but if the deep state indeed tried to assert control over it, IS-P managed to remain independent. Once IS-K was dumped by the deep state, following the fall of Kabul in Taliban hands (see below), IS-P too was completely free to move against the Pakistani state. IS-P and IS-K collaboration strengthened and even IS-K resumed attacks inside Pakistan on a significant scale.[237] Reportedly the two governors met for the first time in Khost (Afghanistan) in early December 2021.[238] The improvement might have started a little earlier, as in July 2021 KP province was transferred back to IS-K, but occasionally IS-P continued to claim attacks taking place within its boundaries.[239]

Until IS-P remained prisoner of IS-K and was forced to keep a low profile in Pakistan, IS-Central had little reason to invest much in it. This seems to be borne out by funding figures provided by IS-P sources. In mid-2020 the perception within IS ranks was that (as of mid-2020) the priority was still reorganizing IS-K, rather than developing IS-P, as IS still saw forthcoming opportunities in Afghanistan due to the US/Taliban peace deal.[240] In 2020 the IS-P received a comparatively modest $22 million and in 2021 it received an estimated at $20–30 million, with a rise towards the end of the year, once IS-P had emancipated itself. For 2022 IS-P was reportedly promised a much bigger budget, $110 million. Some 30 per cent of the funding accrued to IS-P from IS-Central, with both private and state donors in the Gulf countries and AQ contributing too; a more modest amount came from Pakistani supporters. The source alleged that AQ contributed to the budget, in order to help IS create a safe haven in parts of Pakistan, that could serve as a backup in the event of both organization being shut off Afghanistan. Funding from the Gulf too increased after 15 August.[241] The 'emancipation' of IS-P from the cautious approach of IS-K to operations in Pakistan and the increased budget (if it did materialize) had not yet translated into a major increase in the pace of military operations as of April 2022; IS activities in Pakistan were still largely attributable to IS-K, operating in Khyber Pakhtunkhwa.[242] However, IS-P carried out some significant attacks in Baluchistan, including against a high-profile state target in March 2022.[243] IS-P reported suffering heavy casualties in the second half of 2021, presumably as a result of intensified operations: 400 killed and some 200 detained. It is quite possible that some of the casualties might have occurred in Afghanistan, supporting IS-K, as the number seems high compared to Pakistani press reports.[244] In the second half of 2021 even the rhetoric of IS-P propaganda hardened against Pakistan, describing it as a British satellite and as an 'Islamic democracy' where the majority is able to 'alter Islam' and its teachings.[245]

The majority of IS-P members were, as of 2020, Pakistanis, especially Pashtuns (typically former IS-K, former TTP). A source indicated that many Orakzai Pashtuns who had fled back to Pakistan after IS-K's defeat in Nangarhar (November 2019) had been invited to join IS in Kashmir.[246] IS-P also attracted former LeJ and other Punjabi jihadists such as LeT members, as well as some Uzbeks and Chechens. One Uzbek was in fact appointed for managing IS-P ad interim, while a governor was being chosen. There were also some 'advisors' from Chechnya, Nepal and Uzbekistan, tasked to help IS-P getting organized.[247]

By 2020, in sum, IS in Pakistan faced a similar predicament as AQ's. Its three South Asian branches (IS-K, IS-P and IS-H) seemed to be facing the choice between accepting dependence on the support of the Pakistani deep state for survival and irrelevance. IS had broken the monopoly of AQ over Pakistani jihadism, but did not manage to establish its own monopoly, or even get close to that. As it will be discussed in detail in the following chapters, as of late 2020 the situation was still in flux. The Pakistani jihadists rarely aligned unambiguously with either global jihadist group, preferring to 'milk' both of them at the same time, or at least keep the second one in reserve, never completely breaking up relations. The only doctrinal difference between AQ and IS that Pakistani jihadists easily appreciated was IS' strong inclination towards Sunni supremacism, but even the supremacists kept their options open. The competition between AQ and IS benefited the Pakistani deep state and the Pakistani jihadists, neither of whom had any interest in a decisive victory of either global jihadist organization. The Pakistani jihadists enjoyed a much wider room of manoeuvre once AQ's monopoly over global jihad in Pakistan was broken. The Pakistani deep state similarly saw its position vis-à-vis the global jihad movement improve and was able for the first time to impose its terms on both organizations. That, however, did not last. As the deep state turned on IS-K in the summer of 2021, the long delayed clash between IS and the Pakistani state was in the offing. Perhaps unexpectedly to the deep state, AQ was also edging towards IS at that time.

Thaw between AQ and IS

AQIS' typical response to the challenge mounted by IS-K in 2014–19 was to try avoiding a clash among jihadist groups, which was easy to achieve in Pakistan, compared to Afghanistan, given the thin presence of the two organizations there. Only later, in 2020, the issue of some form of relationship with IS-P arose and AQIS started negotiating some form of coordination or division of labour with IS-P. 'Our leaders are busy negotiating with them and finding a solution', said an AQ commander.[248] The mild rapprochement with IS was also encouraged by 'some donors from UAE, Saudi and Bahrain and Kuwait', although donors from Qatar opposed such rapprochement.[249]

They say, we must not support Daesh because it's a tool of external intelligence agencies and it's not stable and will be eliminated very soon. However, we want to continue relations with Daesh because they can support our mission in Afghanistan.[250]

During 2020 the Pakistani deep state also encouraged AQIS to cooperate closely with IS on Kashmir and AQIS seemed ready to do so, even if AQ had already been helping groups in Kashmir from 2013 onwards.[251] An AQIS source acknowledged that relations with IS improved during 2020 due to the Taliban peace deal with the Americans:

We're both interested in strengthening relations with each other. We need one another since situation is changing rapidly in Afghanistan. Our main plan is to come closer with Daesh and build a strong base in eastern Afghanistan Nuristan province.[252]

By the end of the summer 2020 relations were getting close enough for the two organizations to decided to establish a new common safe haven in Nuristan; AQIS even decided to establish a new headquarter there. AQIS agreed to support IS-K financially for getting ready to an offensive against the Taliban in the east and northeast, aimed at establishing a sizeable safe haven for the global jihadists there.[253] Eventually in 2021 AQIS also agreed to support IS-P, with the related aim of setting up a back-up safe haven in case the one in eastern Afghanistan did not hold (see also previous section).[254]

Most Western observers were still seeing the Afghan Taliban and AQ as closely aligned as late as 2021, encouraged by a UN assessment (in turn based on inputs by the intelligence services of members states operating in and around Afghanistan).[255] However, we know from the Abbottabad papers that bin Laden and more in general Al Qa'ida had been distrusting the Taliban from at least 2007, when Mullah Dadullah died in suspect circumstances, if not earlier, and that al Zawahiri in particular expressed in 2010 the view that a US-Taliban agreement would 'render al Qaeda impotent'.[256] AQ's doubts only grew more serious from the time they signed their agreement with the Americans and informed AQ that it would have to accept limitations to its freedom of manoeuvre and action in the future. The series of hits against AQ leader (Hamza bin Laden, Asim Umar, Abu Moshin al Masri just to mention the most important ones) aroused the suspicion that elements of the Taliban leadership were tipping off the Americans about the locations of AQ leaders in order to improve relations with the Americans.[257]

It was not a smooth path for the alliance of IS and AQ in Afghanistan, however. AQIS was still reeling from the loss of LeJ and 'some other minor groups', which used to be close to AQIS and then realigned with IS.[258] Reaching an understanding was therefore not easy. There were doubts within AQIS' ranks, concerning the trustworthiness of IS-K. Some members opposed the deal, citing the bitter fighting involving IS and AQ affiliates in Syria. Despite the improving relations, in fact, AQIS was quite worried about the growing closeness of IS-H with LeT and JeM.[259] In the end the predominant view turned out to be that AQIS did not really have any option.[260] The only realistic alternative would have been to move all assets to Pakistan, but that was rejected as the Pakistani 'deep state' was trusted even less than IS-K (see also *Breakthrough 2014* – above):

Obviously, Pakistan is a slave and puppet country. We cannot trust them fully. We know that they have closer relations with Americans. If we move our people to Pakistan, they will arrest or share info with Americans.[261]

Indeed, the convergence of AQ and IS in Afghanistan slowed after the return to power of the Taliban in August 2021, as AQ developed some illusions that the Taliban would want to maintain close relations with it, after relations with Washington took a dive. Then the process of AQ and IS coming together accelerated again towards the end of 2021 as the Taliban were clearly edging quite close to China and Russia, two unacceptable partners for AQ. By December 2021, one AQ source stated clearly that AQ and IS were coordinating in eastern Afghanistan and that some AQ members were under the 'protection' of IS.[262]

3

The TTP: Bastard offspring of global jihad

The origins of the TTP

From Pakistani Taliban to TTP

The pro-Taliban Deobandi groups discussed in Chapter 1 started going 'rogue' in late 2001 as the Pakistani authorities decided to collaborate with the Americans in the operation that overthrew the Taliban Emirate. This is when the 'Pakistani Taliban' emerged as a variety of separate groups, coagulating small bands of fighters in parallel in a variety of locations, without central leadership. These groups formed around veterans of Afghanistan, who had fought on the Afghan Taliban's side, and mobilized support for the Taliban Emirate first and then for the remnants of the Afghan Taliban, who after the collapse of the Emirate had mostly taken refuge in Pakistan.[1]

According to one of the TTP leaders, the process of formation of a group that could unite all Pakistani Taliban started in 2002, when the Pakistani army started operations against 'jihadist forces' along the Afghan border.[2] These groups had in common their sympathy for the Afghan Taliban and hostility to US intervention in Afghanistan, as well as (to various degrees) criticism of the conduct of the Pakistani government towards the Americans and jihadist groups such as AQ and others. By 2003 the Pakistani Ministry of Interior estimated at 5,000 the number of militants present in FATA, but the number kept growing afterwards.[3]

Overall as many as 40,000 militants might have been involved in the mobilization, according to the higher end estimates. Even the lowest end estimates talk of 15,000 Pashtun tribesmen from the tribal areas of Pakistan, on top of thousands of Pashtuns from the settled areas and smaller numbers of Punjabis.[4] The lowest end estimate would make close to 0.5 per cent of the population of the FATA of the time, or 1 per cent of the male population. Although the TTP later earned a reputation for assassinating tribal elders, it has also maintained close relations with local actors in its areas of activity, especially initially. In Malakand the TNSM had initially the support of the local landlords, even if that did not last long.[5]

The Pakistani Taliban emerged therefore as a rather wide movement originally. However, the mobilization was quite disorganized. In 2002–3 the bands of tens to a few hundred men were completely loose and there was no organizational structure bringing the bands together. The bands operated individually in Afghanistan. By 2004, however, some of the local leaders managed to consolidate their influence and power, forming local insurgent organizations with hundreds or even a few thousand members. The first Pakistani Taliban leader able to co-opt several groups of Pakistani Taliban was Nek Mohammad, who was leading a large group in South Waziristan by 2004.[6] Nek Mohammed had fought in Afghanistan and was in contact with bin Laden and other AQ members.[7] Others followed, but the process was rife with disputes and rivalries. The example of the Ahmedzai Wazir is illustrative. The influential Mullah Nazir was not even able to unite all the Ahmadzai Wazir groups:

> In the Ahmedzai Wazir tribe, 'there were 14 groups of Taliban until November 2006, but after the appointment of Mullah Nazir as commander, all of them were brought under one leadership. Two Taliban commanders, Ghulam Jan and Ifthikar, do not accept Mullah Nazir as commander'.[8]

This resulted in quite a few insurgent organizations or networks emerging in parallel, bringing many of the Pakistani Taliban groups together at the agency or regional level. This unmanaged process was rife with long-term consequences. It is worth noting here the impact that the separate formation of Haqqani network, aka Miran Shah Shura, had on the Afghan Taliban – it remained a constant factor of disunity.[9] Arguably the existence of several separate, regionalized insurgent organizations before the TTP was formed should impact negatively on the long-term cohesiveness of the TTP.

By 2007 there were a few tens of these insurgent organizations/networks, each gathering from a handful to several tens local groups. Eventually most of these organizations first coagulated together at the agency level and then merged into the TTP of Baitullah Mehsud, because he had the support of the 'Arabs and AQ' and also because he was by far the most powerful of the local leaders, having between 5,000 and 20,000 men, depending on the source.[10] The main groups that merged into the TTP were:

- A faction of Hafiz Gul Bahadar's HuJI (North Waziristan's Waziris).
- The Tehrik e Nafaz e Shariat e Mohammadi (TNSM) of Fazlullah and Faqir Mohammed. Tribally the TNSM was a mix of Mohmand, Mehsud, Afridi, Shinwari, Yousafzai and Achekzai and even some Punjabis.[11]
- The Mehsud Pakistani Taliban, led by Baitullah Mehsud.
- The Darra Adamkhil Pakistani Taliban, led by commander Abdullah.
- The Bajaur Pakistani Taliban, led by Abu Baker Mufti.[12]
- The Ahmadzai Wazir group led by Mullah Nazir, which however was to quit soon.[13]

The fragmented origins of the TTP per se do not set it apart from the Afghan Taliban, which also had similar origins. However, in the case of the Afghan Taliban a leadership trying to pull the disparate groups together was formed earlier, essentially within eighteen months at most of the insurgency starting.[14] Among the Pakistani Taliban it took six years, allowing the different component groups to develop separate identities.

AQ and the birth of the TTP

From June 2002 onwards the Pakistani army started intervening in the FATA against elements involved in raids inside Afghanistan, and especially those operating against US forces there.[15] The Pakistani Taliban, whether involved in the Afghan raids or not, reacted to what they considered an intrusion into the tribal areas. Noor Wali Meshud described the consolidation of the Pakistani Taliban into larger groups and eventually into the TTP as motivated by the desire to defend tribal autonomy.[16] By early 2004 there was open warfare between many of the Pakistani Taliban groups and the Pakistani army. Rana and Gunaratna describe a situation in 2004 in which the Afghan Taliban were initially (May) pushing their Pakistani tribal sympathizers to put military pressure on the Pakistani authorities, opposing Nek Mohammed's signature of the Shakai agreement with Islamabad.[17]

By September the Afghan Taliban's position had reportedly shifted and they were asking their Pakistani sympathizers to stop attacking the Pakistani army. According to these authors, who do not cite their sources, the Afghan Taliban, who were still reorganizing themselves, still had a lot of influence on these Pakistani Pashtun networks and could even 'appoint' their agency-level commanders, negotiating between their tribal components. During 2004, as a result of the first Pakistani army operations in the tribal areas, the pro-Afghan Taliban Pakistani networks were beginning to see divergent views between those in favour of accommodation with the Pakistani authorities (such as originally Nek Mohammed and Baitullah Mehsud, and later Mullah Nazir and others) and those in favour of exacting revenge against them (such as originally Abdullah Mehsud and later Baitullah Mehsud, who had changed his mind). It is not clear what was the role of the Afghan Taliban in driving the emergence of these differences. The shifting positions suggest that tribal politics might have played a role in determining the alignments, but there seems to have been a genuine 'policy debate' going on as well. Even the foreigners were divided. While AQ's elements in the tribal areas were at this point reportedly supporting the Afghan Taliban's view, IMU leader Tahir Yuldash advocated retaliation against the Pakistani army. Eventually these debates originated a conflict. In March 2007 Mullah Nazir ordered the expulsion of the Uzbeks from Waziri areas of Waziristan, and the clashes started.[18]

The Pakistani authorities intervened in support of Mullah Nazir. The intervention was seen as the biggest success of the Pakistani security agencies in those early years of the Pakistani Taliban movement, as it allowed them to gain indirect influence in parts of Waziristan. This outcome was probably not unexpected as far as the Qaidists in the tribal areas were concerned. As mentioned above, they appear to have been trying to avoid the intra-jihadist confrontation. The Arabs quit Waziri territory in order to avoid clashes with groups opposed to foreign presence and in order to maintain the pre-eminence of the Afghan front. As tension between pro-foreign militants Dawrs and anti-foreign militants Waziris was building up, many Arab jihadists relocated to Mehsud territory, under the protection of Baitullah and Abdullah Mehsud.[19] The Afghan Taliban were reported to have first tried to mediate between the two Pakistani Taliban factions, eventually unsuccessfully.[20] Then the Afghan Taliban reportedly mediated between Mullah Nazir and the Pakistani army, implicitly siding against the Uzbeks. Given that the Afghan Taliban had close relations with AQ at that time, this could be taken as a further confirmation that ultimately the Qaidists in the tribal areas too did not want to see the Pakistani Taliban start a conflict with the Pakistani authorities and would rather abandon the Central Asians to their fate.[21] According to a Qaidist publication, the position of AQ was that the Central Asians had been told to respect the rules set by the 'amir':

> Non-Pakistani groups like Uzbeks, Turks, Turkman, and others must not cross the boundaries drawn by the Emir concerned with Pakistan and tribal areas.[22]

At this stage (the pre-TTP years) AQ elements already had a significant influence in the tribal areas. The global jihadists in the tribal areas had little cash in comparison what the flows of money that would characterize the region later, but still enough to buy local support and strengthen pro-foreign militant groups within the Pakistani Taliban galaxy, who would eventually coalesce into the TTP.[23]

It should be noted that at this point in time AQ's assets in Pakistan had already been targeted in several raids by the Pakistani security forces, sometimes jointly with US counter-terrorism (see Chapter 2). Hence, if the sources are right, the caution shown by AQ leadership is even more noteworthy and should be taken as further indication of the determination with which the Qaidists in the tribal areas in 2002–6 opposed the option of opening a jihadist campaign against Islamabad. At the same time, AQ's relations with the Pakistani 'deep state' were still uncertain to say the least, despite the 2005 agreement with ISI elements (see Chapter 2).

The establishment of the TTP in December 2007 was however exactly a declaration of jihad against Islamabad, with the stated aim of imposing a Shari'a-based regime in all of Pakistan. The very emergence of the TTP cemented the split between anti-Islamabad Pakistani Taliban and at least some of the pro-Islamabad ones, although the latter would soon be getting out of it. Was there a direct Qaidist role in pushing for the formation of the TTP? Did the Qaidists change their attitude towards the Pakistani authorities in 2007, moving to a more confrontational approach? And if so, why?

Stenersen sees Baitullah Mehsud as gradually building a relationship with AQ from 2004 onwards. Stenersen does not think AQ ever really trying to steer away from confrontation with the Pakistani authorities, but believes that by 2007 AQ's position of focusing on Western targets in Pakistan had changed and that it started now advocating a fight against the Pakistan state. Stenersen acknowledges that just months earlier AQ managed to avoid a confrontation with the Waziri tribesmen who were rebelling against the Central Asian jihadists, with the support of the Pakistani authorities. Was AQ, as Stenersen says, trying to become more influential within the Pakistani jihadist environment, by jumping on the Lal Masjid bandwagon? Her argument is that AQ might have found among local and foreign jihadists in the FATA an environment favourable to global jihadist ideas, as these were after all groups that had largely been fighting other people's jihads already.[24]

As discussed in Chapter 2, AQ's relationship with the ISI was still highly unstable and incoherent in 2005–8 and 2007 was a peak in the turbulence. AQ's rhetoric versus Islamabad undoubtedly became very aggressive in 2007 (see also Chapter 2). The anonymous author of the AQ booklet (*c.* 2006) had already identified the need for the Pakistani Taliban of uniting behind a Pakistani leader:

> *It is necessary for Jihad in Pakistan that local Taliban and Mujahidin Groups to agree on one leadership [...]. The ideal scenario for this unity is for the Pakistani Mujahidin to unite under the leadership of Mullah Muhammad 'Umar, may God protect him. Hypothetically, if this is difficult to achieve now, then it is necessary to select a temporary leader for Jihad. We can achieve such agreement and unity gradually, through the formation of consultative councils that include a Pakistani Mujahid elite in the first phase, and in light of experiments results in this phase, suitable future steps will be taken.*[25]

AQ and TTP sources confirm that Baitullah Mehsud and the nascent TTP in general were establishing good relations with the foreign jihadists, in their struggle against the Pakistani state.[26] A TTP source confirmed that 'it was with the money of AQ that Baitullah Mehsud formed the TTP'.[27] But if the Qaidists clearly seem to have had an important role in the formation of the TTP, what was the purpose?

A view by Sulaiman is that Baitullah was driven by the desire to build a vehicle for his own aggrandisement as the 'Mullah Omar of Pakistan'.[28] While this is likely to have been a factor, it does not explain why so many ended up following Baitullah into the TTP. Franco and Yusufzai describe the emergence of the TTP as a strategy of tribal and organizational consolidation, in opposition to efforts of the Pakistani security agencies to play divide and rule with the Pakistani Taliban, exploiting the tribal and personal rivalries.[29]

> *Treating the FATA like a section of the Muslim Ummah, and the tribals as a single community of believers, the brains behind the TTP were able to introduce a mutual assistance mechanism designed to break the government's strategy, which was based on the tribes' structural propensity for internal conflict.*[30]

'Tribal and organizational consolidation' works as an explanation of the perspective adopted by the Pakistani Taliban local leaders. Despite heavy-handed tactics by the Pakistani army in the tribal areas, the radicalization of the Pakistani Taliban was, according to Kerr, more due to the Lal Masjid crackdown in 2007 (and to the incessant drone strikes in the tribal areas) than to Pakistani army atrocities in the tribal areas.[31] The Lal Masjid incident created the momentum for some Pakistani Taliban leaders to mobilize support around a project (the TTP) that was clearly in opposition to the Pakistani state.[32] In a sense, the emotional wave created by the Lal Masjid episode consolidated the influence of jihadist *rhetoric* among Pakistani TTP leaders, first and foremost Baitullah Mehsud.

'Strategic consolidation', Baitullah's self-aggrandisement, the emotional wave surrounding the Lal Masjid incident all played a role in the emergence of the TTP. AQ elements acted as enablers, but what did it gain from it? Going back to Stenersen's point concerning AQ seeing the tribal areas as an environment favourable to global jihadist ideas, an AQ source dating to sometime before the formation of the TTP indicates how the author saw potential in the tribes of the FATA, if they could be organized and managed by the jihadists, for a mass mobilization into the ranks of the jihad movement:

> *The main power that must be relied upon in Pakistan after God almighty is tribal power; unlike other parts of Pakistan, the British and their regimes were never able to implement total hegemony over the tribal belt. That is why we do not see a total collapse of the natural order among people, tribes, and societies of tribal areas, like we see in areas under government control in Pakistan. The Republican system that the British wisely implemented has broken the strength of tribes in other Pakistani communities [...]. That is why it is the only region that Jihad can transform to become a strong popular movement; the whole society there can join Jihad. So if our military and Islamic missionary worked hand in hand on a straight path ... it will suffice to just signal, so that thousands of people will march to the Jihad arena in the company of their mighty army. [...] Therefore, we say that tribal power is the real and natural one that we could rely upon after God almighty. That is why force preparation is not the real challenge that Jihad leadership must confront. Their challenge lies in organizing and coordinating the available and loose raw force in order to achieve a legitimate objective, and this is the operation that Abu Bakr Naji names as the Management of Savagery.*[33]

It is not so much that the Qaidist author saw the tribals as naturally more inclined towards jihadism; he rather saw them as easy to mobilize rapidly and easily thanks to the persistence of tribal structures. As the Qaidist author acknowledged, the real problem was exactly 'organising and coordinating' this 'raw force', which was the Pakistani Taliban of 2002–6. The author of the booklet was clear about the fact that the Pakistani Taliban needed unity.[34] The centrifugal forces among the Pakistani Taliban were always strong, and it took the emotional wave of the Lal Masjid incident in 2007 to generate a centripetal movement of even greater strength, at least temporarily.

It has been alleged that AQ 'orchestrated' the Lal Masjid incident in order to get a jihad against the Pakistani state going. This was on the basis of the presence of some AQ associates in the mosque.[35] There is no conclusive evidence of this allegation; Stenersen, for example, does not believe AQ 'made' the Lal Masjid incident.[36] As we have seen in Chapter 2, at that time AQ was only just beginning to coalesce into a relative coherent entity even within Pakistan, so even the participation of some AQ members would not be evidence of a decision of the leadership to get involved.

To sum up, the formation of the TTP was the result of the converge of the desire of at least the local AQ operatives' desire to organizing its tribal allies into a powerful force and of the local TTP allies to push the Pakistani army back from the tribal areas. The 'high temperature' generated by the Lal Masjid incident offered the opportunity for these convergent interests to reach the fusion point. As it should be expected in such emotional moments, the rhetoric surrounding the merger was flying much higher, but it did not necessarily mean much.

Semple described the formation of the TTP as the actual starting point of a significant Pakistani insurgency in its own right (as opposed to being a mere spill over of the Afghan one):[37]

The announcement of the TTP was a declaration that the ameers were no longer simply an appendage of the Afghan insurgency. It gave them a vehicle to pursue and articulate aims that diverged from those of the Afghan Taliban. In the TTP, the ameers had a vehicle to challenge the Pakistani state, while professing loyalty to Mullah Omar, whose own forces were obliged to avoid antagonising the same state.[38]

As AQ's local operatives had consolidated their tribal allies into a seemingly powerful TTP, what use did it intend to make of it? In Chapter 2 it was argued that one of AQ's main priorities was the Afghan jihad. The other main priority was protecting its own leadership. The latter was, in what turned out to be a precarious way, dealt with through the 2005 agreement with ISI elements, which took bin Laden to Abbottabad. Instead, the growing pressure of the Pakistani authorities on the tribal areas endangered the infrastructure AQ operatives and allied groups had set up to support (and influence) the Afghan Taliban. From what was discussed in Chapter 2 we can develop the hypothesis that AQ's operatives wanted to protect that infrastructure and the best way of doing so was by raising the cost to Pakistan, through the TTP. In this optic, the TTP was meant to make it harder for the Pakistani security forces to encroach in the tribal areas, and also to raise a wider threat to the Pakistani establishment, strengthening AQ's negotiating position with an eye to a future, more comprehensive trade off than the 2005 deal.

AQ was certainly advertising its relationship with the TTP, featuring them in its propaganda videos, and by 2009 TTP leader Hakimullah seems to have been happy to let AQ manage propaganda for the TTP, whereas under Baitullah the TTP was managing its own propaganda operations.[39]

What evidence do we have that AQ or part thereof intended to use the TTP as a tool for achieving more limited aims, such as forcing the Pakistani authorities to abandon support for the US effort in Afghanistan, as opposed to overthrowing the Pakistani state? In the following sections the following issues will be addressed:

- Was the TTP seriously committed to AQ's global jihad?
- Did the TTP try to mount a serious threat against the Pakistani state, and what was AQ's role in that?
- Why did not AQ start developing a more organic relationship with the TTP, along the lines of one of the models described by Meldelsohns (see *Introduction*)?
- What did AQ make of the TTP as a jihadist organization?
- How did AQ try to 'manage' (influence, grow and direct) the TTP?

The nature of the TTP's jihad

The TTP and global jihad

TTP's support for AQ's campaigns

From the early days of the TTP, the leaders of the anti-Islamabad TTP factions were often making 'global jihadist' statements and expressing support for the foreign fighters.[40] These even included statements about joining the jihad in Kashmir.[41] Are pro-AQ pronouncements by Pakistani Taliban to be interpreted as being genuine demonstrations of commitment to global jihad? It is worth noting that even the pro-Islamabad factions of the Pakistani Taliban allowed Arabs, Central Asians and Chechens to hang around (with the exception of Mullah Nazir's campaign against the Central Asians).[42] Their rhetoric was still 'global-jihadist'. One of them, for example, stated in a meeting:

> Q: Do you want to take war to foreign countries?
> A: Yes why not, the people who are killed in Palestine, who are they, are they not Muslims?[43]

Similar statements were made by other signatories to the 2012 agreement with the Pakistani authorities.[44] One of the most prominent pro-Islamabad leaders, Mullah Nazir, having thrown the Central Asians out of the Wana area in 2006, publicly stated his support for global jihad.[45] Abbas described Mullah Nazir's statement as a tactical move to win support at a time when he was fighting foreign fighters in the Wana region, but many AQ members have been killed over the years in Mullah Nazir's territory, suggesting that his statement was not mere rhetoric.[46]

Mangal Bagh and his Lashkar e Islam (LI) mostly militated among the pro-Islamabad groups and even when aligned with the TTP mostly only skirmished lightly with the Frontier Corps. LI stood out for years among the Pakistani Taliban galaxy for their weak or absent links to global jihadist groups and even to the Afghan Taliban. Perhaps this is what contributed to make many observers doubt Mangal Bagh's ideological commitment.[47] Indeed, even AQ sources rated Mangal Bagh as a 'well-known thug' and a 'common man', with little more than a link to the Tabligh movement.[48] Yet, even a senior member of LI stated in a meeting that for him the foreign fighters were welcome: 'We have a good relationship with them because they are our guests'. He also added that he was ready to continue jihad beyond Afghanistan.[49]

All this suggests that global jihadist rhetoric, common currency in Pakistani Taliban circles and even familiarity with foreign fighters did not necessarily per se mean much in practice, and cannot be taken as evidence of strong links to global jihadist organizations, such as AQ.

The TTP did move some way beyond mere rhetoric. It was volunteering for attacks in America and Europe, although their actual participation in such operations remained always very limited, with not a single successful attack in a Western country ever being delivered.[50] Over a period of almost twenty years, the few failed attempts that have been linked to the TTP do not represent an output that per se would have provided a rationale for AQ to keep up its support to TTP, especially considering the size of that support (see *The long-term AQ support for the TTP* below).

The biggest TTP contribution to the cause of global jihad remains to date its intervention in Afghanistan. Afghan Taliban sources claim that close to 20,000 Pakistani volunteers died up to 2013 fighting alongside them; of these a substantial number were Pakistani Taliban.[51] However, even the TTP's intervention in Afghanistan is not without qualifications. Helping fellow Pashtun Taliban in Afghanistan was not such a 'global' step for the Pakistani Taliban to take, given the ethnic and territorial contiguity. Moreover, while at the beginning of the Afghan insurgency the Pakistani Taliban were unmistakably there to help, by 2013 they were largely there to escape Pakistani repression. The contribution given by the TTP was also limited by its refusal to embed with the Afghan Taliban, contrary to what some other pro-AQ groups did, such as the IMU. TTP units maintained their own chain of command and did not integrate under the Afghan Taliban's one.[52] A TTP commander presented the previous year of fighting (2013) as a mix of fighting against the Afghan security forces and Lashkar e Taiba, the latter supported by the Pakistani army. In that year, his contingent had lost about 100 men fighting the Afghan security forces and the Americans and about 60 men fighting Lashkar e Taiba.[53] It should also be noted that LeT has also been maintaining close relations with AQ (see Chapter 3 below), so in the eyes of AQ fighting against it might well have offset some of the praise earned for fighting against the Americans.[54]

The TTP also contributed to global jihad in terms of sending volunteers to AQ's flagship project of post-2011, the Syrian civil war. Already on 14 July 2012 the TTP agreed to send volunteers to Al Nusra and the first contingent was dispatched soon afterwards. Reports of Pakistani volunteers getting killed in Syria started getting more frequent by the year's end, and by 2013 news agencies and specialist media reported TTP getting involved in the Syrian fight, sending 'hundreds' of volunteers there.[55] As the end of 2014 approached, the TTP reportedly had already sent 1,000 volunteers to Syria, with plans to send hundreds more, as claimed by the TTP itself and confirmed by the Pakistani authorities.[56] TTP won indeed the praise of AQ for doing so, except that these volunteers soon transferred their loyalty to IS, turning from the pride of the TTP to a source of embarrassment.[57]

The TTP attested its global jihadist credentials in some other ways too. Jadoon and Mahmood noted that in recent years the TTP started advertising an interest in female jihadists for 'martyrdom operations', presumably mimicking global jihadist practices.[58]

'Global jihadist' credentials were also enhanced by the hospitality provided to the Central Asians and other foreign fighters, which was discussed above already. Another example of such hospitality is that of the Chinese jihadists. In 2009–10 TTP started welcoming a number of Hui Chinese and Uyghurs in its ranks, led by Abu Omar Seyfiddin.[59] For the TTP this was also, and perhaps primarily, a way to irritate the Pakistani authorities, always sensitive to anything that might raise the brows of their Chinese allies. In fact, not all jihadist circles were impressed by the TTP's hospitality. By the admission of one of the Chinese hosts, some donors to global jihad groups later criticized the Huis and Uyghurs for staying with the TTP, inviting them to join the Islamic State instead, because

> *TTP operates in Pakistan and they are working against Pakistan. They are not doing real Jihad.*[60]

In sum, one thing is to say that the TTP was influenced by AQ and other jihadist groups, and another to say that AQ's long-term investment in it was justified by its gradual absorption into the global jihadist fold. The TTP definitely appears to have drawn its *narrative* from AQ cadres operating in the tribal areas of Pakistan. This does not mean that the TTP absorbed AQ's *ideology*. Semple concludes that by and large the TTP

> remains a classic terrorist group that, through acts of violence and propaganda, periodically manages to insert issues onto the national political agenda and to limit the options available to constitutional actors. [...] Without an overhaul of Pakistan's approach to counter-terrorism and proxy warfare, the TTP will be likely to sustain terrorist violence across Pakistan and ensure that the Pakistan-Afghanistan frontier area remains a hub for regional terrorism.[61]

For 'classic' terrorist group Semple clearly intends not a global jihadist organization. Taken as a whole, the TTP was paying little more than lip service to the cause of global jihad, in exchange for funding that accounted for a substantial portion of its budget. What the TTP was essentially concerned about was (at least initially) the fate of the Afghan Taliban, the autonomy of the tribal areas and the imposition of a Taliban-style regime in FATA and NWFP, and ideally in the rest of Pakistan as well.

The limited interest of the TTP in AQ's global jihad was eventually confirmed in 2020 when its leader, Noor Wali Mehsud, refused to join the new global jihadist alliance, taking shape around AQIS and IS-K, and tried to maintain decent relations with the Afghan Taliban.[62] The TTP's refusal to form the new alliance was a significant blow as its 3,000–4,000 men in Afghanistan would have given that alliance a major boost in eastern Afghanistan. By 2021, no doubt for pragmatic reasons as well, Noor Wali was openly stating that the TTP's fight was limited to Pakistan and was denying any link to AQ.[63]

TTP and the Islamic State

What was discussed in the previous section does not rule out that within the TTP there might have been constituencies somewhat more genuinely drawn towards global jihad. It was mostly these constituencies that were involved in the expeditionary TTP force to the Middle East. Eventually such constituencies ended up being attracted by the global jihadist competition to AQ. As mentioned above, the TTP sent volunteers to Syria, and they fell under the influence of what would become IS. As they went back to Pakistan or Afghanistan, that influence started spreading to other TTP members. According to TTP sources, during 2014–15 alone, as many as 4,000–4,500 members of TTP defected to IS-K, mostly coming from factions marginalized by Fazlullah.[64] This figure might be inflated and is certainly not uncontested, however. An IS-K source acknowledged the presence of just 1,130 ex TTP within IS-K ranks at the end of 2015, that is, just a quarter of the figure above, although there might also have been significant casualties in the meantime.[65]

As discussed in *Competition for AQ* (Chapter 2), essentially the Pakistani branch of IS, known in 2014 as TKP, was formed by some of the anti-Fazlullah dissidents within the TTP, angry that TTP leader Fazlullah was cutting them off funding and resources. Most of the original members of TKP were Orakzais and Mehsuds, but later the TKP was strengthened by the arrival of a large group of Afridis, mostly from the ranks of Mangal Bagh's Lashkar e Islam.[66]

As the influence of the veterans coming back from the Middle East spread, the ideological commitment of the growing number of defectors to IS became more questionable. Overall, the jury is still out over whether the TTP defectors were attracted by the global jihadist ethos of IS, or by its financial wealth, or again by its reputation of unstoppable success. TKP sources claimed that Pakistani army pressure in North Waziristan contributed decisively to push many TTP members to join the TKP, perhaps in protest at the lack of support they were receiving from the TTP leadership.[67] Typically, TTP members accused defectors to IS of being motivated by money, as well as by the belief that IS would not be as aggressively targeted by the Pakistani government as TTP was being.[68] IS-K members by contrast insist that defections from TTP occurred because of differences with Fazlullah, tribal differences (with many Orakzais and Mehsuds joining IS-K) and contrasts between clerical networks.[69] All this suggests non-ideological motives for at least a substantial number of those joining.

One former TTP member who defected to IS-K provided somewhat of a global jihadist blueprint for TKP/IS-K:

> [A] difference is this that TTP is not against Shi'as, but TKP is against Shi'as. Another difference is this that TTP is fighting against the Pakistani government, but we are fighting against Pakistan's government, against the Afghan Government, foreigners, Shi'as, and the same we plan to fight against Iran and Central Asian governments.[70]

In practice, however, IS-K ended up fighting almost exclusively against the Afghan Taliban and to a lesser extent against the Pakistani and Afghan Shi's communities.[71] Although a substantial number in the original core had been to the Middle East, to many other TTP members who switched side to IS-K, its global jihad ideology might well have represented a cover for indulging in a different form of parochialism, pursuing rivalries with other TTP members and with the Afghan Taliban.

The position of the TTP itself vis-à-vis IS was for a long time ambiguous. IS-K sources claims that Fazlullah negotiated joining IS-K for some time, before cutting off links.[72] TTP sources usually denied any negotiations over joining, but admitted that top-level negotiations about finding a modus vivendi took place. Two TTP sources claimed that at one point the TTP announced its support for IS-K, but the Afghan Taliban and AQ complained and TTP retracted. Reportedly AQ warned the TTP leadership that it would cut funding and relations with TTP if it were to negotiate with IS-K. AQ also expressly requested Fazlullah to publicly denounce Al Baghdadi as not a real Caliph.[73] Eventually he did: in spring 2015 the TTP released a tract by Abu Usman Salarzai, criticizing Al Baghdadi's claim to the Caliphate and praising AQ leaders.[74] Soon TTP propaganda against IS-K started building up:

> Their jihad is not a real jihad. You can see they did a lot of cruel actions and activities with common people in Nangarhar province and in Orakzai Agency. For example, they killed innocent people, small children, women and they did adultery with innocent people by the name of wedlock.[75]

The pressure exercised by AQ might explain why the TTP was keen to publicize occasional violent skirmishes between the two groups in Afghanistan and Pakistan in 2015–16. IS-K sources, by contrast, tended to deny such skirmishes were taking place.[76]

Again, the TTP's interest in IS appears to have been of a quite pragmatic nature, rather than ideological – the expectation of IS financial support in exchange for help in setting up IS-K in the critical first several months of its existence.

Although the original TTP/IS-K talks fizzled out relatively rapidly, sources admitted that relations between the middle ranks of the two organizations continued after 2015 and some TTP members were still tempted by the idea of defecting to IS-K.[77] Indeed defections kept taking place, as discussed in *The fragmentation of the TTP* below.

In a much changed context, the new TTP leader, Noor Wali Mehsud, resumed talks with IS-K in 2019. At that time when even AQIS was negotiating with IS-K, both TTP and AQIS worried that the Afghan Taliban would sign a deal with the Americans and betray AQ and its allies.[78] The TTP was seeking some form of cooperation, but once again Noor Wali was asked to pledge to the Caliphate, which he refused to do, despite lobbying by senior IS figures in Syria. Relations between IS-K and TTP however improved in 2019–20 as a result of the former weakening and becoming more inclined to find allies (as opposed to absorbing them).[79]

In early 2020 the TTP leader, Noor Wali Mehsud, accepted to re-open talks with IS-K, in the wake of Afghan Taliban-US talks, which resulted in the 29 February 2020 agreement. The talks between IS-K and TTP in early 2020 focused on the IS-K's request that TTP contribute fighters to a counter-offensive in eastern Afghanistan against the Afghan Taliban. While this represented a much more modest demand than had been the case in 2019, the TTP refused also because of its reasonable relations with the Afghan Taliban and its vulnerability to an Afghan Taliban counter-offensive. By the summer of 2020 all negotiations had been dropped.[80] There was at this point so little appetite for close relations with IS-K that ex TTP, JuA and HuA commanders, who had merged into IS-K, were banned from rejoining the TTP in the wake of the JuA and HuA merge agreement, because they were 'distrusted'.[81]

None of this talking and negotiating amounted in any case to any serious TTP interest in global jihad as such, and was instead due to the shared need to secure a safe haven in Afghanistan.

The distrust just mentioned highlights how the longer-term intentions of IS-K were still believed to be spreading its ideology within the TTP ranks and then cannibalizing it, as it had done in 2014–18. The TTP leaders in the end started seeing the IS-K as a Pakistani ISI and Saudi project, meant to undermine the TTP in line with previous attempts to splinter it.[82] Some TTP donors in Saudi Arabia and Qatar switched to supporting IS-K as well, intensifying the competition.[83] As negotiations faltered, as it had been the case earlier, according to one TTP source, IS-K indeed resorted to its old policy of reaching out to TTP commanders for recruitment. This time it targeted commanders in Orakzai, Bajaur and Swat, but also in Afghanistan.[84] It was however not very successful:

I too was contacted by a TTP commander who is now with IS-K and told me to leave TTP because TTP is divided in several groups and doesn't have the power as it had before. He told me that IS-K is supported by Arab Mujahideen and it has more facilities for doing Jihad than TTP. I rejected his offer but later I heard that several other TTP commanders also have been contacted by IS-K in Afghanistan.[85]

As late as 2019, one source alleged that the faction of Hakimullah Mehsud (Sheharyar) was closest to IS-K and was lobbying for talks between TTP and IS-K.[86] At the same time, the new branch of IS in Pakistan, IS-P, was also reaching out to TTP commanders in various parts of Khyber Pakhtunkhwa. TTP sources claim that most of the commanders rejected the invitation.[87] That TTP commanders were being sought is also confirmed by IS-P sources, according to which during the summer of 2020 some TTP commanders were in talks with IS-P to join, in exchange for being appointed to senior positions.[88] That as of October 2020 these negotiations had borne no results yet bears witness to the fact that IS branches were losing the power of attraction fast, both in its ideological and material dimensions.

After the re-establishment of the Emirate in Afghanistan in August 2021, TTP and IS-K adopted a position of 'neither friends nor foes' to each other.[89] However, when TTP negotiated with Islamabad in November 2021, IS-P seized the opportunity for trying to attract its hardline members.[90] One IS-P commander confirmed that:

When the cease-fire ended, we met with some of the TTP commanders. We talked about the current government of Pakistan. We told the TTP commanders that Pakistani officials are not trustworthy at all. We told them that we have to fight against them shoulder to shoulder, we told them we must bring the Shari'a to Pakistan, we told them we must bring down this westernised regime as soon as possible.[91]

Within the ranks of TTP, there continued to be uneasiness about Afghan Taliban intent, in the wake of US withdrawal, a possible interim government in Afghanistan, and Taliban readiness to comply with Pakistani demands of banning TTP from Afghan territory after the took power.[92] No defections occurred during 2021 and in any case the attraction of IS-K was less ideological than pragmatic: it would have been a useful ally if relations with the Afghan Taliban had got complicated.

IS-K was more successful in establishing alliances with some of the splinters of the TTP. JuA in particular maintained close relations with IS-K until 2019 and has appeared supportive of the 'Caliphate' in its media outlets. In September 2014 JuA was reported to have declared its allegiance to Al Baghdadi, but later JuA sources denied this had ever been the case.[93] IS-K did ask the leader of JuA to pledge to IS, but he managed to avoid that and maintain just an alliance with IS-K. JuA agreed to cooperate with IS-K in Afghanistan and sources in TTP also confirm their close relationship and military alliance even in Nangarhar.[94] However, although an IS source claimed a degree of cooperation when it claimed the Quetta Hospital attack of August 2016 was carried out by IS-K and JuA together, a JuA source rejected claims by IS-K that it cooperated with it in Pakistan. Relations between IS-K and JuA worsened after a major IS-K defeat in Nangarhar (Afghanistan) in November 2019. JuA itself took serious casualties and suffered desertions while fighting alongside IS-K in Nangarhar.[95]

IS-K sources acknowledged some months of blackout with JuA after that, but then claimed relations had resumed in the summer of 2020. However, in September JuA merged back into the TTP (see *Reuniting the TTP under Noor Wali* below), and agreed to cut off all links to IS-K. Hizb-ul Ahrar (HuA), which had split from JuA (see *The fragmentation of the TTP* below) followed a similar parable, in fact maintaining a close relationship with JuA throughout its existence, despite having split out of it.[96] The closeness of JuA and HuA to IS-K appears to have at least in part to have been motivated by ideological contiguity (*The fragmentation of the TTP* below), although IS-K was supporting them financially and logistically as long as they fought alongside it. The refusal to merge with IS-K seems however to indicate a residual degree of pragmatism in these two groups. As soon as IS-K lost the ability to support them, they negotiated a merger with the TTP.

Among the Pakistani Taliban groups that did not merge into the TTP in 2007, LI was reported to have entertained at times good relations with IS-K at least in Nangarhar, and often coordinated with them.[97] Some sources also report that the Tariq Geedar Group, which is part of the TTP, had also at times been collaborating with IS-K in Nangarhar, but a senior IS-K source firmly denied this.[98] Both groups stood out among the many splinters and faction of the TTP for having been repeatedly accused of links to the security agencies of Afghanistan and India (see below) and undoubtedly they did enjoy a degree of hospitality by the Afghan authority. Their relationship with IS-K, if it was real, should therefore be ascribed to mere pragmatism.

In conclusion, the TTP was mostly paying lip service to global jihad and to the extent that there were people within it, who had some genuine interest in the cause, it eventually benefited IS more than it did benefit AQ. The vision of global jihad that appears to have predominated within TTP ranks was typically parochial and had more to do with anti-Shi'ism than with anti-Americanism. This aligned it with IS-K, rather than with AQ.

The TTP's threat to the Pakistani state

If the TTP was not much of a player in the world of AQ's global jihad, was it at least able to mount a credible jihad against the Pakistani state? TTP activities were largely confined to areas with a large Pashtun population: FATA, KP, Karachi and northern Baluchistan.[99] It was able to carry out small attacks, typically targeted assassinations, in some of Punjab's cities, including Islamabad.

In fact, the TTP struggled to even produce a coherent vision for Pakistan, let alone global jihad. Semple assessed that

> *The TTP has never taken the trouble to elaborate its vision for a Shari a-based Pakistan. [...] Members of the TTP identify themselves as belonging to and acting in solidarity with a broader movement of militant Islamists. This informed the Hakeemullah critique of the Pakistani state – cooperation with the US in counterterrorism amounted to treachery against the mujahideen.*[100]

Even at the local level the TTP's *political* programme looked quite thin:

> The TTP could more credibly aspire to dictate change in the core areas where it has mobilised. Its component groups have engaged in short – lived campaigns of Islamisation in areas which they have taken over. [...] But these have not amounted to a credible programme of Islamisation. Instead they have focused on developing and protecting their armed forces and empowering TTP affiliated commanders and, to a lesser extent, associated ulema.[101]

Noor Wali Mehsud, the leader of TTP from 2018 onwards, provided the most sophisticated statement of the TTP's struggle from within the ranks, when in 2017 he described the TTP's struggle as a 'defensive jihad' as well as a struggle for the 'implementation of Shari'a'.[102]

The leadership of TTP was young and mostly uneducated, especially at the beginning. Baitullah Mehsud, the founder of TTP, was uneducated and became leader at the age of about thirty-five. Hakimullah Mehsud, who succeeded him, was thirty-three and had just some madrasa education. Only Fazlullah and Noor Wali had completed a madrasa curriculum. Noor Wali is the only one with an intellectual profile. Fazlullah was forty-four at the time of being selected as leader, while Noor Wali was forty.[103] While the first generation of TTP leaders was inexperienced and uneducated, they could have enlisted more help from like-minded groups (see below, *Little effort to import know-how*).

The high degree of organizational fluidity and the lack of a consolidated leadership (even compared for example to the Afghan Taliban) prevented the maturation of the TTP into an effective organization.[104] Mobilization was to a considerable extent driven by the desire for revenge against the Pakistani army, and the TTP struggled to turn that into a longer term ideological thrust.[105] Below is a discussion of how the TTP leadership failed to keep it united and to turn it into an organization capable of achieving its stated aims. The poorly organized, constantly divided Pakistani Taliban kept looking like a *movement* more than as an *organization*, despite the creation of the TTP. The TTP's internal rivalries turned it into a rather dysfunctional insurgent organization, turning it into a potential liability to AQ, as discussed in *The TTP's vulnerability to co-optation* below.

The fragmentation of the TTP

The TTP never managed to pull together all the Pakistani Taliban factions, even for a short period of time. In particular, LI was reportedly involved in the 2007 talks, but stayed out of the merger.[106] LI largely drew its members from Afridi tribesmen in Khyber, although it also attracted a sprinkle of volunteers from Swat and Punjab.[107] Reportedly Mangal Bagh had good relations with JuI, the original source of Deobandi militancy. LI often cooperated with the TTP, but tension emerged with TTP leader Fazlullah (2013–18) after LI appeared to flirt with IS-K in Nangarhar and a substantial portion of LI defected to IS-K.[108] The relationship of LI with TTP improved however once Noor Wali Mehsud took over, and they started cooperating in the field.[109]

More importantly, the groups that did join the TTP never fully merged into it. Mullah Nazir's group was special in that it joined very briefly at the time of the foundation of the TTP, and quickly separated again; part of it rejoined after Nazir's death in January 2013, while most of the rest joined the Afghan Taliban.[110] As one commander in South Waziristan noted, the TTP was never really fully unified and already under Baitullah Mehsud and Hakimullah Mehsud its core was divided into four main factions (excluding Mullah Nazir's), which were not really integrated together:

- Fazlullah's TNSM in Swat. After being chased from Swat in 2009, the group moved to other areas. By 2013 the group was active in Swat, Malakand, Dargai, Chenagi, Bajawar and Chitral, as well as in the Afghanistan provinces in Kunar, Nuristan and Nangarhar.[111]
- Baitullah and Hakimullah Mehsud's organization in Waziristan.
- Commander Abdullah's organization in Darra Adamkhil.
- Abu Baker Mufti's organization in Bajaur.[112]

A fifth group, Hafiz Gul Bahadur's, was sitting at the margins, sometimes in and sometimes out, depending on how negotiations with Islamabad were going. Despite the unifying intent and the centralizing ambitions, the TTP really looked like a rather loose federation of groups, where

> *fighters would have been able to move freely within the TTP-controlled areas to provide reinforcements or support as needed, without having to transit through government-controlled settled areas. At the same time, the government would lose the possibility of negotiating in one agency while fighting in another, as the TTP would only negotiate or fight as a whole.*[113]

Szrom provided a similar description:

> *They agreed on these objectives and pledged to support each other in time of need. It was a sort of collective security unit, where they can resolve differences and fight for their common goals.*[114]

Nonetheless, even the 'federative' character of the TTP was not loose enough for many of the thirty-eight to forty organizations that did join the TTP in 2007, either directly or as part of the main factions described above. By 2011 the TTP six factions or groups had left already (Figure 2), not counting Mullah Nazir's group.[115] The TTP started losing pieces already during 2007, when the Tariq Geedar group was formed in 2007 in Darra Adam Khel by Omar Mansoor. The group remained close to the TTP until JuA emerged (see below).[116]

In 2008 three more splits took place. In Bajaur one of the allies of Faqir Mohammed split to form his own group of young militants, known as Karwan e Naimatullah, in 2008. The groups knew a rapid decline into obscurity after his formation.[117] In 2008 another split occurred, as Jaysh e Islami was formed by Qari Ali Rehman, a Yusufkhel TTP member. Wari Rehman had previously been close to Faqir Mohammed, but

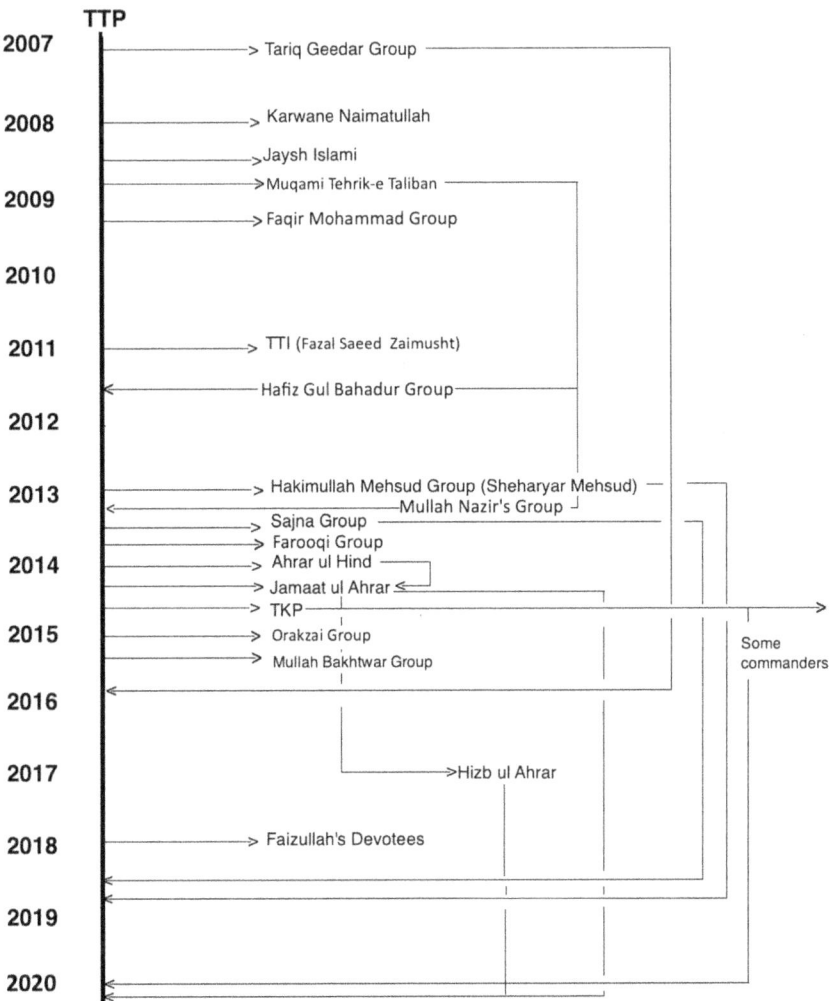

Figure 2 Splinters and mergers of the TTP, 2007–19.

was upset by his agreement with Islamabad. This group too did not fare well and disappeared from the chronicles.[118] The third split of 2008 was that of the Muqami Tehrik e Taliban (Local Taliban Movement), formed in June by Ahmadzai Wazir and Uthmanzai Wazir Taliban, alarmed by the rising power and influence of Baitullah Mehsud. The Movement counter-balanced Baitullah's power with the power of two top Waziri commanders, Hafiz Gul Bahadur (who became leader) and Mullah Nazir, who had left the TTP earlier.[119] Later Bahadur rejoined the TTP, parting ways with Nazir; after Nazir's death in 2013 his group too in part rejoined the TTP.[120]

In 2009 Faqir Mohammed negotiated a new deal with Islamabad after the army had entered Swat valley, taking a substantial part of the TNSM with him. Faqir Mohammed would become the most prominent pro-Islamabad Talib in the subsequent years and several allies of the TTP followed Faqir Mohammed in the coming years, at least temporarily (Tehrik Taliban Punjab, JeM factions, LI, SSP factions and the majority of LeJ).[121] By 2012 these groups had formed the pro-Islamabad alliance led by Faqir Mohammed.[122] By 2013 this alliance had, according to its leader, 6,000 men fighting in Afghanistan alongside the Afghan Taliban, especially Dost Mohammed of the Peshawar Shura, but the majority of these came from groups other than TTP.[123]

Faqir Mohammed's deal with Islamabad caused another split, with an anti-Islamabad faction emerging in Bajaur in opposition to Faqir Mohammad under the leadership of Jamal ud Din Dadullah.[124]

Another minor split occurred in 2011, when Fazal Saeed Zaimusht split away in June in Kurram and formed Tehreek e Taliban Islami (TTI), accusing the TTP of indiscriminate violence against civilians. At that time the split was interpreted as having been engineered by the Pakistani security services, as Saeed was signing a peace agreement between Sunnis and Shi'as in the agency. There were also reports that Saeed wanted to keep the taxes he was collecting locally.[125] TTI disintegrated when Zaimusht was assassinated in December 2016 and many of his men went over to the Haqqani network of the Afghan Taliban.[126]

It is however in 2013–14 that the TTP went close to disintegrating, following the contested selection of Fazlullah as leader. Many Mehsud commanders did not accept Fazlullah as leader and separated from the TTP, alleging that he was unable to lead it.[127] One of them was Sheharyar Mehsud, who formed the faction also known as TTP North Waziristan or as Hakimullah Mehsud's group.[128] Before this faction was weakened by numerous defections to IS-K, at the peak of its strength it might have had over 5,000 members, according to one source.[129] Maulana Wali Mohammad replaced Sheharyar after his death in February 2020.[130]

At about the same time as Sheharyar's faction, another Mehsud faction led by Khan Saeed Sajna and also known as 'TTP South Waziristan' split away.[131] TTP sources say that Sajna was the leading candidate for the succession to Hakimullah, but his earlier inclination towards talks with Islamabad undermine him in the race with Fazlullah, losing him the support of even many Mehsuds.[132] Sajna was killed in February 2018, but his faction survived.[133]

Not only the Mehsuds were turning against Fazlullah, but also hardliners of various tribal background. Ahrar ul Hind split from TTP in February 2014, taking a hardline position on any possible peace agreement with Islamabad (which Fazlullah was instead considering). The group was led by Maulana Umar Qasmi, previously close to SPP. Ahrar ul Hind was reported to have links to Central Asian militants and reportedly recruited mostly Punjabis.[134]

After a few months Ahrar ul Hind joined JuA, another group of hardliners which split in August 2014.[135] This new group, more substantial than Ahrar ul Hind, criticized the TTP for having lost its path. Leader Omar Khali Khorasani accused Fazlullah of not following the rules of the TTP.[136] The best known among them was spokesperson Ehsanullah Ehsan, although the leader was Omar Khalid Khorasani. JuA claimed to have attracted TTP groups from the tribal agencies of Mohmand, Bajaur, Khyber and Orakzai, and the districts of Charsadda, Peshawar and Swat, but its core was in fact in Dara Adam Khel. In 2015 JuA was operating in Malakand Agency, Momand Agency, Khyber Agency, Orakzai Agency, Kurram Agency, as well as in Nangarhar and Kunar Provinces of Afghanistan.[137] After 2014 JuA established relations with IS-K, which was providing financial and logistical support. At one point the leadership of the group was reportedly considering merging into IS-K. It was also considering moving its main base to Nangarhar, where it was already carrying out joint operations with IS-K.[138]

In 2015 it was the time of the group of Mullah Bakhtwar, who split from the TTP over differences with Fazlullah and formed a group of perhaps 400 members, of which half were Pakistanis (mostly former TTP Afridis from Bara, Tera, Jamroad and Landi Kotal), a quarter freshly recruited Afghans and the rest Central Asians from various groups.[139] The group later joined IS-K (see *Competition for AQ* above).

In 2017 a faction led by Mukkaram Khan split off JuA, claiming to reject its use of indiscriminate violence, and took the name of Hizb ul Ahrar (HuA). HuA was mostly based in Nangarhar and Kunar of Afghanistan.[140]

Going back to the TTP, in November 2013 a group of pro-AQ hardliner led my Mawlavi Farooqi split as well (see also *AQ explores alternatives* below).[141]Yet another group of hardliners split in 2014 to join IS as discussed in *Competition for AQ* above. They formed the TKP, which would some months later merge into IS-K. Initially TKP was present in Miran Shah, Bano, Bajawar, Hongu, Orakzai and Kurram.[142] In 2015 another group of Orakzais split from TTP to join TKP/IS-K, followed by some Afridi groups in Khyber and by several commanders of Fazlullah (from Swat) in 2019.[143]

Finally, at some point in 2018/19 another split of 'Devotees of Fazlullah' took place, made of some 1,000 opponents of Mufti Noor Wali as leader (2020). As the name suggests, these were loyalists of Fazlullah, who resisted the Mehsud restauration at the helm of the TTP.[144]

There were also some other splinters as well, of which so little is known that they have not been discussed in detail here. One, for example, was a group called Fedayaan Baitullah Mehsud, which might have gathered 400–500 fighters, with a specialization in suicide bombing.[145]

Not all of these splits took place on good terms and infighting was far from uncommon within the Pakistani Taliban.[146] But what drove the fragmentations of the TTP?

Narrow horizons: Tribalism and personalism

Among the causes of the TTP's extreme proclivity to fragmentation was the inability of its leaders to rise above personal and local feuds. TTP members have been tending to interpret their internal divisions in tribal terms. Mullah Nazir's breaking ranks with others Pakistani Taliban in 2006 (before the TTP was even formed) is generally attributed to Ahmadzai Wazir's resentment versus Mehsud dominance within the TTP.[147] Then Yusufzai explained the Wana Taliban internal split, again involving Mullah Nazir, with sub-tribal rivalries.[148] It was telling that even TTP leader Baitullah

Mehsud could not operate freely in the Wana area, territory of the Ahmadzai Wazir sub-tribe within the same agency of South Waziristan. The TTP had to maintain a separate command chain in the Wana area.[149]

Even in the election of Hakimullah as TTP head, the alignments were reportedly on a tribal/sub-tribal basis: the Bahlozai Mehsud supported Hakimullah, while the Manzai Mehsud supported Wali ur Rahman.[150] When Fazlullah was elected with the support of several Mehsud commanders, despite being a Yusufzai, those opposed to him were so upset that they cut off their relation with Fazlullah, claiming that TTP was made by Mehsud tribe and the leader of TTP should be always from the Mehsud tribe.[151] That left permanent resentment among Fazlullah's followers:

> *when Maulana Fazlullah became the leader of TTP, the Mehsud tribe because of their selfish attitude destroyed TTP unity. The wanted to hold the leadership of TTP forever and did not want to give chance of leading the TTP to other tribes. [...] The TTP was not made only from Mehsud tribe.*[152]

Yusufzai explains the centrifugal pressure of the tribes with the fact that the TTP components were

> *under pressure from their tribes and communities not to become involved in wider conflicts that could transform their areas into battlegrounds and contribute to their suffering.*[153]

Another common explanation, offered by TTP members for the fragmentation of the movement, has been the impact of personal rivalries. This is evident in the case of the South Waziristan Taliban. After Khalid Sajna and Sheharyar Mehsud split from Fazlullah's TTP in 2014, Sajna was selected as leader, causing Sheharyar to separate from him and form his own faction. There was even fighting between the two groups.[154] Elsewhere, the split of HuA from JuA was also in part allegedly due to personal rivalries.[155] Indeed after criticizing JuA for its use of indiscriminate violence, HuA allied with IS-K, an organization hardly renowned for its rejection of indiscriminate violence, casting doubts on the substance of its claims.[156]

Most splits among the Pakistani Taliban seemingly took place over the relationship with Islamabad, but sometimes personal rivalries appear to be looming behind this justification. For example, Abdullah Mehsud's faction started opposing Baitullah in South Waziristan on the ground that it was fighting the Pakistani authorities, although Abdullah himself had been a great supporter of resistance against Islamabad before.[157]

Deals with the Pakistani military were done and undone also on the basis of intra-Pakistani Taliban rivalries. For example, when Mullah Nazir launched his campaign against the Central Asians, his rival Haji Omar threatened to pull out of his own deal with the Army, signed in November 2004, if the army kept supporting Nazir.[158]

Factionalism and personal rivalries among leaders were not simply verbal matters. Infighting was common even at the local level. In Mohmand agency, for example, clashes between two TTP factions ended up with the killing in 2008 of one of the contenders, Shah Sahib.[159] Some sources even allege that in the wake of Baitullah Mehsud's death, the TTP was on the verge of violent infighting, with several candidates to succession jockeying for power. Only the mediation of Serajuddin Haqqani prevented a collapse into a TTP civil war.[160]

Lack of ambition: Weak organization

The TTP's rhetoric claimed to have set its sights on the Pakistani state, but it did not develop an organization capable of confronting it. Its organization resembled that of the early post-2001 years Afghan Taliban. Local commanders had 'ownership' of their men and the groups that they led were the building blocks of the TTP and of its internal factions. For example, the group of commanders who formed TKP in 2014 each took alongside his small coagulation of bands of fighters: Khalid Mansoor in Banu took 200 fighters, Shahidullah Shahid took his 280 men, Mufti Hassan in Kuram joined with his 180 fighters, Maulana Gul Zaman in Khyber Agency joined with 320 fighters, Hafiz Dawlat Khan in Hangu joined with 260 men, Hafiz Sayed Khan in Orakzai joined with 210, Abdul Bahar Mehsud in Waziristan with 420 and Maulana Abu Bakr, who was commander of TTP in Bajawar, now joined with Tehrik e Khalifa with 190.[161] This was particularly the case of the TTP's 'army', that is, the armed groups that were operating in full daylight in the FATA and parts of KP. The TTP's 'guerrilla' force, based in the cities and in areas of weak TTP presence and operating underground, appears to have been more integrated together.[162]

The Afghan Taliban gradually evolved after 2003, introduced the rotation of senior commanders and developed after 2005 a mobile army, under the orders of the central leadership, not of local commanders.[163] The TTP instead never evolved towards a greater centralization of its military assets. When it decided to create a dedicated unit for freeing TTP prisoners, for example, it ended up creating a new group, called Ansar ul Aseer, which became another faction owned by its leader Adnan Rashid.[164] The regional leaders always had the freedom to order military operations in their areas as they pleased, although the Amir had the power of summoning them if something went wrong and Baitullah in a few occasions told them off.[165] These leaders were also free to organize their men as they saw fit for military operations. All they were asked to do was reporting back to the Amir any operation they carried out. The larger operations had to be confirmed with the Amir in advance, but their tactical implementation was completely in the hand of the regional leaders.[166]

> *When there were important and huge military operations for sure [Baitullah] was the man to decide and without his decision no regional leaders had permission to launch military operations.*[167]

The basic set of rules to which the entire TTP was bound, including the regional leaders, was basic. The main ones were:

- *avoid civilian casualties inside the FATA and KP areas,*
- *do not misuse the TTP for own benefits,*
- *do not make relation with Jihadist groups whose goals are not similar to the TTP's,*

- *be honest in tax collection,*
- *obey to the leader of TTP and the TTP Shura,*
- *the field commanders should be obey their regional leaders,*
- *stay clear of links with the Pakistan government,*
- *follow the rule of Shari'a.*[168]

At the time of announcing the formation of the TTP, the stakeholders stated that that they would be submitting to the centralized command of Baitullah Mehsud.[169] Although it has been repeatedly claimed that the TTP was from the start a decentralized umbrella organization, that was not what Baitullah had intended. On the basis of the rules he had himself come up with,

> *Baitullah Mehsud had the power to control fight everywhere, had the power to change any group commanders without permission of the Shura, had the power to order any regional TTP leader in FATA and KP to do this or fight here or send fighters or other military staff.*[170]

> *He was making most of his decisions alone, except some more important ones, such as changing the rules, or when he received offers of negotiations from Pakistan's government.*[171]

As Fazlullah put it in 2008, he was waiting for Baitullah's decisions as Amir, before taking action following the expulsion of TNSM from Swat valley.[172] But while in the TTP decision-making was in principle concentrated in the hands of the Amir, in practice he did not have the power to impose his authority on the other stakeholders. Not even Baitullah had the right to replace the leaders of the founding groups.

> *Baitullah Mehsud could not change or remove Mullah Fazlullah, who was the head of TTP in Swat of Pakistan, and Baitullah could not change Omar Khalid Khurasani who was the head of TTP in Momand Agency.*[173]

Baitullah relied on his charisma, on the authority deriving from AQ's endorsement and on the emotional wave of support created by the Lal Masjid incident, but he did not shape a structure that would allow for long-term centralized authority. In the event of one of the regional leaders disobeying Baitullah, he could only try to convince him to come back to the fold, or expel him from the TTP.[174]

The TTP stakeholders agreed that the TTP's judiciary would have authority to implement Shari'a and TTP rules within the TTP. Whether the courts really had all this sway is questionable.[175] In 2010, AQ cadres had to remind the TTP that issuing judgements based on tribal traditions was a 'terrible crime'.[176]

The discrepancy between the autocratic ambitions of Baitullah and the lack of an organization able to enforce its decision was to emerge as a problem. Shaikh Mahmud and Shaikh Yahya seemed to have already identified in 2010 the tendency of the Amir of TTP to disregard the regional amirs as a major source of trouble: for example, summoning TTP members for a meeting directly, without going through the regional amirs, 'will create problems, because the local Amir will lose the respect of his team members'.[177] In general the two Qaidist authors criticized the tendency of the draft TTP charter they were analysing to be heavy handed in dealing with any dissent.

This discrepancy between concentrated decision-making and diffuse power would not necessarily have been a critical problem in itself, except that the TTP leadership set its aims very high – a direct confrontation with the Pakistani state. Relative to the strength of the TTP, the combined Pakistani army/Frontier Corps deployment was no lesser challenge than US/NATO/Afghan security forces were for the Afghan Taliban. The latter adapted, the TTP did not (at least until 2018–20, see below).

The TTP did establish a central shura (council), composed of about forty of its most notable leaders and stakeholders (at least at the time of its foundation), with an amir, a deputy amir and a general secretary at the top, along the model of the Afghan Taliban, and a system for election of its Amir by the Shura.[178] It also developed a code of discipline, again following the model of the Afghan Taliban. According to Elahi, the TTP even had a meritocratic system of appointments based on 'not only the length of time spent in the organisation but also the performance'.[179] Elahi does not quote his sources, but in any case this should not be understood to mean a system of meritocratic appointments from the top down. If there was any kind of meritocracy, it was just for a few top positions at the help of the TTP (fifteen senior positions, according to Elahi), as local branches had a large degree of autonomy. In fact, different factions of the TTP organized themselves differently. Even in Waziristan, it was the local leadership that appointed military commanders to different regions, which responded to 'the supreme commander of the local Taliban and the Taliban Shura (consultative council) of their respective tribe'.[180] It seems unlikely that other, more peripheral areas would allow the top leadership to appoint local commanders.

Some functional differentiation developed within the TTP, with specific units tasked with duties such as intelligence collection and counter-intelligence, collection of revenue and maintenance of law and order. Reportedly the TTP, at least in Baitullah's time, had a thick network of informers throughout the FATA and most of KP, extending also into the government apparatus.[181] The TTP also had its own judiciary, again following the Afghan Taliban model, although this existed already before the TTP was formed in some areas such as Waziristan, where Baitullah Mehsud established it in 2005, and in Swat.[182]

However, many crucial aspects of the TTP's organization remained very weak, even compared to the Afghan Taliban. A former TTP commander who went over to IS-K noted that in the TTP

> our logistics was weak, our finance was weak, and our weapons and ammunitions very weak. [...] We can say that when we were with TTP, we did not have logistics at all. In that time food was not provided to us. We were eating in the houses of the people. Our other equipment and logistics were not good.[183]

These weaknesses emerged as a major flaw when serious fighting with the Pakistani army started. While the Afghan Taliban also started out with a weak logistics, they gradually improved it over the course of their jihad; not so the TTP.[184]

When direct clashes with the Pakistani army predictably started going bad, the TTP opted for terror tactics, often indiscriminate, but did not make much progress in terms of viable asymmetric tactics on the battlefield under Baitullah's, Hakimullah's or Fazlullah's leadership. For example, contrary to the Afghan Taliban it did not rely much on mines against the Pakistani army; over 2011–17, 81 per cent of the casualties of IEDs in Pakistan were civilians.[185]

One particularly important aspect of the TTP's organization is fund raising. The Afghan Taliban relied like the TTP on a mix of locally raised revenue and external support. In the case of the Afghan Taliban, external contributions were largely predominant throughout their insurgency, allowing the central leadership to manage centrifugal tendencies.[186] While a precise comparison is hard to make, due to data being often absent or unreliable, it seems clear that the TTP suffered from erratic and unreliable external funding. The TTP invested disproportionate resources in local fund raising, relative to its size. It targeted all legal and illegal businesses and raised taxes from local residents. The TTP's local fund-raising operations appear to have been among the best organized aspects of its activities:

> *The TTP leadership in FATA monitors the fundraising campaign closely, and has punished operatives who embezzle funds. In early 2013, TTP chief Hakimullah Mehsud reportedly ordered his men to kill his former Karachi leader, Sher Zaman Mehsud, for stealing money that was collected through extortion and bank robberie.*[187]

TTP activities in Karachi were largely focused on fund raising.[188] A TTP source claimed in early 2016 that almost 4,000 of the TTP's members were based in cities, almost entirely focused on fund raising and logistics (14 per cent of total).[189] Other sources have proposed even higher figures. In October 2012, a report submitted to Pakistan's Supreme Court claimed that 7,000 TTP militants had infiltrated Karachi, which seems quite inflated.[190] The regional leaders of the TTP had autonomy in tax collection, only being required to report to the leadership about their revenue and transfer a percentage. After Baitullah Mehsud's death fouling even these basic rules became common.[191]

The TTP's focus on local fund raising might have been the result of insufficient or unreliable external funding. AQ helped Baitullah Mehsud launch TTP in 2007, and remained a source of funding throughout, but was never in a position to bankroll the TTP entirely. Soon allegations started flourishing that the TTP had found 'inappropriate' sources of funding. It became common for non-Mehsud factions within TTP to accuse the Mehsuds of having connections with India's intelligence services. One senior TTP source dated the start of support coming from suspiciously sounding 'Afghan businessmen' to 2007; that was reaching Baitullah and after his death Wali ur Rahman. Unsurprisingly this support allegedly continued for the anti-Islamabad faction, but never reached the pro-Islamabad one.[192] As late as 2015 one source indicated that about 44 per cent of the TTP budget was coming from other suspiciously sounding sources such as 'mujahidin in Afghanistan' and 'Muslim circles in India'.[193] The Pakistani security services have of course been claiming all the time that foreign funding is in fact coming from Indian intelligence.[194] A member of the Farooqi Group, critical of the TTP, stated openly that he believed these allegations were true.[195] Several other TTP sources mentioned funds coming from 'Afghan businessmen'.[196] Within the TTP there were still as late as 2020 accusations that the Sheharyar faction had been receiving support from the Indian security services for fighting against JeM and LeT in eastern Afghanistan.[197] Allegations were also made by anti-Mehsud TTP members that several other Mehsud commanders and even some commanders of JuA and HuA have links to RAW or to the Afghan NDS.[198] What AQ might have thought of these allegations is not known, but it was likely not impressed very positively. The existence of funding flows from abroad, whatever their nature, must in any case have made AQ aware that the TTP was not entirely loyal to it.

Aside from the source of funding, another noteworthy point is the dispersed character it seems to have taken, targeting factions and even individual commanders, rather than going through the TTP leadership. This would favour the fragmentation of the TTP.

AQ funding and private contributions from the Gulf were unreliable and fluctuated a lot, on top of being quite limited compared to the amount flowing to the Afghan Taliban. The salary paid by the TTP to his members appears to have been somewhat lower than what the Afghan Taliban paid, at $84.[199]

In sum, the unreliability and fragmentation of external funding forced the TTP to stretch its reliance on local fund raising, which was even more decentralized in nature, to the point where it created an additional risk of 'criminalization'. The political and ideological aims of the TTP were at risk of being overridden by business interests, causing further fragmentation. Fredholm in fact describes the Mehsud Taliban (in contrast to the Waziris such as Bahadur and Nazir) as 'fundamentally criminal gangs', who used Islam 'as a mere pretext for their activities'.[200]

> *Some witness reports suggest that Baitullah and Hakimullah in fact had spent more time as petty criminals in Karachi than with the Afghan Taliban, but having failed to gain a reputation in the city, had chosen to return to Waziristan.*[201]

Fredholm believes that the Mehsud factions of the TTP were more involved in criminal activities than other TTP factions, although he also says that with Baitullah as leader criminal activities spread to much of the TTP.[202] Khattak also portrays the TTP as ridden by rivalries over the control of streams or revenue, and infiltrated by gangs.[203] Acharya, Bukhari and Sulaiman also point out that the Pakistani Taliban recruited 'hardened criminals' for the purpose of raising funds through criminal activities, and re-organized them to work more efficiently.[204]

> *Reportedly, the Pakistan Taliban have created a number of 'commando squads,' each having five to eight cadres. These units are tasked with the assignment to loot banks, snatch vehicles belonging to civilians, government, and various nongovernmental organizations (NGOs).In return, the Pakistan Taliban pay them a fixed amount as percentage of the 'bounty' and assure them that if they are caught by the law enforcement agencies, they would get them free by putting pressure on the government or by exchanging troops taken hostage with the government.*[205]

Although LI was not part of the TTP, Khan identified similar dynamics and argued that LI that was essentially a criminal and drug network, although with the ability to portray itself as a 'strong advocate for the poor' and railing 'against the traditional tribal maliks (tribal elders) and rich who collect government favors for themselves'.[206]

On this basis, Semple believes that

> *The movement is self-serving. The proceeds of crime are required to sustain the mujahideen and that in itself is justification enough for the kidnapping or extortion which it is engaged in. Because the TTP lacks any credible aspiration to establish an Islamic system, which would require some form of regulation of criminal activity, the TTP has been free to consider all activities which generate funds for the mujahideen as legitimate.*[207]

The TTP might have used criminals for its own purpose and then ended up being in part at least hijacked by them. As 'business' interests rose in importance, the unity and sense of purpose of the TTP weakened. The unwillingness or inability of the TTP leadership to centralize fund raising to a higher degree added another element of structural weakness and lessened its already limited leverage vis-à-vis the component groups.

Little effort to import organizational know-how

As discussed above, the TTP never developed a solid organization, capable of maximizing its capabilities in confronting the Pakistani state. It is not the case, however, that the TTP had no models to follow, or that help was not available. To be fair, the Afghan Taliban benefited very extensively after 2003 from the advice and training imparted by Pakistani, Iranian and Arab advisers.[208] Instead, the TTP enjoyed only limited support from a handful of advisers from AQ and AQ allies. A former TTP member recalled how 'in that time our people were also not professional and we did not have a lot of advisers'.[209] Hundreds of TTP members received training in Syria by IS, but then joined IS-K and did not therefore contribute much new know-how to the TTP.[210]

The TTP shared considerable proximity with the Afghan Taliban, especially early on, and often imitated their organization. It should be assumed that some Afghan Taliban organizational know-how was transferred to TTP. Still, the Afghan Taliban were widely seen as not being keen on the TTP from the beginning and Mullah Omar was said to be against the formation of the TTP, which risked complicating the relationship of the Afghan Taliban with the Pakistani security services. The peak of the Quetta Shura's engagement with the TTP was in 2009 when it played a crucial role in the formation of the Shura Ittehad al Itefaq, which was meant to reconcile pro- and anti-Islamabad Taliban.[211] At that point the Afghan Taliban's Quetta Shura promised to help TTP logistically in Afghanistan, but the killing of Baitullah a few months later and a conflict over the killing of some of Nazir's men led to the collapse of the Shura.[212] After that the word of the Afghan Taliban carried little weight with TTP, in part because many of them became convinced that Mullah Omar had died in 2009 and therefore their bond of obedience was dissolved.[213] Whereas in 2007–8 it was conceivable that Mullah Omar would 'fire' the TTP leader,[214] by 2013 the TTP had rejected the idea that Mullah Omar (had he been alive) had any authority over them.[215]

> in 2009 we did one agreement with the Quetta Shura and we said we will help them in the Afghan fighting, but when Biatullah Mehsud was killed, this agreement was also dismissed and we focused on operations in Pakistan. The TTP is neither under the control of Omar nor of the Quetta Shura. This is not possible that they are supported by the Pakistan government, and we are opposed to the Pakistani government. If TTP was under their control, then we would not be fighting the Pakistani government.[216]

As one interviewee put it, 'Mohammad Omar's role is zero in TTP.'[217] Soon, some Pakistani Taliban were criticizing the Afghan Taliban for their close relationship with the impious Pakistani government: 'jihad knows no borders' was the frequent criticism laid at the Afghan Taliban.[218] Already in 2008 the Afghan Taliban thought it opportune to declare that the Afghan and Pakistani Taliban were separate entities, probably in order to avoid getting entangled in its internal conflicts and in its conflicts with the Pakistani authorities.[219]

The delay in informing the world of the death of Mullah Omar was a major source of friction between Afghan Taliban and TTP's leadership, which felt humiliated.[220] The TTP was reluctant to acknowledge Akhtar Mohammad Mansur as the successor to Mullah Omar and therefore as their counterpart:

> Mansur is not like him. He does not have a place in the people's hearts. He spent most of his times in the smuggling of heroin and narcotics. Mullah Akhtar Mohammad Mansur is not acceptable for us.[221]

As a result of this and of other issues, including the TTP's rejection of efforts by the Afghan Taliban to mediate a reunification of the Pakistani Taliban and peace with Islamabad, the TTP by 2012 did not have a very good relationship with the Quetta Shura of the Taliban, preferring to work with the shuras of Peshawar and Miran Shah (Haqqanis), despite their links with the ISI.[222] By 2016 the TTP still maintained relations with the Haqqanis, with the Northern Shura and some factions in Quetta Shura, but relations were no longer very close as the Afghan Taliban had to outwardly privilege relations with pro-Islamabad Pakistani Taliban and groups like LeJ and JeM.[223] The TTP continued to occupy Afghan territory on the basis of agreements with the Afghan Taliban, even if only its factions reconciled with Islamabad (such as Faqir Mohammad's) kept fighting alongside the Taliban. Essentially, the bulk of the TTP was neutral in the Afghan conflict.

In 2020, at a time of poor relations between the Haqqani network and the Pakistani deep state, the Haqqanis invited the TTP to relocate from eastern Afghanistan to the Haqqani's turn in south-eastern Afghanistan, from where they started intensifying operations in Waziristan.[224] According to a TTP commander, AQ played a very important role in the rapprochement between TTP and Haqqani network in 2020.[225]

In late 2021 Noor Wali Mehsud made an open claim that the TTP was a branch of the Islamic Emirate of Afghanistan, which was immediately denied by the official spokesman of the Afghan Taliban. Noor Wali might have simply implied that by acknowledging the Taliban's leader as Amir al Muminun, as it never ceased doing, the TTP placed itself under its umbrella. He might have wanted to benefit as much as possible from the fall out of the Taliban's victory in Afghanistan. He might also have tried to make it harder for the Taliban to undermine him vis-à-vis the Pakistani authorities, by reducing his freedom of manoeuvre inside Afghanistan (hence the shift Taliban reaction).[226]

Although tension between TTP and the Haqqani network of the Taliban arose when the latter mediated between Islamabad and non-TTP Taliban factions such as Hafiz Gul Bahadur's group and others, they seem to have mended fences quite quickly. Due to strong tensions between Kandahari Taliban and the Haqqanis, relations with the Kandahari Taliban actually improved while Noor Wali was having his own rift with the Haqqanis.[227]

As for the transfer of know-how from AQ, little is known. AQ has a record of having formed local jihadist elites in other areas of operations and one of its cadres even proposed something similar for Pakistan around 2005–6:

Jihad against America, the west, and their supporters in tribal areas and Pakistan, even the whole world, necessitates that the Mujahidin have a sufficient number of staff – at least thirty – who are experts in understanding enemy forces, their military theories, their philosophy, and methods. [...] Also, the Mujahidin need experts knowledgeable of Pakistani forces and its tactics. That is why it is unavoidable to select 25 – 30 youths from various groups and train them for at least three or four months, where they will study such subjects in details. Those personnel will become an asset to the Mujahidin, and by their guessing of future enemy plans in changeable circumstances, they will become a means of transforming the Mujahid trend to its correct path before it is too late. They will assume leadership positions in the future.[228]

It is not clear, however, whether AQ tried to or in any event succeeded in implementing such training efforts in Pakistan. The AQ author of the booklet quoted above believed that it was up to AQ to transfer a doctrine of jihad to the Pakistani Taliban:

Pakistani Mujahidin ranks totally lack any clear war theory that links them intellectually and operationally on any level, whether they are tribal areas, Taliban or associations or Mujahidin organizations from outside those areas. All of them fell prey to intellectual disintegration, whether they are Mujahidin affiliated with various associations or Mujahidin from the same association, you will find different analyses of events and a different impression about the enemy, and different operational priorities expressed by all of them. And because of such differences and theoretical disintegration, their strength in the practical field is scattered in various directions, and have evaporated. It became difficult for Mujahidin as a whole to obtain and agree upon a clear objective. [...] Therefore, the Mujahid leadership must first establish a clear war theory; then, gather Pakistani groups and all local Taliban leaders, by convening lengthy meetings with them.[229]

Occasionally the TTP media would recognize the role played by AQ advisers. In April 2015, for example, Umar Media praised two AQ cadres killed in US drone strikes for the role in mentoring and training the TTP.[230] However, there are also indications of friction between AQ and TTP, about the former's efforts to advise the TTP. AQ's cadres were very sensitive over their role as mentors and guides of the TTP. In one letter to Hakimullah, the authors causticized him for having called AQ's members 'guests':

> We want to make it clear to you that we, the al Qa'ida is an Islamist Jihadist organization that is not restricted to a country or race, and that we in Afghanistan swore allegiance to the Emir Mullah Muhammad (('Umar)) who allowed us to carry Jihad. Those that call us as guests do that for political reasons and don't base this attribute on the Shari'a.[231]

The issue resurfaced again later. In 2010 Shaykh Mahmud and Shaykh Abu Yahya objected to the draft TTP Charter containing a statement about 'The Immigrants are not to interfere in any local issues'.[232]

The embattled TTP leaders could do little to meet AQ's expectations. Faced with loss of territory following the military offensive of 2014, Fazlullah opted to start a campaign of targeted assassinations even beyond the tribal areas. He minimized the impact of territorial losses:

> Taliban have spread to all corners of the country, everyday someone is being targeted in the country [...] And as far as losing territory is concerned, Taliban are fighting guerilla [sic] style war which is not limited to one place, so territory doesn't even matter.[233]

The new asymmetric campaign of the TTP represented the acquisition of new military skills, but the loss of territory did not prove as insignificant as Fazlullah claimed. Chased away from their turfs, the TTP factions accelerated their centrifugal movement, as discussed in *The fragmentation of the TTP* above.

In sum, whatever exchange of know-how between Afghan and Pakistani Taliban might have taken place, it declined rapidly after the early years. Some modest transfer of know-how between AQ and TTP appears to have taken place at the top level, with little evident impact. But the opportunity was there and even after relations turned rather sour with the Quetta Shura, links survived with the shuras of Peshawar and Miran Shah, as well as with AQ. The know-how received by TTP volunteers in Syria migrated with them to IS-K early on. Overall, the TTP received little support that could help it strengthen its organization and inform its policymaking, but this appears to have been as much as a choice as a misfortune. Again, the 'lack of ambition' of the TTP's leadership, highlighted above, stands out.

The TTP's vulnerability to co-optation by state agencies

It is difficult to compare directly American-led counterinsurgency in Afghanistan and Pakistani counterinsurgency. However, one difference stands out. The Pakistani used divide and rule and co-optation tactics with the TTP much more ruthlessly (and apparently effectively) than the Americans and the Afghan government did with the Afghan Taliban. Pakistani intelligence appears to have been quite apt at manipulating the Pakistani Taliban groups, pitting one against the other.[234]

The presence of foreign militants, especially Central Asians, proved divisive for the Pakistani Taliban, some of whom alleged that the foreigners were interfering locally. Important portions of the Pakistani Taliban were pushed towards seeking an accommodation with the Pakistani authorities, while others opposed such deal.[235] The Pakistani authorities were prompt in exploiting any opportunity offered to them to sow divisions within the Pakistani Taliban.

The Pakistani authorities were effective in co-opting Pakistani Taliban with the argument that Pakistan needed their assistance and they could become its defenders, and leveraging their anti-Americanism:

> *We told the Pakistani government that we will defeat America in Afghanistan and also solve the problems of Pakistan and India in Kashmir if they would really help us.*[236]

> *The government of Pakistan understands now that America is against them. We benefited a lot from the Bajaur incident, in which 24 Pakistani soldiers were killed. [...] Now the government of Pakistan understands that it is the Taliban who are protecting Pakistan.*[237]

One way used for shaming the TTP in their struggle against Islamabad was to pit other jihadist groups against them, such as LeT. TTP and LeT never had good relations from the beginning due to the close relationship of LeT to the Pakistani authorities and to its Ahl e Hadith orientation. Often the two groups fought each other.[238] TTP relations with the Deobandi JeM by contrast remained good.[239] One TTP source explained that

> *TTP has good connections with most of the Jihadist groups in Pakistan like JeM, SSP, LeJ, Jundullah and all other Jihadist groups, which are doing Jihad in the name of Shari'a. TTP is not in fight with any Jihadist group that follows Deobandism in Pakistan and in Afghanistan.*[240]

Militarily, the Pakistani army was able to achieve considerable numerical superiority against the TTP. Initially the Pakistani authorities hoped to be able to rely on the FC, but once that failed the army was deployed and it was able to crush the TTP in most areas. With the army moving in, the TSNM was rapidly displaced from Swat valley.[241] The TTP's weak, decentralized military command and control system, and its unsophisticated tactics, discussed above in *Lack of ambition*, never enabled the TTP to exploit the weak spots in the army's deployment, nor to react quickly to the army's moves.

The deals negotiated by the Pakistani authorities have been strongly criticized.[242] However, in Swat like in Waziristan the Pakistani authorities successfully split the Taliban by accepting to negotiate with them, even if the very idea of negotiating with the militants was controversial in Pakistan. Only for a short period the formation of the TTP seemed to have an impact: the military activities of the Pakistani Taliban increased in 2007–8 and no Taliban leader kept insisting on the exclusion of the foreign militants.[243] But the Pakistani security agencies remained effective in co-opting portions of the TTP and soon the TTP started dividing between those in favour of a deal with Islamabad and those in favour of jihad in Pakistan. It is beyond the scope of this book to discuss the details of Islamabad/Pakistani Taliban deal making, but as of 2013 a TTP source estimated that some 20 per cent of the Pakistani Taliban manpower was locked in agreements with Islamabad.[244]

Few of the Pakistani Taliban leaders stayed clear of making deals with the Pakistani authorities, at one point or another. Mullah Nazir's group, which was stubbornly pro-Islamabad in 2006–8, by 2009 had turned hostile to Islamabad, mainly on the ground of the continuous drone strikes, which Islamabad could or would not prevent.[245] After Nazir's death in a drone strike, his group disintegrated in factions that joined the TTP, the Afghan Taliban or reconciled with the authorities.[246] Most other top leaders shifted back and forth at least once. Even the most prominent early Pakistani Taliban leader, Nek Mohammad, had his own deal in 2004, before a US drone strike killed him.[247] In 2005–6 Baitullah Mehsud, who would turn into the Pakistani army's enemy number 1, was not averse to reaching a modus vivendi with the army, and negotiated a short-lived agreement with them in 2005 (Sararogha).[248] Later in 2008 he negotiated two more deals with the Pakistani army.[249] Among Baitullah's successors, Hakimullah Mehsud 'two-three times prepared to negotiate with Pakistan's government'.[250] Fazlullah signed a deal with Islamabad in May 2008, even if it lasted only a few months.[251] The 2012 agreement involved part of the TTP, led by Faqir Mohammed, LI, part of the TNSM, the Punjabi Taliban and the Peshawar Shura of the Taliban, which these groups agreed to support militarily on the Afghan battlefield.[252] The deal however collapsed in 2013.[253] Szrom sees Hafiz Gul Bahadur as making deals alternatively with hardliners like Baitullah Mehsud and with the Pakistani army, in order to maintain his territory and power.[254]

Mangal Bagh (leader of Lashkar e Islam) explained the dynamics behind the deals with Islamabad as driven by US drone strikes:

we have lost many of our leaders to American drones. These attacks push us towards making peace with the Pakistan government and start operations against the Americans in Afghanistan.[255]

The drone strikes did not stop following the 2012 deal, and Mangal Bagh, among others, rejoined the opposition to Islamabad. This was not an isolated example. Indeed, the most contentious point in negotiations with Islamabad tended to be the Pakistani Taliban request that US drone strikes should stop.[256] The 2008 agreement signed by Bahadar lasted only six months before it collapsed. Bahadar and his men had fought against the Pakistanis in 2005–8, before negotiating the 2008 agreement. During this period, they stopped sending fighters to Afghanistan. In 2007 he had accepted that unity was the only way to respond to Islamabad and acceded to the TTP. The 2008 agreement collapsed because Islamabad 'did not maintain its promises', especially with regard to stopping US drone strikes.[257]

The repeated peace deals signed by Pakistani Taliban leaders and the Pakistani authorities seem to suggest that whatever the influence of foreign jihadists, either it produced something less than a permanent ideological shift, or the foreign jihadists were not consistently advocating jihad against the Pakistan state. The anti-Islamabad thrust generated by the Lal Masjid episode appears to have started waning relatively soon. The TTP's call to jihad was not compelling enough for its component groups to unite, or to make the effort to improve organizationally.

The ability of the Pakistani security services to co-opt TTP factions was eventually compromised not by the organizational power or ideological thrust of the TTP, but by the relentless US drone strikes against pro-Islamabad drone strikes. The main group of Pakistani Taliban aligned with Islamabad, the Local Taliban Movement, started collapsing after the Americans killed its most important commander, Mullah Nazir, in 2013.[258]

By 2013 the bulk of the Pakistani Taliban had consolidated again in an alliance of anti-Islamabad groups, led by Wali ur Rehman and describing itself as TTP tout court:

- TTP Rehman faction (Mehsuds)
- Part of Mullah Nazir's group (Waziris)
- TTP Bahadur faction, North Waziristan (primarily Waziris, Ismail Khel, Sadar Khel, Achekzai)
- TTP Dadullah faction (Bajaur)
- TNSM – Fazlullah faction
- Minority LeJ splinter.[259]

This alliance was mostly active in Dera e Ismail Khan, Miran Shah, Wanna, Shabaz Khel, Bannu and Bahakkar.[260] The Pakistani authorities kept trying their co-optation tactics and in 2013 (two months before the meeting) the Pakistani authorities were trying to reach out to the alliance led by Wali ur Rehman through Maulana Fazlur Rahman (Jama'at ul Ulema's leader), senior Afghan Taliban figures, Sayed Hafiz (leader of LeT) and former TTP leader Faqir Mohammed, now the highest profile Pakistani Talib aligned with Islamabad. The Pakistani authorities released some prisoners in a gesture of good will, but reportedly Wali ur Rehman imposed conditions such as freeing all Pakistani Taliban prisoners, a level of support similar to that offered to the Afghan Taliban, the withdrawal of the Pakistani army from the tribal areas, the closure of the ISAF transit route to Afghanistan and the stopping of drone strikes in Waziristan. Sayed Hafiz reportedly offered guarantees that if the Pakistani army were not to keep its side of the bargain, he would pull all his men from the Kashmir front, but these conditions were too onerous for Islamabad.[261]

Again, the American drones were the key obstacle. Mangal Bagh, the leader of Lashkar e Islam, at that time aligned with Islamabad, later agreed that Wali ur Rehman's demand in 2013 had been a just one:

I think that they will not reach to any agreement because Wali Ur Rehman first point to Pakistan government is to stop American air attacks. This is so tough for Pakistan to stop such attacks. We also agree with this claim of Wali Ur Rehman.[262]

As predicted by Mangal Bagh, the negotiations failed. Then Fazlullah became leader. Concerning negotiations with the Pakistani authorities, he adopted an intransigent line, demanding that Pakistan be close to all US activities (including logistics) before he would even start peace talks with Islamabad.[263] LI itself turned against Islamabad in 2015.

Still the Pakistani army had made substantial gains by then against the TTP. By 2013 what was left of Faqir Mohammed's pro-Islamabad Pakistani Taliban had even stopped supporting the Afghan Taliban and were fighting alongside LeT against their former TTP colleagues and the Afghan security forces.[264] Their overall role was negligible, but the divisions had been sowed within the anti-Islamabad Pakistani Taliban as trust between leaders had been damaged. The military power of the TTP had been broken.

The large-scale military operations of 2014 (Zarb e Azb) are acknowledged by the TTP to have inflicted a serious blow. A commander estimated that the TTP lost 2,000–3,000 men due to that operations, between those killed, those who would be pushed to defect to IS, and those who left the fight and went home.[265] However, the decline in TTP activities after 2014 was arguably as much the result of its structural weakness, as of the counterinsurgency efforts of the Pakistani state. In 2010–14, the TTP had been able to carry out 200–400 attacks per year, although with considerable fluctuations. In 2015, the number fell to below 100 and in 2016–20 it always remained under 50. The year 2018 was the lowest point, with just twenty-one TTP attacks.[266]

From AQ's perspective, therefore, the TTP must have appeared as a poor vehicle for a jihad against the Pakistani state from Hakimullah onwards, if not earlier. More than that, the constant bickering of TTP factions and their readiness to make spurious alliances clearly represented a liability for AQ. Why then did AQ keep supporting it?

AQ's relationship with the TTP

The extent of AQ's long-term support for the TTP

As mentioned already in *AQ and the birth of the TTP* above, it is likely that the relative wealth of the foreign jihadists might have played a role in wooing the Pakistani Taliban: in the early years (2002–7) the limited resources of the foreigners nonetheless looked like substantial amounts of hard currency in the tribal areas. The spending power of the global jihadists helped the pro-Afghan Taliban campaign and maximized the influence of the global jihadists.

AQ operatives also played a substantial role in getting the Afghan Taliban's insurgency itself off the ground. But the Afghans rapidly managed to diversify their sources of support, to the extent that AQ's contributions were marginal by 2009.[267] It has been a different story for the TTP. According to an AQ source, AQ operatives were also providing advice and training.[268] AQ was definitely an enabler, whether or not it was the prime mover.

The Pakistani Taliban did to some extent follow their Afghan colleagues in diversifying their sources of revenue, as their networks got organized and expanded. The literature on the TTP's 'shadow economy' is relatively abundant. Pakistani government sources alleged the TTP galaxy was collecting in 2009 some $50 million in 'taxes'. Burki too put the central budget of the TTP at $45 million in 2009, presumably factoring in only 'tax' revenue; according to him the rule was that the component groups would contribute 50 per cent of their own income to the TTP coffers and keep the rest, implying a significantly higher total revenue.[269] The 2010 draft charter of the TTP also said that the regions should give 50 per cent of their tax collection to the central TTP leadership.[270] The TTP would exploit whatever source of revenue existed locally, such as smuggling, mines, timber, tolls, fines, zakat, kidnapping for ransom, extortion, looting, contributions from businessmen and diaspora Pakistanis.[271] The 2010 draft charter of the TTP openly endorses the practice of kidnapping for ransom, as long as done only for the cause of jihad. The Charter openly recognizes that in the past TTP members had been using ransom for personal benefit.[272] An official estimate proposed the following breakdown for 2012–13:

- 20 per cent of TTP funding came from criminal activities;
- 50 per cent came from donations and extortions;
- 30 per cent from the drug trade.[273]

Much of the TTP organization outside its core areas was actually dedicated to fund raising.[274] Fund raising and taxation occurred not only in FATA and PATA, but in Karachi, Lahore and other cities too.[275] These fund-raising efforts absorbed a substantial portion of the TTP's manpower. At the beginning of 2016, according to a TTP source, 3,760 of its members were in the cities, mainly Peshawar and Karachi, but also Islamabad, Quetta, Lahore and others. Aside from a few hit teams, these were not fighters, but support elements.[276]

Estimates of the TTP budget available in the public domain ignore the external contributions. This is probably because at least 'taxes' levied from the population can be estimated to some extent. According to TTP and AQ sources, however, external contributions do seem to have made up a large portion of the TTP's budget. The TTP would have no particular interest in making fake claims in this regard, given that it would better serve propaganda purposes to portray the organization as self-sufficient. Nonetheless, TTP sources say explicitly that AQ has been supporting the TTP. They also say that the level of funding fluctuated. Estimating the level of AQ funding is hard because it might not just be direct cash payments, and could involve deliveries of equipment and even of goods to be traded for profit.[277] One source indicated that AQ supplied $45 million to TTP in 2015 compared to $25 million gathered by the TTP through 'taxes' and $55 million for other external sources.[278] These figures, if correct, would indicate that in 2015 AQ accounted for about 36 per cent of all funding to the TTP. This is a percentage that is way higher than AQ's contributions to the Taliban, which in 2014 were estimated at 16 per cent of their total revenue.[279] These figures are likely to be a mix of funds raised by AQ lobbyists on behalf jihadist allies and of cash from AQ's own budget, which appears to have grown dramatically after the first difficult post-9/11 years. AQ used its brand name and well-established contacts in the Gulf monarchies and elsewhere to mobilize funds much more effectively than local jihadist causes could have done. In addition, well into 2013 an anti-Pakistani TTP source indicated how they were still close enough to Central Asian and Chechen militants to receive funding from them, although probably it amounted to little overall.[280]

Moreover, by 2015 the TTP was not just much more dependent on AQ funding than the Afghan Taliban, but was also moving away from greater financial independence. A TTP source indicated that in 2015 TTP finances were in decline and indeed the figure for tax revenue provided by the source is much lower than what Burki estimated for 2009 ($25 million vs $45 million);[281] Burki also wrote that a decline in TTP tax raising started already in late 2009 and Elahi too supports the idea of a decline as the crackdown intensified. The Pakistani Taliban factions by the end of 2009 were facing serious problems, as businessmen were being threatened by the government for supporting the Taliban.[282]

The financial crisis of the TTP worsened in subsequent years, as TTP territorial control shrank and tax collection dived. AQ had not abandoned the TTP, however. In late 2016 a TTP commander denied any problem between AQ and TTP and claimed that 'they are still helping and supporting us in logistic and finance'.[283] At about the same time an AQ source in Afghanistan essentially confirmed that, rating the TTP as the top recipient of AQ funding in the region, followed by LeT and JeM.[284] Both sources however omitted to provide any figures. In reality another AQ source indicated in 2017 that yes the financial relationship was still there, but AQ too had been reducing its funding and by 2017 this was down to $28 million/year. Aside from AQ reducing its own contributions, it might also be that the 'donors' to the cause of the Pakistan Taliban were losing interest – not hard to believe considering the latter's performance. It might also be that AQ's lobbyists were working harder for other causes at that point. In part the decline was due to the fact that AQ was trying to maintain relations with some of the TTP's hardline splinters as well; for example in 2016 it reportedly paid $2 million to JuA.[285] AQ continued supporting JuA in subsequent years and was still doing so in 2020 and even embedded its groups in JuA's units.[286]

In sum, AQ used its fund-raising 'services' to gain leverage over the TTP; at times it reduced funding in order to exercise pressure over the TTP leadership and push it towards change and reform.

What did AQ make of the TTP as a jihadist organization?

AQ's critique of the TTP

The need to fund some of the TTP splinters was however not the only reason for the decline in AQ support to the TTP itself. The TTP was not functioning very effectively from the AQ's perspective. More than its modest contribution to global jihad, the TTP came under AQ scrutiny for its tendency towards fragmentation, which made infiltration by rival groups and intelligence agencies much easier, and for its strategy and tactics. As early as 2005–6 an AQ writer had noted:

And until we agree on unity, enemy infiltration within our ranks will remain easy, and it will not be difficult for infiltrators to hamstring our advance.[287]

The factionalized TTP was easy prey to the infiltration of not just the Pakistani security agencies, but reportedly of the Afghan and Indian ones as well (see about the 'mujahidin in Afghanistan' and 'Muslim circles in India' above in *Long-term AQ support*). From AQ's point of view, that was a very risky vulnerability; potentially any foreign security agency could be able to infiltrate the TTP. This should of course be viewed in the context of the regular killing of TTP leaders and AQ operatives by US drones. While the TTP could still serve its purpose of creating an insecure environment, where AQ could operate more easily, it could hardly be trusted for the protection of AQ members. The AQ decision to relocate its leaders away from the tribal areas is likely to have had to do with this too (see *Renewed primacy of Afghanistan 2014–16* above).

The tendency towards fragmentation was thus definitely a major concern of AQ. Says an AQIS cadre that

We are disappointed by the TTP and its never ending divisions. In the past year, we have continuously worked with TTP leaders to end differences and division and worked to strengthen the group and achieve ambitions. […] The current leadership must take charge and overcome the challenges and align the group's policies with the policies of AQ and AQIS. Without proper policies and procedures, the group will not overcome the current quagmire situation.[288]

Flaws in the weak institutionalization of the TTP were evident to the trained eyes of AQ advisers. Sheikh Mahmud and Sheikh Aby Yahya of AQ criticized the draft TTP charter for not clarifying what the procedure for the selection or dismissing of the Amir was, what the criteria for selecting him and the Shura were, and what procedures should be in place if he was incapacitated. They insisted that a fixed set of rules should be in place.[289] The two cadres suggest a process as inclusive as possible:

There is no doubt that the best way is to consult with the decision makers, the people in power, the Amirs of the groups, and then to consider the public opinion.[290]

The two Qaidists recommended appointing a deputy amir with the specific role of 'manag[ing] affairs for a specific period of time till the Shura meets and appoints a new Amir'.[291] This recommendation was later incorporated by the TTP. They also criticized the absolute power the draft charter attributed to the Amir, on the basis that it is preferable to

abide by the opinion of the majority to avoid whimsical decisions and avoid decisions based on absolute personal cravings, because a true decision is more likely to be based on the opinion of the majority.[292]

They also raised the issue of the need for the Amir to be accountable:

> *The document didn't cover the subject of calling the Amir to account, which is an important issue that we should give more priority to than the atheists who call their president to account, do. The Emir is nothing but a human being who does the right thing, makes mistakes, oppresses others, and is a just person. Thus there should be a way to have him account for his actions in front of the Shura Council. It is a fact that the Amir has his own rights and duties, and if he neglects or manipulates his duties, and doesn't give them due attention, then he has to be brought to account through a clear and disciplinary procedure.*[293]

The two cadres also seem to imply that Hakimullah being neither knowledgeable nor experienced, and facing complex issues,

> *[is] obliged, and by that I mean absolutely obliged to abide by the opinion of the majority members of the Shura Council. If a tie occurs, then the Amir's opinion counts.*[294]

Otherwise, the two cadres predicted:

> *The procedure that was mentioned in the organizational structure will undoubtedly result in a conflict and will have the Amir side with the sect that agrees with his opinions, and that will result in a grudge, hatred, and in discrimination; which are evils that are expected to take place, and thus it is a must to shut the door that leads to it.*[295]

Shaikh Mahmud and Shaikh Yahya also criticized the lack of a detailed criminal code, raising the risk that the poorly institutionalized fine system would

> *[open] the door wide open for reckless jihadist people to unjustifiably seize the money of the people and collect it in an easy way; and more so if the person in charge is an ignorant person seeking revenge.*[296]

Shaikh Mahmud and Shaikh Yahya also expressed the fear that the arbitrary use of the TTP intelligence system could harm the TTP itself and lead to purges and stressed that the intelligence committee should 'work hard for the movement without being influenced by the wishes of the Amir or of a prominent person while they are performing their duties'.[297]

Shaikh Mahmud and Shaikh Yahya also noted that even the duties and tasks of the TTP judiciary were only superficially discussed in the draft 2010 charter.[298] Evidence has emerged that Osama bin Laden himself sharply criticized the indiscriminate tactics of the TTP, while his men privately attacked the TTP's ideology, its methods and its behaviour, and even threatened public exposure.[299] Hakimullah was a particular target for AQ, which viewed with horror his lack of religious education and pretentiousness. Hakimullah seems to have resented AQ's interference and retaliated calling AQ members in the tribal areas 'guests', as opposed to 'brothers' as it was in vogue among fellow jihadists.[300] Several damaging practices were highlighted, such as:

killing the normal Muslims as a result of martyrdom operations that takes place in the marketplaces, mosques, roads, assembly places, and calling the Muslims apostates.[301]

As late as 2017, AQ/AQIS was still using what it considered some the TTP's capital mistakes in its 'do not' list:

We consider it absolutely wrong to cause blasts in public gatherings, including masjids, funerals, markets, and courtrooms, where there is a possibility of hurting common Muslims. We consider it a must to avoid even hitting permissible targets in such places, because such operations may hurt the Muslims masses [...]. [The wives and children of the apostates'] mere relationship to them does not prove their apostasy or their fighting against the mujahideen; rather, the default ruling of their wives and children is that they are Muslims. [...] The established educational system is corrupt and carved by the Kuffaar. However, we consider targeting educational institutions extremely wrong and un-Islamic, because in Muslims countries and in Muslim-majority areas, the teachers, the students, and other individuals affiliated with them are generally Muslims.[302]

AQ might also have objected to the TTP's indiscriminate violence against Shi'as in Pakistan. Implicitly the 2010 draft TTP charter considers Shi'as and Ismailis as non-Muslims, when it forbids targeting Muslims for ransom, but allows the targeting of 'Agha Khans' and Shi'a merchants. At that time, however, AQ cadres did not pick up this issue.[303] That AQ objected to these tendencies seems however to be supported by Khan Said Sajna's allegations that TTP was alienating AQ and drifting towards sectarianism, when he split from TTP in May 2014.[304] The TTP had traditionally good relations with the sectarian SSP, due to shares Deobandi roots, although these deteriorated somewhat after 2014, as SSP started warming to IS-K. The same applies to the other main sectarian groups, LeJ.[305] The relationship with the SSP might have strengthened anti-Shi'ism in the TTP. Hakimullah, who had led TTP in Kurram before becoming leader, had particularly close links to SSP and fought Shi'as extensively in both Kurram and Hangu.[306] Qari Ussain, another high-profile Bahlozai Mahsud, had been in SSP before joining TTP.[307] Strongly anti-Shi'a feeling seem to have been common among not just the hardliners. Faqir Mohammad, for example, after reconciling with Islamabad expressed his happiness about attacks against Shi'as in an interview.[308] Many of the TTP members most hostile to Shi'as defected to the newly established IS-K in 2014–19 (especially Orakzai Taliban), but it is not known whether AQ's pressure against sectarianism played a role in this wave of defections or not.[309]

The number of the TTP's terrorist attacks in Pakistan declined after Fazlullah took over the reins of the organization from Hakimullah in 2013 (Figure 3). The number of victims of terrorist attacks (as opposed to the number of attacks) kept climbing in 2014 largely due to a single attack, against the Peshawar school, but then it started declining too (Figure 4). It is unclear whether bin Laden's complaints against the TTP's indiscriminate tactics had anything to do with this decline in terrorist attacks. The decline started over three years after his death, but AQ might of course have kept up the pressure on TTP after the Abbottabad raid. Other likely causes of the decline

The TTP: Bastard Offspring of Global Jihad   103

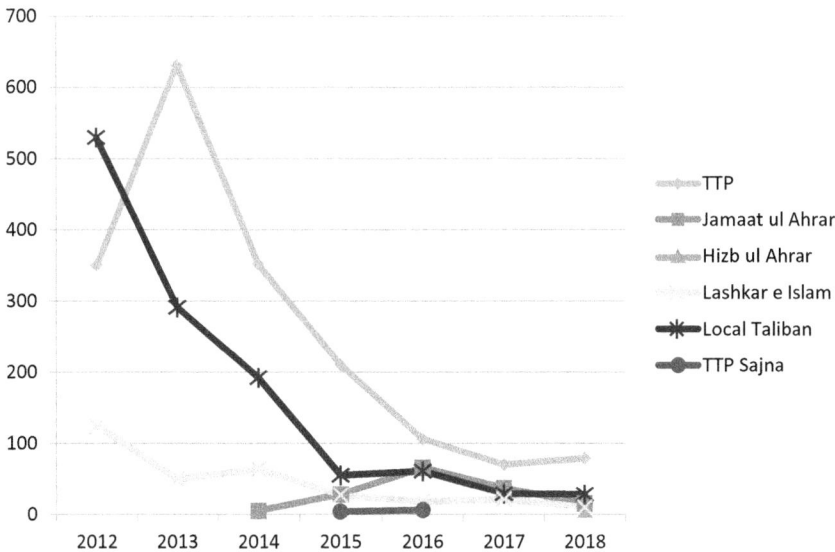

Figure 3 Terrorist attack by TTP and related organizations, 2012–18.
Source: PIPS.

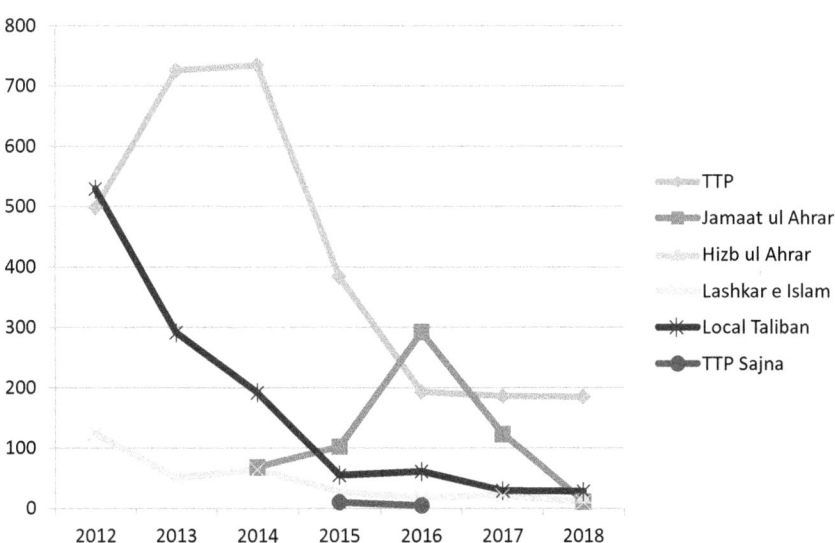

Figure 4 Victims (killed) of terrorist attack by TTP and related organizations, 2012–18.
Source: PIPS.

include the successful offensives of the Pakistani army, which reduced the TTP's capabilities inside Pakistan, and the internal fragmentation that led some of the most active terrorist cells to leave TTP and join JuA.

On the basis of the existing evidence, it is not possible to categorically state that AQ objected to TTP indiscriminate violence because it went against its understanding with ISI elements and its plans to widen that understanding. Given what was discussed in Chapter 2, however, this is a distinct possibility. AQ managed to maintain close relations with groups such as LeT and JeM, which also collaborated very closely with the Pakistani military establishment, at the same time as it stayed close to the TTP, which was the main armed opposition to Islamabad.[310] Some effort to narrow the gap between these groups and between TTP and the 'deep state' appears likely.

Sectarianism and indiscriminate violence were not the only objections that AQ had towards TTP. It seems that AQ operatives questioned the 'jihadist professionalism' of the TTP leadership as well. A source in the pro-Islamabad faction of the Pakistani Taliban explained that when Hakimullah was temporarily removed from the leadership of TTP in 2009, the fact that he was wounded was only one of the reasons. The other reason was that Hakimullah had lost the trust of AQ. Wali ur Rehman was the new AQ favourite, allegedly because of his better education (studied in Egypt) and capabilities.[311] AQ sources also pointed out the weak institutionalization and loose practices that characterized the TTP, whose impact was particularly dramatic in Hakimullah's time because he lacked Baitullah's charisma. For example, forcing everybody to swear allegiance to Hakimullah was highlighted by AQ critics as bound to cause infighting.[312]

Concerning the Central 'Enjoy what is Just and Forbid Evil' Committee, whose duty was to monitor respect and implementation for the Shari'a, Shaikh Mahmud and Shaikh Yahya were disparaging:

> We regret to note that this isn't what is taking place, and that there are never ending complaints being received from the regions under the control of Taliban. [...] Whoever compares the love and support extended here in Waziristan to Jihad and the Mujahidin during the early years, and to that of today's hate and annoyance, will definitely become aware of the failure of our policies in gaining the people to our side and in dealing with them.[313]

While the TTP's opposition to Islamabad was in line with AQ's interests (forcing Islamabad to contain its efforts to eradicate AQ first and then to reach a modus vivendi), its extreme violence was not, nor were its internal divisions. But throughout the period taken into consideration (2002–20), AQ appears to have judged that even this somewhat dysfunctional relationship was worth pursuing.

The TTP's role in AQ's strategy

AQ never rated the TTP among its favourite partners in South Asia, despite its size. When mentioning the groups from which AQIS was recruiting second tier members, a source contacted in 2019 mentioned the Afghan Taliban, Lashkar e Taiba and LeJ, but not the TTP.[314] Another AQIS source estimated at 5 per cent the percentage of non-core members who belonged to TTP, a low share considered that the TTP was together with LeT the largest jihadist organization in Pakistan.[315]

This is not so surprising, considering what discussed in *AQ's critique of the TTP* above. It is likely that the TTP's vulnerability to infiltration by and co-optation by intelligence agencies advised against absorbing many of its members into even AQ's second tier. The role of TTP in AQ's strategy would appear to have initially been to provide some protection to AQ operatives and leaders, and create an environment where these operatives would have found easier to operate. The TTP, by simply being there, provided a deterrent against the Pakistani authorities not to do more in-depth hunting of AQ members along the Afghan border. For AQ, whose options were very limited, this still had some value.

So far, a number of aspects of AQ's relationship with Pakistani actors have been established in this volume. As discussed in Chapter 2, AQ's propaganda outburst against Islamabad in 2007 is likely to have been the result of the emotional wave created by the Lal Masjid incident impacting on the existing complex relationship with the Pakistani 'deep state'. From AQ's perspective, there were jihadist energies waiting to be captured in that emotional wave of mobilization, energies that AQ could have turned into a way of expanding its influence and strengthening the coalition of forces committed to AQ's agenda of supporting the Afghan jihad and protecting AQ's assets in Pakistan. Whatever the rhetoric, an all-out jihad against the Pakistani state was not in AQ's interest, and indeed even in the realm of possibilities. AQ operatives must have seen the value of staying close to the Pakistani Taliban networks, whichever direction they were taking, and riding the tiger of their anti-Islamabad radicalization. It then offered its services to the Pakistani deep state, mediating between it and the jihadists. The Qaidists might also have hoped to reap some benefit from presiding over the strengthening of those militant networks in the tribal areas, which acted as hosts and protectors of AQ, through the formation of the TTP. It was a risk it had to take, for want of better options. If AQ had allowed a gap to open between itself and those networks, its thin structure along the border would be left completely exposed.

If there was a conscious, coherent AQ strategy to push Pakistan off the coalition with the United States, as hinted by Rassler (see Chapter 2), it needed tools that could apply pressure on Pakistan, and the TTP was the best such tool available to AQ.

If this interpretation of AQ's attitude vis-à-vis the 'deep state' is correct, the findings so far can be summed up stating that to AQ the TTP was:

- A tool to exercise pressure on the Pakistani state;
- A protection force for AQ's assets and leaders in Pakistan, when AQ members were hosted in the tribal areas.

As discussed in Chapter 2, after various ups and downs AQ managed to improve its relations with the Pakistani state. We know from *The extent of AQ's long term support for the TTP* above, that AQ continued supporting the TTP even after it reached an understanding with the 'deep state'.

Moving now on towards answering additional questions on AQ's TTP agenda, several points need to be clarified. On the basis of the interpretation outlined above, one might wonder why AQ continued supporting the TTP even after its leaders were offered safety by the Pakistani authorities and the 'deep state' had fully engaged on the Afghan Taliban side. The explanation proposed here is that AQ kept the TTP alive as a spare option, in case the 'deep state', which it never fully trusted, turned against it again. So the TTP to AQ was also

- A deterrent against any renewed deep state effort to go after AQ's leaders, after these moved out of the tribal areas.

This interpretation also has the advantage of explaining why AQ sided with the pro-Islamabad Taliban. If AQ had intended to force Pakistan to abandon its strategy of collaboration with the United States, wouldn't it have made sense for it to encourage a pro-Islamabad shift within the TTP, as Pakistan started turning away from collaboration with the United States and Washington-Islamabad tension started growing? This would have made sense also because the pro-Islamabad Pakistani Taliban were fighting alongside the Afghan Taliban, and the anti-Islamabad ones decreasingly so. But not trusting the 'deep state' to keep doing the right thing indefinitely, AQ seemingly concluded that it needed to retain some deterrence. By remaining one of the main sources of funding to the TTP, AQ enabled it to continue its 'jihad' versus Islamabad.[316]

Another question that arises from the interpretation proposed a few lines above is why AQ continued supporting the TTP after the latter's campaign against Islamabad started faltering after 2013. The explanation just put forward offers an answer to this question too: even in its state of disrepair, the TTP still served AQ's purpose as a deterrent. In fact, an ineffective, but not yet completely dysfunctional TTP served AQ's purpose even better by then, as it made the continuing links between the two organizations more tolerable for the 'deep state'.

AQ's efforts to 'manage' the TTP

If AQ needed the TTP to survive at least as a potential threat to the Pakistani state, it would have needed to carefully monitor its evolution. AQ neither needed the TTP to reach an understanding with Islamabad, nor it to implode as a result of its dysfunctionality or of the repression of the Pakistani state. The TTP had to be managed.

A complete picture of how AQ tried to manage the TTP is of course not available. However, some information is there about AQ's efforts to intervene in the TTP's internal affairs. It seems clear that despite having cadres deployed to advise the TTP, for long years AQ did not improve the organizational skills of the TTP much, whether by design or by default (see *Little effort to import organizational know-how* above). The AQ advisers however also tried to influence TTP policymaking. The sections below review how successful they and AQ's leaders were in this regard.

Mediating between TTP and the 'deep state'

According to an internal source, AQIS did try to mend fences between the TTP and the 'deep state', but its efforts were not successful and in fact fruitless, to the extent that it had to keep the depth of its relationship with TTP secret:[317]

> we are constantly urging TTP leaders and members to stop Jihad against the Pakistani state, but they're not ready to accept this, since they have deep enmity with the Pakistani state. The Pakistani ISI is pressing our leaders to stand against the TTP, but we told them we do not have any relations with the TTP. Our relations with the TTP are kept secret.[318]

This should be intended as keeping the extent of AQ's support for the TTP secret. As the source further explained that the 2014 deal with Islamabad allowed AQ to maintain some relationship with the TTP as long as it did not mean supporting it against the Pakistani state.[319]

> Our relations with TTP are based on a separate agreement in which we support the group only against infidels and our enemies, not Pakistan. TTP accepted that our support will not be used against the state of Pakistan and its people. [...] We are helping the Pakistani government. We give updated information about TTP to Pakistan.[320]

The source said that the relationship of AQIS with the TTP is akin to the relationship of Islamabad with the Americans:

> The Pakistani government also maintain relations with our enemies like the Americans, but we never told them that it's compromising the deal we have.[321]

AQ clearly did not exercise on the TTP all the pressure it could have, for example completely withholding funding. Even when AQ did reduce funding to the TTP, the sources never mentioned restraining its activities against the Pakistani state as a reason for that (see *The extent of AQ's long-term support to the TTP* above). It is difficult to escape the feeling that AQ might have paid little more than lip service to its commitment to try and rein in the TTP.

Clearly, TTP retained some use for AQ even if it threatened its relationship with the 'deep state'. One such use was, as discussed above, the role of deterrent vis-à-vis the deep state, but there was at least another one. As the Afghan Taliban signed a peace deal with the United States and started talks with the Kabul authorities, the fate of global jihadist groups in the region started appearing more uncertain than ever. In September 2020 a document emerged, in which the Afghan Taliban had offered the TTP safe haven inside Afghanistan, in exchange for guaranteeing that they would not carry out hostile activities against Pakistan and for registering all TTP members with the Quetta Shura. The TTP however rejected the draft agreement, on the ground that several of its 27 points went against the TTP's policies and aims. Negotiations were still going on as of September 2020.³²² The TTP had no plans to transfer forces from Afghanistan to Pakistan either as the TTP still considered Afghanistan much safer than Pakistan for his men. Until the tribal areas were freed, says the source, the TTP will need to use its bases in Afghanistan. In fact, as of September 2020 the TTP was building yet another base in Kunar. TTP sources seemed confident that some deal could be worked out with the Afghan Taliban.³²³

> *I am sure that Afghan Taliban will not force TTP to leave the territory of Afghanistan when they reach in a peace agreement with Afghan government.*³²⁴

Afghan Taliban sources were not so optimistic, nor was former TTP and former JuA Ehsanullah Ehsan.³²⁵ AQIS had not signed the deal proposed by the Afghan Taliban either. It is not hard to imagine that AQ would see the TTP's presence along the Afghanistan-Pakistan border as an insurance policy, in case the Afghan peace talks were successful. Indeed, a source indicated that AQIS was actively discouraging the TTP from signing the deal with the Taliban, even threatening the TTP with cutting all support if it were to sign.³²⁶

AQ and the pro-Islamabad Pakistani Taliban

A remarkable aspect of AQ's relationship with the TTP and more in general of the Pakistani Taliban was keeping the rival factions of the latter and all the other Pakistani jihadist groups (pro- and anti-Islamabad) together in their support of the Afghan jihad, which until 2014 at least was the primary strategic aim. Shaikh Mahmud and Shaikh Yahya seem to imply that peace deals with Islamabad were permissible as long as based on consensus within the TTP.³²⁷

Reconciling the differences and the rivalries must have been problematic, but it was to some degree managed. The pro-Islamabad Pakistani Taliban avoided discussing the issue of the anti-Islamabad TTP with the Afghan Taliban in order to avoid friction, and the Afghan Taliban do not seem to have been interested in such debates either.³²⁸ Privately Peshawar Shura Taliban told anti-Islamabad TTP commanders that they disliked the presence of LeT, JeM and LeJ on Afghan soil, but they would not raise the issue with the Pakistani security services in order to avoid Pakistani retaliation. Instead, the Peshawar Shura Taliban would express their appreciation for both TTP wings.³²⁹ These 'arrangements' survived ISI efforts to disrupt them. Anti-Islamabad TTP sources alleged that the Pakistani ISI infiltrated its own men among their ranks to start violent incidents with the Afghan Taliban and generate friction; one such commander and his men were reportedly killed by the Taliban in Kunar in 2013, after the anti-Islamabad TTP tipped the Peshawar Shura off.³³⁰ Exactly what role AQ played in setting up these arrangements is however not known.

Throughout the post-2006 period (that is when the division between pro-Islamabad and pro-Islamabad factions of the Pakistani Taliban emerged), no evidence of direct AQ support for the Pakistani Taliban signing deals with Islamabad emerged. It is not actually clear to what extent AQ was maintaining relations the pro-Islamabad Pakistani Taliban. The only evidence of a relationship is an AQIS source, which claimed in 2019 that the group of Mullah Nazir was allied with it.[331] Sources in the pro-Pakistan factions say that they were raising funding through 'taxes', Afghan Taliban contributions (for fighting in Afghanistan) and foreign countries like China (presumably interested in preventing instability in Pakistan).[332] AQ was never mentioned as a source of funding. No AQ source mentioned any pro-Islamabad Pakistani Taliban group among the main recipients of AQ support. It is worth mentioning that, while AQ does not seem to have 'punished' the TTP for being unable to prevent the defections from TTP of pro-Islamabad groups, defections to IS-K were taken more seriously. AQ definitely felt more threatened by IS-K than by the pro-Islamabad Taliban.[333]

The pro-Islamabad Taliban's neglect by AQ came despite their engagement on the Afghan Taliban's side. In fact, overall the contribution of the pro-Islamabad Pakistani Taliban to the Afghan Taliban's war effort is likely to have been overall greater than that of the TTP. For example, in 2012 an agreement was reached (sponsored by the Pakistani ISI), according to which the pro-Islamabad Pakistani Taliban, led by Faqir Mohammad, agreed to fight in Afghanistan. According to the terms of the agreement, the ISI handed over large quantities of weapons to the Faqir Mohammed's men, for redistribution in Afghanistan. According to one source, 60,000 weapons were passed to the Taliban.[334] Even during the phases in which relations between AQ and the Pakistani military were improving (2008–11, 2016, 2019–), AQ seems to have been doing little for the Pakistani Taliban allied with Islamabad, while it was handing out tens of millions of dollars every year to the TTP.

Part of the answer is likely to be that the pro-Islamabad Pakistani Taliban received sufficient support by the Pakistani 'deep state' and did not need AQ's help. The absence or low level of AQ support for the pro-Pakistani Taliban confirms nonetheless that AQ's primary reason for supporting the TTP was not, at least after the early years, its role in the Afghan jihad (see Chapter 2 and *The TTP's role in AQ's strategy* above).

AQ explores alternatives to the TTP

For the purpose of getting a more reliable protection for its leaders, in November 2013 AQ encouraged (with the endorsement of some donors in the Gulf) one of the TTP's senior commanders, Maulana Abdul Rahim Farooqi, to split away and form his own group of about 700 men. AQ fully funded the group and used it for the protection of its camps and of its cadres in Pakistan and Afghanistan. After the split AQ did not try to mediate between Farooqi and the TTP, confirming that it was not displeased at all with the split.[335] AQ reportedly sent one of its few Pakistani Pashtuns core members, Mawlavi Babar Swati (ex TTP, with AQ since 2011), to join Farooqi in a senior position. The Farooqi Group positioned itself as verbally close to AQ's agenda of exporting terrorism to Western countries, but like the TTP doing in fact little, except protecting AQ. Compared to TTP, the Farooqi Group did little even in Pakistan and Afghanistan. Its sole purpose seems instead to have been escorting and protecting AQ operatives.[336]

AQ appears therefore to have seen in Farooqi and his men somebody it could trust better for its own security than the rest of the TTP and the decision to favour the emergence of the new splinter was reportedly taken by AQ's regional chief Yasin al Suri himself.[337] Farooqi, in reality, had his own reasons for quitting the TTP, and these appear to have had little to do with ideology. He originally joined the TTP in 2008 in his original area of Batkhela, Malakand District, and was reportedly close to Hakimullah Mehsud, serving also as TTP head of Mohmand Agency. After the killing of Hakimullah, Farooqi decided to leave the TTP as he could not get along with Fazlullah and took some men with him; others joined later as they too developed issues with Fazlullah. Some disaffected LeT Punjabis also joined.[338]

It soon turned out that the Farooqi Group was not immune from the problems affecting the TTP. Although the group was claimed by AQ to be under its complete control and despite fully funding it, Farooqi repeatedly refused to obey orders from AQ, that he did not like, such as carrying out offensive operations against IS-K in Kunar, Afghanistan. Then some commanders of the Farooqi Group defected to IS-K, seriously upsetting AQ.[339] AQ might have drawn from the experience the lesson that there was no real alternative to the TTP in the tribal areas and that its deficiencies reflected the society and culture of the region.

AQ's role in keeping the TTP together under Fazlullah

However inexperienced at the beginning, the leadership of the TTP kept trying through the years to prevent the disintegration of its organization, and negotiated various re-unification efforts. AQ, for its part, although it might have not provided much or any help to the pro-Islamabad Taliban, is more likely to have tried to bring them closer to the TTP. Already the first TTP leader, Baitullah Mehsud, tried to re-absorb the Local Taliban Movement by signing an agreement in February 2009 with Mullah Nazir and Bahadur, for the formation of a new council called *Shura Ittihad ul Mujahideen,* essentially an alliance of TTP and Local Taliban, allowing the latter to stay out of the fight with the Pakistani authorities.[340] This was the first time a TTP leader accepted an even looser alliance to keep the Pakistani Taliban united, although clearly it was meant as an ad hoc measure.

The task of keeping the TTP together grew more daunting over time. Many of the smaller splits melted away without trace once their leaders were killed, usually by US drone strikes, but the bigger splits proved durable. The peak in the centrifugal tendencies within the TTP was reached in 2014–15. Having been selected leader in a very controversial way, Fazlullah appeared initially to be risking the disintegration of the TTP (see *The fragmentation of the TTP* above). This prospect scared even the central leadership of AQ. In 2015, according to an AQ source, AQ's decided to curtail funding to punish the TTP for its failure to prevent a major outflow of its commanders and fighters towards IS-K.[341] However, according to an AQ source by late 2016 AQ was beginning to worry about the viability of the TTP and ordered the finance commission to increase allocations again in the future.[342] It is not clear whether 2017 actually saw an increase in AQ allocations to the TTP, but this renewed concern of AQ for the TTP might go some way in explaining how Fazlullah managed in 2016–17 to keep most of what was left of the TTP somehow together.

Given the concerns expressed by AQ's leaders about the tendency of the TTP to fragment, one can assume that AQ might have played a role in encouraging Fazlullah to seek compromises in order to keep what was left of the TTP together. There is however no direct evidence of AQ's involvement. What is known is that Fazlullah started making systematic efforts to soften the opposition to his leadership, if anything else because he faced much more widespread opposition than any other leader before him. Fazlullah managed to keep the Sheharyar and Sajna factions from splitting completely away. They remained de facto independent, but found common ground with Fazlullah in their common rejection of Faqir Mohammed's deal with Islamabad.[343] Despite reassurances by many TTP commanders, that Sajna and Fazlullah were on the same page, one senior TTP source admitted that

> the TTP is not completely unified behind Fazlullah. There are some leaders and commanders who [...] are still in competition with Maulana Fazlullah, [...] such as Mangal Bagh, Sajna Mehsud, Commander Wali Khan and Khalid Mansur.[344]

Fazlullah also negotiated with the various TTP splinters, even putting in principle his own job at stake. Fazlullah achieved a few successes in this regard. The Tariq Geedar group, which had survived the death of its leader, de facto reintegrated in the TTP in 2016.[345] In 2015/16 Fazlullah also managed to negotiate a reunification with JuA and even the first merger with LI, on the basis of Fazlullah agreeing to have another leadership selection process. The two groups cooperated with the TTP while waiting for a new leader selection process for the merger. Fazlullah kept postponing the new leadership contest, claiming that continuing Pakistani army operations in the FATA and PATA made it impossible.[346] Fazlullah's reluctance to go through a new leadership contest resulted eventually in the failure of the two mergers. JuA turned hostile, while LI continued cooperating with the TTP, even if it stayed out of it.[347] The net result of Fazlullah's efforts was therefore an alliance with LI and the re-integration of the Tariq Geedar Group, and a peaceful co-existence with the Mehsud factions of Sajna and Sheharyar.

Overall in 2017–18 the TTP was at its nadir. Fazlullah directly controlled only what was left of his own TNSM faction after the defection of Faqir Mohammed in 2009. That means probably about 2,000–3,000 fighters (Figure 5).[348] He could then coordinate with perhaps another 2,000 fighters of LI and of the Tariq Geedar Group (Figure 6).

At the end of Fazlullah's tenure at the top of the TTP, the TTP was 'almost dead' and

> there was no management between the TTP leadership and the TTP commanders and members active in Pakistan and in Afghanistan. Every commander and leader of TTP were running their own groups and factions without any consultation with the TTP leadership.[349]

That state of disarray had encouraged many TTP commanders and fighters to join IS-K.

AQ pushing for reform?

In 2018 another TTP crisis came about, kick-started by the killing of Fazlullah in an American air strike on 24 June. al Zawahiri in an audio message sent his condolences

112   *Jihadism in Pakistan*

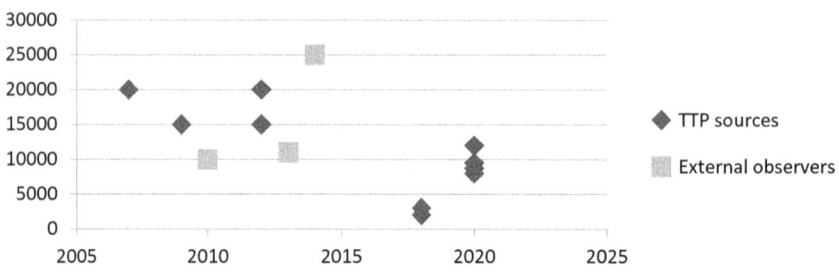

Figure 5 Estimates and claims of TTP fighting strength, 2007–20 (excluding splinter groups).[350]

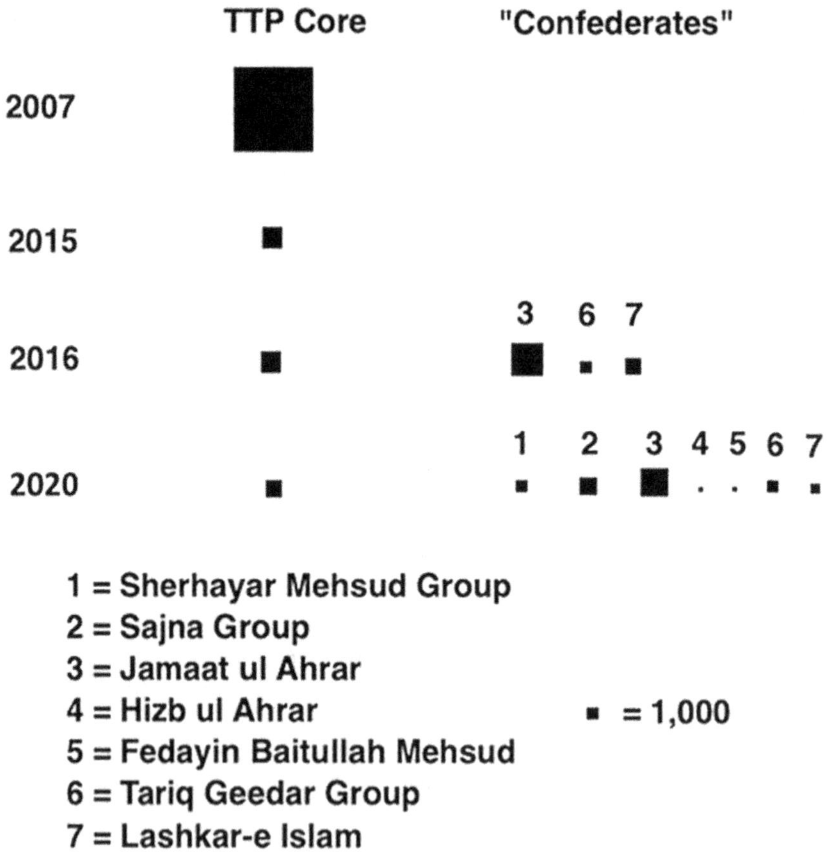

```
              TTP Core        "Confederates"

2007            ■■

2015            ■

                                3   6   7
2016            ■               ■   .   ■

                                1   2   3   4   5   6   7
2020            ■               .   ■   ■   .   .   ■   ■
```

1 = Sherhayar Mehsud Group
2 = Sajna Group
3 = Jamaat ul Ahrar
4 = Hizb ul Ahrar   ■ = 1,000
5 = Fedayin Baitullah Mehsud
6 = Tariq Geedar Group
7 = Lashkar-e Islam

Figure 6 The changing structure of the TTP (fighters by faction).[351]

to the TTP and stated that al Qa'ida as always will remain the brother of TTP and will help the TTP in Pakistan.'[352] But after some months TTP was beginning to experience a new wave of defections to IS-K, this time of Fazlullah's men, who objected to the treatment reserved for them by new leader Mufti Noor Wali Mehsud, whom they accused of trying to restore Mahsud domination of the TTP (see *The fragmentation of the TTP* above).

Again, TTP sources were insisting in 2020 that they maintained good relations with AQ throughout and that AQ continued supporting TTP without hindrance or hesitation.[353] An AQIS source confirmed that the organization was still having 'close contacts and cooperation with the TTP' in 2020.[354] But these vague statements were hiding the fact that after Fazlullah's death the financial situation of the TTP soon became critical again. 'For the last two years TTP has been in financial trouble', said a TTP commander in 2020.[355]

The renewed crisis of TTP seems to have prompted talks between AQ and TTP. In spring 2019 a member of the TTP council visited commanders in Afghanistan, inviting them to stay with TTP because a massive increase in funding was on its way.[356] That promise appears to have been premature. Re-establishing a level of funding sufficient for TTP to recover has been new leader Noor Wali's biggest challenge. The TTP in 2019–20 continued collecting taxes from households in parts of North and South Waziristan, and from some business all over the old FATA. It also kidnapped people for ransom.[357] None of this amounted to much and most importantly was decentralized in nature, not helping the central leadership in strengthening its influence and power. Noor Wali's options were limited therefore, and he had to appeal to external donors, including AQ, for additional support. Noor Wali worked hard to bring back the donors who had deserted the TTP in Fazlullah's years, achieving some success at least with AQ and some Arab donors.[358]

AQ eventually in 2019 agreed to increase its funding and started lobbying donors in the Gulf to support the TTP.[359] A TTP commander reported in March 2020 that 'just a few months ago very high-ranking officials of al Qa'ida came to South Waziristan and visited our activities and also met with Mufti Noor Wali Mehsud', and interpreted the development as a reaffirmation of AQ support. At about the same time a delegation of Arab donors to AQ visited South Waziristan as well, met the leaders and toured the training camp.[360] The pattern of AQ cutting funds to the non-performing TTP, until it reached a critical state and AQ was forced to come to its rescue, appears to have been repeated again.

This funding, which accrued directly to Noor Wali and the coffers of the TTP, gave him a re-distributional power that helped in keeping the factions linked to the leadership. As of September 2020, the main source of funding to the TTP was reported to be Saudi private donors, interested in 'caus[ing] the collapse of the corrupt Pakistani government and in establish[ing] an Islamic government based on Islamic Sharia'. These donors appeared to be driven by anti-Americanism, but did 'not give directions or orders on what to do'. The reunification of TTP was believed to be enhancing the reputation of Noor Wali with the donors, which a TTP source believes would eventually lead to an increase in funding.[361]

The role of AQ might have been even greater than just supplying (crucial) funding. One source in AQIS even claimed that the organization had been able to

influence the selection of the new TTP leaders. During the appointment of new leaders such as Emir Noor Wali Mehsud and Mufti Hazrat [Noor Wali's deputy], our leaders played very important role. They worked with TTP leaders and encouraged them to set aside their differences and accept AQ decisions. In fact, TTP is dependent on us for the selection of new leaders. TTP leaders are always respecting our leader's decisions.[362]

Fazlullah's successor Noor Wali had his own group of loyal Mehsud fighters, somewhat smaller than Fazlullah's TNSM faction. The base on which to rebuild the TTP was therefore not greater than Fazlullah's. Moreover, continuing army operations against the TTP caused the overall strength of all TTP faction to shrink by as many as 3,000 men in 2018–20, through losses and desertions.[363] But Noor Wali was also the most thoughtful of the TTP leaders up to that point and set out to roll out a more systematic overhaul of the TTP's organization, whereas up to Fazlullah ad hoc approaches had prevailed. Noor Wali won the leadership contest promising the TTP's Leadership Council that he would reunite the TTP and make it powerful again.[364]

One of Noor Wali's innovations was a new code of conduct, which built in a 'confederative' structure, requesting member to be loyal to their 'factional leaders', who in turn would be loyal to the TTP leader. Each component group was asked to form a six-member council in order to interface with the TTP's Supreme Council.[365] The leadership retained the right to mobilize fighters from the different local commanders for major offensive operations:

Military Shura will devise a war plan for the area considering the strength of Mujahideen and enemy and geographical features of the terrain, on the instruction of Supreme Shura. If the Military Shura decides to neutralize the strength of enemy in an area and for this mission If they need to assemble the Mujahideen, then it is compulsory for the Mujahideen to obey them. Military Shura will bound every group to provide armed brothers for the targeted area according to their capacity.[366]

The structure of the military operations, however, was decentralized, the local TTP commanders and governors having enough freedom from leadership council to run their own military structure and military plans in their areas. The governors were made answerable not to the leader alone, but to a new commission of six members.[367] In 2021 Noor Wali announced the establishment of a 'central military training centre', which all TTP would be able to attend, again suggesting a model a leadership offering central services, but without prevaricating over its component groups.[368]

Intra-factional disputes were expected to be resolved locally, with transfers used as punishment where this was not achieved. The new code also aimed for clear lines of authority, in an effort to improve discipline and reduce internal infighting. Six-member shuras were to be established in each locality, introducing therefore a principle of collegial leadership at all level, and a military court system was introduced to punish abuses committed by the members. The code also forbade attacks against soft targets, such as schools. Attacks against Shi'as without other cause were banned and the use of suicide attacks reserved for very important targets, to be selected exclusively by the top leadership. Unauthorized relations with external groups (read IS) were also banned.[369] The new rules of engagement appear to have been implemented.[370]

Violence against civilians was discouraged.[371] Reportedly Mufti Noor Wali 'always advises the TTP commanders to be very careful with the Muslim civilians during our operations in Pakistan'. The source points the finger at JuA as having been much more ruthless with civilians than the TTP.[372]

> *Because of the Muslim civilian victims during suicide attacks and bombing against the Pakistan army and the Christian and unbelievers in Pakistan and in Afghanistan, TTP reduced its suicide attacks and bombing and is focusing more on guerrilla attacks and face to face fighting against the Pakistani government, which cause less civilian casualties.*[373]

The TTP warning of an offensive in South Waziristan was thus described as dictated by humanitarian concerns:

> *Recently TTP asked the villagers of the tribal areas, especially the Mehsud tribe in South Waziristan, to move to a safe area because TTP will launch a huge operation against the government army, so that during the operation the villagers will not get hurt.*[374]

One TTP Mehsud member argued that Noor Wali had a record of opposing 'any kind' of attacks against civilians before he was appointed leader, dating back to the time of Baitullah Mehsud's leadership, when Noor Wali was head of the TTP's judiciary. Reportedly Noor Wali often clashed with Baitullah over the attacks against civilians and advocated stricter rules of engagement.[375] These reforms were in line with what AQ operatives had been suggesting for years. Given the help in securing funding and the role in getting Noor Wali selected as leader, it would be surprising if AQ had not played a significant role in driving these reforms as well.

Reuniting the TTP under Noor Wali

The decentralized model adopted by Noor Wali was meant as a cure for the disintegration of Fazlullah's time.[376] Fazlullah had started his mandate trying to implement Baitullah's template of relatively centralized leadership, despite having considerably fewer means, power and support than Baitullah ever had. Noor Wali accepted that such a model was not implementable, as Mahmud and Abu Yahya had pointed out years earlier (see *AQ's critique of the TTP* above). On the basis of this 'confederative' approach, Noor Wali managed to consolidate the good relations and close cooperation with LI that Fazlullah already achieved before getting killed.[377] He also established good relations with JuA and with HuA and his forces started carrying out joint operations with them.³⁷⁸ This was an important achievement as by 2020 JuA was the biggest splinter of TTP movement (Figure 4).³⁷⁹

After long years of shedding members in favour of a variety of competing insurgent groups, there were some signs of an inversion in tendency. Already in late 2019 and early 2020, some TKP members rejoined TTP, HuA and especially JuA after the defeat of IS-K in Nangarhar.³⁸⁰

Noor Wali sought to bring JuA and HuA back into the TTP, but initially they refused because they seemed to be running strong.³⁸¹ Noor Wali renewed his offer after the November 2019 defeat of IS-K in Nangarhar, when both JuA and HuA (allied to IS-K) suffered heavy casualties. This time TTP and JuA and HuA started negotiating in earnest. AQIS helped TTP negotiate the re-merger of JuA and HuA into the TTP.³⁸² At that point the two groups had lost the logistical support of IS-K and became unable to sustain their operations. They also realized they did not stand a chance of successfully re-entering Pakistan alone. Reportedly JuA and HuA merged into the TTP without conditions and took an oath to accept all TTP rules. They also accepted to cut off all relations with IS-K. A TTP commander in eastern Afghanistan confirmed that JuA and HuA units fully merged into TTP.³⁸³ The deal is likely to have included some guarantee that JuA's leader, Omar Khalid Khurasani, would be appointed to a senior position in TTP. The rumours were in September 2020 that he would be named TTP leader for his home area, Khyber, where the TTP intended to re-establish a presence.³⁸⁴

In July 2020 what was left of the Punjabi Taliban, the faction of Asmatullah Mawya, also merged into the TTP. In early August, a small LeJ faction named after Ameer Usman Saifullah Kurd also merged into the TTP. By October, there were some 300 former LeJ members within the ranks of TTP.³⁸⁵ A couple of other smaller jihadist groups based in Waziristan also merged into TTP.³⁸⁶

There were allegations that Sheharyar was killed in 2020 on Noor Wali's orders because his links to India were making him too independent and difficult to control.³⁸⁷ His colleagues however seem to have thought otherwise, and to have linked his death to a campaign of targeted assassination of TTP cadres in Afghanistan, probably facilitated by the US military.³⁸⁸ The Sheharyar group eventually rejoined the TTP in October 2021. A minority of what was left of Fazlullah's faction agreed to cooperate with Noor Wali as well.³⁸⁹ Noor Wali also sought to remobilize into the TTP members who left the struggle when the tide was against the TTP. 'Negotiations' were ongoing with such retired commanders, according to a TTP source, while a Pakistani scholar was told by local journalists that a campaign of intimidation against former members reluctant to rejoin was going on.³⁹⁰

One sympathetic source in the Sajna faction estimated that Noor Wali reunified 90 per cent of what was left of the TTP.³⁹¹ Only among Maulana Fazlullah's Devotees, who split exactly because of Noor Wali's appointment, inevitably there was still strong criticism of Noor Wali. One of them saw the confederative approach as a weakness, as it did not translate into a high striking power (read large-scale terror attacks):

> From the time that Mufti Noor Wali Mehsud became the leader of TTP, he has not even finished making unity among the Mehsud tribe's TTP factions. [...] Now most of the supporters and fighters of Shehrayar Mehsud are against of him, lots of fighters of

Khalid Sajna are not loyal to him, the other factions from Swat and Jama'at ul Ahrar, our groups the Devotees of Moulana Fazlullah [...] all have problems. ... From the time that Mufti Noor Wali Mehsud became the leader of TTP, he couldn't manage any huge attack against Pakistan.[392]

This critic asserted that only half of the Mehsud members of the TTP were under Noor Wali's direct control. The rest were just in good terms with him, but were not taking orders from him.[393] In reality, as discussed above, Noor Wali appears to have settled for a new organizational model, having verified that implementing Baitullah's model was impossible. One of Noor Wali's supporters thus explained:

Mufti Noor Wali Mehsud [...] worked a lot to make the TTP united again under his control. He was succeeded to at least make a unity between the different factions of TTP, but couldn't bring all of them under his own control. Different factions of TTP like JuA, Hakimullah Mehsud's or Tehrik Taliban Pakistan, South Waziristan or Swat TTP and other factions have agreed to ally with TTP, but they will have their own freedom, will not come under order of Mufti Noor Wali Mehsud. They are friends and fight together against Pakistan's government and against Americans in Afghanistan when there is need, but the factions have their own policies.[394]

A source close to Noor Wali reported that while the Khalid Sajna group has already been 'integrated' back in the TTP, as of September 2020 Noor Wali was still negotiating with the Orakzai, Swati, Bajaur factions of TTP, as well as Hafiz Gul Bahadur's group in North Waziristan and several individual leaders who defected to IS-K, trying to get them to merge back into the TTP. Some senior commanders of Bahadur joined TTP in 2020, leaving Bahadur behind.[395] The signature of the Taliban-US peace deal added a new urgency to the negotiations for a full reunification, in order to be in a position to recapture Pakistani territory, should the TTP be expelled from Afghanistan.[396]

Noor Wali might have had his own merit in all this reunification work, but a source in the splinter Devotees of Maulana Fazlullah indicated that AQ was also mediating between the different TTP factions in order to seek a full TTP reunification, a role that it seems to have been playing for some time.[397] This is another indication of the guiding and mentoring role that AQ was finally really able to play with the TTP's leadership.

Except for those TTP groups which joined the Islamic State and the TTP does not appear to want back, by end 2021 there was little left to reunify:

- Hafiz Gul Bahadur's group, traditionally very close to the Haqqanis, operating between North Waziristan and Afghanistan's south-eastern provinces. Bahadur's group was cooperating tactically with TTP as of December 2021 and his group and TTP had been in good terms, negotiating reunification, for some time. A source within the group estimated its strength at 1,000–1,500 in late 2021, while a TTP source estimated its strength at just 200–250. TTP talks with Bahadur's group had started already in mid-2020 but stopped twice.
- The deceased Mawlawi Nazir's group, now reduced to just a few hundred men, also based between south-eastern Afghanistan and South Waziristan.

- A coterie of old commanders based in KP's Swat district, who belonged to a group led by Maulana Fazlullah, the deceased predecessor of current TTP leader Noor Wali Mehsud. These commanders might have a few hundred fighters between them.
- A group led by Faqir Mohammad, who was recently released by the Taliban from an Afghan prison. Reportedly 800 former TTP members were released with him, but it is not know how many are still loyal to him.[398]

In addition, Noor Wali Mehsud has also been negotiating with (LI), which had never joined the TTP in the first place. LI might have had a few hundred members left as of end 2021, having seen a steep decline after its leader Mangal Bagh was killed in a bomb attack in Afghanistan's eastern Nangarhar province in January 2021. During the November–December 2021 ceasefire, Noor Wali reportedly managed to convince several small TTP commanders inside the tribal areas to rejoin TTP as well.[399]

A new strategy for the TTP

Under Noor Wali the TTP appears to have adopted also a more realistic aim than overthrowing the Pakistani state, that is, freeing the tribal areas from the Pakistani army.[400] This was an aim that some Gulf donors seem to have found appealing:

> *They want TTP to continue its Jihad against Pakistan's army and government to free the tribal areas from army and government and run a Shari'a system there.*[401]

Thanks to the ongoing reunifications, in 2020 Noor Wali was able to re-escalate military activities.[402] By 2019 there were some signs of a modest TTP resurgence, with an increase in guerrilla attacks in Waziristan.[403] Then a total of 149 attacks were claimed in 2020. In the first quarter of 2021, sixty-one attacks took place. By the third quarter, the number of attacks had reached ninety-four. Until the ceasefire was declared in November (see *A new strategy for the TTP* below), 2021 was showing a further massive intensification of the violence (twenty-four attacks were claimed in October alone).[404]

A pro-Noor Wali source had estimated the total number of TTP fighters at 9,000–12,000 in March 2020. By September he had revised that number up to 13,000, of which 3,000 were in Afghanistan (after the merger of JuA and HuA).[405] At the same time another TTP commander, also loyal to Noor Wali, estimated the total strength of the TTP under Noor Wali after the merger at about 11,000–12,000, of which 3,000–4,000 were in Afghanistan.[406] These numbers do reflect an upward trend, but are uncertain, because the factions merging back into TTP likely inflated their actual fighting strength in order to win better appointments for their leaders in the unified TTP structure. By the end of 2021 TTP sources had a more sober assessment of the actual fighting strength of the TTP, placing it at 10,000 fighters.[407]

Given the context, Noor Wali's approach of using his confederation of Pakistani Taliban to wage a guerrilla war (as opposed to the TTP's earlier approach of taking over large portions of territory) seemed the only viable one. As he was making progress in its reunification priority, by the end of the summer of 2020 Noor Wali's ambitions seemed to be getting bigger. The TTP, aware of the unpopularity of the merger of the FATA into the Pakistani state, announced in 2020 that it opposed it.[408] The TTP was in September 2020 moving groups from all over Pakistan to South Waziristan, reportedly in preparation for a large offensive. Even some groups in Afghanistan were placed in a state of readiness, in case they were needed in Waziristan. The intent appears to have been to re-establish safe areas in South and to a lesser extent North Waziristan, exploiting also anti-Islamabad resentment among the Pashtun population.[409] Sources in LeJ confirmed seeing an increase in the pace of TTP operations, especially in South Waziristan.[410]

In the longer run the TTP strategy appears to be evolving towards re-establishing some type of autonomy for the tribal areas (hence courting Pashtun nationalist sentiment), even if it reportedly gave up on re-establishing the FATA as such,[411] and introducing a Shari'a-based government there. TTP rhetoric became more sympathetic to Pashtun nationalist groups.[412] There were also allegations that TTP established links to Baluchi nationalist groups.[413]

These aims implied a negotiated path. TTP sources have been reporting that already in 2020 the Haqqani Network faction of the Afghan Taliban tried to kick-start peace talks between the TTP and the Pakistani government, but without success due to the distance between the two sides in terms of negotiating positions.[414] Noor Wali Mehsud's demand have consistently been the implementation of sharia (Islamic law) nationwide, the release of TTP prisoners, TTP control over the tribal areas of the FATA, and the withdrawal of the Pakistani military from these areas.

Noor Wali might have felt that he needed more bargaining power to succeed in getting what he wanted from Islamabad. In part that was provided by the decision of the re-established Taliban Emirate in Afghanistan to keep allowing a TTP safe haven inside Afghanistan. A wave of TTP attacks against Chinese targets might also have been a way of gaining leverage in future peace negotiations with the Pakistani government, given the failure of the TTP in getting any concessions from Islamabad in 2020. A bomb attack in Khyber Pukhtoonkhwa on 14 July targeted a van transporting Chinese workers, killing nine of them, while an earlier 22 April attack targeted the hotel in Quetta where the Chinese ambassador to Pakistan was staying. The ambassador was not at the hotel at the time and no mention of China or the ambassador was made in the TTP claim of responsibility for the attack, but the message was clear. At least two more smaller attacks against Chinese interest took place in 2021. The TTP denied targeting Chinese interests.[415]

Noor Wali Mehsud was then in a stronger negotiating position when he was invited by the Haqqani Network to resume talks with the Pakistani government after the Taliban seized Kabul in August and had agreed to do so; he had in fact reportedly even formed an ad hoc delegation. However, these preparations collapsed when the Pakistani government decided to instead start talks with smaller Pakistani Taliban factions in late August. This included the Bahadur faction, the Nazir faction, the remnants of LI and remnants of fighters loyal to Maulana Qazi Fazlullah and Faqir Mohammed. Overall, therefore, the talks between Islamabad and Bahadur's little coalition of factions and groups did not really break much new ground. Faqir Mohammed and Nazir had reconciled with Islamabad years before. Bahadur also repeatedly reached ceasefires with Islamabad and so did Lashkar e Islam.[416]

Noor Wali Mehsud interpreted the talks as an attempt to weaken the TTP and ordered the intensification of military operations in Pakistan in retaliation. Noor Wali Mehsud appears to have been suspected an attempt to lure away some of the groups he had just reunited with into separate deals with Islamabad.[417] Islamabad's talks with Bahadur did not anyway make significant progress. All that the Pakistani government had to offer was amnesty and the release of prisoners, in exchange for disbandment and reintegration of the insurgent groups and their cutting links to any other insurgent group.[418]

In the last week of October, however, Noor Wali Mehsud also resumed talks with the Pakistani government. Noor Wali demanded that sharia should be implemented nationwide, that all militant Islamist prisoners be released and that the army be withdrawn from the tribal areas. In two weeks the two delegations were able to agree on a one-month ceasefire, in exchange apparently for the release of a number of TTP prisoners, according to Pakistani media.[419] Although Noor Wali had dropped the demand of a nationwide implementation of Shari'a during the 2020 talks, by 2021 he and the TTP leadership reportedly felt that the TTP's position had strengthened and his position shifted towards one of 'Shari'a in the tribal belt now, permanent ceasefire and long-term talks for a country-wide negotiations to follow'.[420] It is likely that various hardline groups having rejoined the TTP in the meanwhile, Noor Wali had to take their view into account as well.

During the negotiations, the TTP handed over to the authorities a list of 102 TTP detainees it wanted to get released, but the authorities refused to release them and instead released a number of other TTP detainees, mostly individuals who had undergone deradicalization programmes. The negotiations rapidly grew to a standstill and the ceasefire was not renewed. On 10 December 2021 the TTP resumed its military operations.[421] In the subsequent months, the TTP was able to exploit rising tensions between the Taliban's Emirate in Afghanistan and the Pakistani authorities, becoming the only Afghanistan-based organization allowed by the Emirate to carry out military operations against a neighbouring country. In the wake of the April 2022 Pakistani air strikes in Afghanistan, which killed tens of civilians, the TTP even started benefiting from a number of Taliban commanders offering weapons and training facilities.[422]

The TTP's trajectory

Baitullah Mehsud was very successful in mobilizing a mass of keen Pakistani Taliban in 2007. In Priestland's terms, he delivered the 'romantic' element of the revolutionary equation.[423] However, he failed in delivering the 'technocratic' element. He created an organization that was rather decentralized at the bottom, but quite centralized at the top – the amir was taking the important decisions, but then had limited ability to impose them throughout the structure. In particular, the amir and the shura of the TTP had the power to decide about war and peace, and to dispose of whatever cash accrued to the top leadership, whether through the local fund-raising system or grants from external supporters.

The TTP under Baitullah Mehsud's 'romantic' leadership decided not just to fight Islamabad, but also to do it with a highly confrontational approach. The TTP controlled vast stretches of the tribal areas and also some of the settled areas. It largely fought for territorial control until it was pushed out of all the areas but those most difficult to control for the army. In the meanwhile, it resorted to indiscriminate terrorist tactics, which proved controversial even within the TTP. Baitullah's decisions would have needed a cohesive organization in order to achieve success. If there was any doubt, the TTP proved that was not such an organization. There was therefore a clear mismatch between ends and means.

By 2019 the TTP had shed virtually all the elements who were not focused on the Pakistani jihad. At the same time, some policy options were by then foreclosed: there was no question anymore of confronting the Pakistani army for territorial control. By trial and error, the TTP leadership had been gradually shifting towards a more sustainable model of insurgency. Noor Wali Mehsud incarnated a less charismatic and less romantic leadership, endowed however with greater technocratic skills to complete the transition by enshrining a more 'confederative' model in the TTP code of conduct. The evolution was towards a more flexible organizational model, able to accommodate a certain variation of policy aims around a common platform of opposition to the Pakistani state. It seemed at that point the only way a small TTP core group, accounting for no more than 20–25 per cent of the TTP fighter strength, could still gather around itself the rest of the TTP factions.

The eventual resurgence of the TTP, while possibly influenced by AQIS, appeared likely to be of limited benefit to the followers of al Zawahiri in Afghanistan and Pakistan. The TTP was happy to receive funds and advice from AQIS, but its political line was still being decided autonomously. Noor Wali refused to sign an agreement with the Quetta Shura in 2020, in the wake of the US/Taliban agreement, but not out of loyalty to AQIS. Noor Wali was not willing to give up its campaign against the Pakistani state, which is what the Quetta Shura was demanding, but also refused to join the new jihadist alliance, taking shape around AQIS and IS-K, and sought to maintain decent relations with the Afghan Taliban.[424] The TTP's refusal to form the new alliance was a significant blow as its 3,000–4,000 men in Afghanistan would have given that alliance a major boost in eastern Afghanistan.

While at least the TTP did not edge close to IS-K, by 2020 its residual value for AQIS was limited to deterrence, in case the 'deep state' decided one day to turn on AQIS. This, despite Noor Wali's greater inclination than his predecessors to follow the AQ blueprint for reshaping the TTP into a more effective organization, highlights the very partial overlap of TTP's and AQ's interests.

Even when in late 2021 AQ were cutting off relations with the 'deep state' and the value of TTP to them was on the rise again, the interests of the two organizations were not entirely coincident. In late 2021 a new dispute emerged over the TTP's cooperation with Baluchi nationalists, which was reported in the press.[425] In public the TTP denied any cooperation was taking place, but one AQ source and a source in an international organization both confirmed that that was the case. According to the AQ source, *those Baluchis groups are involved in some kind of action, which are against Islam for example human trafficking and drug-trafficking. So, we requested the TTP to end their relations with the Baluchis groups because they are not fighting for Islam. But, the TTP is saying that at the moment we need the Baluch because they are against the government and in the same time the Baluchis are supporting the TTP as well.*[426]

Another possible area of divergence was the issue of negotiations with Islamabad. It is not completely clear how committed the TTP leadership ever was to a negotiated settlement, but as discussed above, negotiations were implicit in the TTP's new strategy of focusing on Khyber Pakhtunkhwa. Contrary to what had been the case then AQ had an agreement with the seep state (2019–21), AQ sources were adamant that AQ was no longer supporting any TTP-Islamabad deal and instead fiercely opposed it.[427]

4

The Sunni supremacists: Deviant allies of AQ

As already discussed above, 2001 was a turning point in the relationship between the jihadist groups and the Pakistani military establishment. The crisis in the relationship with the United States because of 9/11 and American intervention in Afghanistan pushed the Pakistani authorities to reduce their exposition in terms of involvement with jihadist groups and in 2002 to stage a crackdown against them. The relationship between AQ and the supremacists was also affected as a result and deepened in 2001–2, when many foreign militants were given safe haven by Punjabi militants.

The three main Sunni supremacist groups in Pakistan during the 1990s and the early twenty-first century have been SSP, LeJ and Jundullah. The origins of the SSP and LeJ were discussed in Chapter 1. Much less is known about the origins of Jundullah. Although a source put the date of formation of Jundullah as 1997, another source put its establishment at March 2003, at the hand of former JeI member Attar Rehman. In any case, the group only became known to the outside world in 2004, when it started claiming attacks in Pakistan. Militant sources put the number of members at the peak of Jundullah's power in 1997–2000 at 7,000–10,000, although the number seems wildly inflated and certainly does not refer the number of active insurgents. Hussain put the number of active terrorists at just twenty in 2004, organized in a single cell. In the early days Jundullah was collaborating closely with Iran's Jundullah, which was one of its main aims. Jundullah's leadership argued at that time that it did not oppose the Pakistani government. Jundullah maintained close relations with LeJ and SSP, from whose madrasa many of its members came. The main difference between Jundullah and the other Sunni supremacists was its Baluchi ethnicity.[1]

Jundullah became associated with TTP in 2009 when it chose Hakimullah Mehsud as its leader. The association ended when Hakimullah was killed. The killing of Hakimullah Mehsud had a strong demoralizing impact on the members and the organization remained leaderless for a full year. Fazlullah did not offer any support to Jundullah, which drifted away. Then its spokesman, Ahmad Marwaat, was appointed as leader, but he was reportedly an ineffective character, which did not manage to raise sufficient funding, leading to the terminal decline of Jundullah.[2]

The ambiguous SSP-LeJ relationship

SSP has not been carrying out any attacks in Pakistan for quite a few years now.[3] Nonetheless, as already hinted in Chapter 1, internal sources say that the SSP was still maintaining close relations with more radical groups, and in particular LeJ, which had split from it in 1996.[4] LeJ sources say the same, unanimously.[5] In fact several SSP and LeJ sources go even further than that and claim that SSP has been treating LeJ as its military wing.[6] The relationship is of course not openly acknowledged:

> *Officially we are not accepting that we are the military section of SSP, but indirectly and unofficially all Pakistan know that LeJ is the military wing of SSP.*[7]

One of the sources explained that

> *SSP members in Pakistan are aware of any military operations of LeJ and its splinter groups in Pakistan and have very close relations with all splinter groups of SSP and LeJ. [...] LeJ and its splinter groups and also the splinter groups of SSP are carrying the military plan of the SSP.*[8]

This does not mean that when LeJ split out of SSP in 1996 there weren't serious issues at stake. The hardliners had genuine differences with the other SSP leaders and that is why they decided to separate.[9] According to one SSP source,

> *There were some arguments between the leadership of the SSP regarding the reduction of violence against of the Shi'a community and against of the Pakistani government on that time. [...] Focusing on a political effort was not acceptable for some SSP leaders, that's why some of them, such as Riaz Basra, Malik Ishaq, Ghulam Rasoul and Akram Lahori, came together and made the militant faction LeJ. [...] For sure in the beginning there were some tensions between the LeJ and SSP, but very soon the tensions were over and [...] LeJ [...] was doing its military activities under the control of SSP leaders and this continues even now.*[10]

In reality, there is evidence that even after the reconciliation between the two groups, the policies of SSP and LeJ did not always align. For example, when in the summer of 2020 LeJ decided to sign an agreement with the Quetta Shura of the Taliban, committing to operate in Afghanistan under its authority, accepting to register its members with the Taliban and to abstain from carrying out operations against other states, the SSP objected:

> *LeJ consulted with SSP before signing deal with Taliban. However, SSP advised LeJ leaders to avoid any kind of a deal and agreement with the Quetta Shura. Still we signed an agreement with the Taliban and this really upset the SSP. At the same time, we have a good relationship with SSP and we do not take any action against each other.*[11]

While LeJ was drifting away from IS-K due to its bad experiences there and from AQ because of its inability to support LeJ adequately in Afghanistan, SSP was preserving its links with both of them. The difference is easily explained with the fact that LeJ needed safe haven in Afghanistan, while SSP did not, thanks to its legal status in Pakistan.[12]

The sectarian supremacists' role in AQ's strategy

As indicated already in Chapter 1, SSP had relations with AQ from the early days of the latter's existence. Initially the connection was 'weak', but

> *after 9/11 and when the Americans attacked Afghanistan, AQ focused more on Pakistani jihadist groups to save its members escaping from Afghanistan during the Americans bombing attacks. [...] The only way for AQ to protect their leaders and important commanders was to hide them inside Pakistan with the help of the jihadist groups.*[13]

Indeed, SSP members were caught by Pakistani police in AQ safehouses.[14] An SSP source described SSP and its militant splinters as 'one of the closest friends of AQ in Pakistan and in the entire region'.[15] This view is confirmed by another SSP member.[16] In 2008 Minister Malik stated that AQ used 'SSP, LeJ and Karachi-based Taliban groups to execute its agenda'.[17]

According to an internal source, AQ became so influential with SSP as to be able to select its most senior figures and to give orders.[18] SSP seemingly started being lured into a global jihadist path. Despite its original focus on Pakistani Shi'as, SSP soon started going global, or pretending to. It was pushed towards fighting against the 'foreign occupiers' by AQ and other jihadist groups. Then it started looking at carrying out attacks in 'the UAE, Europe, and other countries where the sinful activities are done'. It also started belatedly getting involved in Iran, supporting Baluchi rebels. Like LeJ, SSP reportedly had a scheme to recruit converts to Islam in Europe.[19] In 2016 an SSP source claimed that the organization had established a presence in Bangladesh, Iranian Baluchistan (supporting Baluchi rebels), in the UAE, in Europe and in Canada.[20]

It is not clear, however, to what extent these SSP activities outside Pakistan were genuine efforts, or phoney ones meant to accommodate AQ, which was a major source of funding. So far, there is no evidence of SSP being involved in any attack in Europe. If the SSP's commitment was phoney, AQ would have not taken too long to realize it. However, as in the case of the TTP's engagement with global jihad (see Chapter 3), this does not necessarily mean that AQ minders would be too upset. The fact that AQ kept supporting the SSP over the years, despite the lack of concrete global jihadist achievements, suggests that it did not. As in the case of the TTP, AQ's main reason for supporting the SSP was another one:

> *One of the main demands of AQ to SSP, in exchange for its support to SSP, was to give safe heaven to AQ members who escaped from American bombing in Afghanistan.*[21]

A secondary reason was obtaining SSP support for the Afghan Taliban's jihad. Getting SSP to engage in global jihad is likely to have ranked well below these two other rationales and perhaps AQ itself viewed its demands in this regard as a cover screen to justify ideologically the engagement, more than a serious need.

As for LeJ, like other Deobandi groups, LeJ too started seemingly harbouring global aspirations. At some point LeJ started sending members to Iran, with 210 already there, alongside SSP members to train Baluchi rebels.[22] According to Mir, there is little doubt that LeJ was attracted to global jihad.[23] A security analyst quoted by the ICG believed that LeJ had a key role in linking AQ, Taliban and sectarian groups

> ... because of its ability to exploit its network of mosques and madrasas in just about every district in Pakistan. [...] In all major terrorist attacks in Pakistan there is irrefutable evidence that the LeJ and SSP were used.[24]

Again, there is some objective evidence of AQ-LeJ relations. In February 2015, for example, ninety-seven militants of AQIS and LeJ were reportedly detained in Karachi.[25] LeJ is known to have trained a number of its members in AQ-linked training camps. Some of its leaders have also trained in such camps in Afghanistan.[26] This clearly suggests that, in the case of LeJ too, AQ expected to obtain protection in exchange for its support.

For years, AQ used to have a strong influence over LeJ and was even able to issue direct orders or to replace leaders.[27] In some ways, the AQ-LeJ relationship was even stronger than the AQ-SSP one: it is worth noting that while AQ had many non-core members from LeJ (about 400 in 2019), it had none from SSP. This is not surprising as AQ needed militants able to operate underground, which LeJ had and SSP had not. It is also worth noting that AQ retained its LeJ non-core members even after it cut off funding to the group in 2017.[28] This suggests that AQ intended to use LeJ not just for protection, as in the case of the SSP, but also for supporting its operations. AQ needed them to strengthen its own position in South Asia and SSP and LeJ collaborated with AQ in Afghanistan, India, Kashmir and Bangladesh.[29]

LeJ's core aim, however, remained to 'finish the Shi'a community or force it to leave the country or accept the Sunni Sharia Law'.[30] The group was not very active in recent years, but it did carry out occasional attacks against Shi'as, such as the August 2021 Bahawalnagar attack, which killed two and injured many more.[31] How did this square with AQ's proclaimed non-sectarian approach?

AQ and sectarian violence

Given AQ's condemnation of sectarian violence, its close relationship with Pakistan's sectarian jihadists appears indeed odd. An AQIS source claimed in 2020 that

> Nobody in our leadership and council is in favour of SSP's and LeJ's anti-Shi'ite violence. Our leaders have been often calling on SSP and LeJ to stop their violence

against the Shi'ite minority of Pakistan. Violence against Shi'ites is not Jihad. It's not allowed in our policy.[32]

One AQIS source attributed the insistence of AQ in criticizing the sectarian violence practices by SSP and LeJ to AQ's relationship with Iran:[33]

> We have good relations with Islamic Republic of Iran, therefore we are trying our best to convince SSP and LeJ leaders and members to refrain from any violence against Shi'as in Pakistan, in particular in Karachi.[34]

There were several rationales for maintaining close relations to both SSP and LeJ, even while they kept carrying out violent attacks against Shi'as in Pakistan. AQ considered that it might be possible to gradually draw the sectarian groups away from their violent campaign.[35]

> We have strong connections with these groups and actively worked to organize their ranks and change them to good jihadist groups in the region.[36]

The source assessed (from the vantage point of 2020) that SSP was quite responsive to AQ's coaching:

> As you may know, in recent times, we have seen significant reduction in sectarian violence in Pakistan. I know that there're demonstration and rallies against Shi'a but overall, we do not see any violence and attacks.[37]

Despite a long AQ-LeJ-SSP relationship, there was in 2016–17 a serious crisis between AQ and the two main Sunni supremacist organizations. This followed an escalation in sectarian violence from 2000 onwards, which AQ, under heavy Iranian pressure, tried to stem without success. The violence had been going on for fifteen years and was past its peak before the crisis exploded (see Figure 7), so it is questionable whether the crisis was caused by the violence. Indeed, there were more contingent reasons for AQ to cut relations at the point. As one AQIS source acknowledged, AQIS was upset that SSP and LeJ were edging closer to IS, and that both groups were refusing to cut relations with it. AQIS's ultimatum went unheeded and for a period AQ cut off relations with both groups. As LeJ allied with IS and even started participating in armed actions against AQIS, the latter decided to restore relations with SSP, in order to use it for influencing LeJ. Reportedly, even the Iranians approved of this move.[38]

An LeJ source indicated in late 2020 that

> the leadership of SSP is trying to convince AQ to make again its relation close with LeJ and do not cut off relations with LeJ because of its support for IS-P, because LeJ is supporting Wilayat Pakistan of Daesh only because both groups have same thoughts about the Shia Community and Iran regime.[39]

Figure 7 Sectarian violence in Pakistan.[40]
Sources: https://www.satp.org/type-of-attack/Sectarian-Violence/pakistan-2018; https://www.satp.org/type-of-attack/Sectarian-Violence/pakistan-2019 and https://www.satp.org/type-of-attack/Sectarian-Violence/pakistan-2020.

The delay in cutting relations with SSP and AQ might also be explained with the fact that AQ had been struggling with 'hundreds and thousands of donors in the Gulf States', who were 'keen to support anti Shi'a groups in Pakistan'. Relations with such donors turned sour 'when AQ leaders developed relations with the Islamic Republic of Iran'.[41]

Bin Laden and al Zawahiri were inclined to remain above the sectarian conflict, but supported sectarian groups nonetheless because of the situation they were in after 2001, in exchange for protection vis-à-vis the Pakistani state. Some AQ members were strongly anti-Shia, such as Khalid Sheikh Mohammad and Ramzi Yusuf, especially Kuwaiti-Pakistanis with support from anti-Shia sheikhs in Kuwait. Ramzi Yusuf was also linked to the Pakistani sectarian groups, like SSP.[42] In addition, given the general trend in the Gulf and in the Arab world towards sectarianism, many AQ recruits had indeed sectarian leanings. By 2006 AQ was fully cooperating in sectarian attacks by LeJ.[43]

The supremacists and the Pakistani authorities

The relationship with AQ was not cost-free for the sectarian supremacists. The SSP was the least exposed. Already in the late 1990s the SSP steered away from carrying out violent actions inside Pakistan and as such it was not affected by the 2002 crackdown, unleashed by Musharraf on a range of jihadist groups. That does not mean that relations between SSP and Islamabad have been altogether easy. SSP sources are not very positive about the relationship, which they describe as 'weak', 'not very good but also not very bad'. Poor relations with Musharraf and Bhutto were followed by good relations with Nawaz Sharif, whose electoral campaign it supported, and then by poor ones with Imran Khan, whom the SSP accused the authorities of 'supporting the Shi'a community'.[44]

Despite differences arising, the relationship between SSP and LeJ was close enough that it should have warranted the attention of law enforcement agencies. To make things worse, the SSP had relations with the TTP and AQ as well. While one source claimed that SSP and TTP had no relations,[45] other sources admitted that TTP (especially Noor Wali) and SSP entertained close connections. Reportedly SSP also maintained close relations with the IMU, another group not popular in Islamabad.⁴⁶ While a source attributed the difficult relationship with Islamabad to the SSP's relations with TTP and AQ, one would have expected the reaction of the authorities versus the SSP to be strong.⁴⁷

Instead, despite a temporary ban issued by Musharraf in 2002, the SSP managed to avoid being seriously targeted by Islamabad for a number of reasons. An important one was that permanently banning SSP and derivatives organization proved too hard due to its large mass base.⁴⁸

Another, related, reason is that it was quite influential politically and had vast networks, which led to its full rehabilitation by Nawaz Sharif after the latter returned to power in 2013. At one point, the SSP agreed with Nawaz that it would renounce violence.⁴⁹

*Nawaz Sharif during his tenure supported SSP a lot and the Punjab government also closed its eyes on several SSP attacks. The visit of Nawaz Sharif to the grave of SSP founder Haq Nawaz Jhangvi led to a closer relationship between SSP and Nawaz Sharif. When Nawaz Sharif became the prime minister of Pakistan for sure SSP stopped attacks against the government because SSP didn't want to compromise Nawaz Sharif's reputation.*⁵⁰

A third reason was that the SSP managed to make itself useful for the Pakistani authorities in Afghanistan, where it deployed the bulk of its armed force, and elsewhere. External estimates of the 'combat strength' of SSP ranged between 3,000 and 6,000 trained militants in 2005–8.⁵¹ Internal SSP sources estimated the organization to have tens of thousands of members and an active strength of SSP of 8,750 men in 2016, of which over 1,200 were deployed in Afghanistan.⁵² Reportedly Mullah Omar had been very close to the SSP leader. In 2020 the SSP still had 'hundreds of volunteers' with the Taliban and there was a 'good connection' between the two.⁵³ The initial evaluation of the US/Taliban deal by SSP was the same as AQ's:⁵⁴

*I think the signature of peace deal with the Americans is a victory of the Afghan Taliban against the Americans troops […]. The SSP will support the Afghan Taliban until they are fighting and as soon as the Taliban run an Islamic government in Afghanistan the SSP fighters will return to Pakistan.*⁵⁵

By the summer of that year, however, relations between SSP and Afghan Taliban started worsening fast as the SSP rejected several requests from the Taliban's Quetta Shura to reach an agreement over the SSP's presence on territory controlled by the Shura. The Quetta Shura wanted to register and exercise full control over the SSP militias, but the SSP refused and started pulling its men out of areas under the control of the Shura. The SSP seems to have been motivated by the new alliance of AQ and IS-K pulling it towards its orbit.⁵⁶ It is not clear what the attitude of the Pakistani deep state was towards this rift, but the SSP's service were hardly needed anymore by the Taliban at that point.

The SSP also deployed some volunteers to Kashmir, again ingratiating itself with the 'deep state'.[57] Its deployment to Kashmir took place in coordination with JeM, with which SSP maintained close relations thanks to the common roots in the JuI.[58]

Last but not least, SSP was also helped by its close relations with the Gulf states, especially Saudi Arabia, which remained the main financial supporters of SSP and LeJ throughout, alongside 'hundreds of Ahl e Sunnat madrasas and businessmen'.[59] The closeness of the Saudis to the Pakistani establishment (up to 2020) is likely to have translated into some tolerance for the SSP's bad frequentations.

LeJ was much more exposed than the SSP. All factions of LeJ have very poor relations with the Pakistani authorities and all aim for 'a Sunni kingdom and Sunni shari'a rule all over Pakistan', says a member.[60] In reality differences emerged among LeJ's factions about the relationship with Islamabad. With the arrival to power of Gen. Musharraf in 1999, the sectarian militants split between those willing to adopt a lower profile, and the hardliners. The majority of LeJ, led by Riaz Basra, decided to continue its terrorist campaign, while a minority led by Qari Abdul Hayye decided to stop the terror campaign.[61] Nowadays the LeJ(aA) faction incarnates the opposition to the Pakistani authorities, while there is still a group that has abandoned the struggle against Islamabad. However, an LeJ cadre indicated that the two main factions were working together under the same leadership and were both opposed by the Pakistani authorities. The leader of LeJ as of mid-2020 was Sayed Safdar Shah (aka Yousuf Mansoor Khurasani) from Punjab. He was in charge of both factions, which can therefore be said to have reunified. In practice for years LeJ(aA) has been the active faction, operating from bases in Punjab, on the Pakistan-Afghanistan border and in southern and northeast of Afghanistan, especially in Zabul Province in south of Afghanistan and Kunduz Province in northeast of Afghanistan.[62]

In reality, by 2017–18 LeJ had ceased carrying out any attacks against the Pakistani state. Reportedly the decision was communicated to the Pakistani authorities, although it is not clear whether there was any formal agreement.[63] The reunification of the al Alami and Hayye factions appears therefore to have taken place on the basis of an opposition to Islamabad in principle only, whereas in practice LeJ was observing a ceasefire. A LeJ commander confirmed:

> *we have got a notice to not attack the Sunni Government until our leadership order us. I don't think so, that this would be because of the mediation of AQ because as far as I hear the relation of AQ is also not good with LeJ since LeJ has been helping IS in Pakistan.*[64]

As in the case of so many other jihadist groups, LeJ(aA) gradually rehabilitated itself by accepting to contribute to the deep state's objectives in Afghanistan. Of the about 3,500 members claimed by all factions of LeJ in 2016, almost 600 were deployed to Afghanistan.[65] Another source estimated in mid-2020 that there were 1,000–1,500 active fighters in LeJ, implying that the Afghan deployment accounted for a large portion of these. Considering the regular rotation taking place, the armed strength of LeJ was largely absorbed by the Afghan jihad.[66] Another LeJ source provided in October 2020 similar figures, putting the number of LeJ members (after a new series of splits, which took away some 450 members) at 1,000–1,100, of which 300–400 in Pakistan and the rest in Afghanistan.[67] The only main attack of LeJ in Afghanistan was on the Ashura celebrations in 2011.[68] However, it fought extensively alongside the Taliban. LeJ established widespread cooperation programmes and still ran joint training camps with the Taliban in 2020, in Zabul, Uruzgan, Kandahar and Khost, despite no longer fighting side by side.[69]

As of 2020, LeJ's military HQ was reportedly in Khak i Afghan district of Zabul province.[70] Initially, like the TTP, LeJ moved into Afghanistan to seek a safe haven there. Contrary to the TTP, however, it never sought accommodation and ceasefire with the Afghan authorities. Instead, LeJ kept fighting alongside the Afghan Taliban throughout, and in particular the ISI-aligned Quetta Shura. In some cases at least, LeJ took part in operations where the ISI was heavily involved, such as the capture of Kunduz in 2015, a fact which suggests some coordination with the Pakistani ISI.[71]

On the negative side (as seen from Islamabad), LeJ(aA) always maintained a close relationship with TTP, even under Mufti Noor Wali.[72] LeJ fighters have been fighting alongside TTP in Afghanistan.[73] An LeJ source describes the TTP as being 'also against the Shi'a community and Sufism'. LeJ and TTP conducted several joint operations in Karachi, Baluchistan and on the Afghan border. Many LeJ members sought protection from the TTP.[74] As mentioned above, two small factions of LeJ even merged into the TTP. Relations remained good even after LeJ agreed to the term sought by the Quetta Shura of the Afghan Taliban, which included abstaining from attacks against the Pakistani state, and the TTP rejected them. According to an LeJ source, the TTP did not object to LeJ signing and kept offering support. Should the TTP be able to recapture significant territory inside Pakistan, stated the source, LeJ would be happy to relocate its forces there.[75] Overall, however, by 2017–18 LeJ seemed to have adopted an attitude towards the TTP that resembled AQ's, that is, to keep the TTP as a spare strategic option, while focusing instead on consolidating an understanding of the deep taste.

An LeJ source explained in 2020 that the organization lost interest in confronting the Pakistani state directly 'because of a lack of fighters' and focused on asymmetric attacks.[76] Although this source implied that the fight against the Pakistani state was not over, it provided a rationale for LeJ(aA)'s turn: simply it did not have the resources to fight the Pakistani state.

Inside Pakistan, LeJ had always focused on attacking Shi'as anyway. At the time of writing LeJ's latest attack in Pakistan was against the marketplace in Quetta, which killed many Hazaras (2019). An LeJ source explains the slow pace of attacks with the preference for large, high-profile strikes.[77] It has been repeated alleged that the Pakistani authorities have supported anti-Shi'a groups, or at least tolerated their activities.[78] The last attack unquestionably targeted at the Pakistani state was against the Punjab minister of interior in 2015, allegedly carried out in coordination with the TTP, in revenge for the killing of Malik Ishaq by the police.[79] The 2016 attack against the Baluchistan police training centre was presented by LeJ as aimed against the many Shi'as studying in that institution. As in the case of AQ, there appears to have been a transition from full confrontation towards cooperation, in which the two sides continued trading blows while negotiating and sometime cooperating. In the case of LeJ, the transition was around 2015–16.

LeJ moved one step closer to the deep state in 2021, when it accepted to fully mobilize its reserves in support of the Taliban's final campaign, eventually sending to Afghanistan almost 3,000 volunteers. As in many other cases discussed here, the relationship was opportunistic and in Pakistan LeJ continued to cooperate with IS-P and share training camps with it.[80]

The case of Jundullah remains much more obscure than either SSP's or LeJ's. What is known is that despite its closeness to TTP and LeJ, Jundullah had contacts with the deep state in its early years and again towards its end, when the deep state encouraged its members to join IS-P (see below).[81]

In sum, the Pakistani deep state tried to manage the Sunni supremacists, containing their violence inside Pakistan and turning them to purposes that fit into the deep state's strategy of covert operations northwards and eastwards. Although there might be multiple causes for the decline of sectarian violence in Pakistan, the deep state's efforts are likely to be one of the causes. The deep state turned the supremacists into clients of the Pakistani state, trading their services in covert operation in Afghanistan and Kashmir for protection and patronage. The deep state might have been even more successful, had it not been for the appearance of a new major actor on the supremacist scene in 2014, the Islamic State.

IS breaks AQ's monopoly

Enter IS-K

Among the Pakistani Sunni supremacist groups, IS-K established between 2014 and 2015 close relations with all three the main groups (SSP, LeJ and Jundullah). IS-K had the closest relations with LeJ and Jundullah. These two organizations and SSP all started negotiating with IS-K soon after it appeared in Pakistan. The leadership of LeJ reportedly met senior IS figures in Saudi Arabia.[82]

Reportedly, the Arab donors to SSP were encouraging SSP members to switch to IS-K, offering in exchange extra funds. Individual members of SSP were also being attracted by the financial offers made by IS-K, which at that time was considerably wealthier than SSP.[83]

SSP lost almost 400 people to IS up to April 2016, about half of which were volunteers who had gone to Syria and Iraq.[84] But as a SSP member noted, SSP being much bigger in terms of membership than IS-P, the idea of merging into it was never seriously considered.[85] But as an SSP member noted, SSP being much bigger in terms of membership than IS-P, the idea of merging into it was never seriously considered.[86] The SSP also wanted to safeguard its legal operations.[87]

The attitude of SSP appears to have been quite opportunistic. SSP tried to maintain good relations with both global jihad organizations. An SSP source claimed in 2016 that his organization had good relations with AQ and IS-K, as well as LeT, IMU, JeM and Afghan Taliban.[88] In their discussions with AQ, SSP leaders were denying having close relations with LeJ, after the latter had got very close to IS-K, although this was quite an open secret.[89]

SSP reaped financial benefits from this two-pronged approach. An SSP source put the organization's budget at $85 million in 2016, at which point both AQ and IS were contributing funds, as well as some Arab sheikhs. In 2015 the budget had been put at $65 million by the source, which implies an increase of $20 million in a single year.[90] AQ's irritation at the SSP's double game appears to have undermined this SSP policy: in 2017 an AQIS source put at $5 million the support AQIS was providing to SSP, which is likely to have represented a serious drop.[91]

As AQ tightened its leash, SSP shifted towards a policy of indirectly supporting IS and encouraging LeJ to collaborate with IS in its place.[92] As one SSP member commented:

IS-K conducted several joint operations against of Shi'a Community in Punjab and Baluchistan with LeJ and of course it was consulted first with SSP.[93]

In this way, SSP managed to remain close to AQ and was still sharing some training centres with it in Pakistan and Afghanistan in 2020.[94] Any faith the leaders of SSP might have had in the future of IS-K was at least temporarily shaken by the string of defeats it suffered in Afghanistan between November 2019 and March 2020. For a period, possibly due to the dislocation caused by those defeats (the leadership of IS-K had to relocate and much of it was captured), even communication between SSP and IS-K was suspended.[95] By mid-2020 some optimism was emerging within SSP that IS-K would recover from its defeats in eastern Afghanistan.[96]

The case of LeJ was different, as it edged much closer to IS-K than SSP. AQ was reportedly greatly disappointed by this. One account has it that LeJ's close relationship with AQ weakened after Maleek Ishaq and Ghulam Rasoul were killed by Pakistani police in Muzafargar. Maleek Ishaq was the liaison between the two organizations and moreover at that time LeJ was also beginning to get close to IS-K. Another account, however, claims that both Maleek Ishaq's and Ghulam Rasool's factions were already negotiating with IS-K before their death.[97] It seems more likely that the shared sectarian agenda and determination to rely on violence provided a strong rationale for IS and LeJ getting closer.

Al Baghdadi himself reportedly had direct, close relations with LeJ, which he then started funding.[98] In fact, the attraction of IS-K towards LeJ impacted on a fraying organization. When Riaz Basra was killed by the Pakistan police attack in 2002, Akram Lahori took the leadership, but immediately he was arrested by the Police of Pakistan in the same year. Maleek Ishaq, LeJ's number 2, became the acting chief.[99] The repression drove LeJ deeper and deeper underground, making coordination between the different units harder and harder. Units and cells started operating more and more autonomously and LeJ became factionalized. A source portrays the splits of LeJ as pre-planned, in order for LeJ to 'have better operation and better activities against the Shi'as community and the Pakistan government'.[100] Another source maintains that the different LeJ factions never fought each other and 'are unity, operating under one formula'.[101] In reality, given that the factions were regionally based and deep underground, the chances of clashing were negligible anyway. By 2020 LeJ sources had counted at least fourteen factions (see Figure 8):

- LeJ (aA), led by Yousof Mansoor Khurasani, and currently responsible for most of its military activities; Yousof Mansoor Khurasani took the leadership after Malik Ishaq was killed by Pakistani Police.
- Qari Abdul Hayye faction, formed in 1999 as Hayye argued in favour of suspending the terror campaign; later reunified with LeJ(aA).
- Akram Lahori Group led by Akram Lahori, who was released from jail in 2011, but again arrested years later and still in jail currently, with a death sentence pending. This faction is no longer active militarily, but negotiated merger with IS in 2015 (even if Akram was in jail).
- The Asif Chotu faction, which disbanded and merged into the Al Alami faction when Chotu was killed by the police in 2017.
- The Naeem Bokhari Faction, led by Naeem Bokhari, was an important member of LeJ, and closely linked to AQ. This faction lost importance after Bokhari's arrest.
- The Farooq Bengali faction, currently active in Karachi.
- Riaz Basra Group, led by Moulavi Mohammad Wasi Lahori and Qari Ikramuddin.
- The Qari Zafar Faction, also closely linked to AQ, joined the TTP after Zafar was killed in a US drone strike.
- Maleek Ishaq Group, led by Qari Osman Ishaq and Qari Haq Nawaz Ishaq. This group reportedly merged into IS-K before Maleek's death in July 2015, although one AQIS source claimed in 2020 that the faction still existed and was aligned with AQIS.
- Ghulam Rasool Shah Group, led by Ghulam Rasool Shah. This group was negotiating negotiated merger with IS in 2015 and apparently continued to do so after Ghulam Rasool's death in July 2015.
- Qari Mohammad Islam faction, as of 2020 still aligned with AQ.
- Wasim Lahori group, which split from LeJ(aA) in 2020 with some 100 members, over the latter's decision to sign a deal with the Quetta Shura of the Taliban and cut off links to IS-K and AQIS.
- The Usman Afridi group, which also split from LeJ(aA) in 2020 with some 150 members for the same reasons as above.
- The group of Sheikh al Hadis Mukhtar Lahori, which as the two groups above also split from LeJ(aA) in 2020 with perhaps 200 members, for the same reasons.[102]

One SSP source indicated that even the Asian Tigers, mostly active in Punjab, part of the Punjabi Taliban and Jundullah (active in Baluchistan and Karachi) are also splinters of LeJ.[103] Except for LeJ(aA), which has hundreds of members, none of the other (active) factions had more than thirty to forty members as of 2020. LeJ(aA) accounted in 2020 for 85–90 per cent of all LeJ activities.[104]

It is far from obvious that this was a case of planned decentralization, rather than a disintegration, given that the different factions took different paths. The arrival of IS-K accelerated the process. As it can be noted, the sources suggested that there might have been at least one policy or ideological difference driving the different factions

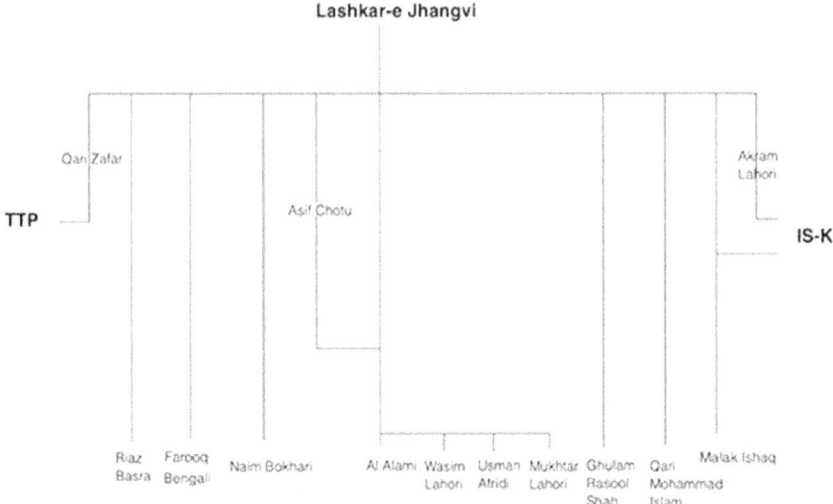

Figure 8 The factionalization of LeJ.
Sources: see text above.

apart, namely the relationship with IS-K and TTP. Three factions (Ghulam Rasool Shah's, Maleek Ishaq's and Akram Lahori's) negotiated a merger into IS-K, and one actually did merge into it (Maleek Ishaq's). Another faction merged into TTP (Qari Zafar's). The argument in favour of a disintegration is also supported by the fact that, as admitted by a source in LeJ, the smaller factions of LeJ reportedly do not maintain close relations with SSP and became criminalized, relying on the kidnapping of businessmen for funding.[105] According to a senior IS-K commander, negotiations over a merger of LeJ(aA) stalled during 2016, as Arab Gulf donors reportedly warned IS-K that they would retaliate if a merger took place and crack down on IS-K activities.[106]

At the end of its alliance with AQ in 2016, according to an AQ source LeJ had a $55 million budget and most of it had been donated by AQ and IS-K. Most of the rest came from some Arab donors.[107] As LeJ(aA) edged closer to IS-K, AQIS cut the funding to it. By 2017 AQIS support had ended.[108] LeJ(aA) did not cut ties to AQIS altogether and tried to remain in good terms with it, but could not avoid AQIS' punishment.[109] Only the remnants of the factions of Naeem Bukhari and Farooq remained completely aligned with AQ.[110]

As of 2020, the Arab donors to LeJ allegedly included the government of Saudi Arabia and UAE, although the latter wavered in its support due to LeJ's agreement with the Quetta Shura in August 2020, while the Saudis endorsed it. The Saudis clearly approved of LeJ's growing distance from AQ and of its friendship with IS. LeJ also allegedly received offers from Qatar to join IS-K in exchange for funding, but rejected those, probably as they would have been incompatible with Saudi support.[111]

LeJ's drift towards IS-K was thus really a function of its anti-Shi'ism and probably of financial incentives from the Gulf, motivated by either hostility to AQ or sympathy for IS.[112] The hatred for Shi'as was the main common ground between LeT and IS-K, but the latter also tried to turn LeJ into a more coherently 'global jihadist' group, advocating operations against the Afghani and Pakistani authorities, and against Europe, Iran and Central Asia. According to one source, as of 2016 LeJ (Lahori) had already started sending members to Europe, in order to build a base there. The source claimed that up to then 110 members had been sent to European countries, mixed among the refugees flowing in that direction. LeJ was also recruiting members in Europe, especially converts to Islam, some of whom allegedly had already been to Pakistan for training in bomb making. Sources claim that LeJ also sent volunteers to Syria and Iraq and Central Asia, and was able to expand recruitment thanks to the subsidies provided by IS-K.[113] However, as in the case of SSP discussed above, given the lack of evidence of any link of LeJ to attacks in Europe and any confirmation of a presence in Central Asia, one suspects that these efforts might have been phoney ones to a large extent, or that they might have been aimed at LeJ's own benefit (recruitment, fund raising), rather than at benefiting global jihad.

Apart from LeJ (aA), LeJ (Lahori) and LeJ (Rasool) being allied to IS-K, there was also an outflow of members towards IS-K, including the already mentioned merger of the LeJ (Ishaq) faction, but also a number of individuals voting with their legs. One LeJ source put the total number of those switching to IS-K at 410 as of February 2016. Many at the point believed that the entire LeJ would end up joining IS-K, something some LeJ factions had at that point been negotiating over for two years.[114] Seven months later a source in IS-K put at 200 the ex-LeJ members active in his organization.[115] Four years later, a source in LeJ put the number at 150.[116] This discrepancies could be due to combat losses, but also to desertions; IS-K was taking high casualties in Afghanistan at that time and many Pakistani IS-K members returned to their home organizations.[117] For example, after the Nangarhar defeat some former LeJ members rejoined LeJ.[118]

LeJ sent hundreds of fighters to fight alongside IS-K in Nangarhar and Zabul. In Pakistan LeJ and IS-K launched some attacks together, such as the Quetta Attack on the Shi'ite community, the attack in Parachinar and others.[119] Although LeJ(aA) extensively cooperates with IS-K against Shi'a targets in Pakistan, it never announced officially its support for it and according to one of its commanders it never cooperated with it in activities against the Afghan government, the Pakistani government or against the Afghan Taliban.[120] This is however a question of interpretations. Another LeJ source admitted that LeJ carried out the attack against the Quetta police training centre in 2016 in cooperation with IS-K, but asserted that the attack should not be considered as aimed against the Pakistani state as the target were the mainly Shi'a students attending the centre.[121]

The fact that IS-K's attacks were usually jointly claimed attacks suggest IS-K was dependent on other groups and especially LeJ(aA).[122] The LeJ (aA)'s spokesperson did claim in 2016 that all its attacks were taking place in cooperation with IS-K.[123]

The relationship between LeJ(aA) and IS-K was damaged by the November 2019 defeat and for several months there was no contact between the two organizations. Still it took some time for the feeling that IS-K was in decline to sink in. LeJ members were looking forward to resuming cooperation in the future.[124] One of the sources even stressed that the alliance with IS-K was still going unquestioned in LeJ and there was faith that IS-K would stage a comeback. This despite LeJ having taken serious casualties while fighting alongside IS-K.[125]

LeJ sources noted however that after the defeats in Afghanistan, the activities of IS-K in Pakistan were reduced.[126] Most importantly, IS-K was soon forced to cut funding to LeJ. By the summer of 2020 the attitude of LeJ finally shifted, as relations with IS-K indeed deteriorated and LeJ opted to align with the Quetta Shura of the Taliban despite the US/Taliban agreement, which not only IS but AQIS too bitterly resisted. The agreement, signed in August 2020, entailed cutting all links of LeJ units in Afghanistan to global jihad. Although LeJ had sought to maintain friendly relations with AQIS, the latter's intensifying relations with the IRGC and with Pakistani intelligence aroused LeJ's hostility. The fact that the Taliban's Quetta Shura, by contrast, was at the same time drifting away from the IRGC and closer to the Saudi monarchy appeared to offer LeJ a better option.[127]

Despite the ideological attraction exercised by IS on LeJ, noted above, the latter's commitment to global jihad proved in the end negotiable.

Enter IS-P

Relations between SSP and IS were resumed in the summer of 2020, as the new branch of IS in Pakistan, IS-P, approached the leaders of SSP. SSP welcomed the establishment of IS-P. The sense among common members and cadres was that SSP was going to cooperate with them.[128] An SSP source expected the organization to establish close relations with IS-P as

> SSP has good relation and supporting all those jihadist groups and movements, which are against of the Shi'as in Pakistan and in the world.[129]

According to another source that there were 'several meetings' between SSP and LeJ and IS-P and IS-Central, all centred about the provision of direct support.[130] In the end, SSP managed to find a point of equilibrium between IS and AQ. SSP members believed that if SSP intensified relations with IS-P, AQ would again object.[131] A source indicated that SSP had decided to 'indirectly' support IS-P.[132] That meant that SSP only intended to support IS-P through its encouragement of LeJ, even if IS-P asked SSP to send madrasa students to its ranks.[133]

Surely AQ must have been aware of SSP's relationship with IS. An AQIS source claimed in July 2020, rather optimistically, that SSP had already cut relations with IS by then and was fully back in AQIS' orbit.[134] But the SSP had said so earlier: AQ was clearly closing one eye and perhaps even two. The rationale for AQ's persistence in maintaining close relations with SSP, despite its ongoing alliance with IS-K, was according to an internal SSP source that

> SSP is one the number one Sunni political party in Pakistan that has hundreds of offices in different provinces of Pakistan and runs hundreds of Sunni Madrasas. That's why AQ considers the political base and military base of SSP in Pakistan and kept a very good relations with SSP.[135]

In other words, SSP provided some political backing for AQ and its wide networks could always be useful offering protection to AQ members in much of Pakistan – no other jihadist group could offer anything comparable.

The fine balancing act staged by the SSP was not replicated by LeJ. While (as discussed above) LeJ in Afghanistan made a deal with the Taliban, which cut off all global jihadists, as far as Pakistan itself was concerned the crisis of IS-K prompted LeJ to approach AQIS in 2020, seeking to re-establish relations, as a result of the faltering star of IS, presumably hoping of receiving funding again. Negotiations were in progress in mid-2020.[136]

At that point AQ appeared optimistic that IS was condemned to marginalization in Pakistan. An AQIS source was dismissive of IS' chances of recovering ground and of gathering all the Sunni supremacists around itself.[137]

> *They're not in position to do this since they have lost almost everything. They do not have the operational capabilities that are necessary for encouraging other groups to join them. At this time, none of these groups like LeJ, SSP, Jundullah are interested in working with IS since they know that IT cannot provide them with funding and other support. Each group is now trying to limit their relationship with IS. We are also working hard to stay close to these groups and prevent them making any further agreement with Daesh.*[138]

However, AQ was aware that LeJ's links to IS had not been completely severed. To the extent that there is still sectarian violence, argues the source, it is because some SSP and LeJ commanders have links to IS. The source claimed that AQ was working to stop even these commanders from continuing in the violent campaign.[139]

In the end, it turned out that AQ dramatically underestimated the residual attraction of IS over LeJ, which ended up opting for IS again, this time its IS-P branch. As of July 2020, one of the LeJ sources did not know of any contact between IS-P and LeJ yet, contrary to what was the case of SSP sources (see above). 'We only heard rumours about it', said the source.[140] Some months later, however, two other LeJ sources were well informed about a series of LeJ/IS-P meetings, which led to a cooperation agreement in Pakistan. LeJ agreed to share its Pakistani bases and training centres (where only non-military training was imparted) with IS-P and even contribute members, weapons and ammunition to IS-P at some point in the future. The understanding was that the enemy was Pakistan's Shi'as, not the Pakistani state.[141] As mentioned above, AQ's ties to Iran were certainly a factor in this choice.

Cutting off links to global jihad in Afghanistan and aligning again with IS in Pakistan does appear rather odd, even if an LeJ source did not see any contradiction between the agreement with the Quetta Shura and the agreement reached shortly later with IS-P.[142] This suggests a considerable degree of opportunism in LeJ(aA)'s attitude. In this, LeJ and SSP did not differ that much.

The impact of the appearance of IS in Pakistan on Jundullah was even greater than on LeJ. Although the Pakistani security forces were reported in 2021 to be worried about IS recruitment among the Brahui/Baluch population, in fact the attraction of IS was felt in Baluchistan from the beginning.[143] The LeJ branch in Baluchistan was strongly attracted to IS-K, and LeJ's operational commander for Baluchistan, Saifullah Kurd, reportedly became IS-K's amir for Baluchistan in the early stages of IS-K implantation there. IS reportedly had early connections with another minor Baluchi jihadist group, Lashkar e Khorasan.[144] Already affected by defections to LeJ, Jundullah started drying out with the emergence of IS-K. Most members joined IS-K, while others just quit and return to a civilian life.[145] By 2013–14, Jundullah only had 200–300 active members. Initially Jundullah hesitated in fully embracing IS-K, because while the latter had a ban on smuggling, Jundullah was very much closely connected with the smuggling world. Then IS-K lifted its ban and the main obstacle to Jundullah's members joining was removed.[146] In August 2016 Jundullah suffered a final blow when the bulk of the remaining members followed an IS-K-sponsored merger with the Iranian Jundullah. The focus of the new organization shifted towards Iran.[147] The few members left and some of those who had quit were later drawn towards IS-K and IS-P. By end 2020 all was left was some circles of sympathizers, without any military activity. Its last significant attack was in 2014.[148]

AQ had had close relations with Jundullah in its early years, then abandoned it once it edged closer to IS. AQ reportedly tried to reactivate Jundullah in 2020, exploiting the crisis of IS-K.[149] As of late 2020, there was no sign that this was being successful.

By 2020 Jundullah had contributed much to the development of an embryonic autonomous fighting capability of IS-K first and IS-P later in Pakistan. As of mid-2020, IS-P has 'tens' of highly qualified cadres, with IT skills and university degrees and are mostly busy in the propaganda field. Among them were non-Pakistanis such as Tajiks, Chechens, Indian Muslims and Bangladeshis, and a few Chechen trainers. The lowest layers are composed of 'hundreds' of Ahl e Sunnat sympathizers and 'many' Ahl e Sunnat Madrasas, which provide day-by-day support. But its fighting wing was still only 16 mobile combat groups of 15–20 men each, with 200–250 fighters in total, most of which were former Jundullah members in Baluchistan, with the rest (including some Tajiks and Indian Muslims) in KP and a very small number in Azad Kashmir.[150] Pakistani government sources confirmed the presence of IS-P elements in the hills surrounding Quetta, even if the put the number in the tens rather than in the hundreds.[151]

The total membership of IS-P in mid-2020 is not known. By the end of 2021, IS-P sources were reporting a total membership of some 6,700, of which 5,000 were deemed to be combat capable. Of the 6,700, some 400 were Arabs and Turks, at least 60 Europeans, plus some Central Asians. Of the about 6,000 Pakistanis, some 2,300/2,400 were Pashtuns and a slightly lower number Punjabis and Sindhis. The number of Baluchis was relatively small in comparison, despite efforts to attract them as discussed above, as there were only some hundreds of them. It is clear that the majority of the 5,000 claimed to be combat capable were not active and substantial proportion of them appears to have been concentrated in some tribal areas, such as Tira, Momand and the two Waziristans, but with a significant presence in Peshawar, Lahore and in Karachi too. Some appear to have taken refuge there from Afghanistan, and others to be reserves and training elements. There was some overlap between IS-P and IS-K claims concerning membership. Source admits that members of IS-P and IS-K in the tribal areas constantly move between the two groups. This probably resulted in some double-counting, implying that the actual number of IS-P members operating under its orders at any given time might in fact be lower than what claimed above, assuming the figures provided were genuine in the first place.[152]

The place of the supremacists in the strategy of IS

IS brought to Pakistan its tested strategy of kick-starting a sectarian conflict as one of the pillars of its strategy, as it would create a large social constituency for itself (among the Sunni population) and embed it in the social fabric of the region for the long term. The relatively long history of sectarian conflict made Pakistan look promising from this perspective. IS-K invested relatively limited resources on sectarianism in Pakistan in 2015–19, as its focus was on Afghanistan.

That was seemingly meant to change with the establishment of IS-P, which according to internal sources intended to attract the different supremacist groups into a single home, so that their aim could finally be realized:

> *Sunnis should rule the country and Shi'a community should either change their religion to Sunnism and accept the real Shari'a or leave Pakistan, lest we carry out attacks and kill them.*[153]

Still, despite a renewed alliance with LeJ, IS-P had not taken off as of end 2020. IS-P started recruiting among Pashtuns in KP and Pashtuns and Baluchis in Baluchistan, then also Punjabis, exploiting Sunni-Shi'a tensions, and Kashmiris.[154] The number of recruits appears to have been modest. The IS central leadership was reportedly negotiating the appointment to the position IS-P governor with various jihadist leaders in Pakistan, in the hope of attracting a leader with a significant following, who could boost the ranks of IS-P. According to a source in SSP, IS-P was talking to 'many influential extremist Sunni leaders in Pakistan to take the leadership of IS-P'.

> *There have been several contacts between the SSP leaders and IS-P and IS leadership in Syria and Iraq, [...] maybe one of the issues of the talks was debating over the leadership of IS-P.*[155]

Most candidates were from the TTP ranks, 'senior leaders unhappy with Noor Wali'.[156] As attracting TTP figures proved harder than expected, IS-P was reportedly considering former TTP and former IS-K commander Sayid Khan.[157] Another name that was mentioned was Yusuf Mansur Khorasani, leader of LeJ.[158] As of end 2021, the decision had not been take yet and Daud Meshud remained in charge as interim governor.

The impact of IS on the relationship of AQ with the Sunni supremacists highlights how SSP, LeJ and Jundullah were primarily clients of AQ. Some aspects of the relationship hint at elements of an alliance, especially the participation of SSP and LeJ in the post-2001 Afghan jihad. But, by and large, SSP, LeJ and Jundullah followed the patronage trail. They tried to milk both IS and AQ for as long as possible, and did as little as possible for the cause of global jihad.

5

Global jihad and the Kashmiri jihad: Co-opting or being co-opted?

The Pakistani state and the 2002 crisis

Year 2001 was also a turning point in the relationship between the jihadist groups active in Kashmir and the Pakistani military establishment. The crisis in the relationship with the United States because of 9/11 and American intervention in Afghanistan pushed the Pakistani authorities to reduce their exposition in terms of involvement with jihadist groups even in Kashmir. From May 2002 onwards the Kashmir operation was put in near freeze, leaving idle thousands of members of Pakistani jihadist groups, of which the main ones were LeT, JeM and HuM. Although the ban on the jihadist groups was weakly implemented, and all were able to continue their activities with some caution, immediately allegations started that Musharraf had betrayed the cause of Kashmir as well, having just betrayed the Afghan Taliban.[1]

The jihadist groups were in a state of panic. According to HuM sources, at that time their contacts in the Pakistani state apparatus were saying that the Americans would put pressure on Pakistan to do to them what United States had done to Afghan Taliban (see also Chapter 2).[2]

The near suspension of the Kashmiri jihad left many members of these organizations unhappy, especially as the freeze turned out not to be short term. Their unhappiness was widely believed to be linked to an increase in terrorist violence inside Pakistan itself, with attacks on Christians, Shi'as and foreigners. As a result, Musharraf tried to appease the jihadist by letting them loose in Afghanistan and by allowing a small-scale resumption of operations even in Kashmir, from the end of 2002.[3]

Some influence of AQ on the Kashmiri jihad had been there from the start (see Chapter 1). During the 1980s and the early 1990s, the ISI had arranged for Kashmiri militants and their Pakistani supporters to be trained in camps in Afghanistan, alongside foreign volunteers who had come to take part in the Jihad against the Soviets.[4] Bonds of friendship and common cause were formed among those training together. From early 2002 onwards, whenever a raid has been conducted in Pakistan against a safehouse, AQ members were found being hosted by militant Pakistanis, primarily from LeT or JeM groups, supporters of the Kashmiri insurgency.[5]

HuM and JeM in disgrace

The leadership of HuM signed a decree in support of 'AQ's ideology', inviting to fight the Americans in Afghanistan and to 'kill the unbelievers and Jews in Pakistan and Afghanistan'. As a result, the relationship between HuM and Pakistani authorities worsened.[6] HuM's leader was detained, reportedly because of the links to AQ, even if he was soon released.[7] The leadership of HuM nearly disintegrated. Of the main leaders, Massud Azhar formed JeM and Asim Umar joined AQ. Farooq Kashmiri entered politics and so did Fazul Rahman Khalil, even if they continued being the top HuM leaders.[8]

One HuM source agreed that the Pakistani authorities might have gradually reduced their support for HuM by virtue of the latter's excessively close and excessively relationship with AQ, but he also gave another reason: the greater effectiveness of JeM had already led to a shift in resource allocation before the Americans got into Afghanistan, so the crackdown was seen as the continuation of a pattern.[9]

In this context it is not surprising that some HuM elements went rogue. Some of them were involved in an attempt on Musharraf's life.[10] The Pakistani authorities nonetheless tried to keep HuM on board and imposed splitting the US-blacklisted Harakat ul Ansar back into separate HuJI and HuM groups (HuJi was rather marginal at this point).[11] The two groups were then rebranded as Ansal ul Umma and Jamiat ul Ansar, as a cover for continuing operations, albeit initially at a dramatically reduced pace.[12]

Although HuM cadres and leaders might have been convinced that the authorities were favouring JeM, the competing group has its own share of trouble post-2001. In the aftermath of Pakistan's cooperation with the Americans in bringing down the Islamic Emirate in Afghanistan, the JeM leadership struggled to maintain control over its commanders, many of whom had established close relations with AQ and Taliban. JeM always incorporated non-Pakistanis among its members, such as Chechens, Arabs, Somalis, Central Asians and Europeans, and was present in some form in Central Asia and some European countries. A member described JeM as 'an international organization'.[13] From its early days the group made global jihadist statements, invoking the destruction of India, Israel and the United States.[14]

When Musharraf tried to restrain the militants in Kashmir in 2001–2, 'a faction of JeM members decided to act in a more defiant fashion that would bring India and Pakistan to the brink of war'. The attack on the Indian parliament in December 2001 was reportedly not sanctioned by Musharraf. As India and Pakistan came close to war in the following weeks, Musharraf was forced to show Washington that he was bringing the Kashmir- and India-focused groups under control. JeM and LeT were banned, while Azhar was detained. Again, the ban was not strictly implemented and the two groups resumed activities promptly under new names, and Azhar was released. But Azhar was losing control of JeM and the majority of JeM's Supreme Council (seven out of ten) demanded his resignation, accusing him of deviating from the path of jihad. The leader of the JeM opposition to Islamabad was Maulana Abdul Jabbar, who started a campaign of terrorist attacks in Pakistan, targeting Westerners, Christians and Shi'as and then against Pakistani state officials as well, allegedly with AQ support. Elements of LeT were also involved, but the biggest chunk of dissident militants was from JeM. By late 2002 Jabbar had formed Jama'at ul Furqaan as a faction in JeM. Then a JeM dissident was involved in a failed assassination attempt against Musharraf.[15] Amjad Farooqi, one the leaders of JeM and reputedly the main link to AQ, was believed to be behind the assassination attempt.[16]

Azhar was indirectly implicated for having called in public for Musharraf's assassination, but was not caught in the repression and then focused on rebuilding his organization, keeping a low profile. Other dissidents who split from JeM with their factions were Gul Hassan and Asmatullah Mauviya.[17] JeM's dissidence stemmed in part from its sectarian leanings. It was involved in sectarian violence and attracted many SSP militants.[18]

Although the crackdown was rather superficially implemented, HuM and JeM were effectively absent from the Kashmir scene for years after the crackdown. The only main jihadist group that was allowed to remain active in Kashmir was LeT.

LeT weathers the 2001 storm

LeT too was targeted in a ban by the Pakistani authorities in 2002 after the attack against the Indian parliament. This ban was recognized as merely cosmetic not only by the Indians, but also by the Americans.[19] The ICG later assessed that LeT coped with the crisis thanks to 'significant support within some bureaucratic circles, and in segments of the civilian police'.[20] LeT was thus able to escape the 2002 ban and to continue its activities, albeit at a reduced level.[21]

Still, according to Kapur, 'many of LeT's members were deeply unhappy about Pakistani support for US policies'.[22] Sources within LeT denied any tendencies hostile to the Pakistani authorities within the organization.

> *Pakistan has an Islamic government, they always supported Islamic Jihadi organizations such as Lashkar e Taiba, Al Qaida, IMU, Islamic Mujahideen, [...] but we must do Jihad in Afghanistan, there are Americans and Westerns, we must do jihad in India to free Muslims from them, we must do jihad in Bangladesh because they are killing Ulema there, we must do jihad in America and Central Asia. So, we can say that Jihad is not duty in Pakistan. If anyone from LeT had been saying that jihad is duty in Pakistan, we would submit him to the Pakistani authorities.*[23]

However, LeT does not appear to have been completely immune from the lure of jihad in Pakistan. Some small groups splintered off and joined jihadist groups opposed to the Pakistan state. These internal tensions, with many militants increasingly disillusioned, reportedly led to the Mumbai strike of 2008, a spectacular attack meant to keep the hardliners in.[24] Several internal crises of varying intensity have been reported. After 9/11 there were divisions over the role of Pakistan in supporting US intervention in Afghanistan and whether jihad was now justifiable in Pakistan. LeT remained loyal, even if it dodged some of the rules imposed by Musharraf, such as not allowing foreign trainees in its camps.[25] In 2007, while the Lal Masjid crisis was at its peak, *a sizeable faction inside Lashkar [...] argued that the outfit should dump its ISI paymasters, join forces with al Qa'ida and shift its theatre of activity from fighting Indian forces in Kashmir to launching attacks against coalition forces in Afghanistan.*[26]

The leadership 'had serious problems in holding Lashkar together and convincing the outfit to fight for Kashmir' and 'worried that if Lashkar spurned the military, it would lose its ISI shield and come under attack from all sides.'[27] Although LeT Hafiz Saeed kept aloof of sectarian killings,[28] there was also a fraction of LeT that harboured hostility towards Shi'as, including senior figures such as Abdul Wahab, Sheikh Waqas, Maulana Farooq Ibrahim, Sheikh Al Hadiths Naveed Jamal, Maulana Ghulam Qadir, Maulana Mohammad Afzal and Sheikh Ahmad Noor Khan.[29]

Mir reports a split in LeT over the decision of Hafiz Saeed to separate LeT from JuD. Lakhvi quit and formed Khairun Naas.[30] Originally however Mir had interpreted the split as a mere attempt to elude the ban.[31]

LeT as whole also 'worked with militant organizations whose interests diverged sharply from those of Pakistan'; 'At times, this amounted to de facto efforts to undermine Pakistani policies'.[32] Reportedly there is evidence of close LeT/AQ ties, and of the ISI turning a blind eye on them, 'as long as [LeT] remains operationally India-focused'.[33] In mid-2003 Hafiz Saeed himself reportedly accused Musharraf of having become 'the biggest enemy of jihad', and wished to see him 'out of the picture'.[34]

LeT in the end still weathered the tension more easily than the other jihadist groups and was rewarded by the ISI with expanded patronage, while the competing Deobandi groups were mostly falling out of favour.[35] Its assets in Pakistan were mostly concentrated in Muridke, where in 2005 were '500 offices, 2200 training camps, 150 schools, 2 science colleges, 3 hospitals, 34 dispensaries, 11 ambulance services, a publishing empire, garment factory, iron foundry, and woodworks factories'. Its more than 300,000 members were led by cadres much better paid than in the civilian sector.[36]

It has been argued that one important reason why LeT enjoyed such a high degree of support and protection from the Pakistani authorities was that it invested much of its energy and resources arguing against violence aimed at the Pakistani state or at Pakistan's citizens and completely rejecting the doctrine of takfir.[37] However, the Deobandi groups did not approve of takfir either and LeT's position concerning the Pakistani state did not stand out much more clearly than those of HuM or JeM. LeT also ingratiated itself to the Pakistani state by offering its help in covert operations even beyond Kashmir. In the Miranshah camp, even before 2005 LeT trained Afghan Taliban as well, transferring bomb making technology to them.[38] From 2005 onwards, the ISI started encouraging LeT to resume operations on Afghan ground. Jamal places at 2008 the date when LeT was ready, after a long preparatory period, to join the new Afghan jihad.[39] However, LeT's role in Afghanistan was noted already in 2006, according to ISAF reports and evidence of recruitment of Afghan refugees in Pakistan.[40]

As of 2013 LeT still had one large training camp in Miranshah (North Waziristan) and two smaller ones in Alipur and Azad Kashmir, where it was providing theoretical training to recruits, before sending them for 'practical training' to Afghanistan.[41] One LeT commander commented about the Taliban in 2013 that 'Our relationship is very necessary for them; we studied professionally and did professional training in Pakistan.'⁴² Over time, however, the LeT deployment to Afghanistan changed in nature, as the Taliban became more and more proficient. Afghanistan became at that point a training ground for LeT recruits, even if in the rhetoric of LeT there remained a commitment 'to bring an Islamic government in Afghanistan'.⁴³

In addition, LeT was also carrying 'special operations' separately from the Taliban in Afghanistan, presumably under ISI orders, and targeting at Indian assets (including Indian NGOs).⁴⁴

However, as it will be discussed below, HuM and JeM too agreed to send fighters to Afghanistan once they were allowed to resume full-scale operations. It is possible that LeT might have agreed to send men to Afghanistan more promptly than the two other organizations, but seems doubtful given the closer contacts of JeM and HuM with the Taliban in the 1990s (see Chapter 1).

Another way in which LeT might have made itself useful to Islamabad is by passing on intelligence about fellow jihadists, according to a member:

> This is LeT's plan, to infiltrate our people into any Jihadist organization, to get information about what they are doing or not doing against the Pakistan Government. The Pakistan Government is also supporting us in this.⁴⁵

The source could of course have been boasting, especially considering that LeT did run into trouble in 2019 (see *The 2019 crackdown* below). Still, it appears very plausible that LeT might have provided this type of service to the Pakistani authorities as well, considering how remarkable LeT's involvement with the Taliban in Afghanistan was. As Bacon noted, LeT never had much sympathy for the Taliban, who were much closer to Pakistan's Deobandi jihadists.⁴⁶ Perhaps the key to the deep state favour enjoyed by LeT after 2001 is exactly in this readiness to share intelligence, which no source has reported about the other jihadist groups.

The US government in those years was of course interested in keeping Pakistan's formal support for its operations in Afghanistan, dependent as it was on its supply routes through Pakistan. As a result, although the US government listed LeT as a terrorist group in 2000, after 9/11 it cooperated with the Pakistani military establishment and took the position that there was no evidence of Pakistani support for LeT and other jihadist groups active against India, despite the evidence that such groups were based in Pakistan and being fully aware of the support provided by the security services.⁴⁷ Essentially the Bush administration did not apply its own rules about hosting terrorists to Pakistan and considered the Kashmir affaire a problem between Pakistan and India.⁴⁸

JeM and HuM back in business

JeM was still threading on a dangerous path in 2007: there were an estimated 200 JeM members at the Lal Masjid when the clashes started.⁴⁹ Remarkably, however, the faltering of the peace process in Kashmir in 2007 gave JeM an opportunity for a comeback. JeM reappeared under the figurehead leadership of Mufti Abdul Rauf, Azhar's brother, while Maulana Masood Azhar remained de facto in charge.⁵⁰

Azhar managed to bring Mauviya back and resumed activities in Jammu and Kashmir on a significant scale in 2009, even if Azhar himself only resurfaced in public in 2014.[51] Abbas commented that 'the military wants to keep alive its strategic options in Kashmir'.[52] The dissidents either dispersed or joined other militant organizations, including the Punjabi Taliban.[53] When JeM resurfaced in 2009, its strength was estimated at 5,000 members, with 1,500–2,000 fighters.[54]

JeM accepted to cut off relations with LeJ when the latter kept its path of confrontation with the Pakistani authorities.[55] JeM instead maintained good relations with the SSP, whose relations with Islamabad were better than LeJ, even if worsening in 2018, after Imran khan became prime minister.[56]

Lieven sees this as a success of Pakistani intelligence, which also co-opted JeM into its activities to support the Taliban insurgency in Afghanistan.[57] At the peak of JeM's campaign in Afghanistan (2017), it had almost 4,000 men there.[58] Apart from providing fighting power, it supported the Taliban with logistical, financial and training, advisory, coordination and intelligence assistance. JeM specialized also in providing suicide bombers.[59] Its activities were supervised by mobile ISI agents/inspectors.[60]

Despite this considerable effort, Afghanistan was not where the average Pakistani member of JeM wanted to be. In May 2018 a source in JeM admitted that as many as 80 per cent of the members and of the leadership would have like to focus on Kashmir and that just 20 per cent was in favour of giving priority to Afghanistan.

At present time, most members of our organization demand to have more activities in Kashmir instead of Afghanistan, since they believe and think that we have done what should be done in Afghanistan and now we must do more work for our own people and the Kashmiris, and overall now they consider Afghanistan a very low priority.[61]

Perhaps due to the lack of strong commitment to the cause of the Afghan jihad, or perhaps because their role in Afghanistan was more to project Pakistani presence and influence than to fight, JeM casualties there appear to have been comparatively light. Although large numbers of JeM members were deployed to Afghanistan than to Jammu and Kashmir until 2019, JeM was still losing more men in Jammu and Kashmir than in Afghanistan. For example, in 2018 according to internal source the group lost 185 members in Kashmir.[62] In 2017, it had lost only 88 members in Afghanistan and in 2016 it had lost 129.[63]

JeM rapidly re-established an extensive infrastructure, even if not as developed as LeT's. In 2018 it had 123 active recruitment offices throughout Pakistan, according to an internal source. In some areas like Bahawalpur of Punjab and Bags and Neelum district of Azad Kashmir, where its presence was strongest, it even had village-level offices.[64] Bahawalpur is also where Azhar had his headquarter, surrounded by a thick network of tens of small training camps, extending into the neighbouring Multan and Rahim Yar Khan districts. JeM also continued to use a network of training camps in the tribal areas on the border with Afghanistan and inside Afghanistan itself, and other camps around Muzaffarabad, in Azad Kashmir. Most of JeM's madrasas also had training facilities.[65]

After the 2001–3 crisis, Azhar appears to have been able to rebuild the organization under his stricter personal control and internal dissidence was eliminated.[66] In JeM's structure, under Azhar were two deputies, one for Afghan affairs and one for Kashmiri affairs, a leadership council of ten members and a number of 'commissions' covering military, financial, logistical, recruitment and provincial affairs.[67]

After 2009 JeM kept growing fast, according to internal sources, at the rate of almost 1,000 men/year, reaching a membership of 11,850 men in 2016. In 2017–18 its growth even accelerated somewhat, taking its membership to 14,300 active members by May 2018. Of those, 12,750 were trained as fighters, a JeM source claimed. The increase was due to expanded ISI financial support. In addition the group had plus perhaps 50,000 simple members, mostly madrasa students.[68] After 2018, however, growth appears to have ceased. By March 2019 JeM claimed to have some 14,300 members, the same number as a year earlier, although the number of those classified as fighters had gone up slightly to over 13,000. Only a small proportion were actually deployed on operations – some 75 per cent was either in training or in reserve in Pakistan.[69]

Like JeM, HuM recovered from the 2001–3 crisis, probably for the same primary reason: the need to intensify operations in Kashmir. Farooq Kashmiri, who was in charge of the organization at the time of 9/11, remained in control. The other reason for HuM's recovery is likely to have been again its willingness to deploy to Afghanistan in support of Pakistan's policies there. In 2016 HuM claimed to have carried out forty-eight operations in Afghanistan, and thirty-eight in 2017.[70] Internal sources put at 2,000 its members in Afghanistan in the summer of 2017, typically shrinking to 800 during the winter of 2017/18.[71] The level of casualties taken in Afghanistan suggests a modest level of military activities, as in the previously discussed case of JeM: forty-five killed in action in 2017 and eighty-eight in 2018.[72] Indeed much of its activity was supporting the Afghan Taliban in training and logistics and tactical advice, including especially in bomb making.[73] Like JeM, HuM was collaborating with the Quetta Shura as well as with the Haqqanis.[74]

In this phase (2007–16), HuM had again access to substantial funding, and by 2016 it had reached the peak of its power, with almost 18,000 active members, if we believe an internal source.[75] HuM had offices in a number of towns and cities in Pakistan and even at the village level in Azad Kashmir and also in Pashtun villages around Quetta.[76] The structure of HuM was similar to that of JeM, with leader Maulana Rahman Khalil assisted by two deputies (Sheikh Helal Ahmad Kashmiri and Maulana Hafiz Tahir Lahory), by a leadership council of five members and four 'commissions' (finance, military, political and logistical).[77]

The rehabilitation of HuM was not due to it cutting off links to AQ. In fact, HuM continued enjoying substantial funding by AQ, which was supporting it with several million dollars a year; in 2015 HuM received $9 million according to an AQ source.[78] HuM also kept some outward commitment to global jihad, posting representatives not only in India and Afghanistan, but also in the Philippines, Malaysia, Indonesia, Thailand and Bangladesh. It recruited from Bangladesh, India, Malaysia, Indonesia, the Philippines, Thailand, Tajikistan, Afghanistan and Somalia.[79] The priorities of the deep state had changed and the desire to intensify operations in Kashmir led to massive increase in the funding committed to HuM. Moreover, as it has been discussed in Chapters 2 and 4, the relationship between AQ and the deep state had also been evolving from 2005 onwards and the latter stopped treating it as resolutely hostile force.

Then in 2016 HuM suffered a sudden drop in funding.[80] It had to release its Afghan fighters, who joined the Afghan Taliban, and its overall size shrank by almost a quarter. The reason for the drop in funding is not immediately clear; perhaps the US drawdown in Afghanistan removed the need for a strong HuM presence there. By 2018 again HuM, like the other groups, was coming under pressure from the Pakistani authorities to increase efforts in Kashmir, and for the summer of 2018 it was planning to reduce its commitment to Afghanistan in order to allocate more resources to Kashmir.[81]

From their beginning, LeT, HuM and JeM had all been clients of the Pakistani deep state. The Pakistani deep state manages to salvage its relationship with the Kashmir-focused jihadists, despite a serious crisis in 2002. It did so by restoring funding for them and by keeping them busy in Afghanistan for years, until operations started getting gradually resumed in Kashmir. Did it do so because it needed them to further its political goals in Afghanistan and Kashmir, or because having created a 'monster' it needed to keep it busy outside Pakistan? Developments occurring in 2018–19 throw some light on these issues.

Global jihad arrives in Kashmir

AQ's trajectory towards Kashmir

As discussed in Chapter 2, the establishment of AQIS represented the beginning of a turn away from Afghanistan towards Kashmir, probably because the Afghan conflict was losing legitimacy and interest after the withdrawal of the bulk of US troops in 2014. Aside from Kashmir, AQIS also intended to get involved in Bangladesh and Myanmar, but the focus was clearly in Kashmir.[82] Global jihad needed a new cause célèbre in South Asia.

AQ, at least since the establishment of AQIS, has tried to insert itself in the diatribe between the Pakistani authorities and the Kashmir jihad lobby, as much as it did with the Afghan jihad. Of course, AQ was positioning itself on the side of those advocating the re-intensification of jihad in Kashmir. AQIS' first leader, Asim Umar, repeatedly criticized the Pakistani authorities for their failure to support jihad in Indian Kashmir. He denounced the Pakistani state, its intelligence agencies, military and law enforcement bodies for acting against 'mujahedeen on behalf of 'infidels' (the United States and allies).[83] At that time (2014–15), AQIS had poor relations with the Pakistani military establishment and was reeling for their presumed cooperation with the Americans in the killing of bin Laden.

Relations with groups active in Kashmir pre-existed, but the new focus led to a more thorough plan. Until 2019, AQ was mostly interested in LeT because of the protection it could afford to AQ members in Pakistan (see *LeT weathers the storm* above), and because bringing a large jihadist organization such as LeT under its umbrella was essential for legitimizing AQ's jihadist leadership. The important of AQ's jihadist legitimacy is illustrated by the hic up in the relationship between the two organizations, when AQ saw significant numbers of LeT members flowing to IS-K in 2016–18, it reportedly cut the level of support to LeT because it was irritated that a significant number of its members joined IS-K.[84] This despite the fact that LeT's cooperation with AQ continued unabated and unchanged. To AQ, the idea that Pakistani jihadist organization could cooperate with both AQ and IS was unacceptable.

It was only when relations between AQIS and ISI warmed again in 2019 that Kashmir and India could really start playing a much bigger role in AQIS' strategy.[85] An AQIS source openly acknowledged that the organization at that point viewed India and Kashmir as much higher priorities than Pakistan or Afghanistan.[86] At this point AQIS's criticism of Pakistani policies towards became much more muted:

> *The Pakistani and Kashmiri groups involved in the liberation of Kashmir issue [...] accuse the Pakistani government of betraying jihad in Kashmir. These groups are continuously pressuring Pakistani state to take sincere and real steps in the issue of Kashmir. Although the Pakistani government is providing significant support, the Kashmiri groups are not totally happy because they say this support is not sufficient or effective. The groups need additional support in intelligence, planning and operations which the Pakistani government is unable to provide at this time mostly due to the high level of Indian build up in the region. The Pakistanis are worried about a full-scale war with India and that's why they're not providing full support to these groups in intelligence, planning and operations.*[87]

At that point the grand plan of AQIS was to help the Pakistani jihadist groups

> *to maintain jihad in occupied Kashmir and further escalate attacks in major Indian cities'. [...] We will target Indian infrastructures, government institutions and besides will aim our attacks on all foreign diplomatic missions and western interests in India.*[88]

This reportedly happened within a context of the Pakistani military establishment gearing up for a renewed Kashmir campaign.[89] In addition, according to the source AQIS' other donors too were putting pressure to get a greater focus on India and Kashmir, again as a result of the change in the status of Kashmir within the Indian Union and the growing tension there, as well as of the '*anti-Muslim steps*' taken by the Modi government.[90]

Not only AQIS supported LeT, JeM, HuM, but it also supported and cooperated closely with a range of Indian and Kashmiri groups, including HM and others, such as:

- Lashkar e Taiba – India branch, which according to an AQIS source had 500–600 members in 2019;
- Ansar Ghazwat ul Hind (about 180 members);
- HuJI (190 members);
- Indian Islami Inqilabi Mahaz (70 members);
- and Ghazwa e Hind Mujahidin (40 members).[91]

The source does not specify where these members were; it should certainly not be assumed that they were all in India or Kashmir. AQIS also had relations with two more groups based in India, Indian Islamic Mujahidin (200 members) and the Muslim United Liberation Tigers of Assam (140 members).[92] Some of these groups had by 2019 de facto taken over by AQIS, which in exchange for support was able to choose their leadership, as in the case of Ansar Ghazwat ul Hind.[93]

It is worth noting that aside from the Haqqani network, which still accounted for 20 per cent of AQIS' non-core members, by 2019 most of the rest belonged to Kashmir-oriented groups: 45 per cent, breaking down as 35 per cent with LeT, 5 per cent with HuM and 5 per cent with HuJI. IS-K, IMU, LeJ and TTP accounted for the remaining 35 per cent. It is worth noting that AQIS did not have non-core members in JeM.[94] Similarly when asked in 2020 to list the groups closest to AQIS, an internal source mentioned mostly groups active in Kashmir: LeT, SSP, TTP, Jama'at ul Ansar al-Shariah, Jama'at Ul Dawah ul Quran, HM, HuM and Ansar ut Twahid Kashmir.[95]

AQIS' take-off was slow, but the growing sectarian tension in India as a result of Modi's policies offered some boost. One source claimed that as religious tensions increased in India, AQIS started attracting recruits much faster: 300 in 2019 versus 130 in 2018.[96]

An AQ source stated clearly that the new strategic focus of AQIS was reliant on its much improved relations with the ISI.

> *The Pakistani authorities are supporting our operations in India and Indian occupied Kashmir. In recent times, they've increased their pressure on our leadership and are progressively asking us to contribute more to the ongoing efforts in Kashmir and provide more training and support to Kashmiri Jihadist organizations. Actually, they have increased their pressure on us after Indian State revoked the special status of Indian occupied Kashmir. The Pakistani authorities are now pledging additional assistance to us.*[97]

The source mentions 'pressure' from the deep state as one of the reasons for the strengthened focus on Kashmir. This suggests that although there was a logic in AQIS coming to see Kashmir and India as it new main theatres of operations, the relationship with the Pakistan deep state was dictating the terms of that engagement.

IS' trajectory before Wilayat Hind

As discussed in Chapters 3 and 4, IS-K has never been very active in Pakistan. This also applies to the jihadists focused on Kashmir, such as HuM, JeM and LeT. Relations were initially hostile. In LeT anti-Shi'a views were not diffuse. Asked to explain why relations of the still forming IS-K with LeT were poor in 2014, an IS-K cadre answered 'because that is the private group of ISI. We do not want to have relations with them'.[98] In public LeT reciprocated by dismissing claims of links to IS-K as Indian propaganda in 2015 and openly condemning IS in 2017 as 'an anti-Islamic terrorist organization'.[99]

Some authors report that Hafiz Saeed 'explicitly labeled groups such as al-Qai'da and the Islamic State as terror groups' and that in early 2016 JuD in an open letter to the public accused 'Daesh' of having harmed the cause of Islam and of considering JuD an enemy.[100] Then in mid-2016,

> JuD's spokesman Attiqur Rahman Chohan remarked that some of the group's personnel had been attacked in a mosque in Peshawar, specifically due to JuD's public rallies in Malakand during which JuD had expressed support for the Pakistani Army and criticized the Islamic State.[101]

The fact that LeT even labelled AQ as a terror group (whereas it had in reality solid relations with it, see above) warns the reader that these statements should be taken with a pinch of salt and might be mere smoke screen. Indeed, despite claims that LeT and IS-K must have been at odds,[102] an internal source acknowledged close relations between LeT and IS-K as early as 2016, although among the leaders only Hafiz Saeed and Abdul Wahab were reportedly favourable to this relationship. 'We also gave some trainers and advisors to them and some of our fighters also joined them.' The relationship was reportedly born out of the pressure of some Saudi and Qatari donors.[103] The rationale for the collaboration was thus described by an LeT source:

> Any organizations against Americans, Westerners, Afghan Government, we are ready to help them. It does not make any difference for us, as long as it is a jihadist organization.[104]

LeT might well have reached an understanding with IS-K after having fought rhetorically with it in 2014, 2015 and early 2016. Even after LeT and IS-K started cooperating, there is some evidence that this was not always endorsed by the ISI. Initially the Pakistani authorities reportedly really opposed LeT sending volunteers to Iraq and Syria, and also the establishment of relations with IS. However, according to a source, the Saudi authorities intervened to lobby in the favour of IS. According to LeT sources, as of October 2016 167 LeT members had gone over to IS in Syria and Iraq, and about 100 joined IS-K in Afghanistan and Pakistan. The flow was reportedly encouraged by the Pakistani authorities, which wanted to use the former LeT members as sources of information about IS. Among those who joined were some relatively senior figures, including Abdul Wahab, former chief of LeT in Kunar, Shaikh Al Hadith Obeidullah, who was an adviser to Hafiz Saeed and joined in Syria, Zarrar Shah, who was a senior commander, and Mufti Iqbal Lashkari, senior commander in Kashmir. During 2016 LeT also started sending some trainers and advisers to IS-K.[105] LeT's donors in Saudi Arabia and Qatar similarly put some pressure on LeT to cooperate with IS-K.[106]

Perhaps this is the more general pattern followed by evolving relationship between LeT and Pakistani authorities on one side, and IS-K on the other: with the help of Gulf donors, the initial hostility gave way to negotiations sometime in 2015 and then forms of co-operations by 2016. LeT was described (contemptuously) as 'the special representative of the Pakistan Government', by a senior IS-K figure, but other IS-K sources indicated that the leadership of IS-K negotiated with it too in order to convince it to join IS-K, or at least to cooperate with it.[107] In its early contacts with LeT, IS-K tried to reassure them that its arrival in Pakistan was not meant to challenge their interests.[108]

Still even after the 2015–16 thaw relations were not idyllic. IS-K propaganda was still assaulting Pakistan as an 'apostate state' in 2018 and branded militant groups active in Kashmir as mere 'agents of Pakistan'.[109] This might again have been a smoke screen, but in 2018 IS-K made an attempt to kick-start activities in Kashmir, seemingly without consulting the ISI or LeT. Establishing a foothold there proved highly problematic: its first leader in Kashmir, Dawood Ahmad Sufi, a Pakistani close to Al Baghdadi, was killed in 2018/19 and his successor, another Pakistani named Ishfaq Ahmad, was killed in 2019/20.[110] Sources in other groups, such as HuM, say that IS turned up in Kashmir in 2018, but then disappeared as they were not welcomed by the ISI. At that point the ISI did not seem to think it needed IS there, or at least not an IS branch it could not control.[111]

The 2018–19 turn: New blood for Kashmir

LeT turns into a potential threat

As of 2013 LeT was still training together with the Pakistani army and receiving support from it.[112] It appeared to be completely in line with the military authorities:

It is clear that if there is no permission from the ISI we can do nothing.[113]

The Pakistani authorities funded LeT throughout.[114]

In reality LeT had been threading a fine line after 2001, trying to keep happy its members, who wanted to hit India hard, and at the same time avoid upsetting the Pakistani authorities, who did not want to be dragged into a war with India.[115] Many members were also drawn towards more radical positions, as it will be discussed below.

Although little evidence of LeT's ties with AQ might have emerged by 2011[116] and authors were continuing to deny the relationship with AQ as late as 2018,[117] the evidence that has accumulated as of 2020 about LeT's links to global jihad is quite compelling. In 2001–5 LeT was mostly busy helping ex-filtrate AQ and other jihadists from Afghanistan and offering them protection inside Pakistan.[118] LeT showed growing interest for Western targets over the years, starting from the Pune German bakery attack in 2010. There were reports of it recruiting and training Western coverts, presumably for attacks in the West.[119]

There is quite substantial evidence of LeT's 'outreach' to jihadist groups around the world.[120] Hafiz Saeed's rhetoric also turned:

In a rally sponsored by JuD in 2010, Saeed urged the leaders and rulers of the 'world of Islam' to meet their responsibilities by adopting the path of jihad and by not bowing to the West. He later declared, 'A big change is taking place in the world. The era of Europe and America is over. The results of the eighth Crusade are about to come out.' In the rally, Afghanistan and Iraq were used as examples to highlight atrocities committed by America and Israel on Muslims across the world and calls were made to all the religious and political parties in Pakistan to unite and fight against American imperialism under the leadership of Hafiz Saeed.[121]

Roul reports that LeT militants 'took to the streets to offer special funerary prayers in absentia and to declare bin Laden a martyr' in 2011 and that speeches and declarations were released, even declaring 'the United States as an enemy of Pakistan'.[122] Tankel also saw good relations between AQ and LeT, and joint training efforts.[123] In 2011 documents recovered in bin Laden's residence in Abbottabad showed that Hafiz Saeed was regularly corresponding with him.[124]

AQ sources confirmed that the organization was supporting LeT. LeT's annual budget was variously estimated at between $50–100 million, allegedly spent mostly on non-military operations.[125] Part of it was supplied by the ISI, and the rest raised from donations and criminal activities.[126] An NDS source claimed in 2020 that the organization raises funds from 'many Arab businessmen', as well as through small contributions from common people in Pakistan and donations from Pakistani traders and businessmen.[127] In addition, even US intelligence believed LeT received funding from the Saudi Arabia, at least up to 2010.[128] LeT sources confirm the above and also add AQ as a source of funding.[129] In 2015/16, according to one of these sources, AQ gave LeT $16 million.[130] AQ also posted advisers to LeT.[131]

Other sources, drawing from Indian government investigations, describe LeT as paying AQIS, not vice versa, at least on occasion.[132] Does this contradict the claims of AQ and LeT sources that AQ was funding LeT? It is not clear in what circumstances exactly the money was used; LeT might have been the best conduit for transfer of funds to AQIS in India. As discussed in *Renewed primacy of Afghanistan 2014–16* above, AQ/AQIS reportedly was mostly raising funds in the Gulf, it was well placed for mobilizing funds there than Pakistani groups, especially before the rise of IS, when its prestige among sympathizers of jihadism was at its peak. Many Pakistani jihadist groups, as highlighted above, were also raising funds in the Gulf. AQ/AQIS, using a different narrative, less focused on specific campaigns and more clearly 'global jihadist', might well have been able to raise funds from different sets of donors.

A source in LeT described in 2016 the relationship with AQ as 'very good from the past to the present'. Among the leaders Abdul Rehman Makki, Hafiz Saeed, Qari Yousaf and Qari Abdul Wahab were described as those most pro-AQ, but reportedly nobody really opposed the relationship. The same source claimed that LeT and AQ trained together in Kunar, Nuristan, Paktika and in Badakhshan, and that AQ provided financial, logistical and other aid.[133]

More than evidence of the ISI opposing LeT's relationship with AQ, the impression that emerged from the evidence discussed above is however of the ISI essentially tolerating the relationship. It seems implausible that the ISI, which must have plenty of informers within LeT, did not detect the stable relationship between the two organizations. As the source put it, the Pakistani authorities were aware of anything LeT was doing because 'LeT is one organization of the Pakistan Government'.[134] Hence, it must have approved of it at least for a long period. The view expressed by an LeT source in 2016 was that the Pakistani authorities did not oppose LeT's relationship with AQ, because they did not see AQ itself as a threat to Pakistan. Quite the contrary:

> *The senior leaders of AQ are kept by Pakistan Government. Those who are against Pakistan Government like TTP, we do not keep relationship with them. We always fight against them.*[135]

The relationship between LeT and another jihadist group like the IMU was somewhat more complicated because of the fact that the latter did not have any agreement with the Pakistani authorities. However, according to the source, the Pakistani authorities were willing to close one eye even on the IMU links as long as LeT reported to the Pakistani authorities any IMU plot to carry out operations inside Pakistan.[136]

Although AQ provided funding to LeT, this was at relatively modest levels considering the size of LeT and of its budget. LeT was never a client of AQ. It was much more depending on the support of the deep state. Hence AQ had little reason for engaging in global jihadist adventures, just to please AQ. Was then LeT's interest in global jihad more genuine than that of TTP, SSP and LeJ, which was discussed in the previous chapters? Were any global jihadist aspirations LeT might have had a source of worry for the Pakistani deep state?

LeT reportedly got involved with the conflicts in Iraq and Syria, sending volunteers to join both AQ and IS there. As of 2016, according to an internal source LeT had 58 volunteers with AQ and 167 with IS. The source also alleged that the Arab donors to LeT were putting pressure for volunteers being sent to join IS.[137]

> *In the past our focus areas were limited to Kashmir and Afghanistan, but that views are changing and in recent times LeT's main focus is turning to global jihad. One thing more, the donors who funds and back LeT demand us such policy and overall a big role in global jihad.*[138]

As discussed in Chapters 3 and 4, the TTP and Sunni supremacists too agreed to send volunteers to Syria and Iraq. While that had the effect of increasing the influence of global jihadism within the ranks of these organizations, the evidence gathered above suggests that these deployments were in fact a cheap way for the leaderships to show their commitment to donors like AQ and IS, rather than heartfelt decisions. Hence, in the case of LeT too we cannot take the despatch of volunteers to Syria and Iraq as a proof of commitment to global jihad.

Lieven believed that 'the Pakistani security forces are now very afraid of the creature they helped create', of LeT 'launch[ing] successful terrorist attacks in the West, with disastrous results for Pakistan's international position'.[139] He noted that 'despite LeT's strategic decision to concentrate on India, there is no ideological barrier to its members taking part in actions against the West.' Already before 2011 LeT members had been implicated in terrorist plots in Europe, North America and Australia, although Lieven believed that 'the group's leadership [did] not seem to have been involved'.[140]

After Lieven published his book, the threat of LeT getting engaged in terrorist activities in the West became more concrete. According to an internal source, LeT started sending members to Europe in 2011. In 2013 the process was detected by the Pakistani ISI and had to be stopped for a period. It was resumed once again in 2014 and was still going on in 2018. The source claimed that up to that point LeT had sent 740 members to various European countries, mostly to the UK. These had been able to recruit locally over 3,400 new members, mainly among Pakistani nationals.[141]

> *The main objective of LeT in sending members to European countries is to strengthen its presence in those countries as well as invite European people to Islam and in case our leadership decide to carry out attacks or do Jihad, then we will be able to easily start jihad there. [...] We want to support and provide assistance to AQ in their operations and attacks in Europe, our goal is to fully support them.*[142]

A Pakistan people smuggler confirmed in 2016 that he had moved some sixty members of LeT to UK and France and to a lesser extent to Italy and Germany. LeT was happy to pay hefty extras to people smugglers for moving its men.[143] Sometimes government officials helped LeT members obtain fake documents, but this could just be corruption.[144] AQ and some donors in the Gulf states were reportedly a driving force in convincing LeT to send people to Europe.[145]

Again, SSP and LeJ too were sending members to Europe, as discussed in Chapter 4. That does not seem to have translated into any visible contribution to the cause of global jihad. The case of LeJ appears somewhat different, however, as there is at least some evidence that the effort was not a phoney one. Aside from Lieven's quote above, and as mentioned already, at one point the ISI reportedly intervened to stop LeT from sending volunteers to Europe.

LeT's global jihadist inclinations might therefore have been a genuine source of worry for the Pakistani establishment. This might not have been their main worry, however. Another point raised by Lieven was the fear of the Pakistani establishment of LeT turning against them:

> *Pakistani officials have told me that their greatest fears of mass revolt in Punjab concern what would happen if Lashkar e Taiba/Jama'at ud Dawa were to swing against the state and use their extensive network to mobilize and organize unrest. This they say is one key reason (along with their anti-Indian agenda, which they do not mention) for not taking the sweeping measures against the organisation that the US is demanding. As the commissioner of one of Punjab's administrative divisions said to me in January 2009: 'We have to worry that if we do what you say and crack down on them that some of them at least will turn to terrorism against Pakistan in alliance with the Taleban. After all, they have the ideology and the training.'*[146]

Lieven believed that 'the Pakistani security forces are now very afraid of the creature they helped create, of its possible sympathizers within their own ranks, and of the dreadful consequences if it were to join with the Taleban and the sectarians in revolt against Pakistan'.[147]

Lieven's assessment is somewhat supported by the initial deep state opposition to LeT's involvement of LeT with IS (see *Before Wilayat Hind* below). At that time the ISI had not worked out yet how to manage IS and might have feared that it would have pushed LeT against the Pakistani state. Another confirmation comes from changes in LeT's recruitment system, which emerged by 2015 or 2016. For some undisclosed reason, in 2015/16 LeT tightened its recruitment criteria, introducing a vetting procedure that included a reference from somebody senior in LeT. Reportedly the changes were the result of LeT having been infiltrated by the 'enemy', as it had far too loose recruitment procedures.[148]

In sum, between 2002 and 2018 the deep state showed some concerns for LeT's global jihadist ambitions, for its interactions with an as yet unknown quantity such as IS, for its loose recruitment practices and for the liability represented by its massive size, much greater than any other jihadist groups supported by the deep state. Overall, however, LeT appeared to have successfully managed to keep relations with both the deep state and global jihadists up to 2018.

LeT and the 2019 crackdown

The seemingly unassailable position of LeT came for the first time under serious threat in 2019, when following the Pulwama district attack, under pressure to achieve a rapprochement with Washington, the PTI government decided to order a new crackdown on jihadist groups. LeT was at the centre of the storm and the Pakistani authorities decreased funding to the Islamic institutions and madrasas of LeT's NGO wing Jamaat ud Dawa, and detained Hafiz Saeed and other key figures such as Abdul Rahman Makki (LeT's number 2), Zarar Shah, Zaki-ur-Rahman Lakhvi and over sixty other members. Several military camps were closed in Azad Kashmir. Overall, according to a commander who defected to IS after the crackdown, the support provided by the Pakistani authorities to LeT was cut by 70–80 per cent.[149]

Many in India and elsewhere were initially dismissive of the crackdown. Even many Pakistani jihadists were, such as this JeM commander:

> The reaction of Pakistan authorities and ISI against LeT is a political game against the foreign countries, which have raised their voices against the Pakistan after the Pulwama attack. Pakistan for keeping its relations with foreign countries, especially with western countries, needs to have play such a game with them, otherwise Pakistan Intelligent (ISI) has very good relations with LeT as they have with JeM.[150]

However, over time the weight of evidence ended up suggesting that at least when Hafiz Saeed was first arrested in July 2019, he was kept isolated and unable to communicate with his followers. A source described this period a 'very difficult time', stressing that Saeed got multiple sentences in Pakistani courts.[151] Another LeT source too denied the crackdown was just a show as far as LeT was concerned:

> this issue was taken very seriously in Pakistan, our training teachers and Mawlawis were very worried about this issue at that time.[152]

A source in HuM confirmed the weakening of LeT after the detention of Hafiz Saeed.[153]

The crackdown reportedly caused some units to defect to IS-K, IS-P, JeM and even the Afghan Taliban.¹⁵⁴ One of the defectors acknowledged that he had defected to IS as a result of the cut in funding.¹⁵⁵ A number of LeT units relocated to Afghanistan in order to avoid the new crack down.¹⁵⁶ A source in the Afghan NDS indicated that at least 200 LeT members had crossed into Afghanistan after the detention of Hafiz Saeed.¹⁵⁷

The paradox is that the Pulwama attack, which prompted the crackdown, had been carried out by JeM, but according to one interpretation

*Hafiz Saeed was on the top wanted list of western countries and [...] the detention of Hafiz Saeed had two purposes for Pakistan. Reason one, to prove to the world and America that the allegation that Pakistan military has good connections with Hafiz Saeed is not true and the second reason was to show to the Americans and Indian governments that Pakistan was complying in arresting the man that America and India had been asking to detain for a long time.*¹⁵⁸

Islamabad hit LeT because it was the most wanted target for Delhi and Washington: this interpretation was largely predominant also within the security apparatuses of Afghanistan and India.¹⁵⁹

Some LeT and JeM sources however describe a different, although not entirely incompatible, process. They say that relations between Hafiz Saeed and the Pakistani military establishment were already deteriorating before the Pulwama district incident. One source in HuM alleged that

*The Pakistan authorities had problems with LeT because of its illegal kidnappings in Kashmir and assassination of important elders in Pakistan and Kashmir. Hafiz Saeed had got several warnings from Pakistan authorities, but he did not heed to them.*¹⁶⁰

A source in JeM agreed that LeT had come into the crosshairs of the Pakistani authorities because of undisciplined behaviour in Azad Kashmir, where kidnappings and harassment of the local population occurred. Reportedly Hafiz Saeed was caught planning a large attack in Jammu and Kashmir after JeM's attack in Pulwama district and at that point the Pakistani authorities decided LeT had to be reined in.¹⁶¹

Disgruntled LeT commanders broke some of the rules set by the Pakistani military for LeT militias to be allowed on Pakistani soil, including carrying out some kidnappings, going violent and even murdering two Pakistani police officers. This caused the backlash against LeT.¹⁶²

Apart from these 'abuses', sources also allege that Saeed was being jealous of what he felt was the growing deep state favour for JeM. Some sources claim that LeT was never in competition with JeM or other 'Kashmiri' groups and that JeM remained on good terms with LeT and kept cooperating with them in Kashmir and in Afghanistan.¹⁶³ This is a rather common line among jihadist groups, despite their obvious doctrinal differences (Ahl e Hadith vs Deobandi vs Salafi vs Islamism), possibly because donors to these groups do not like to see or hear about infighting among jihadists. Other sources, however, admit that there was jealousy between the two organizations, and even between LeT and a somewhat resurgent HM:

> *The tension between Pakistan military and intelligence service (ISI) with Hafiz Saeed started around one or one and half year ago and the tension was because of the lesser attention of Pakistan military and ISI towards LeT, while the training camps and madrasas of JeM and HM in Pakistan were being improved. Hafiz Saeed who was very angry on this issue and also worried. Then he raised his complaint with the Pakistan military and ISI, but the complaint raised tension between Hafiz Saeed and Pakistan military instead of fixing the problem.*[164]

The source, a former LeT commander, who left after the crackdown, acknowledged that

> *JeM has been leading the jihad against the Indian army in Jammu and Kashmir for a long time. And JeM is doing a very good job in recruiting Afghans for Kashmir. These were the reason why Pakistani military and ISI put more attention to improve JeM facilities in Pakistan.*[165]

A second source confirmed that tension between LeT and the Pakistani military establishment first rose because the perceived favouritism towards JeM, which according to LeT leaders and cadres allowed JeM to take the lead in the Kashmiri jihad.[166]

> *When you see that one group is treat very well and gets more access, services, logistics and funding and the other group is not treated well while both groups are fighting for the same purpose, this made the leaders and commanders of LeT upset.*[167]

Another source confirmed that JeM maintained throughout the 2019 crackdown a much better relationship with the Pakistani authorities than LeT, and that it was better supported, even if he does not agree that this might have been the reason for the spat between LeT and the Pakistani authorities.[168]

Even an AQIS source indicated that

> *Lately, there're some differences among Pakistani intelligence and LeT, which caused a little frustration in overall Pakistani liberation efforts in Kashmir.*[169]

According to one of the sources, between late 2018 and early 2019 the Pakistani military had already started seizing and closing some of LeT's camps around Muzafarabad, such as Sherkot, Dollai and Shawali, and in Mirpur (Gorhan Jundile, Fagosh) and some others. Several Islamic schools and hospitals of LeT were also closed.[170]

When the Pakistani authorities decided that they had no option but to crack down on the jihadists, they seem to have chosen to make a scapegoat of LeT because of the already deteriorating relations. Even a JeM commander agreed that LeT was hit disproportionally hard.[171] This view is shared by another JeM commander:

> *When we attacked the Indian army in Pulwama district, we officially announced and took the responsibility of attack, the Pakistani intelligence service could arrest*

Moulana Saheb Masood Azhar, they know where he is but did not arrest him, this mean that still they support him very much.[172]

A confirmation of the fact that the crackdown on LeT might have been caused by growing distrust by the authorities comes from the fact that, according to the retired member, while his combat group had no resources, it was being harassed by the police and had to disband, other LeT groups, 'that get direct orders and support from the Pakistan military in Kashmir and in Afghanistan', seemed unaffected.[173] An Afghan NDS source also viewed Pakistani support for LeT inside Pakistan as having collapsed, while continuing for units active inside Afghanistan.[174]

In this context, the Pulwama district incident was only important because it led to the pressure on the Pakistani authorities to crack down on the jihadists.

Even LeT, however, was not completely frozen. Ten religious institutions controlled by LeT and tens of madrasas were left open, especially in Muzaffarabad and Lahore, and LeT remained active in Kashmir.[175] One internal source estimated in February 2020 that there might still be 6,000–7,000 LeT fighters, mostly in the two Kashmirs.[176] The numbers actually deployed to Afghanistan, Indian Kashmir or to the camps just across the border in Pakistan were of course much less. Another former cadre, who had left two months before being interviewed, estimated the number of 'deployed' fighters at 1,500–2,000, compared to 2,500–3,000 before the arrest of Hafiz Saeed.[177] NDS sources estimated the numbers in 2020 higher, at 3,000–4,000.[178]

Interestingly, while the Pakistani authorities were cracking down on LeT, they were reaching a new deal with AQIS. This alone confirms that LeT's relationship with AQ was not the issue, as already discussed in the previous paragraph. An AQIS source confirmed that. At the peak of the crisis, LeT even threatened to cut off relations with Islamabad. According to the source, an AQIS mediation played a role in mending fences. AQIS had been very worried about the break-up.[179]

The dynamics of the crisis between LeT and the deep state appear to confirm the assessment made in the previous paragraph, that the size of LeT made any sign of potential disloyalty or indiscipline on its part particularly threatening for the Pakistani establishment. The more hardline elements in LeT had little patience left for the Pakistani authorities, especially after Imran Khan ascended to the premiership:

The problem is that the Pakistan government and Imran Khan have become the servants of America and sold the country to the Americans. […] Until the servant and dog of America Imran Khan is in the power, I think relations between LeT and the Pakistani government and intelligence agencies will not get better.[180]

LeT had to be cut down to size and brought back in line.

HuM and the 2019 crackdown

The 2019 crackdown did not just hurt LeT. As discussed in *JeM and HuM back in business* above, there were signs that HuM was starting to fall out of favour again already in 2016–17. By early 2018 an internal source estimated its strength to have declined from the 17,900 of early 2016 to about 14,000 men, of which 11,800 were fighters.[181] The periods 2015/16 and 2016/17 were reportedly years of heavy cuts, when HuM had to pull out most of its forces in Afghanistan, and release its Afghan fighters. It decided to concentrate efforts on Kashmir.[182] According to the same source, HuM benefited from a funding blip in 2017/18, when it received 42 per cent more than in 2017/17, but even at that level ($17 million according to the internal source) it was not in a position to compete with JeM for the primacy of the Kashmir jihad.[183] The sources of funding were similar to the other Kashmiri groups: the ISI, AQ, donors in the Gulf states, some Islamic charities and private citizens.[184] As it can be seen, in HuM's case too, funding underpinned the 'good relations' with AQ; reportedly Rahman Khalil maintained direct contacts with AQ's leadership.[185] HuM coordinated with LeT even in Afghanistan and maintained thoroughly good relations with them.[186]

Despite the generous treatment offered by the ISI up to 2016, in HuM too part of the leadership kept feeling that Kashmir should have been their priority throughout, not Afghanistan, and that Islamabad should allocate more resources for the jihad in Jammu and Kashmir. Among them senior figures such as Sheikh Helal Ahmad Kashmiri, Maulana Sa'adatullah Kashmiri and Maulana Abdul Jabar. With them was 70 per cent of the membership, according to one source. But the top leaders, including Rahman Khalil and Commander Zafar Iqbal Kashmiri, lined behind the Pakistani authorities and accepted that 'we should give equal attention to both Afghanistan and Kashmir'.[187] The lack of enthusiasm for the Afghan jihad therefore does not appear to have turned into a source of friction with the Pakistani authorities.

Despite seemingly burgeoning relations, in 2019–20 the situation precipitated for HuM and funding almost completely dried out. An HuM source put the problem down to mismanagement and the inability of the leadership to turn the sympathy earned among Pakistani officials and among donors in Pakistan and in the Gulf into actual funding.[188] In general sources insist that support for HuM was not discontinued due to friction between HuM and ISI. Connections with the Pakistani army were still good as of 2020.[189] Another HuM source described the relationship with the Pakistani authorities as 'weak, but not bad'.[190]

> *In the 1990s, the main supporter of HuM was the Pakistan authorities and intelligence services. Fazul Rahman Khalil still has connection with Pakistan army and Pakistan intelligent service (ISI). But HuM does not get any funds from Pakistan authorities.*[191]

Perhaps the declining support received by HuM was simply the result of the fact that after 2015 HuM carried out no major attack in Kashmir and as of mid-2020 had no plans to carry out one.[192] The superior efficiency and aggressiveness of JeM once again overshadowed HuM, relegating to marginality, especially after its services in Afghanistan also became redundant.

By 2020 even a member of HuM considered it to be de facto defunct; he pointed out that the organization says that it maintained only a token military presence in Afghanistan and Kashmir, perhaps as little as 100 active militants in total.[193] The fifty to sixty fighters it had in eastern Afghanistan in 2020 were on stand-by for deployment to

Kashmir, hosted by the Taliban.[194] HuM units in Afghanistan and Kashmir were only able to operate by relying on other jihadist groups for support, such as the Taliban, as HuM could not longer afford a support network of its own.[195] As of 2020 HuM was hardly carrying out any political activities either, even its magazine was not being published any more. 'HuM is almost dead', said another member. The announcement of Moulana Fazul Rahman Khalil that he intended to join the Tehreek e Insaf party had a strong demoralizing impact on the membership and many quit.[196]

HuM behaved like a client of the Pakistani state. In 2018, when it was still in the good graces of the deep state, HuM reportedly cut all relations with LeJ, and then even with SSP, which a source branded as 'our enemy', for reasons unknown but likely related again to SSP's poor relationship with the new cabinet of Imran Khan.[197] However, by 2020 that had all changed, after HuM itself had been cut off state patronage. Two other HuM sources claimed in 2020 that HuM again had good relations with fellow Deobandi LeJ and SSP.[198] There was no sense however within HuM that the organization was up for a clash with the ISI and as a member of HuM put it:

> *all these militant Islamic groups fallow the same strategy and the same ideology and in many points they help each other by leading of Pakistan intelligent service.*[199]

That the near demise of HuM might have been due to its poor military performance is also confirmed by the fact that AQ too stopped funding it at about the same time.[200] Reportedly, AQ ceased its support for the same reason:

> *There are connections with AQ but not like before, in fact we were one of the best partners of the AQ in the area. According to my information, still there are some contact between our leaders and AQ, but due to us not having military activities, their support has been stopped.*[201]

As in the case of the TTP, discussed in Chapter 3, AQ seems to have decided to intervene to rescue the failing HuM. As of mid-2020, the leaders of HuM were planning to re-launch their organization over the summer, redesigning its military organization and changing its image. An internal source said that the proposal for the re-launch came from AQIS.[202] At the time of writing there was no evidence yet that a HuM resurgence was actually taking place.

The rise of JeM: Just a stopgap?

By contrast, the crackdown looks to have been the usual façade for JeM. JeM's leaders were told 'to stay quiet for some time until the situation get better between Pakistan and western powers', said one JeM source.[203] Another JeM source echoed by saying that 'JeM was told by the Pakistan authorities to reduce the violence in Kashmir against the Indian military, because due to the last attack in Pulwama, Pakistan had come under pressure of other countries'.[204] The JeM belief that the Pakistani authorities were very much behind them was not shaken:

> *JeM is the power of Pakistani government against India in Kashmir and against of the world countries. The Pakistani government without these jihadist movements is nothing. There is no worry among JeM's leaders and ISI has close contacts with JeM.*[205]

The new crackdown on LeT and HuM in 2018 therefore did not seriously affect JeM. Azhar went underground, reportedly under the protection of the ISI.[206] A JeM civilian cadre commented that the Pakistani ISI has decreased its relations with JeM, 'but its not like LeT'.[207]

Why was JeM spared from the crackdown? A source inside JeM acknowledged that within JeM extreme views had not gone extinct, even among the top leaders:

> *there're some JeM leaders who are proposing to cause a full scale war among Pakistan and India, such as Maulana Masood Azhar, Mawlana Farooq, Abdul Rashid and some others. [...] The only possible way to reach [the goal of freeing Kashmir] is to get Pakistan and India into a full scale war over Kashmir.*[208]

True to JeM's global jihadist ethos, in 2019 it also reportedly had small contingents abroad, especially in Somalia (some 350 men) training and advising Ash Shabaab.[209]

More discretely than Hafiz Saeed, even within JeM complaints were being made about insufficient support for the insurgency in Jammu and Kashmir by the Pakistani authorities, claiming that 'the Pakistani government has been spending the budget of Kashmir in Afghanistan'.[210] JeM's leader lobbied privately Pakistani government officials for an increase to the Kashmir operations budget, but as of 2018 they had only obtained vague promises.[211]

Why was JeM spared then? LeT had specific issues with the Pakistani authorities, as discussed above, while HuM increasingly appeared as too ineffective in the increasingly tough Kashmiri environment. JeM appears to have been seen by the Pakistani deep state as the most effective organization on the Kashmir front, perhaps with good reason. Its activities in Afghanistan had confirmed its military skills. A former LeT cadre acknowledged that 'JeM is doing very good activities in Afghanistan in the eastern provinces of Nangarhar, Nuristan and Kunar'.[212]

Between 2019 and 2020, Kashmir recovered its priority for JeM at the expense of Afghanistan. The transition occurred quickly. JeM's focus in March 2019 was still definitely Afghanistan, where more than 3,000 of its members were deployed 'fighting shoulder to shoulder along with Islamic Emirate of Afghanistan and AQ against infidels and aggressors such as Americans and NATO countries'. Many of these members were deployed to Afghanistan after completing their training in Pakistan to earn tactical experience.[213] Although Afghanistan was at that point still clearly the priority, JeM had been able between 2018 and 2019 to overtake LeT as the main insurgent group in Kashmir. At the time of the Pulwama incident (14 February 2019) the main insurgent groups active in Jammu and Kashmir were:

- JeM.
- LeT.

- HuM.
- Groups linked with Al Qaeda.
- Asim Omari Group.
- Indian Mujahidin Group, which according to some reports was fully funded by LeT in its early years at least. IM carried out many attacks in India from 2005 onwards.[214]
- Student Islamic Movement of India.[215]

These groups reportedly all cooperated with each other. Their combined strength inside Jammu and Kashmir was estimated by a JeM source as 1,900–2,000 men. That according to the source represented a modest increase on a year earlier, when there were estimated 1,500–1,600 insurgents.[216] What these numbers actually mean is not entirely clear: Indian intelligence sources claim these numbers are inflated if they mean to represent the number of insurgents actually inside Indian Kashmir. These figures would make better sense if they included the insurgents based in the camps just across the border, ready for infiltration.[217]

The better funded JeM claimed to be improving its contacts inside Jammu and Kashmir, and improving its structures.[218] It was able to bring the number of its fighters in Jammu and Kashmir from some 600 in early 2018, to almost 1,000 in March 2019, according to the claim of an internal source (note again the comments above about how to assess these numbers).[219] On this count, JeM alone accounted for 50 per cent of the jihadist fighting strength on the Kashmir front. The bulk of the other members were based in Azad Kashmir, on call to be sent to battle (some 7,400 in May 2018).[220]

The limited surge in insurgent operations in Kashmir was thus mostly the result of a higher involvement of JeM. According to an internal source, 'the pressure of Pakistani military authorities on our organization', 'asking us to increase the level of violence and operations [inside Indian-controlled Kashmir]', prompted JeM into action.[221] The source believed that the Pakistani authorities hoped to undermine Modi's electoral campaign in India by embarrassing him in Kashmir. JeM was selected as the best organization to deliver the effect and agreed to pull 500 men out of Afghanistan in late 2018 in order to redeploy them to Jammu and Kashmir.[222] Donors in the Gulf states also supported Pakistani demands.[223]

> *The Pakistani government authorities had a meeting with our leaders in order to explain their request and talk about a calculated response to the Indian attacks. Moreover, our relations with Pakistani state and ISI are much deeper and closer, therefore, there is no need for explanation.*[224]

The shift in support away mainly from HuM but also from LeT and towards JeM translated into a bigger budget. According to internal sources, the trend started in 2018, when the funds increased by 38 per cent, reaching $33 million.[225] In 2019 a new 86 per cent increase took place, taking the budget to over $60 million. The ISI alone was at that point contributing $33 million, with Gulf donors (mainly Saudi Arabia) giving another $14 million and AQ $10 million. Other smaller donors made up the rest.[226]

The trend seemed to be one of more resources being invested in JeM in Jammu and Kashmir to offset the pull-out from Afghanistan.[227] Another explanation for the decision to escalate tension in Kashmir, provided by a JeM source, is the desire of Islamabad to obtain more support from China vis-à-vis India.[228]

Whatever the reasons for the desire of the Pakistani authorities to up the pressure in Kashmir, the attack in Pulwama in February 2019 was a turning point. The most successful attack against the Indian security forces in several years, it caused the death of forty police agents. The retaliatory Indian airstrikes on 26 February 2019 proved a turning point. After the Indian airstrikes, the Pakistani authorities 'swiftly' asked JeM to slow down operation in Kashmir in order to avoid the risk of a direct confrontation with India.[229]

Even after the 2019 de-escalation was fully implemented, in mid-2020, an internal source put the number of JeM fighters in Kashmir at 600 fighters, as opposed to 400 who belonged to LeT.[230] JeM kept therefore the lead, if these figures are correct. Afghanistan, at the same time, was rapidly losing importance for JeM.[231] As of 2020, JeM was rarely participating in direct clashes alongside the Taliban, and was instead busy carrying out separate operations.[232] JeM agreed with the Taliban that it would pull out its remaining forces from Afghanistan by the time the Americans were completing their own withdrawal.[233]

JeM's position vis-à-vis the Pakistani state was that of a client, as in the cases of HuM, LeT and the Sunni supremacists. Like LeJ, JeM had been tempted to emancipate itself from the patronage of the Pakistani state in 2002–3. As in the case of LeJ and (later) LeT, the deep state taught a harsh lesson to JeM and forced it to fall back in line. After its rehabilitation in 2007–9, JeM toed the lice and did its best to compete with the other organizations active in Kashmir in terms of military prowess.

In sum, the Pakistan deep state demonstrated in 2019 being able to maintain control over jihadist groups, including the largest of them all, LeT. This argues against the hypothesis, ventilated in the previous section, of the deep state being cowed into supporting the jihadists again, after the 2002 crackdown, because of their sheer power and influence within Pakistan.

JeM's military kills made it useful to AQ too and as of 2019 the two organizations were still in close relations with each other. Two sources, including a senior JeM commander, described AQ as 'one of our main allies in the fight against infidels and aggressors'.[234] The relationship with AQ was underpinned by the funding that the latter was providing to JeM. In 2019, for example, according to an internal source, AQ contributed about 16 per cent of JeM's budget of over $60 million.[235] AQ sources confirmed that the organization was supporting JeM, for example, supporting it to the tune of $8 million in 2015/16.[236] AQ also posted advisers to JeM.[237]

LeT's partial rehabilitation in 2020

Even at the peak of the crisis between LeT and Islamabad some of the sources thought that the crisis would be only temporary. This was the view, for example, of a former LeT commander, who was retired because of the cut in funding.[238] This view was shared by a JeM cadre, who believed the deep state 'doesn't want to destroy LeT' and that the crackdown on the groups active in Kashmir was temporary and functional to the need to normalize relations with Washington.[239] An AQ source too expressed his optimism that the depth of the relationship between LeT and the Pakistani military would lead to a quick resolution:[240]

It's not easy for LeT and the Pakistani authorities to completely change their course of action, since both are closely connected with each other. I see many Pakistani ISI generals, officers, operatives and retired IGs in LeT.[241]

Indeed, by mid-2020 reports started emerging that relations between LeT and the Pakistani authorities were normalizing, and cooperation between the two was restarting. This time the partnership reportedly was with MI (Military Intelligence), not the ISI. After several months Saeed was allowed access to his LeT comrades, including through face-to-face visits in jail. Zaki ur Rahman Lakhvi was released from detention and sent to Azad Kashmir, with Saeed supervising from jail thanks to telephone and internet access. He was however detained again in early 2021.[242] Reportedly Hafiz Saeed still had contacts with his armed field commanders in Jammu and Kashmir and even in Afghanistan from his jail.[243]

Hafiz Saeed reportedly made a number of other changes at the top levels of the organization in 2016, but these seem not to have been enough. Abdul Rehman Makki, who had been the military commander, was, for example, sent to focus on Jammu and Kashmir, but was later detained in 2019.[244] Even sources not privy to any negotiations between LeT's leader and the Pakistani authorities had a sense that Hafiz was acknowledging that LeT had underperformed and needed to improve in order to re-enter the graces of the Pakistani army. Nobody seems to believe that Hafiz Saeed could really lose control of the organization; at most, the possibility of a figurehead operating under the control of Hafiz was seen as not unrealistic, as a way to speed up the rehabilitation of LeT.[245]

Then, according to two LeT sources, in May–June 2020 relations between LeT and the military improved further, LeT was told to 're-organize groups inside the camps for sending them to Kashmir' and funding was resumed, although not on the same scale as before Hafiz Saeed's detention. LeT reportedly agreed to squeeze as much as possible from the budgets of its offices and local business, institutes, hospitals and madrasas for contributing to the cost of the Jihad in Kashmir.[246] The MI started funding LeT and also allowed 'foreign Islamic NGOs' to start transferring funds to LeT again.[247] A third LeT source confirmed that in the spring of 2020 LeT and the Pakistani authorities signed an entire range of new agreements regulating the relationship between the two in a much more thorough way than it had been the case earlier.[248] With the agreements signed, the Pakistani authorities resumed their funding and logistical support and released foreign funds (which therefore clearly were being channelled through the authorities).[249]

Even at this point, however, the relationship between the Pakistani services and LeT had not reached back what it used to be during its golden years:

We don't have the same relation and friendships as we had before and the cooperation of Pakistan authorities with LeT is also not like before.[250]

LeT gained additional points with the Pakistani deep state by agreeing to fully mobilize in support of the Taliban's final offensive in Afghanistan, between May and August 2021. Already in the winter 2020–1 LeT was sending unusually high numbers of fighters, after years of limited presence in Afghanistan, but as the Taliban's forces ended up stretched thinner and thinner by the unexpectedly fast advance, LeT's leadership agree to mobilize its reserves and ended up sending some 7,500 volunteers in total to fight alongside the Taliban.[251] The Pakistani deep state provided direct support, according to an LeT source:

> Pakistan Military Intelligent Service has one military officer with every group of LeT, which was sent recently to Helmand and Kandahar provinces. Pakistan's ISI was the coordinator of the recent fight in south of Afghanistan.[252]

The cooperation of LeT with the Taliban was clearly opportunistic and dictated by the concerns of the deep state. At the same time as it was supporting the Taliban, LeT was cooperating with IS-K in Kabul and Logar.[253] Then, as soon as the deep state dumped IS-K in the second half of 2021, LeT turned against IS-K and attacked it in Kunar and Nangarhar and also asked all its former members in IS-K to leave it and rejoin LeT.[254]

As LeT seemed to be cooperating satisfactorily with the deep state, as of May 2021, LeT sources were foreseeing the release of Hafiz Saeed 'in a few years', while they were confirming that

> He runs the group from inside of the jail with more communication of Pakistan military Intelligent services. He has access to receive guests and visit his faction members and also has access to talk with all its commanders and members in Afghanistan and Pakistan.[255]

Although AQIS might have played a role in the rehabilitation of LeT (see *LeT and the 2019 Crackdown*), the main beneficiary risked being AQIS' rival, IS, through its IS-P and IS-H branches. In any case, that expectation was seemingly betrayed when Hafiz Saeed was sentenced to thirty-one years in prison in April 2022, in a context of fast veering of Pakistan towards the United States, after PM Imran Khan lost the support of the army.[256]

Enter IS-H

IS and the deep state converge on Kashmir

In 2015 pro-IS activists were beginning to form networks in parts of India, around an activists who had formed a group called Junood ul Khilafa e Hind (JKH).[257] However, already from 2014 onwards young Keralis were joining in as volunteers in Iraq, Syria and Afghanistan; several were killed in Afghanistan.[258] IS-K claimed some very limited activities in Kashmir in 2017–18, and the police admitted IS had some presence in Jammu and Kashmir, even in in reality these were the work of local freelance sympathizers.[259]

Overall, as of early 2019 IS in India seemed to amount to little, despite the media hype. The formation of Wilayat Hind as a new province in May 2019 and its IS branch IS-Hind (IS-H) did not seem to immediately change things, as it took quite a while for IS-H to take even the first organizational steps. Some minor attacks were claimed in May–June 2019 and then again in February–April 2020, but according to an IS-K source IS-H had not started its military activities yet as of April 2020, although it was recruiting. It might well have opportunistically attacks carried out by others, possibly by sympathizers within other groups. Throughout 2020, genuine IS-H activities appear to have been confined to propaganda operations.[260] Contrary to IS-P, IS-H appears to have been intended to recruit Kashmiris and Indians. IS-P sources claimed that IS-H was doing well in 2020 in recruiting among young Kashmiris, attracting hundreds, especially university students. IS-P reportedly sent some of its members (around ten) to assist IS-H organize in Azad and in Indian Kashmir.[261] Although IS-P was investing also on Sunni supremacism in Pakistan (see *IS breaks AQ's monopoly* above), jihad in Kashmir was also high on the agenda:

We will focus on Kashmir and release our Muslim brothers from the unbelievers, which are Indian army and Indian government. In fact, Kashmir struggles is our main and important goal to release our Muslim brother from the cruelties of Indian army.[262]

Another IS-K source said that IS-P was already in the process of establishing camps in Azad Kashmir as of mid-2020.[263]

IS-P and IS-H turned from mere projects to actual organizations thanks to a strong involvement of the Pakistani deep state. In the first half of 2020 the ISI reportedly started co-opting IS-K members as recruiters of volunteers for Kashmir from within the ranks of IS-K itself. These recruitment efforts were reportedly not authorized by the leadership of IS-K. At the same time the ISI directly approached the IS-K leadership and put it under pressure to send members to Kashmir, essentially transferring them to either IS-P or IS-H.[264] As IS activities in Kashmir weakened, the ISI appears to have identified an opportunity and decided to send in a new IS branch, that it could control. IS sources accused the ISI of having hijacked the organization, creating a branch with ex members taken from Afghanistan and Pakistan.[265] Groups allegedly recruited by the ISI deployed to Kashmir, claiming to be IS. These groups were reportedly trying to be recognized by the Caliphate as legitimate IS. An HuM source believed that because of notorious close association of LeT, JeM and HuM with the ISI, the Pakistani authorities were trying to get a new wave of violence in Kashmir with a 'virgin' group like IS.[266]

IS-K had its own scheme for identifying volunteers for Kashmir, managed by Ismail Kashmiri, a close collaborator of Governor Aslam Farooqi, until he was arrested in Afghanistan in April 2020. This was managed without ISI involvement and in cooperation instead with HuM of Kashmir, Fazal Rahman Khalili group and some other Kashmiri groups. This scheme was stopped after the arrest of Ismail Kashmiri.[267]

These efforts point to the fact that, although in not entirely coordinated ways, both ISI and IS were moving towards re-opening a Kashmir front for IS, under the banner of IS-H. IS-P was also involved in this process, having been designed in part at least as a support structure for IS-H. While it might be true that the first IS-H groups to be formed for Kashmir might have been put together by Pakistani intelligence, it seems clear that the genuine IS was not far behind.

The two efforts might have started separately, but soon converged. The relationship between the Pakistani deep state and IS-P/IS-H thus appears to have key to the IS-P/IS-H project. One LeT source specified that it was the MI that in 2020 was providing support to IS-P and IS-H.[268] An IS-P source acknowledged that IS-P has relations with the 'Pakistani army'.[269] Another IS-P source acknowledged in July 2020 that Pakistani intelligence was already working with IS in Kashmir, supporting IS-H:[270]

> *Any jihadist group that forms in Pakistan, Pakistan intelligence assesses it to find its use. One of the main focuses and purpose of IS-P is to fight against Indians in Kashmir, to free Kashmir from Indians. In this regard Pakistani intelligence is working very hard in creating its own loyalists inside IS-P to fulfil its own aim and propose in Kashmir against Indians. For sure sometime and some place Pakistani intelligence will stand against IS-P, but Pakistani intelligence wants IS-P to become more powerful in Kashmir rather than in Baluchistan.*[271]

The consensus in LeT circles was that the Pakistani authorities looked at IS-P and IS-H as tools to relaunch the jihad in Kashmir, while pretending not to be involved. One source believed that given sufficient funding, IS-H and IS-P could bloom into the main jihadist group active in Kashmir, 'bigger then LeT or JeM and others'.[272]

A source in IS-K accused 'those members of the IS leadership encouraging their members to move to Kashmir' of having a 'close relationship with Pakistan's intelligence service'.[273] Already in April 2020 an IS-K commander was describing the IS-P/IS-H project as a joint ISI-IS project. The main feature of the project, he added, was to be supported by virtually all the Pakistani jihadist groups, which had relations with the deep state: IS-K, LeT, LeJ, JeM, JuA and SSP, all of which would be contributing fighters.[274]

The deep state herds global jihadism towards Kashmir and India

A few months later, an IS-P commander confirmed that IS-P was working to bring together Pakistani jihadist networks, in support of the nascent IS-H.[275] Some LeT commanders joined IS during the period it was in disgrace, initially because LeT has mistreated them. Soon, however, they started joining because LeT was encouraging to do so.[276] An LeT source said that one of the agreements signed committed LeT to help IS-P and IS-H improve their capabilities, provide training for its fighters and support their units once they deployed to Kashmir. The source indicated that the IS-P and IS-H trainees sent to the LeT camps were recruited by the Pakistani authorities themselves.[277]

According to a source, there were no complaints in LeT about the new relationship with IS-P and IS-H.[278] Quite the contrary, in LeT there was optimism that IS-P and IS-H would not diminish the pot of resources allocated to it by donors and MI because of the conviction that the two branches of IS would be funded by the Caliphate, still perceived to be very resourceful. At least, donors had not given any sign that they might want to shift support yet.[279] Despite being forced into it, an LeT trainer described the new relationship with 'global Jihadist movement' IS as 'a big chance for us'. Should IS succeed in Kashmir, he said, LeT and other groups active in Kashmir would be proud of having helped it. He too believed that the deployment of IS to Kashmir was funded by the Caliphate with its 'huge resources' and that this would make a difference for the jihad there.[280] This suggests that LeT rank-and-file were told by September 2020 that the jihad in Kashmir was being taken over by IS.

An AQIS source confirmed that he also saw LeT getting quite close to IS. Despite the rapprochement, AQIS was worried about the growing cosiness between LeT and IS.[281]

> *They're organizing meetings monthly. We have talked and discussed this hot issue with LeT senior leaders but unfortunately, they did not accept our concerns and said that they are not ready to halt relations with IS anytime soon.*[282]

Worse still for AQIS, it was not just LeT getting closer to IS. JeM started edging closer to IS later than LeT. As late as May 2018, one of the sources was still claiming that JeM had no relations with IS.[283] In August, however, an LeT source was already claiming that JeM had started sending members to Europe, following pressure by IS.[284] By March 2019 even a JeM source acknowledged that JeM had established better relations with IS-K in Afghanistan.[285] An IS-P source confirmed that its organization had by the summer of 2020 'good relations' with JeM.[286] At least two LeT sources confirmed in September 2020 that JeM was also involved in supporting IS-P/IS-H and helping them getting organized. Both LeT and JeM were in any case told by the ISI to help IS-P and IS-H set up camp in Kashmir. The same applied to other groups active in Kashmir with the support of ISI. As of mid-2020, some 150 trainees had reached the camps.[287]

HuM too flirted with IS-K for some time, but by early 2018 the relationship had ended and all contacts had been cut, possibly under AQ pressure.[288] It might well be that HuM's refusal to engage with IS led to it being finally abandoned by the deep state.

As of September 2020, IS-H was still very much work in progress. Among else, it did not have a governor yet. One LeT source hinted that even LeT and JeM commanders were being considered for the top IS-H job.[289] As for IS-P (see Chapter 4), the choice of governor was understood to be a decisive card to play in establishing the hegemony of IS among the Pakistani jihadist groups. The emerging framework was one of the Pakistani deep state supporting the IS-H/IS-P claim to hegemony of Pakistani jihadism, presumably not out of sheer love for IS, but out of the conviction that the IS branches in Pakistan had been tamed and IS was still a brand strong enough to maximize the impact of any operation in Kashmir. With the collapse in deep state-IS-K relations in the summer of 2021, even relations with LeT and JeM waned (see also *Competition for AQ*' in Chapter 2).[290] However, LeT retained some relationship with IS-P and with

IS-H, with one source describing this as 'cooperation'.[291] Another LeT source described the cooperation in these terms:

> LeT has some contacts and cooperation with IS-P like logistical support, sometimes providing fighters from the Madrasas and also sometime sharing training centres. [...] According to my information, IS-H is active in Jammu and Kashmir and even in Baluchistan by deep support of LeT and JeM and LeJ. IS-H without support of these three organizations is nothing in Pakistan.[292]

The place of Kashmir in global jihad

The 'regionalization' of AQ largely meant reorientation towards a regional conflict (Kashmir), as opposed to an international one (Afghanistan). While AQ invested considerable resources on groups active in Kashmir after 2002, Kashmir itself was not a top priority for AQ in South Asia for many years. Only after the apparent US disengagement from Afghanistan did AQ start turning more seriously towards Kashmir and India, as symbolized by the formation of AQIS. It is not immediately obvious that jihadist groups such as LeT and JeM played a significant role in pushing AQ towards Kashmir. However, the weight of the evidence is that the Pakistani deep state did.

That the Pakistani deep state might have wanted AQIS to get more and more involved in Kashmir made sense, as AQIS could contribute skills badly needed in the more and more challenging environment of Kashmir: essentially, sophisticated terror techniques. But from AQIS' perspective, Kashmir replacing Afghanistan as the main focus of activity seemed a poor trade off, and certainly a major step away from the fight against the 'far enemy' and against the 'puppet' regimes of the Middle East. In a sense, therefore, AQ might have been dragged by Pakistan into getting involved in Kashmir more deeply than it would otherwise have done, in a manifestation of the agent-principle dilemma discussed in the *Introduction*.

AQIS had probably little choice – the deep state was hosting its leaders in Pakistan and wanted AQIS involved in Kashmir, while Kashmir also offered an opportunity for very necessary fund raising. AQ needed to appear involved in a cause célèbre of the Muslim world in order to keep raising plentiful funding, and the Afghan conflict was starting to lose its jihad aura due to the American drawdown. The sense, however, is still that of AQ being co-opted into the Kashmir conflict, rather than furthering its attempt to consolidate its hegemony over the global jihad movement in South Asia.

This was therefore a case of expediency, as it seems to have often been the case for AQ in South Asia. What made things even worse for AQ was the fact that AQIS did not achieve much in Kashmir and in India from the perspective of the Pakistani deep state. By 2019, as AQIS was agreeing to intensify efforts in Kashmir and India, the deep state was becoming nervous about figuring out a viable strategy to keep up pressure on India, without starting a war with it and without compromising its already difficult relations with Washington. AQIS did not have much time to make an impact, before the deep state had decided that IS better served its purposes there.

From the perspective of AQ, that IS could take the lead in Kashmir with the support of the Pakistani deep state was indeed a potentially ominous development. It signalled that the deep state was beginning to view the IS brand as more powerful than AQ's and within the context of the waning Afghan jihad such a development had the potential to hand a clear lead to IS in the whole subcontinent. The move highlighted how the deep state was the dominant partner in the relationship with AQ and how AQ was a risk to ending up a mere client of the deep state, as opposed to the ally it aspired to be. It should be noted that AQIS sought to outwardly maintain an independent posture in Kashmir, claiming to be aiming for a jihadist effort independent of Pakistani support.[293]

It is worth noting at this point that the Pakistani ISI appeared to be preventing global jihadists from getting involved in Kashmir in the late 1990s.[294] At time of tension between AQ and the Pakistani deep state, AQ would dust off old accusations about the lack of determination of the Pakistani authorities in pursuing jihad in Kashmir.[295] This begs the question of the wisdom, from the long-term perspective of the deep state, of getting IS involved in Kashmir. The short-term benefit of a renewed 'plausible deniability' of a Pakistani role in stocking up the conflict there made sense, but if IS-H and IS-P were to be too successful in Kashmir and India, they could become hard to control for the deep state and not just in Kashmir and India, but also in Pakistan itself. A single major successful attack, comparable to the Mumbai bombings of 2008, would make it hard for the deep state to restrain the global jihadists even in the presence of dangerously high tension with India at the border. Perhaps even more worryingly in the long term, funding to IS branches would be boosted, enabling them to scale up recruitment and organizational efforts even inside Pakistan.

The impact on IS-H of the rapidly worsening relations between IS-K and the deep state (see *IS-K and the Pakistani State* and *Wilayat Pakistan* above) was not yet clear at the time of writing, but it must have raised the type of worries mentioned above within the ranks of the Pakistani deep state. The take-off of Wilayat Hind certainly appeared slow from the vantage point of mid-2022.

Conclusion

Why did the Pakistani deep state keep relying on jihadist groups?

When jihadism was fashionable

The reasons why the Pakistani state got engaged with jihadist groups were fairly clear even before the author started writing this book. In the final decade of the Cold War, in the 1980s, engaging with jihadist groups was fashionable and fully acceptable, even a matter of pride. Even today, despite some embarrassment, the Afghan jihadists of the 1980s are seen as a different matter altogether from the post-2001 ones. The 1980s jihadists have been since described as jihadist/nationalists, focused on winning the Afghan jihad. The concept of global jihad had not become current yet. In reality, some of the groups sponsored by the Pakistani security services (and by others such as the US government, the Saudi government and others) were already into exporting jihad: the various Pakistani groups which joined the fray, but also several of the Afghan groups who dominated that jihad. The case of Hizb e Islami is obvious as that group later sent volunteers to Azerbaijan and supported groups active in Kashmir. Even more moderate groups, however, had links to foreign jihadists abroad, such as Ittehad e Islami, Jami'at e Islami and the various Khomeinist groups. The 1980s worked very well for the Pakistani deep state, and it is no wonder that it felt natural the same approach could be used to undermine Indian control over Jammu and Kashmir.

The 1990s: Global jihadism seemingly under control

The Kashmir campaign gradually became much more controversial internationally, especially as global jihad started becoming a recognized movement and Western targeted started being attacked. This seems to confirm Kapur's analysis:

> *Ironically, the more successful the sponsor state's militant campaign has been, the more likely these problems are to emerge. A successful campaign is likely to be characterized by an able militant force and a significantly damaged adversary. These characteristics increase the likelihood that the militants will be able to exceed the sponsor's control and that the adversary will be highly motivated to inflict retaliatory harm on the sponsor.*[1]

The real question is then why the Pakistani deep state continued pursuing the path of sponsoring jihadist movements even once they started becoming toxic in the West. In the 1990s, the Pakistani deep state was in fact showing restraint. Openly 'global jihadist' groups were being kept out of Kashmir, while the deep state did not entertain direct relations with those based in Afghanistan and sometimes harassed them. This approach seemed to be working, until 9/11 struck.

The impact of 9/11 and of the US intervention in Afghanistan

At that point the Pakistani establishment was oriented towards abiding to American demands and sought to crack down on global jihadists and their Pakistani sympathizers. The expectation in Islamabad and in Rawalpindi was that Pakistan's sacrificing of a client government (the Taliban's emirate) would be rewarded by allowing it to retain significant influence in Kabul, counterbalancing the rapidly rising influence of Iran and India. However, despite pressure from Pakistan, its influence in Kabul during the first post-9/11 years remained negligible. The Americans moved to curtail Iranian and Russian influence, but that if anything benefited India and certainly not Pakistan.

At the same time Musharraf's crackdown on foreign jihadists and their Pakistani sympathizers and allies was proving more destabilizing than expected. The price Pakistan was paying was higher than planned, and the rewards were hardly any. From 2005 onwards the deep state started working to pacify the jihadist networks, probably initially exploring controversial paths autonomously from the country's top leadership. In 2003 already the deep state had started supporting the Afghan Taliban insurgents, in retaliation for the failure of the Americans to grant more influence to Pakistan and to contain India's. Soon the idea emerged of getting the foreign jihadists and their Pakistani supporters fight in Afghanistan alongside the Taliban, allowing them to discharge their anger and at the same time serve Pakistan's interests, killing two birds with one stone.

Bringing the jihadists under control?

By offering Pakistan as a base for jihadist operations in the neighbouring country the deep state also hoped to discourage them from turning against the Pakistani state itself. Indeed, the only time when the Pakistani deep state lost control of its jihadist proxies is when it was forced to shut or contain their operations in both Afghanistan and Kashmir/India, following US intervention in Afghanistan in 2001. It is probably not by accident that the turn away from cooperating with the United States happened after the Lal Masjid incident, which represented the peak in the confrontation with the jihadists. In a sense, Pakistan was trapped in the relationship with the jihadist groups that its deep state contributed so much to create.

After this first crisis in the relationship with the jihadists, which culminated in the Lal Masjid incident, the deep state seemingly recovered confidence in its ability to 'manage' the jihadists. By 2009 the jihadists had mostly been brought back under control, with the exception of LeJ and TTP, which seemed to have been reduced to a marginal actor inside Pakistan or on their way to be.

That was not the end of the confrontation of the deep state with the jihadists. What drove LeT's increasingly arrogant behaviour vis-à-vis its patrons in the Pakistani deep state in 2018–19 is not clear, but the deep state emerged victorious from this confrontation as well. The deep state appeared at that point to have demonstrated its ability to teach a lesson to any misbehaving jihadist group. US pressure to dismantle the jihadist networks helped the deep state renegotiating the terms with the jihadists to its own favour.

The resurgence of the TTP in 2020–2 was therefore a major blow to the deep state, compounded by the loss of influence over the Afghan Taliban, turned Emirate again in August 2021. The sense of a crisis in the relationship with the jihadist was compounded by worsening relations with AQ and IS-K, as well as by the emergence of IS-P as a significant challenge.

From the standpoint of spring 2022, the calculus of the deep state, of being able to get away with extensive cooperation with jihadist groups, could still be argued to have proven substantially right. The resurgent TTP was still well below the 2007–10 peak, LeT and the other main Pakistani jihadist groups appeared to have been tamed, AQ/AQIS had not resumed violent attacks, despite having broken off the 2020 agreement, and IS had not been able to start a campaign of Sunni supremacist violence comparable to that of SSP and LeJ in 2007–15. The trend, however, was no longer positive, but negative on all three counts. The real risk of the strategy of co-opting the global jihadists was that they and their Pakistani partners could end up being strengthened in the long run. The calculus of the deep state, and eventually even of top policymakers in Islamabad, was that Pakistan was already engulfed in a major militant wave in 2002–7 and that it could hardly get worse than that. This is the benchmark for evaluating the success of the strategy.

The risk of damaging relations with Western powers

It was undoubtedly a dangerous path that Pakistan took, and its relationship with the Taliban did in the end damage US-Pakistan relations considerably. The Pakistani authorities might have calculated that eventually the Americans would need to mend fences with Islamabad again, sooner or later. In the end Western powers did prove reluctant throughout to call out Pakistan's relations with global jihadists, also proved right, despite some bad moments. The nuclear power status of Pakistani might have something to do with this. Another rationale for this caution could well be the declining Western interest in global jihadism, except when it represented a direct threat or when it suited wider geopolitical concerns (as highlighted by the different attitude towards Iran's links to listed terrorist organizations).

Overall, the deep state did a good job of keeping its plausible deniability more plausible than it was the case with the Taliban. That proved to be enough, at least until 2022, to allow Western powers rehabilitating Pakistan after short periods of threatened pariah status. The ultimate risk to Pakistan was that one of jihadist clients or collaborators could get caught carrying out a terror attack in Europe or the United States, but risk was averted so far.

What does global jihadism have to offer to national jihadists?

From the perspective of the jihadist groups, allying with both AQ and the Pakistani state was not as incompatible as it would appear at first sight, given what was discussed throughout the book about the on and off cooperation between AQ and the deep state. That such double alliances could survive even periods of bad relations between AQ and the deep state could indicate that conflict between AQ and the deep state was seen as temporary or remediable. Serious crises took place in 2002–7 between jihadist groups and the Pakistani state. Even then, the dominant belief was that it was all due to Musharraf's and his policy of cooperating with the Americans. Musharraf would go, one way or another, and the relationship would then resume a more traditional pattern. Indeed, it did.

That the Pakistani jihadists might have offered hospitality and support to the global jihadists entirely out of ideological sympathy is hard to believe, especially over a period of twenty years. Even the group closest to AQ, the TTP, was unequipped to launch a sophisticated jihad against the Pakistani state. It retaliated to Pakistani army incursions into the tribal areas with a campaign of increasingly indiscriminate terror. AQ did not approve, not on humanitarian grounds, but because it saw this unsophisticated campaign as doomed to fail, as it did. Whatever AQ might have thought of the Pakistani Taliban initially, over the years it must have learned that they would struggle to grow into a competent insurgency. AQ seems to have seen the Pakistani Taliban a relatively primitive and not especially promising proto-jihadist movement, but at the same time saw potential in it as a force that would help igniting an insurgency in Afghanistan, that would cover AQ's back in the tribal areas and that would serve as a useful tool for pushing the Pakistani military towards an accommodation with AQ and away from cooperation with the Americans. It took years before AQ's pressure on the TTP to change course bore some results, and only because changes within the TTP itself had made it more receptive to AQIS' advice.

Other jihadist groups supported by AQ, such as SSP and LeJ, were not entirely consistent with AQ's ideology, principles and aims either. AQIS sources have been claiming that the decline in sectarian violence in recent years was due to their lobbying of the Sunni supremacist groups. The supremacists remained hard to herd, but these groups fulfilled roles in AQ's effort to protect itself and to promote the Afghan jihad. LeT is a special case; its Ahl e Sunna ideology should have placed it especially close to AQ, but it was very guarded in its collaboration with AQ, perhaps because the deep state was trying to avoid the risk of a hijacking by AQ.

There is another possible rationale for LeT keeping some distance from AQ. A more convincing explanation for the collaboration of some many Pakistani groups with AQ first and with IS later could be a transfer of organizational and technical know-how, but this is not so likely in the case of groups that had already received generous infusions of know-how from the deep state, in order to enable them to operate effectively in Afghanistan and most of all in Kashmir. Only the Sunni supremacist groups could have seen value in a transfer of know-how, but there is little evidence that their capabilities increased significantly after 2001.

The value of global jihadism to the local jihadist groups in Pakistan remains therefore difficult to explain unless we accept what it is alleged in this book, based on jihadist sources, that AQ and IS were offering significant amounts of funding. This appealed to poorly funded jihadist groups for obvious reasons, but also to better funded ones because it allowed diversification of funding and therefore potentially greater autonomy. The ultimate proof of this financial relationship (beyond what alleged by the sources used in this book) will always be hard to provide, but this is the most convincing explanation of why otherwise well-funded and rooted organizations collaborated at all with AQ.

The emergence of IS' competition provided a useful test of the relationship between AQ and its local allies. From AQ's point of view, the results of the test were not flattering. In Pakistan, virtually no jihadist group stayed fully loyal to AQ, and by 2020 the majority were closer to IS than to AQ, even if later most of them drifted back to AQ. These groups were all distributed along the allies–clients spectrum, but mostly clustering near the clients end of it.

It can be concluded therefore that the main impact of AQ and IS in South Asia was to empower local jihadism by acting as fund-raising agencies, which thanks to the grand cause of global jihad were more effective in fund raising than the local jihadist groups would have been, each on its own. Some transfer of know-how is also likely to have happened, but it appears to have been less important. The cause of global jihad per se continued to have limited attraction in South Asia and its ideological drive does not seem to have helped recruitment significantly, with more parochial causes remaining largely predominant.

AQ: Carving a strategy out of expediency

AQ might have expected and even desired a US intervention in Afghanistan after 9/11, but certainly it did not expect the Taliban's Emirate to collapse so swiftly. This was a serious miscalculation, which exposed AQ to an existential challenge. Thrown against the Pakistani border, AQ had at that point limited options and was in a completely disorganized state. Its operatives, faced with a leadership that until 2006 was completely absent and even later struggling to lead effectively, resorted to expediency. They needed to cooperate closely with the Afghan Taliban and with the Pakistani Taliban, despite all the deficiencies that AQ was identifying in them. The need to work out a modus vivendi with the Pakistani authorities soon became clear to the AQ operatives as well, despite the leaders being jealous of AQ's independence. Within such a challenging context, AQ managed quite well in not only surviving as an organization, but even dramatically expanding its influence and contributing to the Afghan Taliban's eventual success in 2021. AQ's toughest challenges were yet to emerge and these would not be posed by the Americans or other 'kafirs'. By 2020–1, the gradual drift of the Afghan Taliban away from AQ and the emergence of the global jihadist competition of IS looked much more threatening to AQ than US intervention in Afghanistan in 2001 had been.

AQ's influence

Paradoxically, or perhaps not, the US intervention in Afghanistan, aimed at destroying AQ, ended up strengthening the influence and presence of AQ in the region. AQ already had extensive contacts with Pakistani jihadists before 9/11, but was prompted by the arrival of the Americans to invest massively in deepening its relationship with the many of these groups. The contrary was also true: the Pakistani jihadists were pushed (by US pressure on the Pakistani state for a crackdown on them) to accept AQ's offers for closer collaboration.

Despite its disorganization, AQ's prospects in South Asia looked therefore good at that point, as the Afghan jihad became for at least ten years the cause célèbre par excellence of the Muslim world, only being overtaken by the Syrian war in 2011. During that decade and even beyond, AQ was able to raise funds (chiefly in the Gulf) to an unseen degree. With this unprecedented wealth not only AQ helped the Afghan Taliban kick-start their jihad, but also succeeded in cultivating deeper and deeper relations with virtually all the Pakistani jihadist groups.

This is not to say that AQ succeeded on all fronts and was not left with substantial dilemmas unresolved. For example, AQ's criticism towards the TTP was primarily aimed at its reliance on indiscriminate violence, probably also because among else it was making relations with Pakistani intelligence harder to manage. However, AQ did not really support the potential shift of the TTP shift towards an accommodation with Islamabad, even if it did try to moderate its policies. While such a shift, if successful, would have made relations with the deep state easier, it would also deprive AQ of a major source of leverage.

The cooperation of the Pakistani state with the US crackdown on AQ certainly translated into considerable pressure on the organization, but AQ managed to weather the storm and deployed a long-term strategy to push the Pakistani 'deep state' away from cooperating with the United States. The path towards an alliance was long and troublesome, but despites highs and lows from 2005 onwards there were many instances and forms of cooperation between AQ and the deep state.

There is little evidence that AQ ever committed seriously to a jihad against the Pakistani authorities for any length of time. The rhetorical assault on Islamabad, which followed the Lal Masjid incident, does not seem to have altered a longer-term pattern of seeking forms of cooperation with the Pakistani military, if not Islamabad. What AQ appears to have wanted was not an alliance, but a relationship that would offer some strategic depth and allow to maximize the benefits deriving from its leverage with jihadist groups, essentially offering additional incentives to the deep state for investing more and more in its campaign to undermine the US mission in Afghanistan. In practice, therefore, AQ succeeded to a least a degree in influencing the deep state too.

AQ's core

The account that emerged throughout the book is one of a rather coherent strategic formulation by AQ, after the initial disarray of 2001–2. Some findings however raise the question of how centralized AQ's operations were and of what role the 'core' effectively had. The 2005 deal between AQ and elements of the ISI, reported by an AQIS source, left no trace in bin Laden's papers. This raises the issue of AQ's disorganized state and of operatives reaching their own deals in Pakistan (as well as elsewhere). Was it 'centralisation of decision and decentralisation of execution', as AQ would claim, or mere expediency? In any case, the fact that fifteen years later an AQIS source had recollections of that and of other episodes suggests a high degree of continuity and coherence in operations, despite a high level of casualties.

After 2011 the organizational state of AQ in South Asia seems to have improved anyway and it appeared rather solidly organized and disciplined. Inevitably having to operate in deep clandestine mode over a very large territory made it impossible for AQ to be completely coherent in its approach. After 2011, therefore, AQ appears to have finally managed to develop a unified strategy, even if this too was gradually losing its way, not least because the considerable length of time over which it was implemented (ten years). Many changes, including unexpected one, occurred during that time span, including the US/Taliban deal of 29 February 2020, which was seen by AQ as a huge blow, although not an unexpected one.

AQ's key aims

Protect its leadership and support jihad in Afghanistan

Surprised by the swift collapse of the Taliban Emirate in 2001, the dispersed AQ operatives had to be expedient. They needed first of all to save its leadership and then to plot a resurgence. The options available to AQ initially in the tribal areas of Pakistan were limited. Bin Laden was not playing any role before 2006 and it took time for AQ to develop a long-term strategy, which to a large extent brought together policies that had already been developed by its operatives on the ground. Among them, the self-preservation of AQ's leadership remained a priority. Neither the TTP was AQ's first choice of a primary partner, nor working out deals with the Pakistani security establishment was an ideal scenario. But both choices were functional to AQ's strategy and were acceptable in the absence of better options.

The same applies to supporting the Afghan Taliban's jihad in Afghanistan, using the Pakistani safe haven largely for the purpose of managing its efforts across the border and for keeping its leaders as safe as possible. A jihadist victory in Afghanistan was also supposed to hand back to AQ a safe haven for its leadership. Although from 2005 onwards AQ operatives first and then the leadership as well managed to reach a series of deals with the Pakistani deep state, which among else offered safety to its leaders and to its small apparatus, the leadership of AQ (apparently unaware of at least the first deal) was not satisfied that its safety had been achieved for good. The Abbottabad raid was a dramatic confirmation that this was indeed the case. Even as late as 2020, instead of indulging in celebrations of the seemingly impending departure of the Americans from Afghanistan, AQ had to worry about its future role in the region. That AQ did not consider re-allocating human and financial resources away from South Asia, exploiting the success of its Afghan Taliban allies, is significant. The importance for AQ of establishing a 'safer haven' for its leadership appears therefore to have remained paramount and was confirmed so by the late 2021 decisions to cooperate with IS in establishing an independent safe haven in Pakistan and to relocate al Zawahiri to Afghanistan. By supporting IS financially and not participating directly in the effort, AQ tried to salvage its agreement with the Pakistani deep state. In parallel, as discussed above, AQ was still hoping that eventually the TTP could establish another safe haven, perhaps in agreement with Islamabad. Pakistan was not deemed to be safe enough because of the lingering fear that the 'deep state' would one day turn against them under US or Chinese pressure. The Afghan safe haven was therefore considered to be essential for increasing the safety of the leadership. This made the US/Taliban trade off (withdrawal vs Taliban cutting off links with AQ) unacceptable for AQ, which thus forfeited a chance to close the Afghan jihad and focus resources and efforts towards fostering a domino effect beyond Afghanistan.

Undermine American will

AQ's decision not to take the US decision to withdraw as a major victory had several motivations, but one is likely to have been (at least if we accept the theory that AQ carried out the 9/11 attacks with the aim of luring the United States into a war in Afghanistan) AQ's original intent was to have the Americans fight a never-ending war in Afghanistan and eventually drain their will to hang on to the Middle East. This married nicely the war against the 'far enemy' with the local conflict in Afghanistan. AQ's propaganda hardly tried to exploit the withdrawal agreement of February 2020 to its advantage initially and by late spring it was facing growing tensions with the Afghan Taliban, who were demanding it to commit to stopping using Afghanistan as a global platform even after the completion of the US withdrawal. AQ had been discretely accusing the Taliban of cooperating with the Americans in targeting its senior leaders for some time as well. Aside from the (short) honeymoon between Americans and Taliban, the very prospect of a Taliban victory was deeply worrying for AQ's leaders, who by then had experienced the 'betrayal' of Al Nusra in Syria. A Taliban regime would inevitably be pushed by geography and economics towards seeking accommodation with sworn enemies of AQ such as China and Russia, if not the United States.

So, the American withdrawal from Afghanistan was an AQ defeat disguised as a victory. If AQ had accepted to leave Afghanistan, or to turn it into an asylum refuge (as opposed to an operational base), it could have exploited the 'US defeat' narrative much more effectively. Instead, AQ was moving towards a tactical alliance with IS-K in Afghanistan, which risked further undermining its efforts to regain the leadership of global jihad. As the Taliban took power unexpectedly quickly, AQ faced the dilemma of whether the consolidation of the new regime was actually in its interest.

This begs the question of what was the residual relevance of South Asia for AQ's battle against the 'far enemy' in 2022. AQ was still able to train recruits in Pakistan and Afghanistan, who could then be deployed to other theatres, where they would be more directly useful against the 'far enemy' or at least the Saudi monarchy, even if it would probably be easier to send such recruits to other locations, such as Syria or Sahel. Other than that, AQ's concern for the 'far enemy' appears to have been eclipsed by other, more immediate preoccupations: protecting its leadership, as discussed above, establishing a jihadist legitimacy and competing for the leadership of global jihad, as discussed below. These aims were to a considerable extent in contradiction with each other: to better protect the leadership and to enhance its position vis-à-vis the Taliban, AQ sought an alliance with IS-K and IS-P and was ready to preside over the implosion of the Taliban's second Emirate, but these policies risked eventually undermining its efforts to reclaim the leadership of global jihad and could potentially even hurt its efforts to maintain 'jihadist legitimacy'. In this sense, as AQ's strategy started unravelling in 2019–20, a renewed drift towards expediency became noticeable.

Jihadist legitimacy

AQ did not find managing its affiliates in Pakistan and Afghanistan much easier than the Pakistani military establishment had. As AQ expanded its influence over jihadist groups, to a large extent by distributing money to them, the 'marginal efficiency' of its investment declined. In other words, as the list of allies expanded, AQ received fewer and fewer additional returns for its investment. Still, like the Pakistani military, AQ did not change strategy. AQ appears to have been almost obsessed by the need to maintain its jihadist leadership in Pakistan (as well as elsewhere), investing considerable amounts just to keep a multitude of jihadist groups outwardly loyal to itself.

Was AQ always content to work together with 'compagnons de route' who were essentially only on loan to global jihad, and in any case to AQ, or did it genuinely harbour the hope and determination of transforming them into solid and dependable global jihadists? The big investment made on them is striking, while AQ instead maintained its direct presence on the ground at very modest levels throughout the conflict and did little to recruit locally. The rationale of this choice is apparent, at least for the 2002–14 period: because AQ was being aggressively targeted by the Americans, building up a large AQ branch would only invite more US strikes and cost higher casualties. Operating as much as possible through local allies offered the possibility of better camouflaging AQ and made American strikes more controversial locally, eventually contributing to push the Pakistani authorities away from close cooperation with the United States.

The creation of AQIS in 2014 was only a marginal innovation in this regard. This is also striking: as the Americans were taking out almost all of their combat troops from Afghanistan and the risks involved in establishing a large AQ affiliate or branch in the region dramatically abated, AQ in the end opted to continue operating largely through allies of dubious reliability and/or trustworthiness. Did this perhaps have to do with the desire of not being seen as a serious threat to the Pakistani state, and of not embarrassing the Pakistani deep state with a 'too obvious' AQ presence? Or was jihadist legitimacy the real prize for AQ? By being able to claim undisputed leadership of jihadism in South Asia, despite the very real differences it had with most of the local groups, AQ could probably further its primary causes in the Middle East by attracting donors. In this sense, the aim of jihadist legitimacy linked the South Asian operations to the Middle Eastern aims of AQ as long as any spare resources were raised for investment outside South Asia. It is not clear, based on available information, whether this was achieved.

AQ and the deep state: Who called the shots?

Despite fifteen years of increasingly frequent cooperation with at least some elements of the deep state, AQ/AQIS still had doubts about the reliability of its allies within Pakistan's intelligence in 2020. If the alliance of the Pakistani military establishment with jihadist groups delivered much to AQ and also damaged in the long run the US-Pakistan relationship, it is also true that AQ's relationship with the Pakistani military was far from being a natural alliance.

Although AQ might have never been genuinely interested in a Pakistani jihad, it could not trust the Pakistani security establishment either, the more so given the high pressure the Pakistanis were under to help the United States hunt down AQ operatives. Indeed, for years after the first partial agreement in 2005, the Pakistani security agencies continued contributing to US anti-AQ operations directly or indirectly, although seemingly on a small scale. The AQ leadership, initially not privy to the deal of its operatives with elements of the ISI, came to accept it as the lesser evil, while it figured out how to improve it.

The degree and forms in which AQ and the Pakistani security forces might have collaborated are not wholly clear, but appear to have varied over time. Much of the time, the arrangements between AQ and the Pakistani deep state seemed akin to an understanding to keep friction as low as possible, a kind of 'Cold War' arrangement where proxies and allies were sometimes engaging in direct conflict, but the two main actors refrained from direct clashes. The exception was the protection afforded by the deep state to AQ's top leaders, starting with bin Laden.

When the AQ leadership eventually managed to read a deal with the deep state, it was a trade off in which AQ abstained from encouraging jihad against the Pakistani state, and possibly even quietly discouraged it, in exchange for protection, limited to its leaders. Understandably, this is not a type of deal that AQ's leadership would want to advertise with its allies or even lower-rank members: the former were often opposed to the Pakistani state and the latter might not have appreciated being left vulnerable, while the leaders enjoyed protection.

Despite this, as AQ contributed to drive a wedge between the US and the Pakistani authorities, it seemed initially that AQ might end up as the main beneficiary of the bargain. The war in Afghanistan, where US policies were until 2018 hurting Pakistan's interests, favoured AQ. The US decision to withdraw from Afghanistan, taken by the Trump administration in early 2020 if not earlier, turned the tables on AQ. The deep state did not need AQ any more in Afghanistan at that point and was now in a position to coerce AQ/AQIS into prioritizing Pakistan's campaign against India and into dealing with the TTP once and for all. AQ seems to have had little interest in India and Kashmir, at least as long as it had to serve Pakistan's interests there. Not only that put further distance between AQ and its Middle Eastern interests, but the operating environment was much tougher than in Afghanistan, making it hard to AQ to score successes that would impact positively on its fund raising. Moreover, by 2020 the deep state seemed intent on making IS its primary global jihadist partner in Kashmir, leaving AQ in a corner.

The quick succession of failures (risk of being relegated to India/Kashmir and being quickly overtaken by IS there as well) highlights again how by 2019–20 AQ's strategy was in disarray, and badly in need of a major overhaul.

From AQ's perspective, trying to maintain good relations with both sides made sense and for a period it appears to have even tried to mediate between the deep state and the jihadists opposed to Islamabad. However, why did the deep state tolerate this? It is hard to believe Pakistani intelligence was unaware of the extent to which AQ supported the anti-Islamabad jihadists, especially the TTP. Hence, the deep state must have considered it necessary to tolerate ongoing AQ relations with TTP and others for one or more of the following reasons:

- because it considered that AQ might still play a benign role at some point, bringing the jihadists back, or
- because it deemed that things would get worse if it pushed for confrontation with AQ,
- or again because it considered AQ's help on other fronts worth the price.

It is not clear how AQ's influence over groups such as LeT and JeM affected their loyalty to the Pakistani state, aside from splinter elements who turned into the Punjabi Taliban in the early post-2001 years. If AQ played an important role in driving the jihadists against the Pakistani state in 2002–5, it also played an important role in mending fences, especially after 2007.

AQ's relationship with HuM, JeM and LeT seemed to be developing relatively free of contradictions until 2016. Despite AQ's limited interests in Kashmir until at least 2014, these groups traded off AQ's support for affording protection to AQ's members and for participating in the Afghan jihad. After 2014 and especially from 2019 onwards, AQ's involvement in Kashmir and with Pakistani groups committed to that conflict initially allowed AQ to consolidate the relationship with Pakistan's 'deep state' and made AQ's leadership confident that its Pakistani safe haven was not under immediate threat. But even this did not last, as AQ faced unexpected competition from IS from 2014 onwards.

The impact of IS

When IS started spreading its influence to South Asia from 2014 onwards, the monopolistic position of AQ with regard to the Pakistani jihadist organizations was quickly undermined. IS was well resourced and arrived in South Asia riding high on the wave of its astonishing successes in the Middle East. Most Pakistani jihadist groups immediately started talks with IS, leaving AQ's drive for jihadist legitimacy badly shattered.

Still AQ stayed away from armed confrontations with IS, in part in order to avoid the delegitimizing impact of jihadist infighting, and in part because IS appeared decisively stronger militarily. AQ's early efforts to contain the rising influence of IS appeared to be in vain and even LeT, the most reluctant of the Pakistani groups, ended up edging quite close to IS. The turning of LeT was particularly ominous for AQ, because it signalled the shift of the deep state towards a closer and closer engagement with IS.

It was only the crushing of the Caliphate in the Middle East, in which AQ played little part, that allowed it to invert the trend. For IS it became much harder to attract Pakistani jihadists and none of the groups that had been negotiating about a merger with it in 2014–16 ended up doing it. As the Caliphate was in decline, the funding accruing to IS-K first and later to IS-P and IS-H was no longer so generous, compounding the recruitment issues. Fast-track jihad soon ceased to be an option and so did IS' insistence that it did not want allies, but was seeking unconditional mergers.

In practice, seven years after its first appearance in South Asia, IS was operationally distinguishable from AQ mainly because of its heavier footprint (thousands vs hundreds, direct action vs train and advise), because of its looser recruitment standards, which made it much easier to join IS in South Asia than AQ, and because of its penchant for extreme violence. Otherwise, the modus operandi of IS did not differ so radically from AQ's anymore. The ideological differences were also thinning, as the immediate establishment of the Caliphate advocated by IS was no longer credible after the fall of Mosul and Raqqa. The main ideological differences were IS' heavier reliance on takfirism and of its Sunni suprematism. The Caliphate's main purpose was by the end of 2021 to preserve the safe haven of IS in eastern Afghanistan, which did not really differ from AQ's.

IS and the deep state's tutelage

IS was able to mobilize sufficient resources to compete with AQ and establish its own pole of attraction. However, no major jihadist group merged into IS. Only minority factions of TTP, LeJ, SSP, LeT and few others pledged to the Caliph. This suggests that the actual ideological attraction was limited, even among the Sunni suprematists. Instead, most Pakistani jihadist groups flirted with IS in order to obtain funding from it, while at the same time trying to maintain the financial flows from AQ as well. IS initially tried to get the various groups to pledge to it, but eventually it had to accommodate them and ended up establishing in a seemingly permanent way a relationship with them akin to AQ's.

Like AQ, IS rapidly started getting pulled toward the deep state. The Caliphate tried regularly to pull its South Asian branches away from the deep state, but the gravitational attraction of the latter remained strong. As in the case of AQ, the on and off confrontation between IS and deep state might well have been part of a negotiating process, in which the two tested each other's strength. Overall, IS was more assertive than AQ and had a stronger footprint, but the latter represented a weakness vis-à-vis the deep state, as the logistical needs of IS branches in South Asia played in favour of the deep state. As of end 2021, IS-K looked once again set on a path of autonomy from and even confrontation with the deep state, but the question lingered on of how viable that could be. It cannot be ruled out that IS too might once again be captured by the deep state's gravitational strength in the future.

Competition in global jihad

The emergence of competitors to AQ in the leadership of global jihad from 2014 onwards was a major blow to AQ's claim to jihadist leadership, especially if true that jihadist legitimacy was its main aim in South Asia (aside from self-protection). If until 2019 AQ could still harbour the hope that the challenge could be fought back and that IS would eventually evaporate from South Asia, by 2020 it was clear that nothing like that was going to happen. Quite the contrary, IS branches such as IS-P and IS-H suddenly appeared to have greater potential than AQIS, thanks to their growing ties with key jihadist groups such as LeT, JeM and LeJ, at that time backed up by the Pakistani deep state. That was happening at a time when AQ's relations with the Afghan Taliban were at an all-time low due to the former's agreement with the United States in February 2020.

The long-term disloyalty of so many of its Pakistani clients (not to speak of the Afghan Taliban) indeed raises questions about AQ's strategy of prioritizing investment on allies and clients. AQ's decision not to invest much in an 'affiliate' branch in South Asia left it in a very weak position in 2020. The bulk of AQ's resources in South Asia went to groups that were either dysfunctional (TTP pre Noor Wali), difficult to control (TTP throughout) or eventually disloyal to various degrees (some TTP factions, JeM, LeT, Jundullah, LeJ, SSP). From the 2020 vantage point, AQ's funding appeared to have been the main factor in attracting jihadist friends, leaving it vulnerable to the competition of the Pakistani deep state and of IS and possibly other actors with pockets deep enough. By 2020, AQ's strategy had shown all its limitations.

AQ's drift

Paradoxically, the need to keep its operations well-funded contributed decisively to lead AQ further and further away from the Middle East. Its leadership had to raise the funds it needed (running into a few hundred million dollars worldwide) by sponsoring causes that were popular among donors, mostly Gulf sheiks. The Afghan conflict reconciled AQ's most direct interest of weakening the American resolve to keep supporting friendly regimes in and around the Middle East. As that war started losing popularity among donors, AQ had to start chasing other conflicts that were becoming popular after 2015, such as (within South Asia) the conflict in Kashmir. Such engagement appears to have been in part opportunistic – the Modi government was beginning to arouse hostility among Indian Muslims and among wealthy donors in the Gulf. But it is difficult to escape the feeling that AQ was becoming to a degree at least prisoner of its alliances: the Pakistani deep state wanted it to up its engagement in India and Kashmir, and so did some of the jihadist groups AQ relied on (LeT, JeM).

The risk for AQ was clearly one of competition for leading global jihad becoming an end in itself, the mirror image of the 'war on terror' declared by Bush in 2001. By virtue of being global, this jihad provided a convenient ideological justification for a US-led never-ending war, and for AQ's leadership to endlessly perpetuate its role and justify its requests for funds to all types of donors. The risk of a self-perpetuating, never-ending war should be obvious: the longer a war runs, the more likely are major, unexpected changes to arise. This risk turned into reality with AQ's loss of the monopoly over jihadist leadership from 2014 onwards.

It is not uncommon for political movements and organization to lose sight of their original aim relatively quickly, as they struggle to achieve what were originally supposed to be intermediate objectives, on the path to final victory. Given the sheer size of AQ's ambitions, getting lost along the very long way to achieve them was always bound to be highly likely.

AQ's vulnerabilities

The crisis of AQ, started by the arrival in South Asia of its Middle Eastern splinter IS, deepened from 2019 onwards as relations with its most important ally in South Asia (the Afghan Taliban) started deteriorating. In the end, the crisis of AQ in South Asia from 2019 onwards was not due to the extensive and protracted American efforts to destroy it, but the Americans deciding to pull out. That changed the local dynamics and AQ struggled to figure out how to successfully exploiting the success of its allies in Afghanistan. AQ could have positioned itself for benefiting from the windfall of American failures in Afghanistan, claiming the Taliban's victory as their own, and accepting to pull out at least of Taliban-held areas, meeting the Taliban's need to regional legitimization and trying to present it as a 'mission accomplishment' withdrawal.

Perhaps AQ's hubris prevented them from adopting a pragmatic and realistic approach. AQ appears also to have been concerned about keeping its leaders in Pakistan, having got wind of the Pakistani army's desire to mend fences with the United States. AQ's leaders were hoping to be able to hang on to a safe haven in Afghanistan, in alliance with IS. That safe haven would at least provide AQ with some leverage vis-à-vis Pakistan. The price to pay was a humiliating alliance with IS in Afghanistan, even if AQ did its best to hide from view. The sense of AQ being pushed into a corner remains difficult to dispel. At that point al Zawahiri was seriously sick, a fact that contributes explaining the strategic disarray AQ found itself in at that point. Developments in 2019–20 in any case highlight how global jihadism turned out to be more vulnerable to internal issues, efforts by its enemies to drive a wedge between it and local jihadists and to contradictions in its strategy, than to the militarized response to it, which the United States adopted after 2001.

Working in tandem?

The alliance that AQ and IS reached in 2020 was supposed to be limited to Afghanistan and it did not eliminate the competition between the two organizations, which kept stealing each other's members. By the second half of 2021, however, the alliance seemed to be expanding into Pakistan as well. AQ seemed to be the junior partner in the alliance, providing funding and support to IS in exchange for the availability of a spare safe haven, should the need arise. However, AQ appears to have sought (with success) to shelter its jihadist allies from the influence of IS, at the same time as it cooperated more and more closely with it. This begs the question of whether AQ was really the junior partner, or whether it was cunningly using the eagerness of IS to take the lead for its own purposes. AQ enabled IS to pursue its aggressive campaigns against the Pakistani state and against the Taliban, while AQ maintained uneasy relations with both of them.

Could the AQ-IS relationship evolve into a virtuous one from the point of view of global jihadism, at least in South Asia? In Afghanistan, the presence of IS-K and the threat it has been representing for the Taliban's Emirate has strengthened the position of AQ vis-à-vis that same Emirate, despite the latter being aware of the relationship that AQ has established with IS-K. By occupying the middle ground between the uncompromising global jihadism of IS and the local jihadism of the Taliban, AQ carved out a new role for itself and might even be better able to serve the cause of global jihadism than by aligning with either. The shared aim of the two global jihadist organizations seemed by 2021–2 undermining the Taliban's Emirate, with IS-K taking violent action and AQ working to undermine it through subversion. The consolidation of the Emirate represented a fundamental threat to both of them.

It remains to be seen whether AQ and IS will be able to cooperate significantly for any length of time, while they quite obviously keep competing to attract local jihadist groups.

Notes

Introduction

1. Kapur, 2017, 10.
2. Kapur, 2017, 10.
3. Kapur, 2017, 10.
4. Topich, 2018, 163–4.
5. Rashid, 2008, 326.
6. Rashid, 2008, 327.
7. Rashid, 2008, 511.
8. Topich, 2018, 164.
9. Rashid, 2008, 511.
10. Kapur, 2017, 10.
11. See among others Stenersen, 2010.
12. For a discussion of this debate see Hellmich, 2011, who tends to lean towards the view that there is no 'core al Qa'ida'. Mendelsohn by contrast accepts the existence of an AQ core. For a recent assessment of the AQ core see Rosenau and Powell. For the most recent intervention in the debate see Gartenstein-Ross & Barr, 2020, who argue that the documents retrieved in Abbottabad after the killing of bin Laden support the view of a centralized core of AQ still existing at that time.
13. Gartenstein-Ross & Barr, 2018.
14. Gartenstein-Ross & Barr, 2018.
15. Gartenstein-Ross & Barr, 2018.
16. Brachman, 2016.
17. Moghadam, 2013, 466–97.
18. Moghadam, 2013.
19. Lahoud, 2022, 284.
20. Bunzel, 2022.
21. Byman, 2014, 431–70, 448–53.
22. Byman, 2014, 448–53.
23. Byman, 2014, 448–53.
24. Stenersen, 2010.
25. Crone et al., 2017, 12.
26. Gartenstein-Ross & Barr, 2018.
27. Gartenstein-Ross & Barr, 2018.
28. Andersen, 2017.
29. Mendelsohn, 2016, 82–3.
30. See Giustozzi, 2022b.
31. Byman, 2014, 448–53.
32. Byman, 2014, 448–53.
33. Byman, 2014, 454.
34. Byman, 2014, 459.

35 Byman, 2014, 459.
36 Forest et al., 2006, 11.
37 Byman, 2017.
38 Kadercan, 2019; Brüggemann, 2016; Byman, 2015; Fishman, 2016.
39 See also Almohammad, 2019.
40 Turner, 2019, 563–86, 566–7.
41 Turner, 2019, 574.
42 Turner, 2019, 568, 571.
43 Kadercan, 2019, 4.
44 Azoulay, 2015, 35.
45 Ness, 2018, 5.
46 Critchley et al., 2016, 9–10.
47 Critchley et al., 2016, 10.
48 Hansen, 2019, 199–200.
49 Azoulay, 2015, 21.

Chapter 1

1   For a background see Coll, 2004; Yousaf and Adkin, 2002; Dorronson, 2005; Roy, 1990; Dimitrakis, 2013.
2   See Sands, 2019. The Jama'st Islami represent a parallel brand of Islamism, separate from the Muslim Brotherhood, but with many similarities.
3   See Dorronsoro, 2005.
4   Bell, 2016.
5   Jamal, 2011, location 271ff; Rana, 2010a, 42–3.
6   Meeting with **K, teacher in an SSP madrasa in Punjab, November 2020.
7   Jamal, 2011, location 540ff; Rana, 2010, 42–5; Zahid, 2015, 67ff; Abou Zahab and Roy, 2004, 47–8.
8   Sareen, 2005, 145–6; Jamal, 2014, 39, 48–9, 56–7, 62–5. On Sayyaf's party see Dorronsoro, 2005, 159.
9   Tawil, 2010; Hamid and Farrell, 2015.
10 Stenersen, 2017, 21.
11 Stenersen, 2017, 26, 115, 166ff.
12 Rana, 2010, 46.
13 On Shi'a mobilization see Nasr, 1999, 311–23; and Abbas, 2010. On the success of SSP see Abou ZahaB, 1999.
14 ICG, 2005, 11. For a context to the rise of sectarianism in Pakistan see Murphy, 2019.
15 Murphy, 2019, 490.
16 Murphy, 2019, 491.
17 Jamal, 2011, Location 556ff.
18 Murphy, 2019, 420; Meeting with M**A, member of SSP, Punjab, July 2020.
19 Murphy, 2019, 420.
20 Gul, 2010, 256.
21 Jamal, 2011, Location 581.
22 Jamal, 2011, Location 582ff.
23 Jamal, 2009, 9
24 Jamal, 2009.

25 Kamran, 2016.
26 Jamal, 2011, Location 575.
27 Meeting with M*, Jhangvi district of Punjab, member of SSP and madrasa manager, July 2020; Meeting with M**A, member of SSP, Punjab, July 2020.
28 Meeting with M*, Jhangvi district of Punjab, member of SSP and madrasa manager, July 2020; Meeting with M**A, member of SSP, Punjab, July 2020.
29 Roul, 2005.
30 Murphy, 2019, 422.
31 Murphy, 2019, 423.
32 Murphy, 2019, 423.
33 Jamal, 2009; Jamal, 2011, Location 618.
34 Jamal, 2009.
35 ICG, 2009.
36 Haqqani, 2005.
37 Haqqani, 2005.
38 Shahzad, 2011, 207.
39 Haqqani, 2005.
40 Kapur, 2017, 75.
41 Kapur, 2017, 75.
42 Kapur, 2017, 85.
43 Kapur, 2017, 86.
44 Haqqani, 2005; Murphy, 2013, 124–6.
45 Haqqani, 2005; Kapur, 2017, 88.
46 Sirrs, 2017, 159–60.
47 Kapur, 2017, 89.
48 Kapur, 2017, 89.
49 Shahzad, 2011, 207.
50 Kapur, 2017, 89.
51 Mir, 2008, 120.
52 Swami, 2007, 179.
53 Jamal, 2011, Location 684ff.
54 Sirrs, 2017, 160–1. On HuM's origins see Mir, 2006, 73ff.
55 Meeting with S*, active member of HuM, Muzaffarabad, June 2020; Meeting with N*, member of HuM in Rawalpindi, June 2020.
56 Meeting with S*, active member of HuM, Muzaffarabad, June 2020
57 Swami, 2007, 195–6; Sikand, 2001.
58 Meyerle, 2008, 167.
59 Meyerle, 2008, 181.
60 Meyerle, 2008, 207.
61 Kapur, 2017, 92.
62 Jamal, 2014, 71.
63 Jamal, 2014, 75.
64 Jamal, 2014, 90.
65 Kapur, 2017, 90–1.
66 Kapur, 2017, 92.
67 Zahab/Roy, 2005, 61.
68 Kapur, 2017, 92; Bose, 2003, 140–7; Tankel, 2011, 63.
69 Meyerle, 2008, 209.

70	Meyerle, 2008, 212.
71	Schmidt, 2011, 95–6.
72	Fair, 2018, 77–8.
73	Lieven, 2011, 325.
74	Meeting with *T*, commander of LeT in Jammu and Kashmir, October 2016.
75	Meeting with ***, former commander of LeT, Kunar Province, February 2020; Meeting with **Q, former LeT training camp manager, Muzafarrabad area, February 2020.
76	Meeting with N*, member of HuM in Rawalpindi, June 2020.
77	Meeting with **D, JeM madrasa cadre, Multan district, April 2020.
78	Jamal, 2011, Location 749ff.
79	Mir, 2008, 149.
80	Abbas, 2005, 214; Sareen, 2005, 175.
81	Zahab/Roy, 2004, 66.
82	Mir, 2008, 149.
83	Meyerle, 2008, 211.
84	Honawar, 2005.
85	Meeting with *B*, JeM commander in Afghanistan, April 2020.
86	Semple, 2014, 3.
87	Nojumi, 2008, 101, 105; Rashid, 2000, 29, 90.
88	Rana, 2003, 275–6.
89	Meeting with **K, teacher in an SSP madrasa in Punjab, November 2020.
90	Rana, 2003, 255–6.
91	Dorronsoro, 2002, 169; Rashid, 2000, 90–1.
92	Rashid, 2000, 92.
93	ICG, 2005, 14.
94	Rashid, 2000, 92.
95	Ahmed, 2011, 284–5.
96	Jamal, 2009.
97	Jamal, 2009.
98	Abbas, 2006; Marwat and Toru, 2005.
99	Dorronsoro, 2002, 169.
100	Rana, 2003, 332.
101	Khan, 2004
102	Wilkinson, 2009.
103	Khan, 2009, 10.
104	Stenersen, 2017, 40ff.
105	Stenersen, 2017, 44.
106	Meeting with **K, teacher in an SSP madrasa in Punjab, November 2020.
107	Stenersen, 2017, 72ff.
108	Stenersen, 2017, 93ff.
109	Stenersen, 2017, 114.
110	Stenersen, 2017, 73, 137. See also Hegghammer, 2020, 203, 395–6; Sirrs, 2017, 123ff.
111	Tawil, 2010, 153; Zahid, 2015, 72.
112	Wilson, 2007.
113	Bhutto, 2007, 405, 411–13.
114	National Commission on Terrorist Attacks upon the United States, 2003, 64.

Chapter 2

1. See Riedel, 2008; Larson, 2011 and Wright, 2007 for the argument that AQ intended to lure the United States into a war in Afghanistan. For the argument that bin Laden miscalculated see Topich, 2018; Bergen, 2011 and Gerges, 2011. For what the Abbottabad papers say, see Lahoud, 2022, cit.
2. For a thorough discussion of the Taliban's military effort, see Giustozzi, 2019.
3. 'Code of conduct: al Qa'ida in the Subcontinent', As Sahab Media, June 2017, 5.
4. 'Code of conduct: al Qa'ida in the Subcontinent', As Sahab Media, June 2017, 15.
5. Lahoud, 2022, cit.
6. Shahzad, 2011, 184–5.
7. Meeting with *O, LeJ member in Punjab, November 2020.
8. Meeting with AQIS agent A** in Karachi, July 2020.
9. Lahoud, 2022, 289–90.
10. Meeting with AQIS agent A** in Karachi, July 2020.
11. Meeting with AQ cadre, 2014.
12. Meeting with A*A*, AQ commander in Kunar, January 2016.
13. Meeting with AQ cadre, 2014; Meeting with Q*, assistant of Taliban leader Akhtar Mohammad Mansur, 2014; Meeting with Q*M, senior Taliban cadre, Pakistan, March 2014.
14. Meeting with Q**, AQIS cadre, eastern Afghanistan, September 2020.
15. Meeting with AQIS agent A** in Karachi, July 2020.
16. Meeting with AQIS agent A** in Karachi, July 2020.
17. Meeting with A*A*, AQ commander in Kunar, January 2016.
18. Meeting with AQ cadre, 2014; Meeting with Q*, assistant of Taliban leader Akhtar Mohammad Mansur, 2014; Meeting with Q*M, Taliban commander, February 2014.
19. Meeting with A*A*, AQ commander in Kunar, January 2016; Meeting with AA**, AQ cadre, eastern Afghanistan, May 2017.
20. Meeting with A*A*, AQ commander in Kunar, January 2016.
21. Meeting with **G, AQ group commander, Kunar Province, April 2016.
22. Meeting with Q*, assistant of Taliban leader Akhtar Mohammad Mansur, 2014.
23. Meeting with Q*, assistant of Taliban leader Akhtar Mohammad Mansur, 2014.
24. Meeting with **S, AQ finance cadre, Pakistan, August 2016.
25. Meeting with AA**, AQ cadre, eastern Afghanistan, May 2017.
26. Meeting with AQ cadre, 2014; Meeting with AA**, AQ cadre, eastern Afghanistan, May 2017.
27. Topich, 2018, 231, 388.
28. Meeting with AA**, AQ cadre, eastern Afghanistan, May 2017.
29. Meeting with AA**, AQ cadre, eastern Afghanistan, May 2017.
30. Meeting with *A, AQ group commander in Jammu and Kashmir, September 2019.
31. For more details see Giustozzi, 2019, 260, figures 2 and 3.
32. Gunaratna and Nielsen, 2008, 31:9, 775–807; Stenersen, 2010; Abou Zahab, 2010.
33. Meeting with AQ cadre, 2014. Also Meeting with Q*, assistant of Taliban leader Akhtar Mohammad Mansur, 2014.
34. Meeting with Q*, assistant of Taliban leader Akhtar Mohammad Mansur, 2014; Meeting with A*A*, AQ commander in Kunar, January 2016.
35. Markey, 2013, 12.
36. 'Jihad in Pakistan …', 2016, 17.

37 'Jihad in Pakistan ...', 2016, 17–18.
38 Meeting with **G, AQ group commander, Kunar Province, April 2016.
39 Shahzad, 2011, 211.
40 Shahzad, inside, 212–13.
41 Basit, 2014, 8–12; Dasgupta, 2015; Reed, 2016, 6.
42 Shahzad, 2011, 119–20, 115.
43 Shahzad, 2011, 120.
44 Basit, 2014; Dasgupta, 2015; Reed, 2016, 6.
45 Meeting with Q**, AQIS cadre, eastern Afghanistan, September 2020.
46 Meeting with Q**, AQIS cadre, eastern Afghanistan, September 2020.
47 Meeting with Q**, AQIS cadre, eastern Afghanistan, September 2020.
48 Meeting with *A, AQ group commander in Jammu and Kashmir, September 2019. On the 'Pakistanisation' of AQ in South Asia see also Coll, 2018, 678.
49 Meeting with AQIS agent A** in Karachi, July 2020.
50 Roggio, 2014; Faber and Powell, 2017, 8.
51 Reed, 2016, 6.
52 The Soufan Center, 2019, 10.
53 Meeting with AQIS agent A** in Karachi, July 2020.
54 Meeting with *A, AQ group commander in Jammu and Kashmir, September 2019.
55 Meeting with *A, AQ group commander in Jammu and Kashmir, September 2019.
56 'Code of conduct: al Qa'ida in the Subcontinent', As Sahab Media, June 2017, 3.
57 'Code of conduct: al Qa'ida in the Subcontinent', As Sahab Media, June 2017, 3.
58 Rafiq, 2014; Reed, 2016, 6.
59 Soufan Center, 2019, 13; Roggio, 2014b.
60 Soufan Center, 2019.
61 'Code of conduct: al Qa'ida in the Subcontinent', As Sahab Media, June 2017, 1.
62 'Code of conduct: al Qa'ida in the Subcontinent', As Sahab Media, June 2017, 15.
63 Meeting with *A, AQ group commander in Jammu and Kashmir, September 2019.
64 Meeting with Q**, AQIS cadre, eastern Afghanistan, September 2020.
65 Soufan Center, 2019, 13.
66 Congressional Research Centre, 2020.
67 Roul, 2020.
68 Meeting with AQIS agent A** in Karachi, July 2020.
69 Rana, 2005, 66–7.
70 Lahoud, 2022, 54–5, 78.
71 Rashid, 2008, 510.
72 Gall, 2014, 201.
73 Gall (Carlotta), 2014b, 78–9.
74 Topich, 2018, 231, 228.
75 Meeting with AQIS agent A** in Karachi, July 2020.
76 Riedel, 2008, 80.
77 Meeting with Q**, AQIS cadre, eastern Afghanistan, September 2020.
78 Meeting with Q**, AQIS cadre, eastern Afghanistan, September 2020.
79 Semple, 2014, 6.
80 Topich, 2018, 356.
81 Giustozzi, 2019, 33.
82 Meeting with Q**, AQIS cadre, eastern Afghanistan, September 2020.
83 Lahoud, 2022, cit.

84 Scott-Clark and Levy, 2017, 690. On Hamid Gul and Afghanistan post-2001 see Hussain, 2007, 81–2; Joshi, 2010; Gall, 2012, 296.
85 'The next chapter: The United States and Pakistan', A Report of the Pakistan Policy Working Group, September 2008, 13–14.
86 Bergen, 2012, 116.
87 Chris Allbritton, Mark Hosenball, 'Special report: Why the U.S. mistrusts Pakistan's spies', *Reuters*, 5 May 2011.
88 'Report of the Commission of Inquiry into the Abbottabad Incident of May 2, 2011', Islamabad, 2013, 40–1, 47.
89 Kiessling, 2016, 224–5.
90 Gall (Carlotta), 2014, 203.
91 Gall, 2014; Schmidt, 2017
92 Morell and Harlow, 2015, 172–3.
93 McNally and Weinbaum, 2016, 5.
94 Hearing before the Committee on Foreign Relations, United States Senate, one hundred fourteenth Congress, second session, 8 September 2016.
95 Obama, 2020 (digital edition), 1650.
96 Coll, 2018, 263.
97 Gall (Carlotta), 2014, 203.
98 'Report of the Commission of Inquiry into the Abbottabad Incident of 2 May 2011', Islamabad, 2013, 40–1, 47.
99 Siddique, 2007; Bergen, 2012, 142, 145.
100 Siddique, 2007; Bergen, 2012, 142, 145.
101 Rassler, 2015.
102 Lahoud, 2022, 101.
103 'Musharraf played havoc with nation', *The News*, 17 February 2009.
104 Meeting with Q**, AQIS cadre, eastern Afghanistan, September 2020.
105 Meeting with Q**, AQIS cadre, eastern Afghanistan, September 2020.
106 Meeting with AQIS agent A** in Karachi, July 2020.
107 Rassler, 2015.
108 Meeting with AQIS agent A** in Karachi, July 2020.
109 Meeting with AQIS agent A** in Karachi, July 2020.
110 Bruno and Bajoria, 2008.
111 Kiessling, 2016, 222.
112 Meeting with AQIS agent A** in Karachi, July 2020.
113 Kiessling, 2016, 226.
114 Gall (Carlotta), 2014, 205. Also Coll, 2018, 570.
115 Lahoud, 2022, 107–9.
116 Scott-Clark and Levy, 2017, 690.
117 Gall (Carlotta), 2014, 206.
118 Meeting with AQIS agent A** in Karachi, July 2020.
119 Coll, 2018, 569.
120 Imran, 2010.
121 Meeting with AQIS agent A** in Karachi, July 2020.
122 Latif, 2011. Seymour Hersh made even stronger claims about the involvement of the Pakistani army in the raid in *The killing of Osama bin Laden*, London: Verso, 2016.
123 'Report of the Commission of Inquiry into the Abbottabad Incident of 2 May 2011'; Barack Obama, *A promised land*, New York: Random House, 2020.
124 Meeting with Q**, AQIS cadre, eastern Afghanistan, September 2020.

125 Topich, 2018, 231, 420.
126 Meeting with Q**, AQIS cadre, eastern Afghanistan, September 2020.
127 Meeting with A*A*, AQ commander in Kunar, January 2016.
128 Hassan Abbas, 'Defining the Punjabi Taliban Network', *CTC Sentinel* 2: 4, 2009.
129 Khan, 2010.
130 Khan (Raheel), 2010c.
131 Meeting with Q**, AQIS cadre, eastern Afghanistan, September 2020.
132 Meeting with AQIS agent A** in Karachi, July 2020.
133 'Punjabi Taliban call off armed struggle in Pakistan', *Dawn*, 15 September 2014.
134 Meeting with AQIS agent A** in Karachi, July 2020.
135 Zahid, 2015.
136 Meeting with A*A*, AQ commander in Kunar, January 2016.
137 Meeting with A*A*, AQ commander in Kunar, January 2016.
138 Meeting with AQIS agent A** in Karachi, July 2020.
139 'Code of conduct: al Qa'ida in the Subcontinent', As Sahab Media, June 2017, 7.
140 'Code of conduct: al Qa'ida in the Subcontinent', As Sahab Media, June 2017, 8.
141 Miqdaad, 2017.
142 Meeting with AQIS agent A** in Karachi, July 2020.
143 Meeting with *A, AQ group commander in Jammu and Kashmir, September 2019.
144 Meeting with AQIS agent A** in Karachi, July 2020.
145 Meeting with AQIS agent A** in Karachi, July 2020.
146 Meeting with *A, AQ group commander in Jammu and Kashmir, September 2019.
147 Meeting with AQIS agent A** in Karachi, July 2020.
148 Meeting with *A, AQ group commander in Jammu and Kashmir, September 2019.
149 Meeting with AQIS agent A** in Karachi, July 2020.
150 Meeting with *N* in Kunar, January 2022.
151 Meeting with AQIS agent A** in Karachi, July 2020.
152 Meeting with AQIS agent A** in Karachi, July 2020.
153 Meeting with Q**, AQIS cadre, eastern Afghanistan, September 2020.
154 Meeting with Q**, AQIS cadre, eastern Afghanistan, September 2020.
155 Meeting with Q**, AQIS cadre, eastern Afghanistan, September 2020.
156 Meeting with Q**, AQIS cadre, eastern Afghanistan, September 2020.
157 Meeting with Q**, AQIS cadre, eastern Afghanistan, September 2020.
158 Meeting with Q**, AQIS commander in eastern Afghanistan, October 2020.
159 Meeting with *N* in Kunar, senior AQ commander, January 2022.
160 Meeting with *N* in Kunar, senior AQ commander, January 2022.
161 Communication with senior Taliban cadre in Afghan MoD, April 2022; communication with Taliban commander in Shorabak, April 2022.
162 Meeting with *N* in Kunar, senior AQ commander, January 2022; Meeting with A** in Kunar, AQIS cadre, December 2021.
163 Communication with senior Taliban cadre in Afghan MoD, April 2022; communication with Taliban commander in Shorabak, April 2022.
164 See for a detailed discussion Giustozzi, 2019. See also Waldman, 2010.
165 Gall, 2014; Schmidt, 2017.
166 See Giustozzi, 2022 (second edition) for a discussion of this issue.
167 Mufti Hassan Swati, quoted in Yusufzai, 2008, cit.
168 Meeting with IS-K leader, June 2015.
169 Osman, 2016 (https://www.afghanistan-analysts.org/wp-admin/post.php).

170 Meeting with elder, Achin, Nangarhar, January 2016; Meeting with IS-K commander, Achin, Nangarhar, August 2016.
171 Rassler, 2015.
172 On Deobandi and Panjpiri Taliban see Feyyaz, 2013a, 84; Feyyaz, 2013b, 9–13.
173 Meeting with IS-K cadre, Pakistan, July 2016.
174 Meeting with IS-K cadre, Pakistan, July 2016.
175 Meeting with IS-K senior commander, Pakistan, January 2017.
176 Meeting with IS-K commander from Jaysh ul islam, February 2016.
177 Meeting with ISI officer, Pakistan, January 2016; Meeting with IS-K senior commander, IS-K senior cadre, December 2014; Waseem, 2016.
178 Meeting with IS-K senior commander, Pakistan, January 2017.
179 Meeting with IS-K senior commander, Pakistan, October 2015; Meeting with IS-K senior commander, April 2015; Meeting with IS-K senior cadre, December 2014.
180 Chishti, 2014.
181 Meeting with IS-K cadre, Pakistan, December 2015.
182 Meeting with ISI officer, Pakistan, January 2016.
183 Amir Mir, 'IS makes inroads into Pakistan'. *Asia Times Online*, 27 June 2016.
184 Sherzad, 2016.
185 Meeting with IS-K commander from Jaysh ul islam, February 2016.
186 Meeting with ISI officer, Pakistan, January 2016.
187 Meeting with IS-K cadre, Kunar, July 2016.
188 Meeting with IS-K cadre, Pakistan, January 2016.
189 Meeting with IS-K cadre, March 2015.
190 Meeting with ISI officer, Pakistan, January 2016; Waseem, 2016.
191 Meeting with ISI officer, Pakistan, January 2016.
192 Arif Rafiq, 'What happened to ISIS's Afghanistan-Pakistan province?', *The Diplomat*, 19 February 2016.
193 Meeting with IS-K senior commander, IRGC officer, Afghanistan, January 2016.
194 Meeting with IS-K cadre, Kunar, July 2016.
195 Meeting with IS-K cadre, Kunar, July 2016.
196 Meeting with IS-K cadre, Pakistan, July 2016.
197 Meeting with IS-K senior commander, **F, IS-K commander in Nangarhar province, June 2020; Meeting with IS-K senior commander, A**, senior IS-K cadre in eastern Afghanistan, June 2020.
198 Pandya, 2021.
199 Johnson, 2016, 4; Mashal, 2019.
200 https://www.reddit.com/r/AfghanConflict/comments/t8qilo/abdul_rahim_muslim_dost_a_key_member_of_the_iskp/
201 The Quetta Police Academy attack was initially attributed to LeJ by the police; the Quetta hospital attack according to IK-K in collaboration with Ahrar, 2016.
202 'Ghani condemns Daesh bombing in Quetta', *TOLOnews*.com, 9 August 2016.
203 Meeting with IS-K senior commander, IS-K, senior commander, Pakistan, January 2017.
204 Meeting with IS-K cadre, Nangarhar, December 2016.
205 **, IS-K Deputy commander, Jurm district of Badakhshan Province, May 2020.
206 Mashal, 7; contact with IS-K source in Nangarhar, June 2017; contact with TKP source, June 2017; Tomlinson, 2017.
207 Meeting with IS-K senior commander, ***S, IS-K cadre, Afghanistan, November 2019.

208 Gohel and Winston, 2020.
209 Meeting with IS-K senior commander, *S*, IS-K commander, north-western Afghanistan, August 2018; Meeting with IS-K senior commander, A**, IS-K district amir, June 2020.
210 Meeting with *S*, IS-K commander, north-western Afghanistan, August 2018.
211 Meeting with IS-K senior commander, ***H, IS-K intelligence cadre, Afghanistan, April 2020.
212 Meeting with IS-K senior commander, *M**, IS-K district-level military leader, Afghanistan, August 2020.
213 For a full account of the fighting, see Giustozzi, 2022, chapter 10.
214 Meeting with IS-K senior commander, ***H, IS-K intelligence cadre, Afghanistan, April 2020.
215 Meeting with IS-K senior commander, QGAA, senior military cadre of IS-K, Afghanistan, June 2020; Meeting with IS-K senior commander, A**, IS-K district amir, June 2020.
216 Meeting with Q*Q, IS-K cadre in Kabul province, March 2021; Meeting with QA*, IS-K commander in Nangarhar, March 2021.
217 Meeting with *K, LeT IED maker and trainer, Muzaffarabad camp, May 2021; Meeting with *M*, Punjabi, LeT cadre in Swat valley, May 2021.
218 Meeting with QE*, IS-K commander in Noor Gul, Kunar, September 2021; Meeting with *S, IS-K commander in Dara Pech, Kunar, August 2021.
219 Meeting with Q**, IS-P commander in Momand agency, December 2021.
220 Meeting with IS-K senior commander, O*, IS-P commander, July 2020.
221 Meeting with*K*, IS-P commander, ex TTP, Baluchistan, July 2020; Meeting with Q*P, IS-P member, Baluchistan (Pakistan), former TTP member, July 2020.
222 Meeting with IS-K senior commander, ***S, IS-K cadre, Afghanistan, November 2019.
223 Meeting with Q**, IS-P commander in Momand agency, December 2021.
224 Ahmed, 2019.
225 Valle, 2021.
226 Meeting with* K*, IS-P commander, ex TTP, Baluchistan, July 2020; Meeting with Q*P, IS-P member, Baluchistan (Pakistan), former TTP member, July 2020.
227 Meeting with Q**, IS-P commander in Momand agency, December 2021.
228 Meeting with Q*P, IS-P member, Baluchistan (Pakistan), former TTP member, July 2020.
229 Meeting with IS-K senior commander, ***H, IS-K intelligence cadre, Afghanistan, April 2020.
230 Meeting with IS-K senior commander, O*, IS-P commander, July 2020.
231 Meeting,with IS-K senior commander, O*, IS-P commander, July 2020.
232 Meeting with IS-K senior commander, Q*P, IS-P member, Baluchistan (Pakistan), former TTP member, July 2020.
233 Meeting with IS-K senior commander, O*, IS-P commander, July 2020.
234 Meeting with IS-K senior commander, O*, IS-P commander, July 2020.
235 Meeting with IS-K senior commander, O*, IS-P commander, July 2020.
236 Sattar, 2021.
237 Meeting with Q**, IS-P commander in Momand agency, December 2021.
238 Meeting with Q**, IS-P commander in Momand agency, December 2021.
239 Official IS-P statement, 6.12.1442 (16 July 2021); Meeting with Q**, IS-P commander in Momand agency, December 2021.

240 Meeting with IS-K senior commander, ***H, IS-K intelligence cadre, Afghanistan, April 2020.
241 Meeting with Q**, IS-P commander in Momand agency, December 2021.
242 Siddique, 2022.
243 Nihad, 2022.
244 Meeting with Q**, IS-P commander in Momand agency, December 2021.
245 Valle, 2021.
246 Meeting with IS-K senior commander, *O, IS-K group commander, Manogai district of Kunar province, April 2020.
247 Meeting with Q*P, IS-P member, Baluchistan (Pakistan), former TTP member, July 2020; Meeting with*K*, IS-P commander, ex TTP, Baluchistan, July 2020; Meeting with *K, LeT IED maker and trainer, Muzaffarabad camp, May 2021.
248 Meeting with *A, AQ group commander in Jammu and Kashmir, September 2019.
249 Meeting with Q**, AQIS cadre, eastern Afghanistan, September 2020.
250 Meeting with Q**, AQIS cadre, eastern Afghanistan, September 2020.
251 Meeting with Q**, AQIS cadre, eastern Afghanistan, September 2020.
252 Meeting with Q**, AQIS cadre, eastern Afghanistan, September 2020.
253 Meeting with Q**, AQIS cadre, eastern Afghanistan, September 2020; Meeting with Q**, AQIS commander in eastern Afghanistan, October 2020.
254 Meeting with Q**, IS-P commander in Momand agency, December 2021.
255 Luce, Dilanian and Yusufzai, 2021; UN Security Council, 'Letter dated 21 January 2021 from the Chair of the Security Council Committee pursuant to resolutions 1267 (1999), 1989 (2011) and 2253 (2015) concerning Islamic State in Iraq and the Levant (Da'esh), al Qa'ida and associated individuals, groups, undertakings and entities addressed to the President of the Security Council', New York, 3 February 2021, S/2021/68.
256 Lahoud, 2022, 36, 94–7.
257 Meeting with Q**, AQIS commander in eastern Afghanistan, October 2020.
258 Meeting with *A, AQ group commander in Jammu and Kashmir, September 2019.
259 Meeting with Q**, AQIS commander in eastern Afghanistan, October 2020.
260 Meeting with Q**, AQIS commander in eastern Afghanistan, October 2020.
261 Meeting with Q**, AQIS commander in eastern Afghanistan, October 2020.
262 Meeting with A** in Kunar, AQIS cadre, December 2021.

Chapter 3

1 See Franco, 2009.
2 Meeting with IS-K senior commander, senior TTP figure M*M, Kunar (Afghanistan), February 2013.
3 Rashid, 2008, 446.
4 H Qazi, 2011; Meeting with TTP commander K*, Kunar (Afghanistan), March 2020; Meeting with **B, Sajna TTP faction, Waziristan, April 2020.
5 ICG, 2013.
6 Zeb Burki, 2010, 188–211.
7 Rana, 2010b, 50.
8 Burki, 2010.
9 For a detailed discussion see Giustozzi, 2019.

10 Meeting with IS-K senior commander, senior TTP figure M*M, Kunar (Afghanistan), February 2013; Meeting with IS-K senior commander, *R, TTP member in South Waziristan, formerly close to Hakimullah Mehsud, November 2020.
11 Meeting with TTP commander SM, Swat, February 2013.
12 Meeting with TTP commander Q**M, South Waziristan, Mufti Noor Wali Mehsud faction, March 2020.
13 Meeting with IS-K senior commander, *R, TTP member in South Waziristan, formerly close to Hakimullah Mehsud, November 2020.
14 See Giustozzi, 2019.
15 Burki, 2010; Puri, 2012.
16 Zahid et al., 2020, 503–25, 511.
17 On the Shakai agreement see Rana, 2010b, 73ff.
18 Rana and Gunaratna, 2007, 93, 93–4, 95, 99, 101; Rana, 2010a, 52–3.
19 Gunaratna and Nielsen, 2008.
20 Gretchen, 2010; Franco and Sandee, 2008', NEFA, 5 March 2008.
21 Sulaiman, 2009.
22 Jihad in Pakistan, 2016, 18–19.
23 See Acharya et al., 2009, 95–108; Franco, 2009a.
24 Stenersen, 2010.
25 'Jihad in Pakistan', 2016, 18–19.
26 Sulaiman, 2009; Stenersen, 2010.
27 Meeting with Q**M, TTP commander loyal to Mufti Noor Wali Mehsud, South Waziristan, March 2020.
28 Sulaiman, 2009.
29 See Yusufzai, 2008; Franco, 2009a.
30 See Franco, 2009a.
31 Rogers, 2010; Kerr, 2011.
32 See Franco, 2009a.
33 'Jihad in Pakistan', 2016, 17.
34 'Jihad in Pakistan', 2016, 17.
35 Gall (Carlotta), 2014, 143.
36 Stenersen, 2010.
37 Semple, 2014, 5.
38 Semple, 2014, 5.
39 Peters, 2010.
40 Meeting with *E, senior TTP figure in South Waziristan, February 2013.
41 'Jihad in Kashmir and Sharia rule in India: Tehrik-e-Taliban Pakistan', *India Today*, 9 January 2013.
42 Meeting with IS-K senior commander, senior TTP figure M*M, Kunar (Afghanistan), February 2013.
43 Meeting with IS-K senior commander, senior TTP figure M*M, Kunar (Afghanistan), February 2013.
44 Meeting with TTP commander, Swat, February 2013.
45 Harnisch, 2009; Roggio, 2011.
46 Abbas, 2007; Roggio, 2009.
47 Perlez and Shah, 2008; Peters, 2010.
48 'Report on our visit', Harmony document captured in Abbottabad, June 2008 (released 2016), p. 4.

49 Meeting with senior Lashkar-e Islam figure *B, Nangarhar (Afghanistan), February 2013.
50 Iqbal and De Silva, 2013, 72–86; Celso, 2014, 171–2.
51 Giustozzi, 2019, figure 8. Lashkar-e Taiba, Jaish e Mohammad and several other groups fought in Afghanistan as well.
52 Meeting with IS-K senior commander, TTP leader M**, February 2013; Meeting with **Y, TTP cadre in Kunar Province, January 2014; Meeting with IS-K senior commander, M*, senior LeI figure, February 2013; Meeting with SM, Swat TTP commander, February 2013.
53 Meeting with IS-K senior commander, S*Y, senior TTP figure in Kunar (Afghanistan), January 2014.
54 Meeting with A**G, AQ cadre, Nuristan (Afghanistan), May 2017.
55 'Pakistan Taliban set up camps in Syria, join anti-Assad war', *Reuters*, 14 July 2013; Rehman, 2013, 9; Burke, 2013.
56 'TTP's support for IS disturbing for Pakistan'. *The News*, 6 October 2014; 'Islamic State influence is growing in Pakistan and Afghanistan', *The Australian*, 2 Nov 2014; Amir, 2016; 'Hundreds of Pakistanis joining Daesh: IB'. *The Nation*, 11 February 2016.
57 Meeting with Q*M, AQ commander, Kunar (Afghanistan), March 2014.
58 Jadoon and Mahmood, 2017.
59 Meeting with A**T, TTP commander, Bajaur, November 2016.
60 Meeting with A**T, TTP commander, Bajaur, November 2016.
61 Semple, 2014, 8.
62 Meeting with *I*, LeJ commander in Afghanistan, October 2020.
63 Jadoon, 2021; Sayed, 2021c.
64 Meeting with M*S, TTP commander in Bajaur, January 2016.
65 Meeting with QAS, TTP commander, Orakzai Agency, December 2015.
66 Meeting with elder, Achin, Nangarhar, January 2016; Meeting with IS-K commander, Achin, Nangarhar, August 2016.
67 Mufti Hassan Swati, quoted in Yusufzai, 2008.
68 Meeting MD**, TTP commander in Momand Agency, November 2016; Meeting with M*S, TTP commander in Bajaur, January 2016.
69 Meeting with QAS, TTP commander, Orakzai Agency, December 2015.
70 Meeting with QAS, TTP commander, Orakzai Agency, December 2015.
71 See on this Giustozzi, 2022.
72 Meeting with ISI officer, Pakistan, January 2016.
73 Meeting with *M, TTP group commander, South Waziristan, September 2020; Meeting with *M*, TTP IED team commander in South Waziristan, September 2020; Meeting with M*S, TTP commander in Bajaur, January 2016; Meeting with QAS, TTP commander, Orakzai Agency, December 2015.
74 Joscelyn, 2015.
75 Meeting with M*S, TTP commander in Bajaur, January 2016.
76 Meeting with M*S, TTP commander in Bajaur, January 2016; Meeting with QAS, TTP commander, Orakzai Agency, December 2015.
77 Meeting with M*S, TTP commander in Bajaur, January 2016; Meeting with QAS, TTP commander, Orakzai Agency, December 2015.
78 Meeting with **, Senior cadre of AQIS, November 2019.
79 Meeting with *, TTP commander in South Waziristan, March 2020; Meeting with Q**M, TTP commander (Mufti Noor Wali Mehsud faction) in South Waziristan,

March 2020; Meeting with K*, TTP commander in Kunar and Nuristan Provinces, March 2020.
80 Meeting with *, TTP commander in South Waziristan (Mufti Noor Wali Mehsud faction), September 2020; Meeting with **H, TTP commander in Kunar Province, former member of Sheharyar Mehsud faction, September 2020.
81 Meeting with *M*, TTP IED team commander in South Waziristan, September 2020.
82 Meeting with M*S, TTP commander in Bajaur, January 2016.
83 Meeting with M*S, TTP commander in Bajaur, January 2016.
84 Meeting with *M*, TTP IED team commander in South Waziristan, September 2020.
85 Meeting with **H, TTP commander in Kunar Province, former member of Sheharyar Mehsud faction, September 2020.
86 Meeting with Q**M, TTP commander (Mufti Noor Wali Mehsud faction) in South Waziristan, March 2020.
87 Meeting with *, TTP commander in South Waziristan (Mufti Noor Wali Mehsud faction), September 2020; Meeting with *M, TTP group commander, South Waziristan, September 2020; Meeting with **H, TTP commander in Kunar Province, former member of Sheharyar Mehsud faction, September 2020; Meeting with *M*, TTP IED team commander in South Waziristan, September 2020.
88 Meeting with*K*, IS-P commander, ex TTP, Baluchistan, July 2020.
89 Meeting with K*, TTP commander, Kunar, December 2021.
90 Valle, 2021.
91 Meeting with Q**, IS-P commander in Momand agency, December 2021.
92 Jamal, 2021.
93 Mir, 2016; Meeting with Q*A, member of JuA, Momand Agency, April 2020.
94 Meeting with IS-K cadre, Pakistan, November 2016.
95 Meeting with *, TTP commander in South Waziristan, March 2020; Meeting with Q**M, TTP commander (Mufti Noor Wali Mehsud faction) in South Waziristan, March 2020; Meeting with Q*A, member of JuA, Momand Agency, April 2020; Meeting with K*, TTP commander in Kunar and Nuristan Provinces, March 2020; Meeting with QA*, TTP member, Khalid Sajna faction, April 2020; Meeting with *K*, cadre of Maulana Fazlullah's Devotees, Kunar Province, April 2020; Meeting with K*, TTP commander in Kunar and Nuristan Provinces, March 2020; Rassler, 2015.
96 Meeting with Q*P, IS-P member, Baluchistan (Pakistan), former TTP member, July 2020; Meeting with*K*, IS-P commander, ex TTP, Baluchistan, July 2020.
97 Osman, 2016.
98 Meeting with IS-K senior commander, Pakistan, January 2017.
99 Jadoon, 2021.
100 Semple, 2014, 7.
101 Semple, 2014, 8.
102 Zahid, 2020, 519.
103 'TTP appoints Mufti Noor Wali Mehsud as chief after Fazlullah's killing', *AFP*, 23 June 2018.
104 On the organization of the Afghan Taliban, see Giustozzi, 2019.
105 Hashmi, 2009.
106 Meeting with senior TTP figure M*M, Kunar (Afghanistan), February 2013. On Lashkar-e Islam, see Basit, 2010, 108ff.
107 Meeting MD**, TTP commander in Momand Agency, November 2016.

108 Meeting with M*S, TTP commander in Bajaur, January 2016; Meeting with M*, senior LeI figure, February 2013.
109 Meeting with *, TTP commander in South Waziristan, March 2020.
110 Meeting with *R, TTP member in South Waziristan, formerly close to Hakimullah Mehsud, November 2020.
111 Meeting with TTP commander SM, Swat, February 2013.
112 Meeting with TTP commander Q**M, South Waziristan, Mufti Noor Wali Mehsud faction, March 2020.
113 Franco, 2009a.
114 Szrom, 2009.
115 Elahi, 2019.
116 https://www.un.org/securitycouncil/content/tariq-gidar-group-tgg
117 Franco, 2009.
118 Rahmanullah, 2010; Franco, 'Part III'.
119 Sulaiman, 2009.
120 See Yusufzai, 2008; Franco, 2009a.
121 Meeting with IS-K senior commander, M*, senior LeI figure, February 2013.
122 Meeting with **, TTP leader, South Waziristan, February 2013.
123 Meeting with IS-K senior commander, senior TTP figure M*M, Kunar (Afghanistan), February 2013; Meeting with IS-K senior commander, M*, senior LeI figure, February 2013; Meeting with TTP commander SM, Swat, February 2013. See also Rehman, 2012, 9.
124 Rahmanullah, 2010.
125 Elahi, 2019, Location 3634; Khattak, 2011; Meeting with **B, Sajna TTP faction, Waziristan, April 2020.
126 Meeting with Q*A, member of JuA, Momand Agency, April 2020; Meeting with **B, Sajna TTP faction, Waziristan, April 2020.
127 Meeting with Q*A, member of JuA, Momand Agency, April 2020.
128 Meeting MD**, TTP commander in Momand Agency, November 2016; Meeting with TTP commander Q**M, South Waziristan, Mufti Noor Wali Mehsud faction, March 2020.
129 Meeting MD**, TTP commander in Momand Agency, November 2016.
130 Meeting with *, TTP commander in South Waziristan, March 2020; Meeting with TTP commander Q**M, South Waziristan, Mufti Noor Wali Mehsud faction, March 2020.
131 Meeting M**S, TTP commander in Momand Agency, November 2016; Meeting with TTP commander Q**M, South Waziristan, Mufti Noor Wali Mehsud faction, March 2020; Meeting with TTP commander K*, Kunar (Afghanistan), March 2020; Meeting with **B, Sajna TTP faction, Waziristan, April 2020.
132 Meeting with S**, TTP cadre, Kunar Province, February 2013; Meeting with MB*, TTP cadre in Laghman Province, January 2014.
133 Meeting with TTP commander Q**M, South Waziristan, Mufti Noor Wali Mehsud faction, March 2020.
134 Rehman, 2014, 5; Meeting with TTP commander Q**M, South Waziristan, Mufti Noor Wali Mehsud faction, March 2020.
135 Meeting with *, TTP commander in South Waziristan, March 2020; Meeting with TTP commander K*, Kunar (Afghanistan), March 2020.
136 Meeting with *M, TTP group commander, South Waziristan, September 2020.

137 Roggio, 2014a; Meeting MD**, TTP commander in Momand Agency, November 2016; Meeting with M*S, TTP commander in Bajaur, January 2016; Meeting with TTP commander Q**M, South Waziristan, Mufti Noor Wali Mehsud faction, March 2020.
138 Meeting MD**, TTP commander in Momand Agency, November 2016.
139 Meeting with IS-K cadre, Pakistan, July 2016.
140 Meeting with Q*A, member of JuA, Momand Agency, April 2020; 'Pakistani Taliban splinter group splits further over tactics', *Associated Press*, November 12, 2017; Meeting with Q**M, TTP commander (Mufti Noor Wali Mehsud faction) in South Waziristan, March 2020; Meeting with **B, Sajna TTP faction, Waziristan, April 2020.
141 Meeting with MN*, group commander of Farooqi group, April 2016.
142 Meeting with ***, IS-K leader, Waziristan, December 2014; Meeting with Q**M, TTP commander (Mufti Noor Wali Mehsud faction) in South Waziristan, March 2020.
143 Meeting with Q**M, TTP commander (Mufti Noor Wali Mehsud faction) in South Waziristan, March 2020; Meeting with QA*, TTP member, Khalid Sajna faction, April 2020.
144 Meeting with *, TTP commander in South Waziristan, March 2020; Meeting with Q**M, TTP commander (Mufti Noor Wali Mehsud faction) in South Waziristan, March 2020; Meeting with TTP commander K*, Kunar (Afghanistan), March 2020.
145 Meeting with Q**M, TTP commander (Mufti Noor Wali Mehsud faction) in South Waziristan, March 2020.
146 Khattak, 2014.
147 Franco and Sandee, 2008.
148 Yusufzai, 2008.
149 Yusufzai, 2008.
150 Mahsud, 2010.
151 Meeting with Q**M, TTP commander (Mufti Noor Wali Mehsud faction) in South Waziristan, March 2020; Meeting with S**, TTP cadre in Kunar Province; Meeting with TTP commander K*, Kunar (Afghanistan), March 2020.
152 Meeting with **B, Sajna TTP faction, Waziristan, April 2020.
153 Yusufzai, 2008.
154 Meeting with Q*A, member of JuA, Momand Agency, April 2020; Meeting with TTP commander K*, Kunar (Afghanistan), March 2020.
155 Meeting with Q*A, member of JuA, Momand Agency, April 2020.
156 Meeting with *K*, cadre of Maulana Fazlullah's Devotees, Kunar Province, April 2020.
157 Burki, 2010.
158 Abbas, 2007.
159 Khan, 2010.
160 Mahsud, 2010.
161 Meeting with *M*, IS-K group commander, Waziristan, September 2016; Meeting with ***, IS-K leader, Waziristan, December 2014.
162 Meeting with *R, TTP member in South Waziristan, formerly close to Hakimullah Mehsud, November 2020.
163 See Giustozzi, 2019 for details.
164 Meeting with Q**M, TTP commander (Mufti Noor Wali Mehsud faction) in South Waziristan, March 2020.

165 Meeting with *R, TTP member in South Waziristan, formerly close to Hakimullah Mehsud, November 2020.
166 Meeting with *R, TTP member in South Waziristan, formerly close to Hakimullah Mehsud, November 2020.
167 Meeting with *R, TTP member in South Waziristan, formerly close to Hakimullah Mehsud, November 2020.
168 Meeting with *R, TTP member in South Waziristan, formerly close to Hakimullah Mehsud, November 2020.
169 'Tribal areas under centralized control', *Daily Times*, 16 December 2007.
170 Meeting with *R, TTP member in South Waziristan, formerly close to Hakimullah Mehsud, November 2020.
171 Meeting with *R, TTP member in South Waziristan, formerly close to Hakimullah Mehsud, November 2020.
172 'Suicide bombers ready: Fazlullah', *Dawn*, 28 July 2008. For the claims concerning the 'umbrella' character of the organization, see Siddique, 2010; Qazi, 2011.
173 Meeting with *R, TTP member in South Waziristan, formerly close to Hakimullah Mehsud, November 2020.
174 Meeting with *R, TTP member in South Waziristan, formerly close to Hakimullah Mehsud, November 2020.
175 Meeting with *R, TTP member in South Waziristan, formerly close to Hakimullah Mehsud, November 2020.
176 Mahmud and Abu Yahya (2010), Harmony Collection, with attached TPP Charter and commentary to it, 9–10.
177 Mahmud and Yahya, 2010, with attached Tehrik-e-Taliban Pakistan (TPP) Charter and commentary to it, 3.
178 Yusufzai, 2008; Szrom, 2009; Basit, 2010, 100.
179 Elahi, 2019, Location 1503ff.
180 Acharya et al., 2009.
181 Meeting with *R, TTP member in South Waziristan, formerly close to Hakimullah Mehsud, November 2020.
182 Rana and Gunaratna, 2007, 80–1; Acharya, 2009; Rana, 2009; Burki, 2010; Hussain, 2011.
183 Meeting with QAS, TTP commander, Orakzai Agency, December 2015.
184 See Giustozzi, 2019.
185 'National C-IED initiatives: Pakistan', *aoav.org.uk*, 2 June 2017.
186 See Giustozzi, 2019.
187 Rehman, 2013, 5.
188 Acharya et al., 2009.
189 Meeting with M*S, TTP commander in Bajaur, January 2016.
190 Rehman, 2013b.
191 Meeting with *R, TTP member in South Waziristan, formerly close to Hakimullah Mehsud, November 2020.
192 Meeting with senior TTP figure M*M, Kunar (Afghanistan), February 2013.
193 Meeting with M*S, TTP commander, Bajaur, January 2016.
194 Elahi, 2019, Locations 2131ff.
195 Meeting with MN*, group commander of Farooqi group, April 2016.
196 Meeting with S*Y, senior TTP figure in Kunar (Afghanistan), January 2014; Meeting with senior TTP figure M*M, Kunar (Afghanistan), February 2013; Meeting with M*Y, TTP cadre, Laghman (Afghanistan), January 2014.

197 Meeting with **B, Sajna TTP faction, Waziristan, April 2020.
198 Meeting with *K*, cadre of Maulana Fazlullah's Devotees, Kunar Province, April 2020.
199 Acharya et al., 2009.
200 Fredholm, 2011, 3.
201 Fredholm, 2011.
202 Fredholm, 2011.
203 Khattak, 2014.
204 Acharya et al., 2009. See also Mahsud, 2010; Feyyaz, 2016, 111–34; Elahi, 2019.
205 Acharya et al., 2019.
206 Khan, 2010a.
207 Semple, 2014, 13.
208 See for details Giustozzi, 2019.
209 Meeting with QAS, TTP commander, Orakzai Agency, December 2015.
210 See Giustozzi, 2018, 127, 131.
211 Sulaiman, 2009.
212 Mahsud, 2010.
213 Meeting with senior TTP figure M*M, Kunar (Afghanistan), February 2013; Meeting with **, TTP leader, South Waziristan, February 2013; Sheikh, 2009.
214 Franco and Sandee, 2008.
215 Meeting with **, TTP leader, South Waziristan, February 2013.
216 Meeting with **, TTP leader, South Waziristan, February 2013.
217 Meeting with IS-K senior commander, M*, senior LeI figure, February 2013.
218 Meeting with S**, TTP cadre in Kunar Province, January 2014.
219 Franco and Sandee, 2008.
220 Meeting with M*S, TTP commander in Bajaur, January 2016.
221 Meeting with M*S, TTP commander in Bajaur, January 2016.
222 Meeting with M*S, TTP commander in Bajaur, January 2016; Meeting with **, TTP leader, South Waziristan, February 2013. On the mediation efforts see Jan, 2010.
223 Meeting MD**, TTP commander in Momand Agency, November 2016; Meeting with MB*, TTP cadre in Laghman Province, January 2014; Meeting with M*S, TTP commander in Bajaur, January 2016; Meeting with MN*, group commander of Farooqi group, April 2016; Meeting with **, TTP leader, South Waziristan, February 2013; Meeting with Q*A, member of JuA, Momand Agency, April 2020; Meeting with TTP commander K*, Kunar (Afghanistan), March 2020; I Meeting with **B, Sajna TTP faction, Waziristan, April 2020; Meeting with *K*, cadre of Maulana Fazlullah's Devotees, Kunar Province, April 2020.
224 Meeting with **H, TTP commander in Paktika, October 2021; Meeting with O*, TTP cadre in South Waziristan, May 2021; Meeting with *R*, small business owner in Gorboz (Khost), March 2021; Meeting with MO, local elder in Sabari (Khost), March 2021.
225 Meeting with *M, TTP commander in Kunar, May 2021.
226 Roggio, 2021.
227 Meeting with **H, TTP commander, Paktika, December 2021; Meeting with TTP commander, Kunar, December 2021; Meeting with **, commander in Hafiz Gul Bahadur's groups, Paktia, October 2021; Meeting with K*, TTP commander in Kunar, October 2021; Meeting with N*, TTP commander in South Waziristan, October 2021.
228 'Jihad in Pakistan', 2016, 19.

229 'Jihad in Pakistan', 2016, 17–18.
230 Roggio, 2015.
231 al-Hasan and al-Libi, 2010.
232 Mahmud and Abu Yahya, 2010, 15.
233 Khurasani, n.d.
234 Szrom, 2009.
235 Sulaiman, 2009.
236 Meeting with **, TTP leader, South Waziristan, February 2013.
237 Meeting with TTP commander SM, Swat, February 2013.
238 Meeting MD**, TTP commander in Momand Agency, November 2016. On the ISI pushing LeT to fight against TTP see Jamal, Transnational jihad, 141–2.
239 Meeting MD**, TTP commander in Momand Agency, November 2016.
240 Meeting with *M*, TTP IED team commander in South Waziristan, September 2020.
241 Hussain (Khadim), 2011.
242 Burki, 2010; Puri, 2012., 54ff, 108–10. For a more positive view see Sulaiman, 2008.
243 Burki, 2010.
244 Meeting with MB*, TTP cadre in Laghman Province, January 2014.
245 Harnisch, 2009.
246 Meeting with **, TTP leader, South Waziristan, February 2013; Siddique, 2018.
247 Burki, 2010.
248 See Franco, 2009a; Burki, 2010. On Baitullah's Sararogha's agreement with the Pakistani authorities see Rana, 2010b, 90ff.
249 Burki, 2010.
250 Meeting with *R, TTP member in South Waziristan, formerly close to Hakimullah Mehsud, November 2020.
251 Hussain (Khadim), 2011.
252 Haider, 2012; Meeting with IS-K senior commander, senior LeI figure *B, Nangarhar (Afghanistan), February 2013.
253 Foschini, 2013.
254 Szrom, 2009.
255 Meeting with IS-K senior commander, senior LeI figure *B, Nangarhar (Afghanistan), February 2013.
256 Meeting with **, TTP leader, South Waziristan, February 2013.
257 Meeting with **, TTP leader, South Waziristan, February 2013.
258 Meeting with **, TTP leader, South Waziristan, February 2013.
259 Meeting with **, TTP leader, South Waziristan, February 2013; Meeting with IS-K senior commander, senior TTP figure M*M, Kunar (Afghanistan), February 2013; Meeting with IS-K senior commander, M*, senior LeI figure, February 2013; Meeting with IS-K senior commander, TTP commander SM, Swat, February 2013.
260 Meeting with **, TTP leader, South Waziristan, February 2013.
261 Meeting with IS-K senior commander, senior TTP figure M*M, Kunar (Afghanistan), February 2013; Meeting with IS-K senior commander, M*, senior LeI figure, February 2013; Meeting with TTP commander SM, Swat, February 2013.
262 Meeting with IS-K senior commander, M*, senior LeI figure, February 2013.
263 Meeting with **Y, TTP cadre in Kunar Province, January 2014.
264 Meeting with MB*, TTP cadre in Laghman Province, January 2014; Meeting with Q*A, member of JuA, Momand Agency, April 2020; Meeting with **B, Sajna TTP faction, Waziristan, April 2020; Meeting with *K*, cadre of Maulana Fazlullah's Devotees, Kunar Province, April 2020.

265 Meeting with *, TTP commander in South Waziristan, March 2020.
266 Jadoon, 2021.
267 See for a detailed discussion Giustozzi, 2019.
268 Meeting with Q*M, AQ commander, Kunar (Afghanistan), March 2014.
269 Burki, 2010.
270 Mahmud and Abu Yahya, 2010, 5.
271 Acharya et al., 2009; Mian, 2009; Sulaiman, 2009; Peters, 2010; Khattak, 2014; Elahi, 2019.
272 Mahmud and Abu Yahya, 2010, 5–6.
273 Elahi, 2019, Location 2065.
274 Elahi, 2019, Location 2065.
275 Rehman, 2012a.
276 Meeting with M*S, TTP commander, Bajaur, January 2016.
277 Acharya at al., 2009.
278 Meeting with M*S, TTP commander, Bajaur, January 2016. The Pakistani security services claim that foreign funding is in fact coming from the Indian RAW, see Elahi, 2019, Locations 2131ff. A member of the Farooqi Groups stated that he believed these allegations were true (Meeting with MN*, group commander of Farooqi group, April 2016). Other TTP sources also mentioned funds coming from 'Afghan businessmen': Meeting with S*Y, senior TTP figure in Kunar (Afghanistan), January 2014; Meeting with senior TTP figure M*M, Kunar (Afghanistan), February 2013; Meeting with M*Y, TTP cadre, Laghman (Afghanistan), January 2014.
279 Giustozzi, 2019, 243.
280 Meeting with *E, senior TTP figure in South Waziristan, February 2013.
281 Meeting with M*S, TTP commander, Bajaur, January 2016.
282 Burki, 2010, 188–211; Elahi, 2019, Locations 215ff.
283 Meeting M**S, TTP commander, Momand Agency, November 2016.
284 Meeting with A**M, AQ commander, Watafoor (Afghanistan), January 2016. On the relationship of AQ with Lashkar-e Taiba, see United Nations Security Council, 'Letter dated 15 July 2019 from the Chair of the Security Council Committee pursuant to resolutions 1267 (1999), 1989 (2011) and 2253 (2015) concerning Islamic State in Iraq and the Levant (Da'esh), al Qa'ida and associated individuals, groups, undertakings and entities addressed to the President of the Security Council'. S/2019/570, New York, 15 July 2019, 15; Tankel, 2010. On Jaish e Mohammed and AQ see Moj, 2015, and Riedel, 2011.
285 Meeting with A**G, AQ cadre, Nuristan (Afghanistan), May 2017.
286 Meeting with Q*A, Jama'at-ul-Ahrar cadre, Momand Agency, April 2020.
287 'Jihad in Pakistan', 2016, 18–19.
288 Meeting with AQIS agent A** in Karachi, July 2020.
289 Mahmud and Yahya, 2010, 1, 3.
290 Mahmud and Abu Yahya, 2010, 1.
291 Mahmud and Abu Yahya, 2010, 1, 3.
292 Mahmud and Abu Yahya, 2010, 1–2.
293 Mahmud and Abu Yahya, 2010, 4.
294 Mahmud and Abu Yahya, 2010, 2.
295 Mahmud and Yahya, 2010, 2.
296 Mahmud and Abu Yahya, 2010, 4.
297 Mahmud and Abu Yahya, 2010, 8–9.
298 Mahmud and Abu Yahya, 2010, 9–10.

299 Nelly et al., 2012. On the TTP tactics see among others Human Rights Watch, 'Dreams turned into nightmares', New York, 2017.
300 Lahoud, bin Laden papers, 111–12.
301 'Mahmud al-Hasan ('Atiyatullah) and (Abu Yahya) al-Libi, 'Letter to Hakimullah Mashud', Harmony document, released 2016 (SOCOM-2012-0000007-HT), 27 Dhu al-Hijjah 1431 (3 December 2010). See also Lahoud, bin Laden papers, 111.
302 'Code of conduct: al Qa'ida in the Subcontinent', As Sahab Media, June 2017, 11.
303 Mahmud and Abu Yahya, 2010, 6.
304 'Taliban infighting escalating in Afghanistan and Pakistan'. *Eurasianet.org*, 30 May 2014.
305 Meeting MD**, TTP commander in Momand Agency, November 2016.
306 Mahsud, 2010.
307 Mahsud, 2010.
308 Meeting with senior TTP figure M*M, Kunar (Afghanistan), February 2013.
309 Meeting M**S, TTP commander, Momand Agency, November 2016; Meeting with QAS, IS commander, Orakzai Agency, December 2015; Meeting with *E, senior TTP figure in South Waziristan, February 2013; Khan (Raheel), 2010b.
310 Meeting with A**M, AQ commander, Watafoor (Afghanistan), January 2016.
311 Meeting with *E, senior TTP figure in South Waziristan, February 2013.
312 al-Hasan and al-Libi, 2010.
313 Mahmud and Abu Yahya, 2010, 10–11.
314 Meeting with *A, AQ group commander in Jammu and Kashmir, September 2019.
315 Meeting with **, Senior cadre of AQIS, November 2019.
316 Meeting with *A, AQ group commander in Jammu and Kashmir, September 2019.
317 Meeting with Q**, AQIS cadre, eastern Afghanistan, September 2020.
318 Meeting with Q**, AQIS cadre, eastern Afghanistan, September 2020.
319 Meeting with Q**, AQIS cadre, eastern Afghanistan, September 2020.
320 Meeting with Q**, AQIS cadre, eastern Afghanistan, September 2020.
321 Meeting with Q**, AQIS cadre, eastern Afghanistan, September 2020.
322 Meeting with *, TTP commander in South Waziristan (Mufti Noor Wali Mehsud faction), September 2020. A copy of the draft deal proposed by the Quetta Shura circulated on social media and was confirmed as genuine by this source.
323 Meeting with *M, TTP group commander, South Waziristan, September 2020; Meeting with **H, TTP commander in Kunar Province, former member of Sheharyar Mehsud faction, September 2020.
324 Meeting with *M, TTP group commander, South Waziristan, September 2020.
325 Ehsan, 2020.
326 Meeting with Q**, AQIS commander in eastern Afghanistan, October 2020.
327 Mahmud and Abu Yahya, 2010, 2.
328 Meeting with MB*, TTP cadre in Laghman Province, January 2014; Meeting with **Y, TTP cadre in Kunar Province, January 2014.
329 Meeting with MB*, TTP cadre in Laghman Province, January 2014.
330 Meeting with MB*, TTP cadre in Laghman Province, January 2014.
331 Meeting with *A, AQ group commander in Jammu and Kashmir, September 2019.
332 Meeting with TTP commander, Swat, February 2013.
333 Meeting with *A, AQ group commander in Jammu and Kashmir, September 2019.
334 Meeting with SM, Swat TTP commander, February 2013; Meeting with TTP leader M**, February 2013.
335 Meeting with M*J, Farooqi Group commander, Malakand Agency, February 2016; Meeting with A**G, AQ cadre, Nuristan (Afghanistan), May 2017.

336 Meeting with M*J, Farooqi Group commander, Malakand Agency, February 2016; Meeting M**S, TTP commander, Momand Agency, November 2016.
337 Meeting with Q*M, Taliban commander, Afghanistan.
338 Meeting with M*J, Farooqi Group commander, Malakand Agency, February 2016; Meeting M**S, TTP commander, Momand Agency, November 2016.
339 Meeting with M*J, Farooqi Group commander, Malakand Agency, February 2016; Meeting with A**G, AQ cadre, Nuristan (Afghanistan), May 2017.
340 Burki, 'Rise of Taliban'.
341 Meeting with A**M, AQ commander, Watafoor (Afghanistan), January 2016.
342 Meeting with A**G, AQ cadre, Nuristan (Afghanistan), May 2017.
343 Meeting with S**, TTP cadre in Kunar Province, February 2013; Meeting with MB*, TTP cadre in Laghman Province, January 2014.
344 Meeting with M*S, TTP commander in Bajaur, January 2016.
345 Meeting MD**, TTP commander in Momand Agency, November 2016.
346 Meeting MD**, TTP commander in Momand Agency, November 2016.
347 'Banned militant group merges into Pakistan Taleban', *Dawn*, 13 March 2015; Meeting MD**, TTP commander in Momand Agency, November 2016; Meeting with M*S, TTP commander in Bajaur, January 2016; Meeting MD**, TTP commander in Momand Agency, November 2016.
348 Meeting with O*, TTP cadre in South Waziristan, May 2021; Meeting with Q*B, TTP cadre, Sajna faction, South Waziristan, March 2020.
349 Meeting with *M, TTP group commander, South Waziristan, September 2020.
350 Sources: Meeting with TTP commander K*, Swat, March 2020 Meeting with Q**M, TTP commander loyal to Mufti Noor Wali Mehsud, South Waziristan, March 2020; Siddique, 2010; Meeting with TTP leader M**, February 2013; Elahi, 2019; Owen Bennet-Jones, 'Pakistan army eyes Taliban talks with unease', *BBC.co.uk/News*, 25 April 2014; Meeting with M*S, TTP commander in Bajaur, January 2016; Meeting with **B, Sajna TTP faction, Waziristan, April 2020; Meeting with *, TTP commander in South Waziristan (Mufti Noor Wali Mehsud faction), September 2020; Meeting with Q**M, TTP commander (Mufti Noor Wali Mehsud faction) in South Waziristan, March 2020; Meeting with K*, TTP commander in Kunar and Nuristan Provinces, March 2020.
351 Sources: Elahi, 2019; Meeting with M*S, TTP commander in Bajaur, January 2016; Meeting with *, TTP commander in South Waziristan (Mufti Noor Wali Mehsud faction), September 2020; Meeting with Q**M, TTP commander (Mufti Noor Wali Mehsud faction) in South Waziristan, March 2020; Meeting with K*, TTP commander in Kunar and Nuristan Provinces, March 2020; Meeting with MN*, group commander of Farooqi group, April 2016; Abbas, 2007; Meeting with Q*A, member of JuA, Momand Agency, April 2020.
352 Meeting with Q*B, TTP cadre, Sajna faction, South Waziristan, March 2020.
353 Meeting with J*, TTP commander, Ladha subdivision of South Waziristan, March 2020; Meeting with Q**M, TTP commander loyal to Mufti Noor Wali Mehsud, South Waziristan, March 2020; Meeting with TTP commander K*, Swat, March 2020.
354 Meeting with Q**, AQIS cadre, eastern Afghanistan, September 2020.
355 Meeting with J*, TTP commander, Ladha subdivision of South Waziristan, March 2020.
356 Meeting with TTP cadre, Shinwar, Afghanistan, June 2019.
357 Meeting with *K*, cadre of Maulana Fazlullah's Devotees, Kunar Province, April 2020.

358 Meeting with Q*A, member of JuA, Momand Agency, April 2020; Meeting with **B, Sajna TTP faction, Waziristan, April 2020.
359 For details see A. Giustozzi, 'al Qa'ida'.
360 Meeting with Q*B, TTP cadre, Sajna faction, South Waziristan, March 2020.
361 Meeting with *, TTP commander in South Waziristan (Mufti Noor Wali Mehsud faction), September 2020; Meeting with *M, TTP group commander, South Waziristan, September 2020.
362 Meeting with AQIS agent A** in Karachi, July 2020.
363 Meeting with *, TTP commander in South Waziristan, March 2020.
364 Meeting with *M, TTP group commander, South Waziristan, September 2020.
365 TTP, 'Operation Manual for Mujahideen of Tehreek Taliban Pakistan', n.d.
366 TTP, 'Operation Manual for Mujahideen of Tehreek Taliban Pakistan', n.d.
367 Telephone contact with TTP cadre, June 2021.
368 Jadoon, Sayed, 2021.
369 JADOON and MAHMOOD, 2018.
370 Meeting with *M*, TTP IED team commander in South Waziristan, September 2020.
371 Khattak, 2021.
372 Meeting with *, TTP commander in South Waziristan (Mufti Noor Wali Mehsud faction), September 2020.
373 Meeting with *, TTP commander in South Waziristan (Mufti Noor Wali Mehsud faction), September 2020.
374 Meeting with *, TTP commander in South Waziristan (Mufti Noor Wali Mehsud faction), September 2020.
375 Meeting with *M, TTP group commander, South Waziristan, September 2020.
376 Meeting with *M, TTP group commander, South Waziristan, September 2020.
377 Meeting with Q**M, TTP commander (Mufti Noor Wali Mehsud faction) in South Waziristan, March 2020.
378 Meeting with Q*A, member of JuA, Momand Agency, April 2020.
379 Meeting with Q**M, TTP commander (Mufti Noor Wali Mehsud faction) in South Waziristan, March 2020.
380 Meeting with Q*A, member of JuA, Momand Agency, April 2020; Meeting with **B, Sajna TTP faction, Waziristan, April 2020; Meeting with *K*, cadre of Maulana Fazlullah's Devotees, Kunar Province, April 2020; Meeting with *, TTP commander in South Waziristan, March 2020; Meeting with QA*, TTP member, Khalid Sajna faction, April 2020.
381 Meeting with *M, TTP group commander, South Waziristan, September 2020.
382 Meeting with Q**, AQIS cadre, eastern Afghanistan, September 2020.
383 Meeting with *, TTP commander in South Waziristan (Mufti Noor Wali Mehsud faction), September 2020; Meeting with **H, TTP commander in Kunar Province, former member of Sheharyar Mehsud faction, September 2020; Meeting with *M*, TTP IED team commander in South Waziristan, September 2020.
384 Meeting with *, TTP commander in South Waziristan (Mufti Noor Wali Mehsud faction), September 2020.
385 Meeting with *, TTP commander in South Waziristan (Mufti Noor Wali Mehsud faction), September 2020; Daud Khattak, 'Whither the Pakistani Taliban: An assessment of recent trends', New America Foundation, August 31, 2020; Meeting with Q*A, member of JuA, Momand Agency, April 2020; Meeting with TTP commander K*, Kunar (Afghanistan), March 2020; Meeting with **B, Sajna TTP faction, Waziristan, April 2020.

386 Sayed, 2021b; Sayed and Tore, 2021.
387 Meeting with *K*, cadre of Maulana Fazlullah's Devotees, Kunar Province, April 2020.
388 Jamal, 2020; Nair, 2020.
389 Meeting with TTP commander K*, Kunar (Afghanistan), March 2020.
390 Meeting with *M, TTP group commander, South Waziristan, September 2020; personal communication with Adnan …, September 2020.
391 Meeting with **B, Sajna TTP faction, Waziristan, April 2020.
392 Meeting with *K*, cadre of Maulana Fazlullah's Devotees, Kunar Province, April 2020.
393 Meeting with *K*, cadre of Maulana Fazlullah's Devotees, Kunar Province, April 2020.
394 Meeting with Q**M, TTP commander (Mufti Noor Wali Mehsud faction) in South Waziristan, March 2020.
395 Sayed, 2021a.
396 Meeting with *, TTP commander in South Waziristan (Mufti Noor Wali Mehsud faction), September 2020; Khattak, 2020.
397 Meeting with A*Y, Mowlana Fazlullah Devotees commander, Kunar (Afghanistan), April 2020; Bill Roggio, 'UN sanctions emir of the Pakistani Taliban', *Long War Journal*, 17 July 2020.
398 Meeting with **H, TTP commander, Paktika, December 2021; Jadoon and Sayed, 2021; Meeting with **, Hafiz Gul Bahadur commander in Paktia, October 2021; Meeting with K*, TTP commander in Kunar, October 2021; Meeting with O*, TTP cadre in South Waziristan, May 2021; Meeting with *M, TTP commander in Kunar, May 2021.
399 Meeting with TTP commander, Kunar, December 2021.
400 Meeting with *M, TTP group commander, South Waziristan, September 2020.
401 Meeting with *M, TTP group commander, South Waziristan, September 2020.
402 Fazl-e Haider, 2021.
403 Khuldune Shahid, 2019.
404 These figures are based on the TTP's own claims. For figures based on data coming from the media and the Pakistani authorities, see Jadoon, 2021.
405 Meeting with *, TTP commander in South Waziristan, March 2020; Meeting with *, TTP commander in South Waziristan (Mufti Noor Wali Mehsud faction), September 2020.
406 Meeting with *M, TTP group commander, South Waziristan, September 2020.
407 Meeting with **H, TTP commander, Paktika, December 2021.
408 Tweet of Ehsanullah Ehsan @EUEofficial1, 16 September 2020.
409 Meeting with *, TTP commander in South Waziristan (Mufti Noor Wali Mehsud faction), September 2020; Meeting with **H, TTP commander in Kunar Province, former member of Sheharyar Mehsud faction, September 2020; Meeting with *M*, TTP IED team commander in South Waziristan, September 2020; Khattak, 2020.
410 Meeting with *O, LeJ member in Punjab, November 2020; Meeting with Q*, LeJ trainer in Punjab, December 2020.
411 'TTP withdraws demand of reversing FATA merger', *The Express Tribute*, 27 November 2021.
412 Rupert Stone, 'A tale of two Talibans', *TRT World*, 5 April 2021.
413 Bezhan and Khattak, 2021.
414 Marty, 2021; Meeting with O*, TTP cadre in South Waziristan, May 2021.

415 Aamir, 2021; Pantucci, 2021.
416 Meeting with N*, TTP commander in South Waziristan, October 2021.
417 Meeting with N*, TTP commander in South Waziristan, October 2021.
418 Meeting with **H, TTP commander, Paktika, December 2022; Meeting with TTP commander, Kunar, December 2021.
419 Jadoon, 2021.
420 Meeting with **H, TTP commander, Paktika, December 2022; Meeting with TTP commander, Kunar, December 2021.
421 Meeting with **H, TTP commander, Paktika, December 2022; Meeting with TTP commander, Kunar, December 2021.
422 Communication with Haqqani network commander, Khost, April 2022.
423 Priestland, 2009.
424 Meeting with *I*, LeJ commander in Afghanistan, October 2020.
425 Bezhan and Khattak, 2021.
426 Meeting with *N* in Kunar, senior AQ commander, January 2022.
427 Meeting with *N* in Kunar, senior AQ commander, January 2022; Meeting with A** in Kunar, AQIS cadre, December 2021.

Chapter 4

1 Meeting with *A, former member of Jundullah, Baluchistan, November 2020; Meeting with Q**, AQIS cadre, eastern Afghanistan, September 2020; Hussain, 2007, 137–8.
2 Meeting with *A, former member of Jundullah, Baluchistan, November 2020.
3 Meeting with M*, Jhangvi district of Punjab, member of SSP and madrasa manager, July 2020.
4 Meeting with M*, Jhangvi district of Punjab, member of SSP and madrasa manager, July 2020; Meeting with M**A, member of SSP, Punjab, July 2020; Meeting with M*P, member of SSP in Khyber Pakhtunkha, August 2020.
5 Meeting with *Q*, LeJ trainer, Punjab, July 2020.
6 Meeting with *A, LeJ cadre, Pakistan, July 2020; Meeting with *O, LeJ member in Punjab, November 2020; Meeting with M**A, member of SSP, Punjab, July 2020; Meeting with M*, Jhangvi district of Punjab, member of SSP and madrasa manager, July 2020.
7 Meeting with Q*, LeJ trainer in Punjab, December 2020.
8 Meeting with M*P, member of SSP in Khyber Pakhtunkha, August 2020.
9 Meeting with **K, teacher in an SSP madrasa in Punjab, November 2020.
10 Meeting with *R*, member of SSP, Peshawar, December 2020.
11 Meeting with *I*, LeJ commander in Afghanistan, October 2020.
12 Meeting with *I*, LeJ commander in Afghanistan, October 2020.
13 Meeting with *R*, member of SSP, Peshawar, December 2020.
14 Burke, 2004, 239.
15 Meeting with M**A, member of SSP, Punjab, July 2020.
16 Meeting with *R*, member of SSP, Peshawar, December 2020.
17 ICG, 2009, 6–7.
18 Meeting with M*M, SSP group commander, Punjab, April 2016.
19 Meeting with M*M, SSP group commander, Punjab, April 2016.

20	Meeting with M*M, SSP group commander, Punjab, April 2016.
21	Meeting with *R*, member of SSP, Peshawar, December 2020.
22	Meeting with MA**, LeJ group commander, Punjab, February 2016; Meeting with M**A, member of SSP, Punjab, July 2020; Meeting with MA**, LeJ group commander, Punjab, February 2016.
23	Mir, 2008, 245ff.
24	ICG, 2009, 6–7.
25	Reed, 2016, 16.
26	Jamal, 2011, Location 556ff.
27	Meeting with MA**, LeJ group commander, Punjab, February 2016.
28	Meeting with **, Senior cadre of AQIS, November 2019.
29	Meeting with Q**, AQIS cadre, eastern Afghanistan, September 2020.
30	Meeting with *A, LeJ cadre, Pakistan, July 2020.
31	'Pakistan police kill three Lashkar-e-Jhangvi terrorists responsible for attacking Shias', *The New Indian Express*, 13 October 2021.
32	Meeting with AQIS agent *A**$ in Karachi, July 2020.
33	Meeting with Q**, AQIS cadre, eastern Afghanistan, September 2020.
34	Meeting with Q**, AQIS cadre, eastern Afghanistan, September 2020.
35	Meeting with Q**, AQIS cadre, eastern Afghanistan, September 2020.
36	Meeting with Q**, AQIS cadre, eastern Afghanistan, September 2020.
37	Meeting with Q**, AQIS cadre, eastern Afghanistan, September 2020.
38	Meeting with Q**, AQIS cadre, eastern Afghanistan, September 2020.
39	Meeting with Q*, LeJ trainer in Punjab, December 2020.
40	https://www.satp.org/type-of-attack/Sectarian-Violence/pakistan-2018; https://www.satp.org/type-of-attack/Sectarian-Violence/pakistan-2019 and https://www.satp.org/type-of-attack/Sectarian-Violence/pakistan-2020.
41	Meeting with Q**, AQIS cadre, eastern Afghanistan, September 2020.
42	Ahmed, 2011, 125–7, 148.
43	Ahmed, 2011, 301–2.
44	Meeting with M*, Jhangvi district of Punjab, member of SSP and madrasa manager, July 2020; Meeting with M**A, member of SSP, Punjab, July 2020; Meeting with **K, teacher in an SSP madrasa in Punjab, November 2020; Meeting with *R*, member of SSP, Peshawar, December 2020; Meeting with M*P, member of SSP in Khyber Pakhtunkha, August 2020.
45	Meeting with M*, Jhangvi district of Punjab, member of SSP and madrasa manager, July 2020.
46	Meeting with M*M, SSP group commander, Punjab, April 2016.
47	Meeting with M*P, member of SSP in Khyber Pakhtunkha, August 2020; Meeting with *, TTP commander in South Waziristan (Mufti Noor Wali Mehsud faction), September 2020.
48	Meeting with M*, Jhangvi district of Punjab, member of SSP and madrasa manager, July 2020; Meeting with M**A, member of SSP, Punjab, July 2020; Meeting with **K, teacher in an SSP madrasa in Punjab, November 2020; Meeting with *R*, member of SSP, Peshawar, December 2020.
49	Meeting with **K, teacher in an SSP madrasa in Punjab, November 2020; Meeting with *R*, member of SSP, Peshawar, December 2020.
50	Meeting with *R*, member of SSP, Peshawar, December 2020.
51	Mir, 2006, 142, 241; ICG, 2005, 14; Roul, 2005.
52	Meeting with M*M, SSP group commander, Punjab, April 2016.

53 Meeting with M**A, member of SSP, Punjab, July 2020; Meeting with M*P, member of SSP in Khyber Pakhtunkha, August 2020; Meeting with M*, Jhangvi district of Punjab, member of SSP and madrasa manager, July 2020.
54 Meeting with M**A, member of SSP, Punjab, July 2020.
55 Meeting with M*, Jhangvi district of Punjab, member of SSP and madrasa manager, July 2020.
56 Meeting with *I*, LeJ commander in Afghanistan, October 2020.
57 Meeting with *R*, member of SSP, Peshawar, December 2020.
58 Meeting with M*, Jhangvi district of Punjab, member of SSP and madrasa manager, July 2020; Meeting with M**A, member of SSP, Punjab, July 2020.
59 Meeting with M*, Jhangvi district of Punjab, member of SSP and madrasa manager, July 2020; Meeting with M**A, member of SSP, Punjab, July 2020.
60 Meeting with *A, LeJ cadre, Pakistan, July 2020.
61 Jamal, 2011, Location 621ff; Jamal, 2009.
62 Meeting with *Q*, LeJ trainer, Punjab, July 2020.
63 Meeting with *O, LeJ member in Punjab, November 2020.
64 Meeting with Q*, LeJ trainer in Punjab, December 2020.
65 Meeting with MA**, LeJ group commander, Punjab, February 2016.
66 Meeting with *Q*, LeJ trainer, Punjab, July 2020.
67 Meeting with *I*, LeJ commander in Afghanistan, October 2020.
68 Meeting with *A, LeJ cadre, Pakistan, July 2020.
69 Meeting with *A, LeJ cadre, Pakistan, July 2020.
70 Meeting with *Q*, LeJ trainer, Punjab, July 2020.
71 Meeting with *Q*, LeJ trainer, Punjab, July 2020. On the battle for Kunduz see Giustozzi, 2015.
72 Meeting with *A, LeJ cadre, Pakistan, July 2020; Meeting with *Q*, LeJ trainer, Punjab, July 2020; Meeting with M**A, member of SSP, Punjab, July 2020.
73 Meeting with *Q*, LeJ trainer, Punjab, July 2020.
74 Meeting with *A, LeJ cadre, Pakistan, July 2020.
75 Meeting with *I*, LeJ commander in Afghanistan, October 2020.
76 Meeting with *A, LeJ cadre, Pakistan, July 2020.
77 Meeting with *Q*, LeJ trainer, Punjab, July 2020.
78 Khattak, 2013; Ahmed, 2011, 149–50.
79 Asad and Asghar, 2015.
80 Meeting with *K, LeT IED maker and trainer, Muzaffarabad camp, May 2021; Meeting with **A member of the Taliban's Military Commission, July 2021.
81 Meeting with *A, former member of Jundullah, Baluchistan, November 2020.
82 Murphy, 2019, 457–8.
83 Meeting with M*M, SSP group commander, Punjab, April 2016.
84 Meeting with M*M, SSP group commander, Punjab, April 2016; Meeting with M**A, member of SSP, Punjab, July 2020.
85 Meeting with **K, teacher in an SSP madrasa in Punjab, November 2020.
86 Meeting with **K, teacher in an SSP madrasa in Punjab, November 2020.
87 Meeting with M*, Jhangvi district of Punjab, member of SSP and madrasa manager, July 2020; Meeting with M**A, member of SSP, Punjab, July 2020.
88 Meeting with M*M, SSP group commander, Punjab, April 2016.
89 Meeting with **K, teacher in an SSP madrasa in Punjab, November 2020.
90 Meeting with M*M, SSP group commander, Punjab, April 2016.
91 Meeting with AA**, AQ cadre, eastern Afghanistan, May 2017.

92 Meeting with M*, Jhangvi district of Punjab, member of SSP and madrasa manager, July 2020; Meeting with M**A, member of SSP, Punjab, July 2020; Meeting with **K, teacher in an SSP madrasa in Punjab, November 2020.
93 Meeting with M*P, member of SSP in Khyber Pakhtunkha, August 2020.
94 Meeting with M*, Jhangvi district of Punjab, member of SSP and madrasa manager, July 2020; Meeting with M**A, member of SSP, Punjab, July 2020.
95 Meeting with M*P, member of SSP in Khyber Pakhtunkha, August 2020. On the defeats suffered by IS-K, see Giustozzi, 2020.
96 Meeting with M**A, member of SSP, Punjab, July 2020; Meeting with M*P, member of SSP in Khyber Pakhtunkha, August 2020.
97 Meeting with *Q*, LeJ trainer, Punjab, July 2020; Meeting with MA**, LeJ group commander, Punjab, February 2016; Meeting with M**, IS-K leader, Kurram Agency, December 2014; Meeting with *A, LeJ cadre, Pakistan, July 2020; Meeting with Q**, AQIS cadre, eastern Afghanistan, September 2020.
98 Meeting with IS-K senior cadre, December 2014; United Nations Security Council, 2016; Meeting with IS-K commander, February 2016; Meeting with IS-K cadre, Pakistan, October 2015; Meeting with IS-K leader, June 2015.
99 Meeting with *A, LeJ cadre, Pakistan, July 2020.
100 Meeting with *A, LeJ cadre, Pakistan, July 2020; Meeting with M**A, member of SSP, Punjab, July 2020.
101 Meeting with *A, LeJ cadre, Pakistan, July 2020.
102 Meeting with MA**, LeJ group commander, Punjab, February 2016; Meeting with M**, IS-K leader, Kurram Agency, December 2014; Meeting with *A, LeJ cadre, Pakistan, July 2020; Meeting with Q**, AQIS cadre, eastern Afghanistan, September 2020; Meeting with *O, LeJ member in Punjab, November 2020; Meeting with *I*, LeJ commander in Afghanistan, October 2020.
103 Meeting with M**A, member of SSP, Punjab, July 2020.
104 Meeting with *A, LeJ cadre, Pakistan, July 2020.
105 Meeting with *A, LeJ cadre, Pakistan, July 2020.
106 Meeting with IS-K senior commander, Pakistan, January 2017.
107 Meeting with AA**, AQ cadre, eastern Afghanistan, May 2017.
108 Meeting with AA**, AQ cadre, eastern Afghanistan, May 2017; Meeting with *O, LeJ member in Punjab, November 2020.
109 Meeting with MA**, LeJ group commander, Punjab, February 2016.
110 Meeting with *A, LeJ cadre, Pakistan, July 2020.
111 Meeting with *I*, LeJ commander in Afghanistan, October 2020.
112 Meeting with *A, LeJ cadre, Pakistan, July 2020; Meeting with *Q*, LeJ trainer, Punjab, July 2020.
113 Meeting with MA**, LeJ group commander, Punjab, February 2016; Meeting with M**A, member of SSP, Punjab, July 2020.
114 Meeting with MA**, LeJ group commander, Punjab, February 2016.
115 Meeting with **M, IS-K commander in Waziristan, September 2016.
116 Meeting with *I*, LeJ commander in Afghanistan, October 2020.
117 On IS-K in Afghanistan see Giustozzi, 2018.
118 Meeting with *A, LeJ cadre, Pakistan, July 2020.
119 Meeting with *Q*, LeJ trainer, Punjab, July 2020.
120 Meeting with *A, LeJ cadre, Pakistan, July 2020.
121 Meeting with Q*, LeJ trainer in Punjab, December 2020.
122 Zahid, 2017; 2015c.

123 Shahid, 2016.
124 Meeting with *A, LeJ cadre, Pakistan, July 2020; Meeting with *Q*, LeJ trainer, Punjab, July 2020.
125 Meeting with *Q*, LeJ trainer, Punjab, July 2020.
126 Meeting with *Q*, LeJ trainer, Punjab, July 2020.
127 Meeting with *I*, LeJ commander in Afghanistan, October 2020; Meeting with *O, LeJ member in Punjab, November 2020; Meeting with Q*, LeJ trainer in Punjab, December 2020.
128 Meeting with M*, Jhangvi district of Punjab, member of SSP and madrasa manager, July 2020; Meeting with M**A, member of SSP, Punjab, July 2020; Meeting with **K, teacher in an SSP madrasa in Punjab, November 2020.
129 Meeting with M*P, member of SSP in Khyber Pakhtunkha, August 2020.
130 Meeting with M**A, member of SSP, Punjab, July 2020.
131 Meeting with M*, Jhangvi district of Punjab, member of SSP and madrasa manager, July 2020; Meeting with M**A, member of SSP, Punjab, July 2020; Meeting with **K, teacher in an SSP madrasa in Punjab, November 2020.
132 Meeting with O*, IS-P commander, July 2020.
133 Meeting with *R*, member of SSP, Peshawar, December 2020.
134 Meeting with AQIS agent A** in Karachi, July 2020.
135 Meeting with M*P, member of SSP in Khyber Pakhtunkha, August 2020.
136 Meeting with AQIS agent A** in Karachi, July 2020; Meeting with Q**, AQIS cadre, eastern Afghanistan, September 2020.
137 Meeting with Q**, AQIS cadre, eastern Afghanistan, September 2020.
138 Meeting with Q**, AQIS cadre, eastern Afghanistan, September 2020.
139 Meeting with Q**, AQIS cadre, eastern Afghanistan, September 2020.
140 Meeting with *Q*, LeJ trainer, Punjab, July 2020.
141 Meeting with *O, LeJ member in Punjab, November 2020; Meeting with Q*, LeJ trainer in Punjab, December 2020; Meeting with Q*, LeJ trainer in Punjab, December 2020.
142 Meeting with *O, LeJ member in Punjab, November 2020.
143 Abbas, 2021.
144 Ayaz, 2017.
145 Meeting with *A, former member of Jundullah, Baluchistan, November 2020.
146 Meeting with *B, commander of Herakat Khalifat Baluchistan of Pakistan, February 2016; Meeting with *A, former member of Jundullah, Baluchistan, November 2020.
147 Meeting with *B, commander of Herakat Khalifat Baluchistan of Pakistan, February 2016
148 Meeting with *A, former member of Jundullah, Baluchistan, November 2020.
149 Meeting with Q**, AQIS cadre, eastern Afghanistan, September 2020; Meeting with *A, former member of Jundullah, Baluchistan, November 2020.
150 Meeting with O*, IS-P commander, July 2020; Meeting with Q*P, IS-P member, Baluchistan (Pakistan), former TTP member, July 2020; Meeting with*K*, IS-P commander, ex TTP, Baluchistan, July 2020; Meeting with O*, IS-P commander, July 2020.
151 Siddiqi, 2021.
152 Meeting with Q**, IS-P commander in Momand agency, December 2021.
153 Meeting with Q*P, IS-P member, Baluchistan (Pakistan), former TTP member, July 2020.
154 Meeting with O*, IS-P commander, July 2020.

155 Meeting with M*, Jhangvi district of Punjab, member of SSP and madrasa manager, July 2020.
156 Meeting with O*, IS-P commander, July 2020; Meeting with*K*, IS-P commander, ex TTP, Baluchistan, July 2020; Meeting with *O, LeJ member in Punjab, November 2020.
157 Meeting with *O, LeJ member in Punjab, November 2020.
158 Meeting with O*, IS-P commander, July 2020; Meeting with*K*, IS-P commander, ex TTP, Baluchistan, July 2020; Meeting with *O, LeJ member in Punjab, November 2020.

Chapter 5

1 Abbas, 2005, 226; Arif, 2011, location 800ff.
2 Rana, 2005, 66–7.
3 Abbas, 2005, 226.
4 Schroen, 2005, 361.
5 Riedel, 2008, 83; Topich, 335.
6 Meeting with S*, active member of HuM, Muzaffarabad, June 2020.
7 Mir, 2008, 125.
8 Meeting with S*, active member of HuM, Muzaffarabad, June 2020.
9 Meeting with N*, member of HuM in Rawalpindi, June 2020.
10 Mir, 2008, 124.
11 Jamal, 2011, Location 684ff.
12 Meeting with N*, member of HuM in Rawalpindi, June 2020.
13 Meeting with *H*, JeM senior commander, Muzaffarabad, March 2019; Meeting with M*M*, JeM group commander in Kandahar, May 2018; Meeting with *B*, JeM commander in Afghanistan, April 2020.
14 Honawar, 2005.
15 Mir, 2006, 45ff; Howenstein, 2008; Mir, 2008, 154–5; Popovic, 2015, 919–37.
16 ICG, 2009.
17 Chalk and Fair, 2005; Sareen, 2005, 175ff; Roul, 2011b, 4; Singh, 2020, 50–2; Zahid, 2020.
18 ICG, 2009; Ahmed, 2011, 119, 133–4, 174.
19 Mahadevan, 2013.
20 ICG, 2009.
21 Kapur, 2017, 93.
22 Kapur, 2017, 108.
23 Meeting with *T*, commander of LeT in Jammu and Kashmir, October 2016.
24 Jamal, Transnational jihad, 113ff.
25 Tankel, 2011, 110–11, 155.
26 Scott-Clark And Levy, 2013, 142.
27 Scott-Clark and Levy, 142.
28 Ahmed, 2011, 285.
29 Meeting with *T*, commander of LeT in Jammu and Kashmir, October 2016.
30 Mir, 2008, 178.
31 Rana, 2004.
32 Kapur, 2017, 109.

33 Soufan Center, 2019, 14.
34 Abbas, 2005, 233.
35 Jamal, 2011, Location 158.
36 Padukone, 2011, 70.
37 Lieven, 2011, 333–4; Fair, 2018, 172–3.
38 Meeting with *A, LeT commander in Chaparhar district of Nangarhar, June 2013; Tankel, 2009, 19–20.
39 Jamal, 2014, 138ff.
40 Tankel, 2009, 19–20.
41 Meeting with *A, LeT commander in Chaparhar district of Nangarhar, June 2013.
42 Meeting with *A, LeT commander in Chaparhar district of Nangarhar, June 2013.
43 Meeting with *A, LeT commander in Chaparhar district of Nangarhar, June 2013.
44 Meeting with *A, LeT commander in Chaparhar district of Nangarhar, June 2013; Meeting with *T*, commander of LeT in Jammu and Kashmir, October 2016; Meeting with JeM cadre, Afghanistan, March 2020.
45 Meeting with *T*, commander of LeT in Jammu and Kashmir, October 2016.
46 Bacon, 2019, 38.
47 See for example US embassy in Delhi, 'Indians worry Lashkar terrorists are thriving in Pakistani Kashmir', diplomatic cable, 2005 November 18, ID:05NEWDELHI8791; US embassy in Islamabad, 'Pakistan reactions to terror in Mumbai', 2008 November 28, ID:08ISLAMABAD3716; 'al Qa'ida in Afghanistan and Pakistan: An enduring threat', hearing before the subcommittee on terrorism, non-proliferation and trade of the committee on foreign affairs, House of Representatives, one hundred thirteenth congress, second session, 20 May 2014.
48 Behera, 2002.
49 Mir, 2008, 159.
50 Mir, 2008, 154–5; Jamal, 2011, Location 766ff.
51 Chalk and Fair, 2005; Roul, 2011b; Singh, 2020, 50–2; Zahid, 2020.
52 Abbas, 2009.
53 Abbas, 2009.
54 Abbas, 2009.
55 Meeting with M*M*, JeM group commander in Kandahar, May 2018.
56 Meeting with M*M*, JeM group commander in Kandahar, May 2018.
57 Lieven, 2011, 275–6, 327.
58 Meeting with M*M*, JeM group commander in Kandahar, May 2018.
59 Meeting with M*M*, JeM group commander in Kandahar, May 2018; Meeting with JeM cadre, Afghanistan, March 2020.
60 Meeting with **D, JeM Madrasa cadre, Multan district, April 2020.
61 Meeting with M*M*, JeM group commander in Kandahar, May 2018.
62 Meeting with *H*, JeM senior commander, Muzaffarabad, March 2019.
63 Meeting with M*M*, JeM group commander in Kandahar, May 2018.
64 Meeting with M*M*, JeM group commander in Kandahar, May 2018.
65 Meeting with **D, JeM Madrasa cadre, Multan district, April 2020.
66 Meeting with *H*, JeM senior commander, Muzaffarabad, March 2019.
67 Meeting with M*M*, JeM group commander in Kandahar, May 2018.
68 Meeting with M*M*, JeM group commander in Kandahar, May 2018.
69 Meeting with *H*, JeM senior commander, Muzaffarabad, March 2019.
70 Meeting with **K, HuM group commander, Kandahar province, February 2018.
71 Meeting with **K, HuM group commander, Kandahar province, February 2018.

72 Meeting with **K, HuM group commander, Kandahar province, February 2018.
73 Meeting with **K, HuM group commander, Kandahar province, February 2018.
74 Meeting with **K, HuM group commander, Kandahar province, February 2018.
75 Meeting with **K, HuM group commander, Kandahar province, February 2018.
76 Meeting with **K, HuM group commander, Kandahar province, February 2018.
77 Meeting with **K, HuM group commander, Kandahar province, February 2018.
78 Meeting with Q*, assistant of Taliban leader Akhtar Mohammad Mansur; Meeting with AQ, 2015.
79 Meeting with **K, HuM group commander, Kandahar province, February 2018.
80 Meeting with N*, member of HuM in Rawalpindi, June 2020.
81 Meeting with **K, HuM group commander, Kandahar province, February 2018.
82 Meeting with AQIS agent $A**$ in Karachi, July 2020.
83 Zahid, 2015B, 115–16.
84 Meeting with A*A*, AQ commander in Kunar, January 2016.
85 Meeting with AQIS agent $A**$ in Karachi, July 2020.
86 Meeting with *A, AQ group commander in Jammu and Kashmir, September 2019.
87 Meeting with **, Senior cadre of AQIS, November 2019.
88 Meeting with *A, AQ group commander in Jammu and Kashmir, September 2019.
89 Meeting with **, Senior cadre of AQIS, November 2019.
90 Meeting with *A, AQ group commander in Jammu and Kashmir, September 2019; Meeting with **, Senior cadre of AQIS, November 2019.
91 Meeting with **, Senior cadre of AQIS, November 2019.
92 Meeting with **, Senior cadre of AQIS, November 2019.
93 Meeting with **, Senior cadre of AQIS, November 2019.
94 Meeting with **, Senior cadre of AQIS, November 2019.
95 Meeting with AQIS agent $A**$ in Karachi, July 2020.
96 Meeting with *A, AQ group commander in Jammu and Kashmir, September 2019.
97 Meeting with *A, AQ group commander in Jammu and Kashmir, September 2019.
98 Meeting with IS-K 5, senior cadre, December 2014.
99 Jadoon et al., 2018.
100 Jadoon et al., 2018.
101 Jadoon et al., 2018.
102 Jadoon et al., 2018; Bacon, 2019.
103 Meeting with *T*, commander of LeT in Jammu and Kashmir, October 2016.
104 Meeting with *T*, commander of LeT in Jammu and Kashmir, October 2016.
105 Meeting with *T*, commander of LeT in Jammu and Kashmir, October 2016.
106 Meeting with IS-K senior commander, *T*, commander of LeT in Jammu and Kashmir, October 2016.
107 Meeting with IS-K cadre, Pakistan, October 2015; Meeting with IS-K cadre, Pakistan, February 2016; Meetings with IS-K leader, June 2015; notebook of IS-K leader, obtained July 2015.
108 Meeting with IS-K cadre, Pakistan, December 2015.
109 Jadoon et al., 2018.
110 Meeting with **, IS-K deputy commander, Jurm district of Badakhshan Province, May 2020; Meeting with IS-K senior commander, *T, LeT commander, Jammu and Kashmir, September 2020.
111 Meeting with N*, member of HuM in Rawalpindi, June 2020; Meeting with S*, active member of HuM, Muzaffarabad, June 2020.
112 Meeting with *A, LeT commander in Chaparhar district of Nangarhar, June 2013.

113 Meeting with *A, LeT commander in Chaparhar district of Nangarhar, June 2013.
114 Meeting with *A, LeT commander in Chaparhar district of Nangarhar, June 2013.
115 Bacon, 2019, 36.
116 Fair, 2011, 29–52.
117 Bacon, 2019.
118 Tankel, 2009, 19–20.
119 Tankel, 2009, 12; Markey, 2013, 102.
120 Jamal, 2014, 145ff.
121 Shah, 2014, 87–104, 95.
122 Roul, 2011a.
123 Tankel, 2011, 110, 196–7.
124 Mahadevan, 2013.
125 Fair, 2018, 95.
126 Jamal, 2014, 251–3.
127 Meeting with NDS officer, Afghanistan, February 2020.
128 US embassy cables: Lashkar e Taiba terrorists raise funds in Saudi Arabia, Sun 5 Dec 2010 12.00 GMT Monday, 10 August 2009, 23:56 S E C R E T STATE 083026, EO 12958 DECL: 08/07/2019, REF: STATE 65044.
129 Meeting with IS-K senior commander, *T*, commander of LeT in Jammu and Kashmir, October 2016; Meeting with ***, former commander of LeT, Kunar Province, February 2020; Meeting with **Q, former LeT training camp manager, Muzafarrabad area, February 2020.
130 Meeting with AA**, AQ cadre, eastern Afghanistan. April 2016; Meeting with A*A*, AQ commander in Kunar.
131 Meeting with IS-K senior commander, Q*, assistant of Taliban leader Akhtar Mohammad Mansur; Meeting with AQ, 2015.
132 Shapoo et al., 2019, 25.
133 Meeting with IS-K senior commander, *T*, commander of LeT in Jammu and Kashmir, October 2016.
134 Meeting with IS-K senior commander, *T*, commander of LeT in Jammu and Kashmir, October 2016.
135 Meeting with IS-K senior commander, *T*, commander of LeT in Jammu and Kashmir, October 2016.
136 Meeting with IS-K senior commander, *T*, commander of LeT in Jammu and Kashmir, October 2016.
137 Meeting with IS-K senior commander, *T*, commander of LeT in Jammu and Kashmir, October 2016.
138 Meeting with IS-K senior commander, A*, LeT cadre, Punjab, August 2018.
139 Lieven, 2011, 335; Bacon, 2019, 42.
140 Lieven, 2011, 336.
141 Meeting with IS-K senior commander, A*, LeT cadre, Punjab, August 2018.
142 Meeting with IS-K senior commander, A*, LeT cadre, Punjab, August 2018.
143 Meeting with **, people's smuggler in Pakistan, August 2016.
144 Meeting with **, people's smuggler in Pakistan, August 2016.
145 Meeting with IS-K senior commander, A*, LeT cadre, Punjab, August 2018.
146 Lieven, 2011.
147 Lieven, 2011, 336.
148 Meeting with IS-K senior commander, *T*, commander of LeT in Jammu and Kashmir, October 2016.

149 Meeting with IS-K senior commander, ***, former commander of LeT, Kunar Province, February 2020; Meeting with IS-K senior commander, **Q, former LeT training camp manager, Muzafarrabad area, February 2020; Meeting with NDS officer, Afghanistan, February 2020.
150 Meeting with *B*, JeM commander in Afghanistan, April 2020.
151 Meeting with *W, LeT trainer, Muzaffarabad, September 2020; Khan, 2020a; 2020b.
152 Meeting with **Q, former LeT training camp manager, Muzafarrabad area, February 2020.
153 Meeting with N*, member of HuM in Rawalpindi, June 2020.
154 Meeting with **Q, former LeT training camp manager, Muzafarrabad area, February 2020.
155 Meeting with ***, former commander of LeT, Kunar Province, February 2020.
156 Meeting with ***, former commander of LeT, Kunar Province, February 2020.
157 Meeting with NDS officer, Afghanistan, February 2020.
158 Meeting with **Q, former LeT training camp manager, Muzafarrabad area, February 2020.
159 Meeting with NDS officer, Afghanistan, February 2020; Personal communication with Indian diplomat, March 2020.
160 Meeting with N*, member of HuM in Rawalpindi, June 2020.
161 Meeting with **D, JeM Madrasa cadre, Multan district, April 2020.
162 Meeting with *W, LeT trainer, Muzaffarabad, September 2020.
163 Meeting with M*M*, JeM group commander in Kandahar, May 2018; Meeting with ***, former commander of LeT, Kunar Province, February 2020.
164 Meeting with **Q, former LeT training camp manager, Muzafarrabad area, February 2020.
165 Meeting with **Q, former LeT training camp manager, Muzafarrabad area, February 2020.
166 Meeting with *W, LeT trainer, Muzaffarabad, September 2020; Meeting with *T, LeT commander, Jammu and Kashmir, September 2020.
167 Meeting with *W, LeT trainer, Muzaffarabad, September 2020.
168 Meeting with *R, LeT trainer, Muzaffarabad, September 2020.
169 Meeting with **, Senior cadre of AQIS, November 2019.
170 Meeting with **Q, former LeT training camp manager, Muzafarrabad area, February 2020.
171 Meeting with **Q, former LeT training camp manager, Muzafarrabad area, February 2020.
172 Meeting with **D, JeM Madrasa cadre, Multan district, April 2020.
173 Meeting with **Q, former LeT training camp manager, Muzafarrabad area, February 2020.
174 Meeting with NDS officer, Afghanistan, February 2020.
175 Meeting with ***, former commander of LeT, Kunar Province, February 2020.
176 Meeting with ***, former commander of LeT, Kunar Province, February 2020.
177 Meeting with **Q, former LeT training camp manager, Muzafarrabad area, February 2020.
178 Meeting with NDS officer, Afghanistan, February 2020.
179 Meeting with AQIS agent *A*** in Karachi, July 2020.
180 Meeting with ***, former commander of LeT, Kunar Province, February 2020.
181 Meeting with **K, HuM group commander, Kandahar province, February 2018.
182 Meeting with N*, member of HuM in Rawalpindi, June 2020.

183 Meeting with **K, HuM group commander, Kandahar province, February 2018.
184 Meeting with **K, HuM group commander, Kandahar province, February 2018.
185 Meeting with **K, HuM group commander, Kandahar province, February 2018.
186 Meeting with **K, HuM group commander, Kandahar province, February 2018.
187 Meeting with **K, HuM group commander, Kandahar province, February 2018.
188 Meeting with S*, active member of HuM, Muzaffarabad, June 2020.
189 Meeting with N*, member of HuM in Rawalpindi, June 2020.
190 Meeting with S*, active member of HuM, Muzaffarabad, June 2020.
191 Meeting with S*, active member of HuM, Muzaffarabad, June 2020.
192 Meeting with N*, member of HuM in Rawalpindi, June 2020.
193 Meeting with N*, member of HuM in Rawalpindi, June 2020.
194 Meeting with N*, member of HuM in Rawalpindi, June 2020.
195 Meeting with S*, active member of HuM, Muzaffarabad, June 2020.
196 Meeting with S*, active member of HuM, Muzaffarabad, June 2020.
197 Meeting with **K, HuM group commander, Kandahar province, February 2018.
198 Meeting with N*, member of HuM in Rawalpindi, June 2020; Meeting with S*, active member of HuM, Muzaffarabad, June 2020.
199 Meeting with N*, member of HuM in Rawalpindi, June 2020.
200 Meeting with N*, member of HuM in Rawalpindi, June 2020.
201 Meeting with S*, active member of HuM, Muzaffarabad, June 2020.
202 Meeting with N*, member of HuM in Rawalpindi, June 2020.
203 Meeting with **D, JeM Madrasa cadre, Multan district, April 2020.
204 Meeting with *B*, JeM commander in Afghanistan, April 2020.
205 Meeting with *B*, JeM commander in Afghanistan, April 2020.
206 Meeting with **Q, former LeT training camp manager, Muzafarrabad area, February 2020.
207 Meeting with **D, JeM Madrasa cadre, Multan district, April 2020.
208 Meeting with *H*, JeM senior commander, Muzaffarabad, March 2019.
209 Meeting with *H*, JeM senior commander, Muzaffarabad, March 2019.
210 Meeting with M*M*, JeM group commander in Kandahar, May 2018.
211 Meeting with M*M*, JeM group commander in Kandahar, May 2018.
212 Meeting with **Q, former LeT training camp manager, Muzafarrabad area, February 2020.
213 Meeting with *H*, JeM senior commander, Muzaffarabad, March 2019.
214 Jamal, 2014, 101ff.
215 Meeting with *H*, JeM senior commander, Muzaffarabad, March 2019.
216 Meeting with *H*, JeM senior commander, Muzaffarabad, March 2019.
217 Personal communication with Indian intelligence official, September 2020.
218 Meeting with *H*, JeM senior commander, Muzaffarabad, March 2019.
219 Meeting with *H*, JeM senior commander, Muzaffarabad, March 2019.
220 Meeting with M*M*, JeM group commander in Kandahar, May 2018.
221 Meeting with *H*, JeM senior commander, Muzaffarabad, March 2019.
222 Meeting with M*M*, JeM group commander in Kandahar, May 2018; Meeting with *H*, JeM senior commander, Muzaffarabad, March 2019.
223 Meeting with *H*, JeM senior commander, Muzaffarabad, March 2019.
224 Meeting with *H*, JeM senior commander, Muzaffarabad, March 2019.
225 Meeting with M*M*, JeM group commander in Kandahar, May 2018.
226 Meeting with *H*, JeM senior commander, Muzaffarabad, March 2019.

227 Meeting with **D, JeM Madrasa cadre, Multan district, April 2020; Meeting with *B*, JeM commander in Afghanistan, April 2020.
228 Meeting with *H*, JeM senior commander, Muzaffarabad, March 2019.
229 Meeting with *H*, JeM senior commander, Muzaffarabad, March 2019.
230 Meeting with *T, LeT commander, Jammu and Kashmir, September 2020.
231 Meeting with **D, JeM Madrasa cadre, Multan district, April 2020; Meeting with *B*, JeM commander in Afghanistan, April 2020.
232 Meeting with **D, JeM Madrasa cadre, Multan district, April 2020; Meeting with *B*, JeM commander in Afghanistan, April 2020.
233 Meeting with **D, JeM Madrasa cadre, Multan district, April 2020; Meeting with *B*, JeM commander in Afghanistan, April 2020.
234 Meeting with *H*, JeM senior commander, Muzaffarabad, March 2019; Meeting with M*M*, JeM group commander in Kandahar, May 2018.
235 Meeting with *H*, JeM senior commander, Muzaffarabad, March 2019.
236 Meeting with AA**, AQ cadre, eastern Afghanistan. April 2016; Meeting with A*A*, AQ commander in Kunar.
237 Meeting with Q*, assistant of Taliban leader Akhtar Mohammad Mansur; Meeting with AQ, 2015.
238 Meeting with **Q, former LeT training camp manager, Muzafarrabad area, February 2020.
239 Meeting with **D, JeM Madrasa cadre, Multan district, April 2020.
240 Meeting with AQIS agent *A*** in Karachi, July 2020.
241 Meeting with AQIS agent *A*** in Karachi, July 2020.
242 Meeting with *W, LeT trainer, Muzaffarabad, September 2020; Meeting with *T, LeT commander, Jammu and Kashmir, September 2020; Meeting with **Q, former LeT training camp manager, Muzafarrabad area, February 2020.
243 Meeting with NDS officer, Afghanistan, February 2020.
244 Meeting with *T*, commander of LeT in Jammu and Kashmir, October 2016.
245 Meeting with ***, former commander of LeT, Kunar Province, February 2020; Meeting with **Q, former LeT training camp manager, Muzafarrabad area, February 2020; Meeting with NDS officer, Afghanistan, February 2020.
246 Meeting with *W, LeT trainer, Muzaffarabad, September 2020; Meeting with *T, LeT commander, Jammu and Kashmir, September 2020.
247 Meeting with *T, LeT commander, Jammu and Kashmir, September 2020.
248 Meeting with *R, LeT trainer, Muzaffarabad, September 2020.
249 Meeting with *R, LeT trainer, Muzaffarabad, September 2020.
250 Meeting with *R, LeT trainer, Muzaffarabad, September 2020.
251 Meeting with *K, LeT IED maker and trainer, Muzaffarabad camp, May 2021; Meeting with *M*, Punjabi, LeT cadre in Swat valley, May 2021; Meeting with **A member of the Taliban's Military Commission, July 2021.
252 Meeting with *K, LeT IED maker and trainer, Muzaffarabad camp, May 2021.
253 Meeting with *K, LeT IED maker and trainer, Muzaffarabad camp, May 2021.
254 Meeting with *K, LeT IED maker and trainer, Muzaffarabad camp, May 2021.
255 Meeting with *K, LeT IED maker and trainer, Muzaffarabad camp, May 2021.
256 Mubasher Bukhari, 'Pakistani court jails Islamist Hafiz Saeed for an extra 31 years', *Reuters*, 9 April 2022.
257 Taneja, 2019, 77 ff.
258 Taneja, 2019, 157.
259 Taneja, 2019, 137.

260 Meeting with *O, IS-K group commander, Manogai district of Kunar province, April 2020; Roul, 2020b; Zahid, 2019.
261 Meeting with Q*P, IS-P member, Baluchistan (Pakistan), former TTP member, July 2020; Meeting with*K*, IS-P commander, ex TTP, Baluchistan, July 2020.
262 Meeting with Q*P, IS-P member, Baluchistan (Pakistan), former TTP member, July 2020.
263 Meeting with *O, IS-K group commander, Manogai district of Kunar province, April 2020.
264 Meeting with **F, IS-K group commander, Shirzad district of Nangarhar province, June 2020.
265 **, IS-K Deputy commander, Jurm district of Badakhshan Province, May 2020.
266 Meeting with N*, member of HuM in Rawalpindi, June 2020; Meeting with S*, active member of HuM, Muzaffarabad, June 2020.
267 Meeting with IS-K senior commander, Q**H, member of IS-K intelligence, Jurm district of Badakhshan province, April 2020.
268 Meeting with *T, LeT commander, Jammu and Kashmir, September 2020.
269 Meeting with Q*P, IS-P member, Baluchistan (Pakistan), former TTP member, July 2020.
270 Meeting with*K*, IS-P commander, ex TTP, Baluchistan, July 2020.
271 Meeting with*K*, IS-P commander, ex TTP, Baluchistan, July 2020.
272 Meeting with *W, LeT trainer, Muzaffarabad, September 2020.
273 Meeting with **, IS-K deputy commander, Jurm district of Badakhshan province, May 2020.
274 Meeting with *O, IS-K group commander, Manogai district of Kunar province, April 2020.
275 Meeting with O*, IS-P commander, July 2020.
276 Meeting with *R, LeT trainer, Muzaffarabad, September 2020.
277 Meeting with *R, LeT trainer, Muzaffarabad, September 2020.
278 Meeting with *W, LeT trainer, Muzaffarabad, September 2020; Meeting with *T, LeT commander, Jammu and Kashmir, September 2020.
279 Meeting with *T, LeT commander, Jammu and Kashmir, September 2020.
280 Meeting with *R, LeT trainer, Muzaffarabad, September 2020.
281 Meeting with Q**, AQIS cadre, eastern Afghanistan, September 2020.
282 Meeting with Q**, AQIS cadre, eastern Afghanistan, September 2020.
283 Meeting with M*M*, JeM group commander in Kandahar, May 2018.
284 Meeting with A*, LeT cadre, Punjab, August 2018.
285 Meeting with *H*, JeM senior commander, Muzaffarabad, March 2019; Meeting with M*M*, JeM group commander in Kandahar, May 2018.
286 Meeting with *T, LeT commander, Jammu and Kashmir, September 2020; Meeting with *R, LeT trainer, Muzaffarabad, September 2020; Meeting with Q*P, IS-P member, Baluchistan (Pakistan), former TTP member, July 2020.
287 Meeting with *W, LeT trainer, Muzaffarabad, September 2020; Meeting with *T, LeT commander, Jammu and Kashmir, September 2020.
288 Meeting with **K, HuM group commander, Kandahar province, February 2018.
289 Meeting with *W, LeT trainer, Muzaffarabad, September 2020.
290 Meeting with *K, LeT IED maker and trainer, May 2021; Meeting with B*, JeM commander, Punjab, January 2022; Meeting with **K, JeM commander Afghanistan, January 2022.
291 Meeting with K*, LeT trainer, January 2022.

292 Meeting with *F*, LeT trainer, January 2022.
293 Taneja, 2021.
294 Desai, 2015; Siyech, 2017.
295 As Sahab Media, 2017, 7.

Conclusion

1 Kapur, 2017, 20.

References

Aamir, Adnan (2021) 'Pakistani Taliban Turn on China', *The Interpreter*, 4 May 2021
Abbas, Hassan (2005) *Pakistan's Drift into Extremism: Allah, then Army, and America's War Terror*, London: M. E. Sharpe
Abbas, Hassan (2006) 'The Black-Turbaned Brigade: The Rise of TNSM in Pakistan', *Terrorism Monitor* 4: 23
Abbas, Hassan (2007) 'South Waziristan's Maulvi Nazir: The New Face of the Taliban', *Terrorism Monitor* 5: 9, 14 May
Abbas, Hassan (2009) 'Defining the Punjabi Taliban Network', *CTC Sentinel* 2: 4
Abbas, Hassan (2010) 'Shiism and Sectarian Conflict in Pakistan: Identity Politics, Iranian Influence, and Tit-for-Tat Violence', CTC occasional paper, September 22
Abbas, Hassan (2021) 'Extremism and Terrorism Trends in Pakistan: Changing Dynamics and New Challenges', *CTC Sentinel* 14: 2, February 2021
Abou Zahab, Mariam (1999) 'Le Sipah-e Sahaba Pakistan (Ssp) Dans Le Penjab Islamisation De La Société Ou Conflit De Classe?', CEMOTI 27, janvier-juin
Abou Zahab, Mariam (2010) 'Frontières dans la tourmente: la talibanisation des zones tribales', *Outre-Terre* 1: 24, 337–57
Abou Zahab, Mariam and Roy, Olivier (2004) *Réseaux Islamiques*, Paris: Hachette
Acharya, Arabinda et al. (2009) 'Making Money in the Mayhem: Funding Taliban Insurrection in the Tribal Areas of Pakistan', *Studies in Conflict & Terrorism* 32: 2, 95–108
Ahmed, Roohan (2019) 'Daesh Looks to Gain Foothold in Balochistan under Ex-Karachi Cop', SAMAA, 18 September 2019
Ahmed, Khaled (2011) *Sectarian War*, Karachi: Oxford UP
Ahrar, Jama'at ul (2016) 'Daesh Claims Attack on Pakistani Police College', *Gulf News*, 24 December 2016
Al-hasan, Mahmud ('Atiyatullah) and (Abu Yahya) al-Libi, 'Letter to Hakimullah Mashud', Harmony document, released 2016 (SOCOM-2012-0000007-HT) 27 Dhu al-Hijjah 1431 (3 December 2010)
Almohammad, Asaad (2019) 'Seven Years of Terror: Jihadi Organisations' Strategies and Future Directions', ICCT Research Paper, The Hague, August
'Al Qa'ida in Afghanistan and Pakistan: An Enduring Threat' (2014) hearing before the subcommittee on terrorism, non-proliferation, and trade of the committee on foreign affairs, House of Representatives, one hundred thirteenth congress, second session, May 20
Andersen, Lars Eslev (2017) 'The Mole and the Mallet', *Connections* 16: 1
As Sahab Media (2017) 'Code of Conduct: Al Qa'ida in the Subcontinent', June
Asad, Malik and Asghar, Mohammad (2015) 'TTP Group Involved in Attack Suicide bombing', *Dawn*, 30 September 2015
Ayaz, Ahmed (2017) 'Islamic State Comes to Balochistan', *The Diplomat*, 11 July
Azoulay, Rivka (2015) 'Islamic State Franchising: Tribes, Transnational Jihadi Networks and Generational Shifts', CRU report, The Hague: Clingendael Institute, April 2015

Bacon, Tricia (2019) 'The Evolution of Pakistan's Lashkar-e-Tayyiba Terrorist Group', *Orbis* Winter 2019

Basit, Abdul (2010) 'Militant Landscape after Miranshah Agreement', in MA Rana et al. (eds), *Dynamics of Taliban Insurgency in FATA*, Islamabad: PIPS

Basit, Abdul (2014) 'Asim Umar – "New Kid on the Block"?', *Counter Terrorist Trends and Analyses* 6: 10 (November), 8–12

Behera, Navnita Chadha (2002) 'Kashmir: Redefining the U.S. Role', Washington: Brookings, October 30, 2002

Bell, Kevin (2016) 'The First Islamic State: A Look Back at the Islamic Emirate of Kunar', *CTC Sentinel* 9: 2

Bergen, Peter L. (2011) *The Longest War: The Enduring Conflict between America and al Qa'ida*, New York: Simon and Schuster

Bergen, Peter L. (2012a) *Manhunt*, New York: Crown Publishers, 116

Bergen, Peter L. (2012b) *Manhunt: The Ten-Year Search for bin Laden – from 9/11 to Abbottabad*, New York: Crown

Bezhan, Frud and Khattak, Daud (2021) 'The Rise of the New Pakistani Taliban', *Gandhara*, 18 May 2021

Bhutto, Benazir (2007) *Daughter of the East: An Autobiography*, London: Simon and Schuster

Bose, Sumantra (2003) *Kashmir*, Cambridge, MA: Harvard UP

Brachman, Jarret (2016) 'The War within: A Look Inside al-Qaeda's Undoing', The JSOU Center for Special Operations Studies and Research (CSOSR)

Brüggemann, Ulf (2016) 'Al Qa'ida and the Islamic State: Objectives, Threat, Countermeasures', Security Policy Working Paper, No. 9/2016, Federal academy for Security Policy

Bruno, Greg and Bajoria, Jayshree (2008) 'U.S-Pakistan Military Cooperation', Washington: Council on Foreign Relations

Burke, Jason B. (2013) 'Syria Conflict: Why Pakistani Taliban Is Pledging Support for Rebels', *The Guardian*, 14 Jul.

Bunzel, Cole (2022) 'Inside the Waning Days of al Qaeda', *Foreign Policy*, 5 June 2022

Burke, Jason (2004) *Al Qaeda*, London: Tauris

Burki, Khan Zeb (2010) 'Rise of Taliban in Waziristan', *Dialogue*, July–September, 188–211

Byman, Daniel (2014) 'Buddies or Burdens? Understanding the Al Qaeda Relationship with Its Affiliate Organizations', *Security Studies* 23: 431–70

Byman, Daniel (2015) *Al Qaeda, the Islamic State, and the Global Jihadist Movement*, New York: Oxford UP USA

Byman, Daniel L. (2017) 'Judging al Qa'ida Record, Part I: Is the Organization in Decline?', Brookings.edu, June 29

Celso, Anthony (2014) *Al Qa'ida Post-9/11 Devolution*, London: Bloomsbury, Kindle Edition

Chishti, Ali K (2014) 'ISIS Is the Talk of the Town', *The Friday Times*, 12 September 2014

Chalk, Peter and Fair, Christine (2005) 'The Re-Orientation of Kashmiri Extremism: A Threat to Regional and International Security', *Terrorism Monitor* 3: 22, November 17

Coll, Steve (2004) *Ghost Wars*, London: Penguin

Coll, Steve (2018) *Directorate S*, London: Penguin

Congressional Research Centre (2020) 'Al Qaeda and Islamic State Affiliates in Afghanistan', Washington, June 24

Critchley, Tom et al. (2016) 'The Nature of Affiliation: Daesh in Africa and the Middle East', Richardson institute, June 2016, 9–10

Crone, Manni et al. (2017) 'Expanding Jihad How al-Qaeda and Islamic State Find New Battlefields', DIIS
Dasgupta, S. (2015) 'Al Qaeda in India: Why We Should Pay Attention', The International Relations and Security Network (ISN), 15 April
Desai, Shweta (2015) 'Exploring Transnational Jihad Roots and Caliphate in Kashmir', New Delhi: CLAWS, January
De Luce, Dan,Dilanian, Ken and Yusufzai, Mushtaq (2021) 'Taliban Keep Close Ties with Al Qaeda despite Promise to U.S.', NBC, 17 February 2021
Dimitrakis, Panagiotis (2013) *The Secret War in Afghanistan: The Soviet Union, China and Anglo-American Intelligence in the Afghan War*, London: Bloomsbury Academic
Dorronsoro, Gilles (2002) 'Pakistan and the Taliban', in Christophe Jaffrelot (ed.), *Pakistan: Nationalism without a Nation*, London: Zed Books
Dorronsoro, Gilles (2005) *Revolution Unending*, London: Hurst
Ehsan, Ehsanullah (2020) 'US Taliban Peace Deal, What Will Be the Future of Other Jihadi Organizations in the Region?', *ehsanullahahsan.blogspot.com*, September 2015
Elahi, N. (2019) *Terrorism in Pakistan*, London: Bloomsbury
Faber, Pamela G. and Powell, Alexander (2017) 'Al Qa'ida in the Indian Subcontinent (AQIS): An al Qa'ida Affiliate Case Study', Alexandria, VA: CNA, October
Fair, Christine (2011) 'Lashkar-e-Tayiba and the Pakistani State', *Survival* 53: 4, 29–52
Fair, Christine (2018) *In Their Own Words. Understanding Lashkar-e-Tayyaba*, Oxford: Oxford UP
Feyyaz, Muhammad (2013a) 'Conceptualising Terrorism Trend Patterns in Pakistan – an Empirical Perspective', *Perspectives on Terrorism* 7: 1
Feyyaz, Muhammad (2013b) 'Facets of Religious Violence in Pakistan', *Counter Terrorist Trends and Analyses* 5: 2, 9–13
Feyyaz, Muhammad (2016) 'Religion, Ethnicity, Social Organizations and Terrorists' Behavior – a Case of Taliban Movement in Pakistan', *Behavioral Sciences of Terrorism and Political Aggression* 8: 2, 111–34
Fishman, Brian (2016) *The Master Plan: ISIS, Al Qaeda, and the Jihadi Strategy for Final Victory*, New Haven: Yale UP
Forest, James J. F. et al. (2006) 'Harmony and Disharmony Exploiting al-Qa'ida's Organizational Vulnerabilities', West Point: Combating Terrorism Center
Foschini, Fabrizio (2013) 'When and Why to Catch a TTP Leader: Faqir Muhammad's Arrest', Berlin: AAN, 24 February
Franco, Claudio (2009a) 'The Tehrik-e Taliban Pakistan', in A. Giustozzi (ed.), *Decoding the New Taliban*, London: Hurst
Franco, Claudio (2009b) 'Part III of a NEFA Special Report: Militant Groups Active in the Bajaur Region', New York: NEFA, August
Franco, Claudio and Sandee, Ronald (2008) 'Developments in the Jihadi Resurgence in Pakistan, January 2008', New York: NEFA 5 March
Fredholm, Michael (2011) 'Kashmir, Afghanistan, India and Beyond: A Taxonomy of Islamic Extremism and Terrorism in Pakistan', *Journal of Himalayan Research and Cultural Foundation*, 15: 3
Gall, Carlotta (2014a) 'What Pakistan Knew about bin Laden', *The New York Times*, 19 March 2014
Gall, Carlotta (2014b) *The Wrong Enemy: America in Afghanistan, 2001–2014*, Boston: Houghton Mifflin
Gall, Sandy (2012) *War against the Taliban: Why It All Went Wrong in Afghanistan*, London: A&C Black

Gartenstein-Ross, Daveed and Barr, Nathaniel (2020) 'How al Qa'ida Works: The Jihadist Group's Evolving Organizational Design', Washington: Hudson Institute

Gerges, Fawaz A. (2011) *The Rise and Fall of al Qa'ida*, New York: Oxford University Press USA

Giustozzi, Antonio (2015) 'Assessing the Taliban's Capture of Kunduz and Its Ongoing Implications', *Jane's Terrorism & Insurgency Monitor*, 16 October

Giustozzi, Antonio (2020) 'Territorial Defeats, Leadership Losses, and Internal Fragmentation Underscore Significant Challenge Faced by the Islamic State in Afghanistan', *Jane's Terrorism and Security Monitor*, 23 July

Giustozzi, Antonio (2022a) *The Islamic State in Khorasan*, London: Hurst

Giustozzi, Antonio (2022b [2019]) *Taliban at War*, London: Hurst (second edition)

Gohel, Sajjan M. and Winston, David (2020) 'A Complex Tapestry of Collusion and Cooperation: Afghanistan and Pakistan's Terrorism Networks', *LSE Blogs*, 5 June

Gul, Imtiaz (2010) *The Most Dangerous Place: Pakistan's Lawless Frontier*, London: Penguin Press

Gunaratna, Rohan and Nielsen, Anders (2008) 'Al Qaeda in the Tribal Areas of Pakistan and Beyond', *Studies in Conflict & Terrorism*, 31: 9, 775–807

Haider, Syed Fazl-e (2021) 'Pakistan's Dual Counter-Terrorism Challenges: Tehreek-i-Taliban Pakistan's Merger and Cross-Border Campaign from Afghanistan', *Terrorism Monitor*, 19: 6, 26 March

Haider, Zeeshan (2012) 'Pakistani and Afghan Taliban Groups Set up Council to Coordinate Attacks', *The National*, 4 January 2012

Hamid, Mustafa and Farrell, Leah (2015) *The Arabs at War in Afghanistan*, London: Hurst

Hansen, Stig Jarle (2019) *Horn, Sahel and Rift Fault-lines of the African Jihad*, London: Hurst

Haqqani, Husain (2005) 'Pakistan: Between Mosque and Military', Carnegie Endowment for International Peace

Harnisch, Chris (2009) 'Question Mark of South Waziristan: Biography and Analysis of Maulvi Nazir Ahmad', www.criticalthreats.com, 17 July

Hashmi, Arshi Saleem (2009) 'The Arabist Shift from Indo-Persian Civilization & Genesis of Radicalization in Pakistan', *Pips* 1, April

Hearing before the Committee on Foreign Relations, United States Senate, one hundred fourteenth Congress, second session, 8 September 2016.

Hegghammer, Thomas (2020) *The Caravan: Abdallah Azzam and the Rise of Global Jihad*, Cambridge: Cambridge UP

Hellmich, Christina (2011) *Al Qa'ida: From Global Network to Local Franchise*, London: Zed Books

Hersh, Seymour (2016) *The Killing of Osama bin Laden*, London: Verso

Honawar, Rohit (2005) *Jaish-e-Mohammed*, Delhi: IPCS

Howenstein, Nicholas (2008) 'The Jihadi Terrain in Pakistan: An Introduction to the Sunni Jihadi Groups in Pakistan and Kashmir', Bradford: Pakistan Security Research Unit, 5 February

Human Rights Watch (2017) 'Dreams Turned into Nightmares', New York

Hussain, Khadim (2011) 'Modes and Scale of Conflict in Pakistan's Swat Valley (1989–2008)', Islamabad: PIPS

Hussain, Zahid (2007) *Frontline Pakistan*, London: Tauris

ICG (2005) 'The State of Sectarianism in Pakistan', Asia Report N°95 – 18 April

ICG (2009) 'Pakistan: The Militant Jihadi Challenge', Asia Report N°164

ICG (2013) 'Pakistan: Countering Militancy in PATA', Asia Report N°242

Imran, Zafar (2010) 'Al Qa'ida's Ambitions in Pakistan: Changing Goals, Changing Strategies', *Terrorism Monitor* 8: 31

Iqbal, Khuram and De Silva, Sara (2013) 'Terrorist Lifecycles: A Case Study of Tehrik-e-Taliban Pakistan', *Journal of Policing, Intelligence and Counter Terrorism* 8: 1, 72–86

Jadoon, Amira (2021) 'The Evolution and Potential Resurgence of the Tehrik-i-Taliban Pakistan', Washington: USIP

Jadoon, Amira and Mahmood, Sara (2017) 'CTC Perspectives: Militant Rivalries Extend to Female Recruitment in Pakistan', West Point: CTC

Jadoon, Amira and Mahmood, Sara (2018) 'Fixing the Cracks in the Pakistani Taliban's Foundation: TTP's Leadership Returns to the Mehsud Tribe', *CTC Sentinel* 11: 11

Jadoon, Amira et al. (2018) 'Challenging the ISK Brand in Afghanistan-Pakistan: Rivalries and Divided Loyalties', *CTC Sentinel* 11: 4

Jadoon, Amira and Sayed, Abdul (2021) 'The Pakistani Taliban Is Reinventing Itself', *South Asian Voices*, 15 November 2021

Jamal, Arif (2009) 'A Profile of Pakistan's Lashkar-i-Jhangvi', *CTC Sentinel*, September, 2: 9

Jamal, Arif (2011) *A History of Islamist Militancy in Pakistani Punjab*, Washington: Jamestown Foundation

Jamal, Arif (2014) *Call for Transnational Jihad: Lashkar-e Taiba 1985–2014*, New Jersey: AvantGarde Books

Jamal, Umair (2020) 'Are US Forces Striking Tehreek-e-Taliban Pakistan Members in Afghanistan for Islamabad?', *The Diplomat*, February 14

Jamal, Umair (2021) 'Will the Taliban Leadership Abandon Its Bases in Pakistan?' The Diplomat, 29 June 2021.

Jan, Reza (2010) 'Taliban Reconciliation in Pakistan: Much Less Than Meets the Eye', www.criticalthreats.com, 30 January

'Jihad in Pakistan … Why? And How?' (2016) Anonymous AQ booklet, written some time before formation of TTP, translated by DNI 2016

Johnson, Casey Garret (2016) 'The Rise and Stall of the Islamic State in Afghanistan', Washington: USIP

Joscelyn, Thomas (2015) 'Pakistani Taliban Rejects Islamic State's "Self-professed Caliphate"', www.longwarjournal.com, May 27

Joshi, Shashank (2010) 'With Allies Like This: What the Wikileaks War Logs Say about Pakistan', RUSI Commentary, 28 July

Kadercan, Burak (2019) 'Territorial Logic of the Islamic State: An Interdisciplinary Approach', *Territory, Politics, Governance* vol 7

Kamran, Tahir (2016) 'Genealogical Sociology of Sectarianism: A Case Study of Sipah-e-Sahaba Pakistan', in Jawad Syed et al. (eds), *Faith-Based Violence and Deobandi Militancy in Pakistan*, London: Palgrave

Kapur, Paul S. (2017) *Jihad as Grand Strategy: Islamist Militancy, National Security, and the Pakistani State*, Oxford: Oxford UP

Katzman, Kenneth and Thomas, Clayton (2017) 'Afghanistan: Post-Taliban Governance, Security, and U.S. Policy', Washington: CRS, 13 December

Kerr, Brian R. (2011) 'Impact of Regional Ideology on Contemporary Warfare in FATA', Islamabad: PIPS, May

Khattak, Daud (2021) 'The Pakistani Taliban Is Back', *The Diplomat*, 9 March 2021

Khan, Ilyas (2004) 'Profile of Nek Mohammad', *Dawn*, Karachi, June 19, 2004

Khan, M. Ilyas (2020a) 'Hafiz Saeed: Will Pakistan's "terror cleric" Stay in Jail?', www.bbc.com/news, 13 February 2020

Khan, M. Ilyas (2020b) 'Pakistan Court Sentences Mumbai Attack Mastermind Hafiz Saeed to 10 Years in Jail', *PTI*, 19 November 2020.
Khan, Mukhtar A. (2009) 'A Profile of the TTP's New Leader- Hakimullah Mehsud', *CTC Sentinel* 2: 10
Khan, Raheel (2010a) 'Militancy and Conflict in Khyber', in Peter Bergen and Katherine Tiedemann (eds), *Talibanistan*, Oxford: Oxford University Press
Khan, Raheel (2010b) 'The Battle for Pakistan: Militancy and Conflict in Orakzai', Washington: New America Foundation, September 2010
Khan, Raheel (2010c) 'Untangling the Punjabi Taliban Network', *CTC Sentinel* 3: 3
Khan, Raza (2010) 'The Battle for Pakistan Militancy and Conflict in Mohmand', in Peter Bergen and Katherine Tiedemann (eds), *Talibanistan*, Oxford: Oxford University Press
Khattak, Daud (2020) 'Whither the Pakistani Taliban: An Assessment of Recent Trends', New America, 31 August
Khattak, Daud (2011) 'The Significance of Fazal Saeed's Defection from the Pakistani Taliban', *CTC Sentinel* 4: 7
Khattak, Daud (2013a) 'A Profile of Lashkar-i-Jhangvi Leader Malik Ishaq', *CTC Sentinel* 6: 1
Khattak, Daud (2013b) 'A Profile of Khan Said: Waliur Rahman's Successor in the Pakistani Taliban', *CTC Sentinel* 6: 6
Khattak, Daud (2014) 'Taliban Turf Wars Block Peace', *Foreign Policy*, 5 March
Khurasani, Miqdad (n.d.) 'Reasons For the Failure of Talks between Pakistan Government and Tehreek Taliban Pakistan', Umarmedia
Kiessling, Hein G. (2016) *Faith, Unity, Discipline: The Inter-Service-Intelligence (ISI) of Pakistan*, London: Hurst
Latif, Amir (2011) 'Pakistan Army Knew about Operation against Osama bin Laden', *GlobalPost*, 05 May 2011
Lahoud, Nelly et al. (2012) 'Letters from Abbottabad: Bin Ladin Sidelined?', West Point: CTC
Lahoud, Nelly (2022) *The bin Laden Papers*, New Haven: Yale University Press
Larson, Eric V. (2011) 'Al Qaeda's Propaganda: A Shifting Battlefield', in Brian Michael Jenkins and John Paul Godges (eds), *The Long shadow of 9/11*, Santa Monica: Rand
Lieven, Anatol (2011) *Pakistan a Hard Country*, New York: Public Affairs
Marty, Franz J. (2021) 'Spike in Violence Follows Failed Negotiations Between the Pakistani Taliban and Islamabad', *The Diplomat*, April 03, 2021
Mahsud, Mansur Khan (2010) 'The Battle for Pakistan Militancy and Conflict in South Waziristan', New America, April 2010
Mahadevan, Prem (2013) 'Lashkar-e-Taiba: Local Organisation, Global Ambitions. CSS Analysis in Security Policy', ETH Zurich CSS, No. 132
Mahmud, Shaykh and Abu Yahya, Shaykh (2010) 'Letter to Hakimullah Mashud leader of the Taliban movement', 27 Dhu-al Hijah 1431 (4 December 2010), Harmony Collection
Mahsud, M. K. (2010) 'The Battle for Pakistan – Militancy and Conflict in South Waziristan', in Peter Bergen and Katherine Tiedemann (eds), *Talibanistan*, Oxford: Oxford University Press
Markey, David S. (2013), *No Exit from Pakistan: America's Tortured Relationship with Islamabad*, Cambridge: Cambridge University Press
Marwat, Fazal-ur Rahim and Toru, Parvez Khan (2005) *Talibanization of Pakistan*, Peshawar: Peshawar Study Centre
McNally, Lauren and Weinbaum, Marvin (2016) 'A Resilient al Qa'ida in Afghanistan and Pakistan', Washington: Middle East institute, August 2016, 5

Mashal, Mujeeb (2019) 'As Taliban Talk Peace, ISIS Is Ready to Play the Spoiler in Afghanistan', *The New York Times*, 20 August 2019

Mashal, Mujib 'Leader of ISIS Branch in Afghanistan Killed in Special Forces Raid', *The New York Times*, 7 May 7

Mendelsohn, Barak (2016) *The al Qa'ida Franchise*, New York: Oxford UP

Meyerle, Gerald M. (2008) *Death by a Thousand Cuts: The Dynamics of Protracted Insurgency in Kashmir and Sri Lanka*, PhD dissertation, University of Virginia

Mian, Asif (2009) 'FATA: Tribal Economy in the Context of Ongoing Militancy', Islamabad: PIPS

Miqdaad, Muhammad (2017) 'Don't Get Stung out of the Same Hole Repeatedly!', An Nasr Media, November

Mir, Amir (2006) *True Face of Jihadis*, Lahore: Mashal

Mir, Amir (2008) *The Fluttering Flag of Jihad*, Lahore: Mashal

Mir, Amir (2016) 'IS Makes Inroads into Pakistan', *Asia Times Online*, 27 June 2016

Moghadam, Assaf (2013) 'How Al Qaeda Innovates', *Security Studies* 22: 3, 466–97

Moj, Muhammad (2015) *The Deoband Madrassah Movement: Countercultural Trends and Tendencies*, London: Anthem Press

Morell, Mike and Harlow, Bill (2015) *The Great War of Our Time*, New York, Boston: Twelve

Murphy, Eamon (2013) *The Making of Terrorism in Pakistan. Historical and Social Roots of Extremism*, London: Routledge.

Murphy, Eamon (2019) *Islam and Sectarian Violence in Pakistan: The Terror Within*, London: Routledge

Nair, Tarun (2020) 'The Resurgence of the Tehreek-e-Taliban Pakistan', *The Diplomat*, July 18

Nasr, Seyyed and Reza, Vali (1999) 'Sectarianism and Shia Politics in Pakistan, 1979-Present', *CEMOTI* 28, 311–23

National Commission on Terrorist Attacks upon the United States (2003) *The 9/11 Commission Report,* New York: Norton

Ness, Marielle (2018) 'Beyond the Caliphate. Islamic State Activity Outside the Group's Defined Wilayat', Combatting Terrorism Center at West Point

Nihad, Ghalib (2022) 'At least Five Security Personnel Martyred, 19 Injured in Sibi Blast: Officials', *Dawn*, 8 March 2022.

Nojumi, Neamatullah (2008) 'The Rise and Fall of the Taliban', in Robert D. Crews and Amin Tarzi (eds), *The Taliban and the Crisis of Afghanistan*, Cambridge, MA: Harvard UP

Obama, Barack (2020) *A Promised Land*, New York: Random House

Osman, Borhan (2016) 'The Islamic State in "Khorasan": How It Began and Where It Stands Now in Nangarhar', Berlin: AAN, 27 July

Padukone, Neil (2011) 'The Next al Qa'ida Lashkar-e-Taiba and the Future of Terrorism in South Asia', *World Affairs*, November/December

'Pakistan: Friend or Foe in the Fight against Terrorism?' (2016) Joint hearing before the subcommittee on terrorism, nonproliferation, and trade and the subcommittee on Asia and the Pacific of the committee on foreign affairs, House of Representatives, one hundred fourteenth Congress, second session', July 12

'Pakistan Policy Working Group' (2008) 'The Next Chapter: The United States and Pakistan', Report, September

Pandya, Abhinav (2021) 'The Pakistan Connection: How ISKP Became Islamabad's Latest Proxy', *The National Interest*, 7 September

Pantucci, Raffaello (2021) 'How China Became Jihadis' New Target', *Foreign Policy*, 22 November 2021
Perlez, Jane and Zubair Shah, Pir (2008) 'Pakistani Forces Appear to Push Back Militants', *The New York Times*, 30 June 2008
Peters, Gretchen (2010) 'Crime and Insurgency in the Tribal Areas of Afghanistan and Pakistan', West Point: CTC, October 15
Popovic, Milos (2015) 'The Perils of Weak Organization: Explaining Loyalty and Defection of Militant Organizations toward Pakistan', *Studies in Conflict & Terrorism*, 38: 11, 919–37
Priestland, David (2009) *The Red Flag*, London: Penguin
Puri, Samir (2012) *Pakistan's War on Terrorism*, London: Routledge
Qazi, Shehzad H. (2011) 'An Extended Profile of the Pakistani Taliban', Washington: ISPU
Rafiq, Arif (2014) 'The New Al Qaeda Group in South Asia Has Nothing to Do with ISIS', *The New Republic*, September 5
Rafiq, Arif (2016) 'What Happened to ISIS's Afghanistan-Pakistan Province?', *The Diplomat*, 19 February
Rahmanullah (2010) 'The Battle for Pakistan: Militancy and Conflict in Bajaur', in Peter Bergen and Katherine Tiedemann (eds), *Talibanistan*, Oxford: Oxford University Press
Rana, Amir (2003) *Gateway to Terrorism*, London: New Millennium
Rana, Amir (2004) 'Jamaat ud Dawa Splits', *Daily Times*, 18 July 2004
Rana, Mohammad Amir (2005) *The Seeds of Terrorism*, London: New Millennium
Rana, Mohammad Amir (2009) 'Taliban Insurgency in Pakistan: A Counterinsurgency Perspective', Islamabad: PIPS
Rana, Mohammad Amir (2010a) 'Evolution of Militant Groups in FATA and Adjacent Areas', in MA Rana et al. (eds), *Dynamics of Taliban Insurgency in FATA*, Islamabad: PIPS
Rana, Mohammad Amir (2010b) 'Post-9/11 Developments and Emergence of Local Taliban Groups', in M. A. Rana et al. (eds), *Dynamics of Taliban Insurgency in FATA*, Islamabad: PIPS
Rana, Mohammad Amir and Gunaratna, Rohan (2007) *Al Qaida Fights Back*, Islamabad: PIPS
Rashid, Ahmed (2000) *Taliban*, London: Tauris
Rashid, Ahmed (2008) *Descent into Chaos*, London: Penguin
Rassler, Don (2009) 'Al-Qa`ida's Pakistan Strategy', *CTC Sentinel* 2: 6
Rassler, Don (2015) 'Situating the Emergence of the Islamic State of Khorasan', *CTC Sentinel* 8: 3 March
Reed, Alistair (2016) 'Al Qaeda in the Indian Subcontinent', The Hague: ICCT
Rehman, Zia Ur (2012a) 'Taliban Recruiting and Fundraising in Karachi', *CTC Sentinel* 5: 7
Rehman, Zia Ur (2012b) 'Taliban Militants Striking Pakistan from Afghan Territory', *CTC Sentinel* 5: 9
Rehman, Zia Ur (2013a) 'Pakistani Fighters Joining the War in Syria', *CTC Sentinel* 6: 9
Rehman, Zia Ur (2013b) 'The Pakistani Taliban's Karachi Network', *CTC Sentinel* 6: 5
Rehman, Zia Ur (2014) 'A Profile of Ahrar-ul-Hind and Ansar-ul-Mujahidin Pakistan', *CTC Sentinel* 7: 5
'Report of the Commission of Inquiry into the Abbottabad Incident of May 2, 2011' (2013) Islamabad
'Report on Our Visit' (2008) Harmony document captured in Abbottabad, (released 2016)
Riedel, Bruce (2008) *The Search for Al Qaeda. Its Leadership, Ideology, and Future*, Washington, DC: Brookings Institution Press

Riedel, Bruce (2011) *Deadly Embrace*, Washington: Brookings Institution Press
Riedel, Bruce (2013) 'Pakistan's Osama bin Laden Report: Was Pakistan Clueless or Complicit in Harboring bin Laden?', Washington: Brookings, 12 July
Rogers, Christopher (2010) 'Civilians in Armed Conflict: Civilian Harm and Conflict in Northwest Pakistan', Washington: Center for Civilians in Conflict
Roggio, Bill (2009) 'Mustafa Abu Yazid Eulogizes Baitullah', *www.longwarjournal.com*, 1 October 2009
Roggio, Bill (2011) '"Good" Pakistani Taliban Leader Nazir Affirms Membership of Al Qaeda', *www.longwarjournal.com*, 4 May
Roggio, Bill (2014a) 'Taliban Splinter Group Jama'at-ul-Ahrar Forms in Northwestern Pakistan', *www.longwarjournal.com*, 26 August
Roggio, Bill (2014b) 'Al Qaeda in the Indian Subcontinent Incorporates Regional Jihadist Groups', *www.longwarjournal.com*, September 5
Roggio, Bill (2015) 'Pakistani Taliban Praises Slain al Qaeda Leaders', *www.longwarjournal.com*, April 15
Roggio, Bill (2021) 'Pakistani Taliban Emir Says His Group "Is a Branch of the Islamic Emirate of Afghanistan"', *Long War Journal*, 15 December 2021
Rosenau, William and Powell, Alexander (2017) 'Al Qa'ida Core: A Case Study', Alexandria: CNA, October
Roul, Animesh (2005) 'Sipah-e-Sahaba: Fomenting Sectarian Violence in Pakistan', *Terrorism Monitor* 3: 2
Roul, Animesh (2011a) Pakistan's Jama'at-ud-Sawa Steps up Campaign of Anti-American Rhetoric', *Terrorism Monitor*, 9: 28
Roul, Animesh (2011b) 'Jaish-e-Muhammad's Charity Wing Revitalizes Banned Group in Pakistan', *Terrorism Monitor* 9: 4
Roul, Animesh (2020a) 'Al Qa'ida South Asian Branch Gravitating toward Kashmir', *Terrorism Monitor*, 18: 8, April 2020
Roul, Animesh (2020b) 'Islamic State Hind Province's Kashmir Campaign and Pan-Indian Capabilities', *Terrorism Monitor,* 18: 22, 3 December 2020
Roy, Olivier (1990) *Afghanistan: Islam and Political Modernity*, Cambridge: Cambridge UP
Sands, Chris (2019) *Night Letters*, London: Hurst
Sareen, Sushant (2005) *The Jihad Factory*, New Delhi: Har Anand
Sattar, Abdul (2021) 'Pakistani Shiites Rally against Murder of Coal Miners by Islamic State', *The Diplomat*, 5 January 2021
Sayed, Abdul (2021a) 'Waziristan Militant Leader Aleem Khan Ustad Joins Tehreek-e-Taliban', *Militant Leadership Monitor*, 11: 12, 5 January
Sayed, Abdul (2021b) 'Tehreek-e-Taliban Pakistan's Latest Merger Enables Renewed Attacks in Pakistan', *Terrorism Monitor* 19: 16, 13 August 13
Sayed, Abdul (2021c) 'Pakistan's Peace Talks with the Pakistani Taliban: Insights from an Interview with Abdul Wali Mohmand', *Terrorism Monitor*, 19: 23, 7 December 2021
Sayed, Abdul and Hamming, Tore (2021) 'The Revival of the Pakistani Taliban', *CTC Sentinel*, 14: 4, April/May 2021
Schmidt, John R. (2017) 'Did Pakistan Really Know about Osama bin Laden's Hideout?', *The Daily Beast*, 13 July 2017
Scott-Clark, Cathy and Levy, Adrian (2013) *The Siege: 68 Hours Inside the Taj Hotel*, London: Penguin
Scott-Clark, Cathy and Levy, Adrian (2017) *The Exile*, London: Bloomsbury
Schmidt, John R. (2011) *The Unravelling*, New York: Farrar, Stroux and Giroux
Schroen, Gary (2005) *First In*, Novato, CA: Presidio Press

Semple, Michael (2014) 'The Pakistan Taliban Movement: An Appraisal', Barcelona: Cidob
Shah, Riddhi K. (2014) 'The AI-Qaeda and the Lashkar-e-Toiba: A Case of Growing Ideological Homogeneity?', *India Quarterly*, 70: 2, 87–104
Shahid, Kunwar Khuldune (2016) 'An Alliance between Islamic State and Lashkare-Jhangvi in Pakistan Was Inevitable', *The Diplomat*, 15 November
Shahid, Kunwar Khuldune (2019) 'The Return of the Pakistani Taliban', *The Diplomat*, 8 October
Shahzad, Syed Saleem (2011) *Inside al Qa'ida and the Taliban*, London: Pluto/Palgrave
Shapoo, Sajid Farid et al. (2019) 'Al Qa'ida in the Indian Subcontinent (Aqis)', The Soufan Center, January 2019, 25
Sheikh, Mona Kanwal (2009) 'Disaggregating the Pakistani Taliban', Copenhagen: DIIS
Sherzad, Rafiq (2016) 'Islamic State Claims Suicide Attack on Pakistani Consulate in Afghan City', *Reuters*, 13 January 2016
Siddiqi, Amjad Bashir (2021) 'After Escape from Afghanistan: Anti-Pakistan Terror Outfits Regrouping in Balochistan', *Dawn*, 27 September 2021
Siddique, Abubakar (2018) 'Waziristan Unrest Sheds Light on Lingering Taliban Influence', *Gandhara.rferl.org*, 8 June 2018
Siddique, Abubakar (2022) 'Pakistan Confronts Growing Threat from Islamic State-Khorasan', *Gandhara*, 11 March 2022
Siddique, Haroon (2007) 'Bin Laden Urges Uprising against Musharraf', *The Guardian*, 20 September 2007
Siddique, Qandeel (2010) 'Tehrik-E-Taliban Pakistan: An Attempt to Deconstruct the Umbrella Organization and the Reasons for Its Growth in Pakistan's North-West', Copenhagen: DIIS Report
Sikand, Yoginder (2001) 'The Changing Course of the Kashmiri Struggle: From National Liberation to Islamist Jihad?', *The Muslim World*, 91, Spring
Singh, Surmukh (2020) *Terror Network*, Delhi: BlueRose Publishers
Sirrs, Owen L. (2017) *Pakistan's Inter-Services Intelligence Directorate*, London: Routledge
Siyech, Mohammed Sinan (2017) 'Al Qa'ida in the Indian Subcontinent (AQIS): Renewing Efforts in India', Washington: MEI, 19 September
Soufan Center, The (2019) 'Al-Qaeda in the Indian Subcontinent (AQIS): The Nucleus of Jihad in South Asia', New York
Stenersen, Anne (2010) 'Al Qa'ida's Allies', New York: New America Foundation
Stenersen, Anne (2017) *Al Qa'ida in Afghanistan*, Cambridge: Cambridge UP
Sulaiman, Sadia (2008) 'Empowering "Soft" Taliban over "Hard" Taliban: Pakistan's Counter-terrorism Strategy', *Terrorism Monitor*, 25 July
Sulaiman, Sadia (2009) 'Hafiz Gul Bahadur: A Profile of the Leader of the North Waziristan Taliban', *Terrorism Monitor* 7: 9
Szrom, Charlie (2009) 'The Survivalist of North Waziristan: Hafiz Gul Bahadur Biography and Analysis', *Critical Threat*, 6 August [Available at: www.criticalthreat.org/palkistan/the-survivalist-of-north-waziristan-hafiz-gul-gul-bahadur-biography-and-analysis.html]
Swami, Praveen (2007) *India, Pakistan and the Secret Jihad: The Covert War in Kashmir, 1947–2004*, London: Routledge
Taneja, Kabir (2019) *The ISIS Peril*, Gurgaon: Penguin
Taneja, Kabir (2021) 'Under the Taliban Bonnet: Al Qaeda–ISKP Rivalry and Its Security', New Delhi, ORF, 16 October
Tankel, Stephen (2009) 'Lashkar-e-Taiba: From 9/11 to Mumbai', London: ICSR

Tankel, Stephen (2010) 'Lashkar-e-Taiba in Perspective', New America Foundation, February 2010
Tankel, Stephen (2011) *Storming the World Stage*, Hurst 2011, 63
Tawil, Camille (2010) *Brothers in Arms*, London: Saqi
TTP (n.d.) 'Operation Manual for Mujahideen of Tehreek Taliban Pakistan'
Tomlinson, Hugh, and Janjua, Haroon (2017) 'Jihadist Factions vie for Control of Afghan Isis', *The Times*, 18 July
Topich, William J. (2018) *Pakistan: The Taliban, al Qaeda, and the Rise of Terrorism*, Santa Barbara, CA: ABC-CLIO
Turner, John (2019) 'The Impact of Islamic State's Ideological Correction Initiative on al Qaeda's Bid for Relevance', *Small Wars & Insurgencies*, 30: 3, 563–86
United Nations Security Council (2019) 'Letter dated 15 July 2019 from the Chair of the Security Council Committee pursuant to resolutions 1267 (1999) 1989 (2011) and 2253 (2015) concerning Islamic State in Iraq and the Levant (Da'esh), al Qa'ida and associated individuals, groups, undertakings and entities addressed to the President of the Security Council'. S/2019/570, New York, 15 July
United Nations Security Council (2021) 'Letter dated 21 January 2021 from the Chair of the Security Council Committee pursuant to resolutions 1267 (1999), 1989 (2011) and 2253 (2015) concerning Islamic State in Iraq and the Levant (Da'esh), al Qa'ida and associated individuals, groups, undertakings and entities addressed to the President of the Security Council', S/2021/68, New York, 3 February
Valle, Riccardo (2021) 'Pro-Islamic State Pakistan Province Media Network Publishes Long-Awaited Magazine Issue', *Militant Wire*, 8 December 2021
Waldman, Matt (2010) 'The Sun in the Sky', London: Crisis States Research Centre
Waseem, Zoha (2016) 'Daesh in Pakistan: An Evolving Militant Landscape – Part I', *STRIFE*, February 6
Wilkinson, Isambard (2009) 'Baitullah Mehsud: The "Good Taliban" Who Became One of Pakistan's Most Wanted Men', *The Telegraph*, 31 March 2009
Wilson, John (2007) 'Lashkar-e-Tayyeba', Pakistan Security Research Unit Brief 12,University of Bradford, May 21
Wright, Lawrence (2007) *The Looming Tower*, London: Penguin
Yousaf, Mohammed and Adkin, Mark (2002) *The Bear Trap*, Barnsley: Pen & Sword
Yusufzai, Rahimullah (2008) 'The Impact of Pashtun Tribal Differences on the Pakistani Taliban', *Terrorism Monitor* 6: 3
Zahab, Mariam Abou and Roy, Oliver (2004) *Islamist Networks: The Afghan–Pakistan Connection*, New York: Columbia University Press.
Zahid, Farhan (2015a) *The al Qa'ida Network in Pakistan*, Lahore: Narratives, 2015
Zahid, Farhan (2015b) 'Al Qa'ida Resurgence: al Qa'ida in the Indian Subcontinent', in Imtiaz Gul (ed.), *From Jihad to al Qa'ida to Islamic State*, Islamabad: Center for Research and Security Studies
Zahid, Farhan (2015c) 'Islamic State Claims Deadly Bus Attack on Karachi Shias – First in Pakistan', *AFP*, 13 May 2015
Zahid, Farhan (2017) 'Lashkar-e-Jhangvi al-Alami: A Pakistani Partner for Islamic State', *Terrorism Monitor* 15: 2, January 27
Zahid, Farhan (2019) 'Two New IS Wilayat in South Asia: IS Reinvigorates Itself in Pakistan and India', *Terrorism Monitor,* 17: 13, 3 July 2019
Zahid, Farhan (2020) 'Death of AQIS-linked Commander Abdul Jabbar: Another Blow to al-Qaeda in Pakistan', *Militant Leadership Monitor* 10: 12
Zahid, Zahid Mehmood et al. (2020) 'Critical Discourse Analysis of Tehrik-e-Taliban Pakistan: An Intertextual Recontextualization', *Pakistan Social Sciences Review*, 4: 2, 503–25

Index

Abu Bakr, Maulana 30, 85
Afghan civil war 23–5, 27
Afghanistan
    AQ strategy 27–31, 33, 51, 62–3, 125–6, 142, 148–9, 152–3, 170, 176–87
    HuM in 147, 160–1
    IS-K in 136–7, 140, 151, 166–7, 169
    Islamic Emirate of 27
    IS-P in 139
    JeM in 146, 163
    jihad movement of 1978 15
    LeJ in 124–5, 130–2, 138, 146
    LeT in 142–5, 152–4, 157, 159, 162, 164–6
    against NATO and Pakistan's armed forces' 34
    NDS 89
    1980 government 1
    1990s civil war 23–5
    Pashtun Taliban 72
    SSP in 129, 132–3
    Taliban presence in 2008 29
    TTP in 67, 71–2, 74, 76, 78, 80, 82–3, 88–96, 100, 107–11, 113, 115–21
    2014–16 29–31
    US intervention 27–9, 33, 65, 123, 141, 148, 174
Afghan jihad 48
    AQ agenda 32, 42, 71, 105, 108, 178, 180, 183
    AQIS in 148
    HuM in 160
    Iranian revolution, impact on 23
    IS in 171
    JeM in 146
    LeJ in 130, 140
    LeT in 144
    in 1980s 173
    from 1978 15
    Pakistan sponsorship 1, 16, 24
    second (2002–) 27–9

    SSP in 140
    TTP support 108–9
    Western support 19
Afghan Taliban
    after collapse of Emirate 65
    AQ support 31, 34, 39, 46, 49, 51, 62, 68, 177–80, 185
    crackdown 157
    disunity 66
    election model 87
    evolution after 2003 85, 89
    global jihadists, volunteering 27
    with HuM 147–8
    insurgency 97
    with LeJ 131, 136
    LeT training 144
    Musharraf's betrayal 141, 174
    1990s civil war in Afghanistan 23–5
    operating route 29
    Pakistani networks 67
    peace deal with the United States 107
    with SSP 126, 132
    with TTP 5, 7, 12, 71–7, 79–80, 82, 85, 87–92, 94–7, 99, 104, 106–9, 119, 121, 175
Afridi tribesmen 52, 66, 75, 79, 83
Ahrar ul Hind 82
Akhtar, Qari Saifullah 23
Al Badr Foundation 18
Al Badr Mujahidin 28
Al Baghdadi 52, 56, 75, 77, 133, 152
Al Falestini, Mustafa Hamid 30
Al Farooq 18
Al Hamid, Abd 30
Al Haq Tigers 18
Ali Rehman, Qari 80
Allah Akbar 18
Al Nusra 7, 73
al Qa'ida (AQ)
    in Afghanistan 27–30, 51, 179–80
    alliance with the TTP 37, 67–71, 93, 97–9

competition with global jihad 185
competition with IS 2020 186–7
conflicts after 2015 185
criticism of TTP 99–104, 178–9
deep state relationship 37, 40–3, 46–7, 50–1, 54–62, 121, 182–4
exploitation of US-Pakistan alliance 39–43
funding sources 28, 31, 89
global jihadism 15–16, 24, 27
impact on Pakistani jihadism 28, 32, 61
IS-K and IS-P alliance 181
with Islamic State (IS) 52–3, 61–3
Jihadist legitimacy 92, 181
local budget 31
local partners 4–9, 71
Pakistani military agreement of 2008–11 48
Pakistan, presence in 27–30, 33, 37–9, 42, 45, 51–2, 105
pragmatists 41, 46
pro-Islamabad Pakistani Taliban 108–9
rapprochement between TTP and Haqqani network 91
recruitment of non-core (second-tier) members 36–7
regionalization 32–7
sectarian violence 126–8
South Asian jihad 28, 37
strategic approaches 9–11, 27–8, 177–9
terrorist activities 3–4
training the Indian Mujahidin 32
tribal elements 67
2014 elements 32
2002–7 violent campaign 56
vulnerabilities 186
war with India 47
al Qa'ida in the Indian Subcontinent (AQIS) 113–14, 116, 121
demography 34
establishment 29, 34
follow up of Lashkar e Zil 35
with IS in Kashmir 62
IS-K negotiation 76
Pakistani local AQ 28
Pakistan-India budget 48
primary task 29

recruiting second tier members 104–5
South Asian allies 31, 33, 35
use Pakistan for operations in India 48
al Suri, Yasin 109
Anjaman Sipah i Sahaba (ASS) 17
Ansar ul Khilafat Wal-Jihad (Partisans of the Caliphate and of Jihad) 52
anti-Islamabad group 49, 68, 71, 82, 88, 90, 96–7, 105–6, 108, 119, 183
AQ Central 3–4, 28, 32–4, 36
Arab jihadists, relocation 67
Atiya 42, 44

Bagh, Mangal 72, 75, 95–7, 111, 118
Bakhtwar, Mullah 52–3
bin Laden, Osama 1, 22, 30, 38, 41, 51, 66, 71, 101–2, 179
  Abbottabad raid 1, 40–1, 44–5
  deal with Pakistan 44
  instrumental attitude 28
  killing in 2011 28
  Lal Masjid affair 42
  2007 crisis 43–4
bombing. *See* suicide bombing
bureaucrats 47

Caliphate
  AQ and 75
  extremist ideology 53
  IS-K funding 56–8, 169
  as legitimate IS 167
  in Middle East 184
  TTP and 76–7
Cardin, Ben (senator) 40

Darul Uloom Haqqania 23
Dawlat Khan, Hafiz 52, 85
deep state. *See also* Pakistan
  AQ relationship 37, 40–3, 46–7, 50–1, 54–62, 121, 182–4
  global jihadism towards Kashmir and India 168–70
  IS-K 55–8, 60
  reliance on jihadist group 173
  Sunni supremacists 132, 164, 184
  TTP 107
Deobandi groups 15–17, 21–4, 52, 65, 79, 94, 102, 126, 144–5, 157, 161
Devotees of Fazlullah 12

drone strike
American 34, 38, 44, 47, 49–50, 93, 95–6, 100, 110, 134
in Nangarhar 53
in Shorabak 51
in tribal areas 69

Ehsan, Ehsanullah 82

Farooqi, Abdul Rahim Mawlavi 83, 109
Farooqi, Amjad 143
Farooqi, Aslam 56, 59, 167
Farooq Ibrahim, Maulana 144, 162
Farooqi Group 88–9, 109–10, 142
Farooqi, Mawlavi 83
Farooq, Ustadh Ahmad 45
Fazlullah, Qasi Maulana 79, 84, 86, 88, 93, 97, 110–11, 114–15, 117, 119
Fazlur Rehman Khalil, Maulana 20
Federally Administered Tribal Areas (FATA) 2, 23, 29, 31, 38, 65, 67, 70, 74, 78, 85, 87, 113, 119

Gall, Carlotta 38, 40, 44
Ghani, Ashraf 57–8
global jihad
after 2001 in Pakistan 28, 31–2, 39, 56, 61–2
AQ's competition 185
JeM in 142–3, 161–4
national jihadists vs. 176–7
in 1990s 173–4
Pakistani relations 1, 3–5, 11
place of Kashmir 148–50, 168–71
relations with Afghanistan 15–16, 24, 27
spending power 97
TTP and 71–4
US presence 142, 148, 174–5, 185–6
Gul Bahadur, Hafiz 80–1, 92, 95, 117
Gul Zaman, Maulana 85

Haqqania, Darul Uloom 23
Haqqani network, aka Miran Shah Shura 36, 57, 66, 82, 91–2, 100, 117, 119, 147, 150
Haqqani, Serajuddin 85
Harakat e Enqelab e Islami 15
Harakat ul Ansar 24

Harakat ul Jihad al Islami (HuJI) 15, 19–21, 23–4, 31, 34, 36, 44, 66, 142, 149–50
Harakat ul Mujahidin (HuM) 12, 20, 23, 28, 31, 34, 36–7, 44
support of 'AQ's ideology 142–3
2019 crackdown 159–61
Hassan, Gul 143
Hassan, Mufti 85
Hizb e Islami 15, 24
Hizb ul Ahrar (HuA) 76, 78, 83–4, 89, 116, 118
Hizb ul Mujahideen (HM) 19–22, 28, 149–50, 157–8
Huis 55, 73

Inter-Services Intelligence/Directorate (Pakistan, ISI), 2, 12, 15, 19–22, 25
with AQIS 149–50
AQ's relationship 33, 37–49, 66, 68, 141, 163, 167, 171, 179, 182
with HuM 161
with IS-K 54, 57–60, 167–8
with IS-P 169
with JeM 146–7, 160, 162
with LeT 144–5, 151–3, 155–6, 158, 165–6
with TTP 71, 76, 91, 104, 107–9, 131
Islamic Movement of Uzbekistan (IMU) 24, 34, 36, 57, 67, 73, 129, 132, 143, 150, 154
Islamic State (IS)
in Afghanistan 77
with AQ 2020 186–7
deep state's tutelage 184
focus on India and Kashmir 37, 166–7
jihadist ethos 75
losing the power 77
in Pakistan 52–4, 77
South Asian influence 183–4
strategic approaches 9–11
supporting AQ in Afghanistan 62
supremacists strategy 140
TTP and 117
in 2014–15 4
Wilayat Pakistan (IS-P), establishment of 35, 58

Islamic State Hind (IS-H) 59, 61–2, 166, 171, 184–5
   deep state converge on Kashmir 166–70
Islamic State in Khorasan (IS-K) 12, 36, 52–3, 93, 110, 113, 116, 121
   action in Kashmir 150–2, 166–8
   Afghanistan defeat 78
   attacks against Chinese interests in Pakistan 55
   attacks against Shi'as 54
   closest relations with jihadists 132–7
   deep state relations 55–8, 60
   defeat in Afghanistan 57
   HuA alliance 84
   in India media 55
   Jaysh ul Islam (Army of Islam) merging with 53
   JuA and 77–8, 83
   logistic obstacles 54
   Orakzais and Mehsuds joining 75
   in Pakistan 53–8, 60–1
   problems with IS-P 58–9
   rival factions 56
Islamic State in Pakistan (IS-P) 12, 35, 53, 57–61
   AQIS and 166
   with ISI 60
   jihad in Kashmir, supporting 59, 167–71, 175
   with LeJ 127, 132
   as prisoner of IS-K 60, 175, 181, 185
   with SSP 137–40
   with TTP 77
Ittehad e Islami 16, 90, 173

Jabha al Nusra 4
Jaish e Mohammed (JeM) 12, 20–3, 28, 31, 34, 37, 42, 46, 56
   AQ agenda 141–3, 183
   with AQIS 149–50, 185
   global jihadist ethos 142–3, 161–4, 170
   with HuM 145–8
   with IS 169
   with IS-H 62
   with ISI 160, 167
   with IS-K 150, 168
   with LeT 144–5, 156–9, 164
   with SSP 130, 132
   with TTP 82, 89, 91, 94, 99, 104, 108
Jama'at e Islami (JeI) 15, 19, 24
Jama'at ud Dawa/Lashkar e Taiba (JuD/LeT) 54
Jama'at ul Ahrar (JuA) 12, 82–4, 104, 107, 116, 118
Jama'at ul Ansar ul Shari'a 34
Jama'at Ulema e Islam (JuI) 23, 44
Jami'at ul Ansar ul Afghaneen 16
Jamiat ul Uloomi Islamiyyah 23
Jammu and Kashmir Liberation Front (JKLF) 19–20
Jaysh e Islami 80
Jaysh ul Islam (Army of Islam) 53–4
Jhangvi, Maulana 17
Jhangvi Tigers 18
Jundullah 5, 12, 32, 94, 123, 132, 134, 138, 140, 185
Junood al Fida 34
Junood ul Khilafa e Hind (JKH) 166

Kandahari Taliban 92
Karwan e Naimatullah 80
Kashmiri, Farooq 147
Kashmiri jihad 18–20
   campaign (2001) 27
   global jihads in 148–50, 168–71
   IS in 37, 62, 166–7
   Lashkar e Taiba (LeT) 143–5
   militants 33
   professionalization 20–3
Khan, Hafiz Dawlat 52, 85
Khan, Hafiz Sayed 85
Khan, Imran 48, 50, 128, 146, 159, 161, 166
Khan, Mukkaram 83
Khilafat Speen Ghar Bakhtwar Group 52
Khorasani, Omar 58, 82, 140
Khyber Pukhtoonkhwa, bomb attack 119
Kiessling, Hein G. 44
Kunduz battle 23

Lal Masjid episode 42, 46, 49, 69–70, 174
Lashkar e Islam (LI) 12, 72, 75, 82, 90, 96, 115, 118–19
   Afridi tribesmen 79
   relations with IS-K 78

Lashkar e Jhangvi (LeJ) 18, 28, 34, 36, 46, 48, 52, 57, 62, 102, 104, 108, 116, 119
Lashkar e Taiba (LeT) 12, 20–2, 24, 28, 31, 34, 36–7, 39, 42, 52, 56–8, 73, 89, 97, 99, 104–5, 108
   crackdown in 2019 156–9
   Kashmir affaire 143–5
   partial rehabilitation in 2020 164–6
   ties with AQ 152–6
Lashkar e Zil 33–5

Mahmud, Sheikh 93, 100–1, 108, 115
Maktab Khidamat al Mujahidin 16
Mansoor, Akhtar Mohammad 44, 91
Mansoor, Khalid 85
Mansoor, Omar 80
Markaz Dawat wal'Irshad (MDI) 16, 21, 24
Masood Kashmiri, Maulana 20
Mawya, Asmatullah 116
Mehsud, Abdul Bahar 85
Mehsud, Abdullah 67, 84
Mehsud, Bahlozai 84
Mehsud, Baitullah 66–7, 69, 79–81, 83–6, 88, 95, 110, 120–1
Mehsud, Daud 59
Mehsud, Hakimullah (Sheharyar) 24, 71, 77, 79–80, 82, 84, 88–9, 93, 95, 97, 101–2, 104, 110, 117, 123
Miqdaad, Muhammad 47
Mohammad, Nek 24, 66–7, 95
Mohammed, Faqir 80–2, 97, 109, 119
Mohammed Yousuf Binori, Maulavi 23
Mujahir Qawmi Movement (MQM) 48
Muqami Tehrik e Taliban (Local Taliban Movement) 81
Musharraf, Perves 28, 38, 43–4
   assassination plots on 38–9
   jailing of Gul 42
Muslim Brotherhood 15
Muslim circles in India 98, 100
Muslimdost, Abdul Rahim 55

National Directorate of Security (NDS, Afghanistan) 12
Nawaz Jhangvi, Haq 17–18
Nazir, Mullah 66–7, 72, 80–1, 84, 90, 95, 109, 119

9/11 attack 6, 8, 27, 99, 123, 125, 141, 143, 145, 147, 174, 177–8, 180
   US intervention in Afghanistan 174
Noor, Wali Meshud 67, 76, 79, 92, 113–21
NWFP 74

Omar, Haji 29, 84
Omar, Mohammad 91
Omar, Mullah 23–4, 69, 71, 90–1, 129

Pakistan. *See also* Pakistani authorities
   Afghan jihad involvement 16
   alliance with the United States against AQ 40–1
   American invasion on 2001 29
   AQ influence 29–30, 33, 37–8, 178–87
   as a base for jihadist operations 174–5
   foreign policy 1–3
   IS-K 53–8, 151–2
   Islamic State's arrival 52–3
   jihadist operations 174–5
   jihadists and AQ leadership 27–8
   main sectarian organizations 17
   against NATO and Pakistan's armed forces' 34
   Shi'a mobilization 16
   Sunni supremacist groups 123–41
   TTP's threat 78–83, 102–22
   2008–14 43–5
   2014–21 45–50
   2016 31–2
   2002 crisis 141
   2002–14 28–9
   Western powers, relationship 175–7
   Wilayat Pakistan 58–61
Pakistani authorities
   American collaboration 65
   AQ and 37–52
   co-opting Pakistani Taliban 94
   global jihadist's relationship 1
   influence of foreign jihadists 96
   IS-K relationship 54–6
   LeT against 21
   monitoring IS activities 53
   support of Mullah Nazir 67
   supremacists and 128–32
   with Taliban 23

Index

Pakistani jihadists
   AQ's influence 11, 27–8, 49, 178, 184
   establishment of AQIS 37, 48
   global relationship 176
   indigenization in 2009 33
   Kashmir insurgency 20–1
   presence in India 156
   relationship with AQIS 48
   2020 situation 61
Pakistani Mujahidin 32–3
Pakistani Pashtuns 2, 109
Pakistani Taliban 7, 24, 31, 34, 39, 41
   Afghan insurgency 73
   allied with Islamabad 109
   AQ support 108–9, 176–7
   conflict with the Pakistani authorities 68
   global step 72–3
   guerrilla war 118
   influence of foreign jihadists 96
   Noor Wali's approach 118–19
   pro-Islamabad factions 108–9
   scattered group 65
   separate identities 66
   TTP's impact 65–70, 72–3, 79, 83–4, 91–9, 120
   from 2002–6 70
Pasha, Ahmad Shuja 44
Pashtun tribesmen 65, 67
Peshawar Shura Taliban 108
pro-Islamabad Taliban 106, 109–10
Provincial Administered Tribal Areas (PATA) 31, 98, 111
Punjabi Taliban (Tehrik e Taliban Punjab) 46, 95, 116, 134, 146, 183

Quetta Shura 29, 90, 93, 121, 124, 129, 131, 135–7, 139

Rahman, Mehmud 53
Revolutionary Guards (Iran) 51

Saeed Khan, Hafiz 16, 22, 52
Saifullah Kurd, Ameer Usman 116, 139
Sajna, Khalid 84, 116
Salafi groups 15–16
Salarzai, Abu Usman 75
Sami ul Haq, Mawlavi 23
Seyfiddin, Abu Omar 73

Shahid, Shahidullah 54, 85
Shah, Miran 91
Shakai agreement 67
Shari'a 45, 77, 86, 118, 140
   implementation 120
Sharif, Nawaz 128–9
Shi'as 53, 60, 82, 102, 115, 127, 131, 133, 135, 137, 141–2
   violence against 54, 102, 115
Shir Haydari, Ali 18
Shura Ittehad al Itefaq 90
Sipah e Sahaba Pakistan (SSP) 5, 7, 12, 15–18, 22–4, 32, 46, 53, 82, 94, 102, 123
   with AQ 125–8
   with HuM 161
   with IS-K 132–7, 168
   with IS-P 138–40
   with JeM 146
   in Kashmir 150
   LeJ relationship 124–5, 155
   with LeT 154
   and the Pakistani authorities 128–30
Soufan Group 35, 37
SPP 82
suicide bombing 18, 34, 46, 55
Sunni supremacists
   AQ with 5, 138, 140
   Baluchi ethnicity 123
   during 1990s 123
   Pakistani deep state 132, 164, 184
   three main groups 123
   TTP and 144
Syrian civil war 73

Tahir Baluch, Maulana Mohammad 53
Taliban. *See also* Afghan Taliban; Punjabi Taliban (Tehrik e Taliban Punjab); Quetta Shura
   Afghan victory 27
   AQ distrusting 62
   fall of Kabul 58
   in 1994 27
   onslaught against IS-K 57–8
   relations with Russia 31
   US peace deal 48, 59, 62, 117, 121
Tanzeem ul Haq 18
Tariq Azam, Mawlana 18

Tariq Geedar Group 78, 80, 111
Tehreek e Nafaz e Shariat e Mohammadi (TNSM) 23–4, 65–6, 80–1, 86, 95–6, 111, 114
Tehreek e Taliban Islami (TTI) 82
Tehrik e Khilafat Pakistan (TKP) 52–3, 74–5, 83, 85, 116
Tehrik e Taliban Pakistan (TTP)
   Afghan Taliban 5, 7, 12
   ambition, lack of 85
   AQ and 37, 64–71, 93, 97–115, 178–9
   assassination of tribal elders 65
   asymmetric campaign 93
   attacks against Chinese targets 119
   deep state and 107
   donors in Saudi Arabia and Qatar 76
   fragmentation 79–85
   global jihad 71–4
   'guerrilla' force 85
   impact of personal rivalries 84
   internal factions 85
   IS-K and 76
   Islamic State and 74–8
   killing in 2008 84
   LI with 79
   local fund-raising operations 88, 120
   Local Taliban Movement 110
   Mehsud factions 89
   negative impact 66
   under Noor Wali 115–18
   operation rules 85–6
   Pakistani army/Frontier Corps deployment 87
   proximity with the Afghan Taliban 90
   re-establishment of the Emirate in Afghanistan 77
   shadow economy/financial crisis 98–9
   stakeholders 86
   thin political programme 79
   as threat to the Pakistani state 78–9
   vulnerability to co-optation by state agencies 94–8

Tehrik Taliban Punjab 82
Turkistan Islamic Party 34

ul Haq Qaseemi, Isra 18
Umar, Asim 48
Umar Media 93
Umar Qasmi, Maulana 82
United States
   Afghan invasion 27–8, 123, 174, 180
   against AQ 41, 50–1, 105–7, 178, 181–2
   as an enemy of Pakistan 153
   first and second Afghan jihad 15, 27
   global jihadism 142, 148, 174–5, 185–6
   9/11 attacks 27, 141
   Pakistan relations 175
   withdrawal from Afghanistan 29, 50
ur Rahman, Wali 88
ur Rahman, Zaki 156, 165
Uyghurs 49, 55, 73

Wali Mohammad, Maulana 82
Wana Taliban 83
war on terror (Bush) 185
Wazir, Ahmadzai 66, 81, 83–4
Wazir Taliban, Uthmanzai 81
Wilayat Hind 58, 150–2
Wilayat Khorasan 52–3, 58–9
Wilayat Pakistan (IS-P) 35, 127, 171
   in Pakistan 58–61

Yahya, Abu Shaykh 86, 93, 100–1, 104, 108, 115
Yusufzai, Rahimullah 69, 83–4

Zaimusht, Fazal Saeed 82
Zakiur Rehman Lakhvi, Maulana 16
Zardari, Asif Ali 17
Zawahiri, Ayman Al 29–31, 36, 38, 41, 44, 48–9, 111, 121, 128, 180, 186
Zia-ul-Haq, Muhammad 18–19
Zia ul Rahman Faroqi, Maulana 18

www.ingramcontent.com/pod-product-compliance
Lightning Source LLC
Chambersburg PA
CBHW050350230426
43663CB00010B/2058